PRAISE FOR
THE BOOK OF BATCH SCR

T0100589

"Playfully written and technically robust. . . . It is a painless introduction to bat files for beginners and an invaluable reference for experts."

—DR. NICOLE ENGELKE, PROFESSOR AND
DIRECTOR OF QUANTITATIVE REASONING,
UNIVERSITY OF NEBRASKA AT OMAHA

"If you *have* to work with Windows, you *have* to read this book."

—NIEL INFANTE, SENIOR ENGINEER, GINKGO
BIOWORKS

"[A] dazzling, factual read mixed with full syntax detail and humor along the way. Highly recommended!"

—DAVE MULLEN, SENIOR IT MANAGER,
WINDOWS ADMINISTRATOR, AND
CYBERSECURITY ENGINEER

THE BOOK OF BATCH SCRIPTING

From Fundamentals to Advanced Automation

by Jack McLarney

no starch
press®

San Francisco

THE BOOK OF BATCH SCRIPTING. Copyright © 2024 by Jack McLarney.

All rights reserved. No part of this work may be reproduced or transmitted in any form or by any means, electronic or mechanical, including photocopying, recording, or by any information storage or retrieval system, without the prior written permission of the copyright owner and the publisher.

Printed in the United States of America

First printing

28 27 26 25 24   1 2 3 4 5

ISBN-13: 978-1-7185-0342-7 (print)
ISBN-13: 978-1-7185-0343-4 (ebook)

 Published by No Starch Press®, Inc.
245 8th Street, San Francisco, CA 94103
phone: +1.415.863.9900
www.nostarch.com; info@nostarch.com

Publisher: William Pollock
Managing Editor: Jill Franklin
Production Manager: Sabrina Plomitallo-González
Production Editor: Miles Bond
Developmental Editor: Jill Franklin
Cover Illustrator: Josh Ellingson
Interior Design: Octopod Studios
Technical Reviewer: Michael Varner
Copyeditor: Kim Wimpsett
Proofreader: Katrina Horlbeck Olsen

Library of Congress Control Number: 2023050702

For customer service inquiries, please contact info@nostarch.com. For information on distribution, bulk sales, corporate sales, or translations: sales@nostarch.com. For permission to translate this work: rights@nostarch.com. To report counterfeit copies or piracy: counterfeit@nostarch.com.

No Starch Press and the No Starch Press logo are registered trademarks of No Starch Press, Inc. Other product and company names mentioned herein may be the trademarks of their respective owners. Rather than use a trademark symbol with every occurrence of a trademarked name, we are using the names only in an editorial fashion and to the benefit of the trademark owner, with no intention of infringement of the trademark.

The information in this book is distributed on an "As Is" basis, without warranty. While every precaution has been taken in the preparation of this work, neither the author nor No Starch Press, Inc. shall have any liability to any person or entity with respect to any loss or damage caused or alleged to be caused directly or indirectly by the information contained in it.

[S]

To Bob Cook, an instructor and mentor
without peer, and to my grandfather Mr. Pete

About the Author

Jack McLarney has been coding professionally since 1999 at companies such as Protective Life Corporation, Fiserv, and The Hartford Financial Services Group. McLarney teaches part-time at Manchester Community College as an adjunct professor of mathematics and has taught at the University of Hartford. He holds an MS in applied mathematics from the University of Connecticut and a BS in electronic engineering technology from the University of Hartford.

McLarney codes in many technologies and is an expert in Batch scripting, or the writing of bat files. When he isn't coding or watching *Star Trek*, he is often running, hiking, or motorcycling on the roads and trails in central Connecticut, where he lives with his wife, Jenn, and their son, Kai, and two cats.

About the Technical Reviewer

Michael Varner is a senior-level architect and programmer. A technology enthusiast since childhood, he has been coding professionally since receiving his BS in computer science from Northern Illinois University in 2000. Varner's experience supporting legacy platforms at companies such as CSC and Fiserv has earned him a reputation for being skilled at optimizing systems in a way that is both functional and elegant.

An avid science fiction fan and YouTube home improvement afficionado, Varner can be found in his free time working on a home theater that includes a full-scale replica of the TARDIS. At home in central Indiana, his companions on his travels include his wife, Sara Jayne, and four daughters.

Any fool can make something complicated.
It takes a genius to make it simple.
—Woody Guthrie

BRIEF CONTENTS

CONTENTS IN DETAIL

22
WRITING REPORTS

23
RECURSION

24
TEXT STRING SEARCHES

25
BAT FILES BUILDING BAT FILES

26
AUTOMATIC RESTARTS AND MULTITHREADING   305

27
AND/OR OPERATORS   325

28
COMPACT CONDITIONAL EXECUTION   335

29
ARRAYS AND HASH TABLES   347

30
ODDS AND ENDS   363

31
TROUBLESHOOTING TIPS AND TESTING TECHNIQUES   375

ACKNOWLEDGMENTS

It takes a larger village than I ever imagined possible to publish a book, so I have plenty of people to thank, and the first without doubt is Jim Artman. We worked together for more than a decade across two companies, where he was the resident Batch scripting expert long before me. Not only did I learn most of what I know about bat files from him, but most of the coding standards and conventions that I've shamelessly passed off as mine were originally his. Without his mentoring, this book would not exist.

I'd also like to thank my technical reviewer, Michael Varner. Although we've never met in person, we worked adjacently on different teams and in different locations for a number of years. After Jim's retirement, Michael was likely my sole bat file peer in the company, so he was the logical choice for the job. He readily accepted the role, and his nuanced suggestions and corrections have been invaluable. It turns out that he has been coding in Batch much longer than me (despite being a decade younger).

A couple of ghost (or unofficial) technical reviewers have also made a large impact on this project: Scott Sauyet and Maya Dobrynin. Neither is an expert in Batch, but both are smart coders with an eye for detail. When one of them told me something wasn't clear, I knew that my explanation was lacking, and Scott even contributed a couple of jokes along with his general coding knowledge. My wife, Jennifer Natoli, and my mother, Barbara McLarney, were my early nontechnical reviewers, and both had very helpful suggestions.

More than worthy of mention is a group of friends with whom I have worked for many years. (The term *work friends* just doesn't capture it.) They may not have aided directly with this book, but the years of shared projects and conversations have contributed to it. I'm not listing them here, because I fear missing someone and ruing it forever, but I will mention Tim Kenney for suggesting the chapter about testing. I resisted at first but eventually realized that the book would have been incomplete without it. Also, Bharath Chintala was a great sounding board for a number of ideas, Bobby Oubre enthusiastically allowed me to use his name as my foil in Chapter 27, and Mike Yorgensen has been nothing but supportive.

I'd also like to thank an early teacher and mentor, the late Bob Cook, and to the memory of Joe Dubois, a long-ago boss who showed confidence in me, I dedicate every bad joke in these pages—but none of the good ones. All who knew Joe will understand.

Another thank-you goes out to my publisher, No Starch Press, for agreeing to work with me and getting this book published. My editor, Jill Franklin, has helped me through this new and exciting experience every step of the way, patiently correcting my placement of the word *only* and helping me overcome my em dash addiction—just one more.

My wife and son have been extremely supportive and understanding of me and this massive time commitment. A favorite author of mine, Malcolm Gladwell, thanked his father, a mathematician, for the gift of seeing him working at his desk doing something he loved. I hope that with my hours writing at the dining room table, I have shared that same gift with Kai, and it in some small way inspires him to find and dedicate himself to his passion.

INTRODUCTION

A book about bat files? Why? Didn't the Aztecs use Batch? Isn't it the Betamax of scripting languages? You should be writing a book about a newer, sexier coding language instead of a Model T repair manual.

I wish that I could dismiss out of hand such protestations as simply the negativism of nattering nabobs, but this is a sentiment I feel compelled to address. Batch isn't new, and the lack of some functionality is mystifying by today's standards, but it's still an immensely useful language that isn't going away anytime soon, especially since it's being packaged with the operating system installed on every Windows computer. While Batch is one scripting language among many, there are still many lines of Batch code being supported by large and small companies, and some tasks truly lend themselves to bat files more than any other language. And as for that lacking functionality—booleans, arrays, hash tables, stacks, even object-oriented design, and more—I'll show you how to build it yourselves by the end of this book.

But the most immediate reason for me personally to write a book about Batch scripting is that after two decades of writing bat files for personal and professional use, I believe that I've gotten to a place where I've learned enough about the topic to share my experiences and insights with a larger community. For many moons, I coded at a company that ran large-scale processes on Windows servers, all of them driven by bat files. Others might have gone with a more modern scripting language, but a coder who preceded me had mastered the art of bat files to such an extent that an alternative to Batch was never seriously considered. I played the understudy role of Robin until his retirement, when I was unofficially elevated to Batman.

Writing Batch code is still an important skill for any coder and even noncoders, but much of the existing documentation is sparse, scattered, and sometimes inaccurate. More so than in other languages, a great deal of experience and experimentation is required to gain proficiency, and I have a unique perspective to share. That's why I wrote this book.

This Book's Audience

This book is not for beginners, nor is it for experts; it's for *both*. I actually hope to reach three groups of people. The first is coders who write, maintain, or otherwise work with bat files on a near daily basis. The second is all other coders who work on a Windows machine, and the third is noncoders who also work on a Windows computer.

The first group, those working closely with Batch, are on the list for obvious reasons. This book is the culmination of two decades of my intense and immersive work in Batch scripting. By the end of this book, you'll have explored several complex concepts, such as creating commands, data structures, operators, and even a coding paradigm that weren't envisioned by the language's creators. I'll work steadily up to that complexity, but I hope that in these pages you'll find everything you need to master the language and the tools to further explore what little isn't here.

If you're in the second group, you likely don't maintain thousands of lines of Batch code, but on a Windows computer you write code in other languages, and you should be at least moderately versed in Batch. This skill allows you to perform some common and repetitive tasks by running a simple (or maybe not so simple) bat file. Animating code written in other languages has its challenges, one of which is that your machine's environment is different from the eventual production environment where the program will execute. To this end, I'll show you how to mimic or simulate another computer's environment with a few lines of Batch code. By the end of this book, I'm sure that you'll find that a bat file is a solution for many issues.

Even noncoders, the final group, can benefit from some Batch code to minimize repetitive tasks such as moving files, merging reports, or connecting to network drives to make Windows Explorer easier to use. Since coding isn't in your job description, your employer is unlikely to load the infrastructure for other coding languages onto your computer so that you can perform relatively simple coding tasks, but everything you need to write and execute a bat file is already on your workstation. The skill set needed to write a bat file is the ability to create a text file, rename it, and type a few lines into it. And if you can double-click a file, you can run a bat file. That's all you'll need (other than this book).

How to Read This Book

Every author, regardless of the genre, envisions their readers sitting by a fire, sipping sherry (or for me a good barleywine, not too sweet), hanging on every word, reading, processing, and reading some more until the book is complete. Well . . . this is a technical book, so a significant subset of my readers will be coders sitting in front of a computer trying to figure out why their damn bat file isn't doing what they want it to do. I've been there and fully appreciate the dilemma, and to aid you, I've organized this book with headings, subheadings, a detailed table of contents, and an index. You can find the section and page that will answer your question, and you can jump right to it, but that isn't the ideal way to read this or any book.

I've structured this book into short and concise chapters. Even if you're trying to solve a particular problem, I recommend reading the pertinent chapter in its entirety, because each one is a bit like a lesson plan. (My day job is coding, but I am trained as a mathematician and have spent more than two decades teaching various math classes at Manchester Community College in Connecticut.)

A typical lesson starts with the basic concept, followed by some simple examples. Then I delve into the complexity of the topic, show uses for the concept, and even explain typical stumbling blocks to avoid. Not every lesson (or chapter) follows that arc, but many do. If you have a question about, say, how to copy a file, I recommend reading Chapter 7 from beginning to end. Skipping to the middle of the chapter is analogous to coming into class 20 minutes late.

I also recommend executing on your own some of the coding examples that I present. Most of the code snippets are quite short and easy to type in, and you can grab the longer ones from the online version of this book. Better yet, modify the code, explore the results, and make it your own.

How This Book Is Structured

Batch is unique in that one single command, the for command, predominates all others to a massive extent, and I've organized this book into three parts, centered around that all-important command. Part I is titled "The Essentials," and it deals with the topics you'll need leading up to the discussion of the for command. The first part includes these chapters:

Chapter 1: Batch   This chapter introduces you to the Batch scripting language as you build what may be your first-ever bat file. I include editing tips, and since Batch is an interpreted language, I discuss the role and importance of the interpreter.

Chapter 2: Variables and Values   This chapter is about defining variables and interrogating their values either for display to the console or for any other use.

Chapter 3: Scope and Delayed Expansion   After you learn how to define where variables can be accessed in a bat file, I'll introduce one of the most intriguing features of Batch, delayed expansion, which impacts how you resolve variables.

Chapter 4: Conditional Execution   The if...else construct is a basic feature of most languages, and Batch is no different. You'll learn how to execute or not execute certain bits of code based on various conditional clauses.

Chapter 5: String and Boolean Data Types   This chapter tackles the tasks of building and concatenating strings, extracting a substring from a larger string, and replacing certain text in a string. I also introduce the first of many tools not intrinsic to Batch that we'll build, namely, booleans or variables that evaluate to either true or false.

Chapter 6: Integer and Float Data Types   You'll learn all the intricacies of adding, subtracting, multiplying, and dividing integers. This chapter also details modulo division as well as octal and hexadecimal arithmetic. I then delve into another data type not intrinsic to Batch: floating-point numbers.

Chapter 7: Working with Files   This chapter handles many of the tasks concerning files, such as copying, moving, deleting, and renaming them, and even creating an empty file.

Chapter 8: Executing Compiled Programs   This chapter explores how to call a program with and without a defined path and, in particular, how the interpreter finds your program when you don't provide a path.

Chapter 9: Labels and Nonsequential Execution   This chapter introduces labels and the role they play in allowing you to direct the code's execution to prior or later commands in a bat file, sometimes even initiating a loop.

Chapter 10: Calling Routines and Bat Files   Expanding on the previous chapter, you'll learn all that's involved in creating callable routines within a bat file and how to invoke one bat file from another.

Chapter 11: Parameters and Arguments   Invoking other code is often of little use if you can't pass arguments to the called code and it can't pass parameters back to you. This chapter delves into all the intricacies of the process, even unearthing the hidden parameter.

Chapter 12: Outputs, Redirection, and Piping   After differentiating between outputs created by the coder and the interpreter, I discuss how to redirect both to either the console or a file, which leads nicely to the technique of piping the output of one command into another and its uses.

Chapter 13: Working with Directories This chapter details how to create and delete directories and how to retrieve a great deal of information about a directory and its contents. I also demonstrate techniques for mapping local and network directories to drive letters.

Chapter 14: Escaping If you want to use a certain character in a string, you'll run into issues if it's a special character having some defined function in Batch. This chapter details the sometimes surprisingly involved solutions to that problem.

Chapter 15: Interactive Batch In this chapter you'll build a fully functional Batch user interface that accepts freeform text from the console and allows the user to select one item from a list, among other features.

Chapter 16: Code Blocks Code blocks are more than just blocks of code. This chapter explores how and why variables in a code block can possess two distinct values. I'll even introduce the naked code block and explain its significance.

Part II is simply titled "The for Command," and as its name more than suggests, it explores the aforementioned for command, which opens up a large batch (pun intended) of functionality. You'll find these topics:

Chapter 17: Fundamentals of the for Command This chapter details the functionality of the for command without introducing any of its options, which is still highly impressive. It creates loops processing any number of input files or text strings, and with the use of modifiers, you'll be able to determine almost everything about a file, other than its contents.

Chapter 18: Directories, Recursion, and Iterative Loops This chapter explores some options of the for command that allow for even more functionality. With one option, the command enumerates through a list of directories instead of filenames. With another, you can recursively process through directories and subdirectories, for instance, searching a folder and all of its subfolders for a file fitting a mask. Another option turns the command into an iterative loop, incrementing or decrementing an index with every pass.

Chapter 19: Reading Files and Other Inputs One last option turbocharges the for command, allowing you to read files. This chapter spares no details about how to parse or reformat each record of a file as you read it. In addition to a traditional file, the command can also read and process ordinary text, either hardcoded or from a variable, and it can even take the output of another command and read it as if it were a file.

Chapter 20: Advanced for Techniques This chapter delves into some impressive applications of the for command, such as embedding commands of another language (for example, PowerShell and Python) into your Batch script. I also discuss some techniques for working around limitations of the command.

"Advanced Topics" is the title of Part III, which discusses various and varied topics, particularly everything that I couldn't address before having the for command in my toolkit. Here's the breakdown:

Chapter 21: Pseudo-Environment Variables   This chapter details pseudo-environment variables, or special variables not always under your control. For instance, Batch has specific variables that hold the date, the time, and the return code of both Batch commands and called programs. I also explain how to safely set some of these variables and share the difference between bat and cmd files.

Chapter 22: Writing Reports   This chapter explains how to format rudimentary text file reports with Batch, complete with header, detail, and trailer records.

Chapter 23: Recursion   Some problems lend themselves nicely to the technique of recursion, which is the methodology where code invokes itself. This chapter demonstrates how to do this in Batch with detailed and interesting examples.

Chapter 24: Text String Searches   This chapter explores many permutations of text string searches. Search files, variables, or hardcoded text for one or more words or literal strings. You'll even find a couple of examples that use regular expressions.

Chapter 25: Bat Files Building Bat Files   This chapter details the intricacies involved in one bat file building a second fully functional bat file with dynamic and static code, while also contemplating what Archimedes would have done with Batch.

Chapter 26: Automatic Restarts and Multithreading   After discussing how to automatically restart a failed process, this chapter uses a bat-file-building bat file to automatically kill and restart a hung process. I also discuss executing multiple threads or concurrencies at once under the direction of a single bat file.

Chapter 27: and/or Operators   It might sound like a basic topic, but Batch possesses neither the and nor the or operator. This chapter builds techniques that mimic these operators for various situations.

Chapter 28: Compact Conditional Execution   This chapter details a compact and funky construct that looks and acts a lot like the if...else construct. I discuss when best to use each after examining the subtle yet significant differences between the two.

Chapter 29: Arrays and Hash Tables   These data structures aren't intrinsic to Batch, but you'll learn how to populate and retrieve data from both arrays and hash tables.

Chapter 30: Odds and Ends   This chapter covers a few disparate topics: file attributes, bit manipulation, querying the Windows Registry, and sorting the contents of a file.

Chapter 31: Troubleshooting Tips and Testing Techniques   I share many tips and techniques for developing and testing bat files that I've picked up over the years.

Chapter 32: Object-Oriented Design   As crazy as it might sound, this chapter delivers the capstone of user-built bat file functionality. I explain the four pillars of object-oriented design before walking through a model that implements them as completely as possible. I hope that seasoned coders find this chapter informative and entertaining.

Chapter 33: Stacks, Queues, and Real-World Objects   This chapter applies the just-learned principles of object-oriented design to build objects implementing the stack and queue data structures.

For each chapter in the first and third parts, I set out to discuss a narrow topic or how to perform a specific task; I don't set out to discuss a specific command, but I'll often introduce one or more commands in a chapter. For each command, I'll explain its function, show you its syntax, and detail its features that I find most useful.

It's my goal that if you're a noncoder, you'll find at least the first two parts readable and informative. Read much further and you might just become a coder.

Other Resources

If you're looking for comprehensive and straightforward explanations of individual Batch commands, go no further than *https://ss64.com/nt/*. It's a great and well-organized resource, and I referenced it extensively while writing this book. This book isn't a list of commands; it's a discussion about how to solve problems with those commands. I usually present the options of a command that I find to be the most useful, but you'll find the full list at this site.

In the (hopefully) rare event that you can't find a solution in these pages, the next best alternative is to tap into the online nerd community. Searching the web for your issue and "bat file" (in quotes) should produce several results. Of the many online forums, I've consistently found the best ideas and suggestions at *https://stackoverflow.com*.

Notes on Style

Most technical books and manuals are dry reads, and I've made every effort to buck that trend. First and foremost, I haven't lost sight of the fact that my primary mission is to explain the technical material that I'm trying to impart. But, for instance, when discussing the sort command, I don't want to sort the likes of Apples and Bananas; it's much more fun to sort the captains of the starship *Enterprise* from *Star Trek*, or at least I think it is. I use a Mad Libs game when discussing parameters, passing different parts of speech as arguments. The chapter on interactive Batch shares bat (or maybe bad) jokes with the user.

Not every chapter lends itself to entertaining examples or a humorous anecdote, but I've made every effort to avoid files containing Record 1 as the first record or a string of pipe-delimited fields defined as field 1| field 2|field 3.

Ideally, I hope to elicit an audible chuckle; I'd be thrilled with a smirk and a nod; and I'd even be happy with an eyeroll and a groan. Boring be damned. I live by the mantra "It's better to be uniquely bad than average." (I wish that I could take credit for this quote, but many years ago our guide on a tour of Benziger Winery in Sonoma County, California, used it to describe the winery's philosophy.)

Batveats

In my experience, Batch has many significant caveats in comparison to other languages. In the pages ahead, I'll often follow seemingly definitive statements about syntax or usage with the word *except*. (For instance, "The ampersand character terminates a command, *except* when followed by a second ampersand or . . .") The English language is unique in that much of its syntax has caveats that just don't exist in other languages—think "*i* before *e* except after *c*." Maybe this makes Batch the quintessentially patriotic American language (or maybe British).

These *batch caveats* are so prevalent that I've taken to calling each one a *batveat* (pronounced bat-vē-ăt, trademark pending). They can be very frustrating for unguided new users, but as these chapters unfold, I'll point out the various batveats that have bitten me in the past so that you can ideally avoid the pain.

Woody Guthrie

The epigraph that I chose for this book is a relatively well-known quote from the legendary artist Woody Guthrie, but I was hesitant to use it for fear of how it might be interpreted. The intent of the quote isn't egotistical, it's aspirational. Woody traveled the United States espousing economic justice while also preaching about the evils of racism and sexism. He didn't do this with dry, boring speeches, but with a guitar and perceptive lyrics that still resonate long after his early death.

Woody Guthrie was trying to bend the arc of history in the direction of social justice, while I'm trying to make an esoteric programming language a little more attainable with prose that is informative, readable, and entertaining. It is my hope that I can contribute to the understanding of a complex topic, and I can only aspire to Woody's sublime example.

For the Love of Batch

Never, never invite more than one Batch coder to a party. One is fine. If we're there without a compatriot, we'll talk about sports, politics, books, movies, and travel like anyone else. But when you put at least two of us together anywhere, you'll hear things like "I recently found a new way to code an or operator in the conditional clause of an if command. Would you like me to share it with you?" We will kill your party.

The optimist will say that Batch is *esoteric*, while the pessimist will say it is *cryptic*. The truth is probably somewhere in between, and you'll find both of these words often in this book. The syntax is distinct from most languages, and the lack of certain functionality makes for imaginative solutions to problems that would be uninteresting in other languages. The upshot is a couple of people sucking the oxygen out of your Super Bowl party with a discussion about different ways to construct a hash table.

I find these puzzles invigorating, and that's a major reason why I enjoy scripting in Batch, while others may find it a chore. Sometimes I really enjoy coding in a language that makes the implementation of a stack a significant accomplishment. To briefly demonstrate just one challenge, the character for the at symbol (@) can be a variable name, and extracting the second-to-last character from its value requires the syntax %@:~-2,1%. That might look more like a curse word in a comic strip than code, and admittedly it does look esoteric, maybe even cryptic, but please don't put this book down out of fear; I promise that it will make perfect sense after just a few chapters.

Being a Batch expert in a room full of coders only moderately versed in the discipline can feel like being a Sumerian priest—one out of a select group of people who can interpret a script and impart its meaning and wisdom to others. But I hold my position not due to a random birthright, and I do not guard the ability to decipher this cuneiform from others out of self-interest. With this book I hope to make high priests and priestesses out of all who want to learn this not-so-ancient script. In the pages to follow, I'll be more than honest concerning issues and frustrations that I've found with the language, but I do love coding bat files, and by the time you've finished reading this book, I hope that I've made a convert out of you.

PART I

THE ESSENTIALS

Just as the Batch universe revolves around the all-important for command, so does this book. Part I will explore the essentials of the scripting language, not the basics, because there's nothing basic about Batch syntax. You'll be able to code many Batch solutions by its completion, but chapter by chapter, you'll feel the gravitational pull of the for command in Part II.

In this part, you'll learn about variables, scope, and data types such as strings, integers, and even floats and booleans. I'll also discuss files, directories, and how to call programs, internal routines, and other bat files. You'll learn about techniques such as piping and escaping, how to build an interactive Batch user interface, and much more.

1

BATCH

If you are reading this book (and I'm pretty sure that you are), you are looking to write some Batch code. By the end of this chapter, you will have done just that, coding and executing what may be your very first bat file.

Along the way, I will introduce the Batch scripting language and its origins in the MS-DOS command prompt, along with the two types of files that contain its source code: the bat and cmd. I'll also discuss editors, which are the primary tools for writing a bat file, and the options available to you. Finally, no introduction to the Batch universe would be complete without an overview of the interpreter.

The MS-DOS Command Prompt

The MS-DOS (Microsoft Disk Operating System) command prompt lives on every computer loaded with Microsoft Windows. If you are of a certain age—that is, if you were around for the infancy of personal computers—you might remember that black rectangle (or an entire screen if you go back to the pre-Windows era) where you entered commands to perform various tasks such as installing or launching programs, or copying or deleting files. The average user rarely if ever deals with this anymore because graphical user interfaces have streamlined those tasks so that they can be performed in a few clicks, but it still exists.

To access the command prompt on your Windows computer, go to **Start** and enter **CMD**, which is short for *command*, in the search box. Hit ENTER, and the MS-DOS command prompt will open. From this prompt you can enter a number of commands. You can execute programs, copy files, or even delete your entire *C:*drive. Don't panic, though; you would have to know the command for that. I won't get into all the possible commands here because that's what this entire book is about, and even it isn't exhaustive, but let's look at one example. Say you're working on a project with several documents in a folder. After working on those documents for a few hours each day, it's a good idea to back up the files onto another drive. To do that, you could enter the single command in Listing 1-1 into the command prompt and press ENTER.

```
xcopy C:\YourPath\*.* D:\YourBackUpPath\ /F /S /Y
```

Listing 1-1: The command to back up some files

Don't worry about the syntax yet (wait for Chapter 7). The important point is that you can enter this command into the command prompt each day to copy all of your files. You might protest that it's far too easy to mistype something in this line, such as one of the two paths or one of those letters following the slashes at the end of the line, whatever the heck those are for. Wouldn't it be easier to use Windows, that is, navigate to one folder, select all, right-click, select Copy, navigate to the other folder, right-click, select Paste, and click to verify the copy? I would agree that this would be easier than typing out the command, but notice that the Windows process involves eight discrete steps and likely a dozen or more mouse clicks.

A third option is easier than both the command prompt method and the click-intensive Windows method. That option is to program with the Batch scripting language.

The Batch Scripting Language

Batch is an unfortunate handle for any coding language, scripting or otherwise. Some popular languages are distinctively named for coffee, gemstones, music notes, or British comedy troupes. Even the much-maligned COBOL has an acronym unique to itself, and when Pascal is mentioned, the 20th-century coding language usually comes to mind before the 17th-century mathematician. At the other extreme of the continuum, the term *batch* is banal; even in the context of computer science, it's ambiguous. *Batch processing* is a generic term for the act of running several jobs or a large batch of data at once and is quite distinct from the topic of this book, Batch scripting.

Microsoft developed the Batch scripting or coding language in the early 1980s for the MS-DOS operating system, and it has been installed on every machine running Windows since 1985. I suspect that somebody at Microsoft who grew tired of typing a repetitive series of commands into the command prompt said, "Wouldn't it be great if we could take these commands and batch them together into a single file that could then be executed quickly and easily?"

Those *batched* commands represented the genesis of Batch, the coding language. Individual commands don't constitute a language; a language is a framework to execute those commands. Batching these commands into a file allowed for branching logic, complex loops, and reusable code—the makings of a real language.

Batch has many uses. Its command line origins make it an ideal language for computer or system administration: creating, copying, moving, and deleting files. Batch can also examine and modify directories and the registry and set up a computer's environment.

A simple bat file can set some variables and execute programs written in many other languages. Batch can interact with a user, displaying information and gathering data. Files can be read, written, and altered. Rudimentary reports can be created, and before long you will see that Batch supports intricate and sophisticated scripts.

Before personal computers became available, other operating systems had their own scripting languages analogous to Batch. Unix shell scripts execute on Unix-based operating systems, and JCL, or job control language, is instrumental to the IBM mainframe. When introducing Batch to new coworkers familiar with the mainframe, I'll dispense with rigor and describe it as "JCL for the PC."

In my experience, knowledge of Batch among coders is broad yet shallow. (An image of a large group of coders, laptops in hand, standing in the kiddie pool with their pant cuffs rolled up, afraid to enter the adult pool, much less its deep end, comes to mind.) Most coders can create a simple Batch application but instinctively fall back onto other languages for more complex problems that could be more easily handled in Batch.

Bat Files

Although the term *batch* is ambiguous, a bat file is known to most coders. A batch of commands is entered into a batch file (shortened to bat file). Hence, a *bat file* is a file containing Batch source code. (A *batphile*, however, is someone with a great enthusiasm for, or even a lover of, nocturnal flying mammals.) When a bat file is executed, a series of the commands it contains is performed until reaching either a command to terminate its execution or the end of the file.

Most Windows files have a file extension at the end of the filename after the dot. Modern Word documents end in *.docx*. Excel spreadsheets end in

.xlsx. Simple text files often end in *.txt*, and PDF files end in . . . well, you have the idea. To distinguish a bat file from other files, it must have a *.bat* extension.

By default, file extensions aren't shown after the filename in Windows, but we'll need them. To show them, look for an option to show filename extensions under the **View** menu in Windows Explorer. If it isn't readily obvious, search the web for "show filename extensions" and your operating system.

Now your files will show their extensions; for instance, your Word documents will likely be suffixed with *.docx*. More important, your bat files will be appended with *.bat*. Many refer to these as *batch files*, but in the pages ahead I'll refer to them simply as *bat files*.

Your First Bat File

Let's create a bat file. To start, right-click on the desktop to bring up the context menu and select **New ▸ Text Document**. Rename the text file to something like *SaveProject.bat*. The name can be whatever makes sense to you, but the file extension after the filename must be changed from *.txt* to *.bat*. Right-click the file, select **Rename**, enter the new name and extension, and press ENTER. A pop-up will likely warn you that changing the extension might cause great harm. It will not; just select **Yes** to confirm. Right-click the new file on the desktop and select **Edit** (not Open; I'll get to that momentarily). It should open for editing in Notepad.

Enter the two lines of text in Listing 1-2 into your bat file.

```
xcopy C:\YourPath\*.* D:\YourBackUpPath\ /F /S /Y
pause
```

Listing 1-2: The entire contents of your first bat file

Change `C:\YourPath\` to the folder you want backed up and change `D:\YourBackUpPath\` to the folder to which you want to save everything. (I am assuming that your backup device, such as a flash drive, is assigned `D:\` as the drive, but it might be something else. If nothing else, just to see this work, you could even define a backup path also on the same drive.) Notice that the first line of code in Listing 1-2 is identical to what we typed into the command prompt in Listing 1-1, but it is now followed by a second line containing a single word: pause.

After investing the effort to put this together, you can reap the benefits. Whenever you want to make this backup in the future, simply execute this bat file. To do so you have multiple options; one is to double-click its icon on the desktop, and another is to right-click the bat file and select **Open**. You might expect **Open** to open the file for editing, but it really executes the bat file.

That's it. A window will open showing all the copied files along with the locations that they were copied from and to. The bat file will hold the window open until you press any key to close it. Without this, the copy would still happen, but the window would likely close so quickly you wouldn't know whether it worked.

WARNING *From time to time Windows file associations aren't assigned properly. That is, Word documents should be associated with and opened by Word. Likewise, bat files should be associated with the Windows program that executes bat files. If your bat file opens in Notepad, for instance, the file association for files with the .bat extension is broken. The fix for this varies depending on the operating system. Search the web for "bat file association fix" along with your operating system to learn how to fix the issue.*

Almost anything that you can type into the MS-DOS command prompt can be coded into a bat file so that it can be executed easily and repeatedly. You don't have to download anything from the internet. Everything you need is already on your Windows machine.

I prefixed the last paragraph with *almost* because certain commands, especially the all-important for command yet to be discussed, have slightly different syntaxes in a bat file versus inside the command prompt. Even more bizarre, a command in a bat file can occasionally produce slightly different output compared to the exact same command entered at the command prompt.

This book is geared to writing bat files, not using the command prompt, so all code listings found in this book will work in a bat file, and all examples of output will be the output of code from a bat file. The help command, also yet to be discussed, will explain any differences in syntax. By the same reasoning, this book doesn't cover commands that are primarily used in the command prompt.

cmd Files

In Listing 1-2 we created a bat file with—I know I'm stating the obvious here—the *.bat* extension. With the release of Windows NT, Microsoft introduced a very similar file with the *.cmd* extension, a file that also contains Batch source code. Any Batch command from a bat file can be entered into a cmd file. In fact, if you rename your first bat file from Listing 1-2 with a *.cmd* extension and execute it exactly as you did the bat file, you'll get the same results.

There are some technical differences concerning how your computer executes the two types of files, but from a user perspective, they are nearly identical. The only significant difference (which I will discuss in Chapter 21) concerns how and when the return code is set, and even then, that difference manifests itself only in a very narrow set of circumstances.

Nearly every mention of bat files throughout this book applies equally to cmd files, but I'll refer to them solely as bat files for many reasons. In common usage among coders, *bat file* is the norm. A file with a *.cmd* extension will often be referred to as a bat file, but the opposite never occurs. The single-syllable word *bat* rolls off the tongue effortlessly compared to its vowelless alternative, which is usually referred to as a "see-em-dee" file, an exhausting three syllables when used often. One last not-so-insignificant reason: the cover art on the book you are holding. A book about cmd files would have been far less eye-catching.

Because cmd files are newer, one could argue that they'll be better supported in the future and are the better option for new development. I can't dispute that, but I still find myself creating files with the *.bat* extension, and Microsoft continues to support both. If cmd files have not supplanted bat files in the past three decades, I don't envision the bat's demise anytime soon.

Editor Recommendations

I mentioned earlier that when you edit your first bat file, it'll likely open in Notepad. Notepad is the barest of bare-bones editors for text files. Word is considered by many to be a bloated monstrosity by this stage of its evolution, but Notepad is just the opposite, devoid of useful features. It can be used for a simple bat file, but before we go any further, I must make the case for getting a better editor. By *editor* I mean a utility that allows you to open (not execute) a bat file in a window to read it and make modifications.

My personal favorite is Notepad++. On first hearing the name I mistakenly dismissed it as a glorified Notepad, but it really is a pleasure to use. Commands, variables, operators, labels, comments, and more items we haven't covered yet are displayed in different colors to aid in readability. Most editors have that, but if you double-click a variable, it highlights not just that variable but also all the other instances of that variable in the file, making it even easier to find misspellings, although misspellings aren't very common with Notepad++ because of its easy-to-use auto-complete functionality. If you enter a variable name such as myVeryVerboseVariableName—first off, shame on you, abbreviations were invented for a reason—the next time you start to type myVe, Notepad++ will subtly give you the option of inserting the remaining 21 characters with a single keystroke.

Notepad++ is very configurable. If you find the orange color for variables a bit too harsh, you can change it to a burnt orange or maybe go in the direction of a mauve. It will also work for dozens of other programming languages, and best of all, it's free. Just go to *https://notepad-plus-plus.org* or search the web for "Notepad++ download," and you are a couple mouse clicks away.

UltraEdit is also a solid editor, and Visual Studio Code is fast becoming a very popular editor for many coding languages, including Batch. You'll find several others on the internet, many of which are free. Download two or three and experiment, but whatever you do, don't settle for Notepad.

The Batch Interpreter

Batch is a scripting language, not a compiled language. Compiled languages, such as Java, Visual Basic, and C# are written in text, but that text cannot be executed. Instead, the coder usually writes the program in an integrated development environment (IDE) where the click of a button or two runs the *compiler* to translate the code into an executable file. The resulting file is not at all human-readable, but it will be quite computer-readable and optimized for execution. The lack of readable text has the additional benefit of hiding any proprietary information from the user.

The next piece of this compiled-code puzzle is the *runtime*; runtimes come in different forms, but a runtime is loaded on a computer and is used to run any executable file written in a specific language.

As a scripting language, Batch is also written in text, but the rest of the process deviates greatly from compiled languages. There is no compiler and no runtime; instead, the *Batch interpreter*, or the *cmd.exe* executable file, effectively handles both roles. (Its 16-bit forerunner was *command.com*.) The Batch interpreter is sometimes referred to as the *command interpreter* or *command line interpreter*, but usually it is simply and unassumingly called the *interpreter*.

The interpreter executes the bat file containing the text. The lack of the intermediate compilation step does have some advantages. Before long, I'll share some interesting Batch techniques available to us precisely because the code is not compiled, but it also presents some challenges to the coder. When a program is compiled, the compiler will catch syntax errors and even make suggestions on how to improve the code. For instance, a compiler will easily catch a missing parenthesis so the coder can fix it in seconds. A missing character in a bat file will not be caught until it is executed by the interpreter, and maybe not even the first time it executes. In this way, the interpreter plays one of the roles performed by a compiler—a very inefficient compiler.

The interpreter is much more analogous to a runtime. When the bat file described earlier in this chapter is opened or executed, a call is being put out to the interpreter to read in the bat file and execute it—or interpret it—line by line. This means that the bat file isn't optimized for execution, and for better or worse, the code is available to any user with Notepad technology. Also, the bat file can be executed on any Windows machine because all such machines are loaded with the interpreter. A curious upshot is that later stages of a particularly long-running bat file can actually be coded as the prior logic is being executed, an impressive albeit not very useful feature.

All modern IDEs also have an animator or debugger, which allows you to execute code line by line, analyzing variables and maybe even altering them. You can set the execution to stop at a particular line or multiple lines. It's a very useful tool for any coder, but Batch doesn't support an animator. The life cycle of a bat file is as follows: it's written, and it's executed. That's the list.

Some scripting languages, such as JavaScript, commonly work both ways—the source code can be run with an interpreter or be compiled into an executable file with products available from multiple companies. Nothing like that is in common use with Batch. Bat files are run only via the interpreter, and it's important to understand what the interpreter is because I reference it often in the chapters ahead.

Summary

In this chapter, I introduced the Batch scripting language, bat files, cmd files, and the interpreter. You wrote and executed a bat file (maybe your first) and learned about editors.

You are now ready to truly start coding. In Chapter 2, you'll learn how to assign values to variables with the oft-used set command and how to resolve or extract those values. You'll also explore a few other commands that are used extensively in the Batch universe, giving you the necessary foundation for building any bat file in the future.

2

VARIABLES AND VALUES

Now that we're ready to start coding, we'll explore variables, values, and the Batch set command, which assigns values to variables. Although these topics may seem trivial if you've coded in other languages, Batch has some unique quirks that are worth noting.

You'll learn how to display the value of a variable in the console to confirm that it has been set correctly. Additionally, I'll introduce the *command separator*, which allows you to enter multiple commands on a single line. I'll also show you how to create remarks and set variables that are saved on your computer and remain available even after the bat file is closed. Finally, you'll learn how to access documentation for any Batch command at the command prompt, a useful skill for anyone working with bat files.

Setting and Resolving a Variable

A *variable* is a named field defining a place in memory that holds a value for later use. Many if not most languages allow, and usually require, variables to be defined as a particular data type, often some sort of text or number, before they can be assigned a value. Batch will have none of this; variables come into existence the first time they are "set" to a value, and that value can contain letters, numbers, and other characters. It's then up to the coder to treat them as certain data types, or not. In Chapters 5 and 6 I'll return to ways to handle data types, but this chapter focuses on the seemingly simple task of assigning a value to a variable.

To consider one example of a variable, a coder might have a field that contains the state of their mood; whether it be for narcissistic or obsessive-compulsive reasons is of little importance. The variable is defined as or named myMood, and two possible values out of many are happy and sad. To set the variable to happy, you would use, obviously enough, the set command:

```
set myMood=happy
```

After this executes, the myMood variable contains the value happy.

If the topic is particularly bewildering, the following command wipes out the prior value and replaces it with a different one:

```
set myMood=nonplussed
```

But how do you know for sure the value of this or any other variable? In Batch, the act of revealing the value of a variable is referred to as *resolving a variable*, and it's usually done by surrounding the variable with percent signs. That is, %myMood% will resolve to nonplussed after the prior set command executes. Now, to actually see the results of resolving a variable, we'll need a bit of a digression—a very important digression.

Displaying the Value of a Variable

In this section, you'll learn how to quickly display the resolved value of a variable on your computer screen, but this technique will be useful for far more than just that. We'll return to it in future chapters to demonstrate many other features of Batch, such as using it as a testing technique, which is instrumental for any Batch coder.

Writing to the Console

To display the contents of a variable on the screen, we need two additional commands: echo and pause. To demonstrate, let's create a small bat file. Open a new folder on your computer, perhaps *C:\Batch*, and in it, create a bat file called *Mood.bat* that contains the three lines shown in Listing 2-1.

```
set myMood=happy
echo My mood is %myMood%.
pause
```

Listing 2-1: The bat file, Mood.bat, displays a resolved variable.

If you double-click or open *Mood.bat*, the bat file should execute, and a black window with white text should appear. This window is the DOS window, or *console*, which is how I'll refer to it throughout this book.

We've already discussed the set command in the first line of Listing 2-1. In this context, the echo command writes out the remainder of the statement, excluding the space succeeding the actual text echo, to the console. The text My mood is and a trailing space is displayed, followed by the contents or the value of myMood—that is, the text happy—and the trailing period. The pause command keeps the console open. Without it, the window would open and close before you could read it.

Listing 2-2 shows everything written to the console when this bat file executes, which is more than you may have expected.

```
C:\Batch>set myMood=happy

C:\Batch>echo My mood is happy.
My mood is happy.

C:\Batch>pause
Press any key to continue . . .
```

Listing 2-2: The console display of the Mood.bat bat file

Each command is preceded with the current directory, *C:\Batch*, followed by a greater-than sign (>) as a delimiter. (You'll learn more about the current directory in Chapter 8. For now, just consider it to be the path of the bat file being executed.)

The first line shows the execution of the set command, and the second shows the execution of the echo command. The third line is the result of executing that echo—that is, the output to the console described in Listing 2-2. You can tell that it's not a command because of the lack of the preceding text *C:\Batch>*. More important, %myMood% resolves to the text happy. The pause command also creates output, the text Press any key to continue . . . , and as the message indicates, the execution is on hold until any key is depressed, at which point the bat file will end, and the console will close. Also, notice that the set command doesn't produce any output since it's just setting the value of a variable—there's nothing to output.

Cleaning Up the Console

One problem with what's written to the console is that it's a mess with commands interspersed with the desired output from the echo and pause commands. In Chapter 12, you'll learn more about the various outputs and how to manage them; here we'll just look at a quick means of cleaning this up.

An echo command followed by the argument off is executed at the top of the *Mood.bat* bat file from Listing 2-1:

```
@echo off
set myMood=happy
echo My mood is %myMood%.
pause
```

This echo off command suppresses not the actual output of the subsequent commands but rather the lines showing that each of those commands is being executed—that is, the line prefixed with the current directory. Also, prefixing the echo command with the at sign (@) suppresses its own execution from being written to the console.

Compared to Listing 2-2, the console display is now much cleaner when the modified bat file is executed:

```
My mood is happy.
Press any key to continue . . .
```

Now we can easily demonstrate how to initialize the myMood variable to the gloomy value and then reset it to the cheerful value:

```
@echo off
set myMood=gloomy
echo My mood is %myMood%.
set myMood=cheerful
echo Now my mood is %myMood%.
pause
```

The result shows the same variable resolved to two different values at two different times:

```
My mood is gloomy.
Now my mood is cheerful.
Press any key to continue . . .
```

As our bat files become more complex, the echo command can send the output to someplace other than the console (see Chapter 12 for more details). Prepending the command with > con explicitly redirects the data to the console:

```
> con echo This will always get to the "con" or console
```

This technique will be very useful in coming chapters to demonstrate what's going on in a code snippet. For the sake of brevity, I won't include the initial echo off and trailing pause commands in later examples, but I encourage you to add them to clean up and hold open the console.

The Idiosyncrasies of the set Command

Setting variables is usually a straightforward topic for most coding languages, but Batch isn't like most coding languages. All Batch coders need to understand the following idiosyncrasies of the set command to avoid some level of future pain.

Case Sensitivity

Closely inspect the following two commands. They look a little different but are functionally equivalent:

```
SET myMood=whimsical
set MYMOOD=whimsical
```

Batch commands and variables are case-insensitive. Here the set command is uppercase in one command and lowercase in the other, but the interpreter treats them both the same. You also could've used Set with no change in functionality. For good measure, sET and SeT also work in the same fashion, but you'd have to be a real contrarian to code in such a manner. Likewise, you can use the myMood, MYMOOD, and mymood variables interchangeably. The value, however, is stored just as it's typed, so it's case-sensitive. If the variable is set to WHIMSICAL, it will be resolved as WHIMSICAL; likewise, if it's set to Whimsical, it will be resolved as Whimsical.

It's all a matter of style and personal preference. I find that many bat files have far too much content capitalized. Capitalization is meant to make something stand out, but nothing stands out when everything is flashing neon. Most Batch coders capitalize all the letters in command names, but in this book I use only lowercase characters for all Batch commands. Also, I greatly prefer camel case variables.

NOTE *Camel case text is easily readable even though it contains multiple words not separated by spaces or other characters. The first letter of camel case text can be either uppercase (head up) or lowercase (head down). But to qualify as camel case, the first letter of all subsequent words must be capitalized with the rest of the word being lowercase. An example of the* head up *variant (also called* Pascal *or* upper camel case*) is* myMood. *The corresponding* head down *variant (also called* dromedary *or* lower camel case*) would be* myMood. *Imagine a camel drinking water with his head down.*

Valid Variable Characters

Most programming languages have strict rules concerning the list of permissible characters in variable names. Typically, numbers and the 26 letters of the alphabet, uppercase and lowercase, are allowed, with just a few special characters to boot. But Batch is unique in that nearly every character on the keyboard is a valid variable name character, although you should avoid using numbers as the first character in a variable name. (While you can set variables named with a leading digit, resolving them is problematic, and I'll explain why in Chapter 3.)

A few characters are illegal because they have specific uses in Batch; for example, the tilde (~), ampersand (&), percent sign (%), and the less-than (<) and greater-than (>) signs are reserved characters, but several others would surprise any coder not already familiar with Batch. The three set commands in Listing 2-3 successfully set these three variables with odd-looking single-character names to their respective descriptions.

```
set ;=semicolon
set @=at
set #=hashtag

> con echo %;% %@% %#%
```

Listing 2-3: Setting variables with odd-looking single-character names

The echo command in Listing 2-3 writes the text semicolon at hashtag to the console.

Even the following monstrosity stores the text This actually works in the variable with a dollar sign, dot, and mismatched brackets:

```
set var$with.odd[chars}=This actually works
```

This variable name demonstrates what's possible, but it's hard to read and not recommended.

Judicious use of such characters in variable names, however, can be a handy tool. For example, a group of related variables might all have a leading or trailing underscore as a visual cue to that relationship; number can be abbreviated as #, which is even more succinct than nbr and clearer than no. Much later in this book I'll use this interesting feature to build arrays and hash tables with meaningful names containing brackets.

Spaces Around the Assignment Operator

The following classic rookie mistake bites most new Batch coders familiar with other languages. Inspect the set command shown in Listing 2-4 carefully.

```
set X = Hello
> con echo The value of X is "%X%".
```

Listing 2-4: Setting a variable with spaces around the equal sign

If you expect the result of the echo command to be

```
The value of X is "Hello".
```

that would be an understandable mistake, but a mistake nonetheless. The result is actually this:

```
The value of X is "".
```

The empty quotes mean that X isn't set or is set to null, meaning nothing at all, not even a space.

NOTE *In Chapter 1, I mentioned that inside the command prompt, the syntax and output can differ in comparison to a bat file, and this is a prime example. The same code entered at the command prompt displays the attempted resolution of the unset variable very differently:*

```
The value of X is "%X%".
```

I won't be noting every discrepancy in the pages ahead, so if you see any future anomalies working at the command prompt, try putting the code in a bat file.

Now, the set command in Listing 2-4 isn't all that complex, and it clearly is setting X to the text Hello, correct? Furthermore, it looks a lot like assignment commands in other more modern languages that would've performed the assignment as desired.

This is our first *batveat* (Batch caveat; see the Introduction for details on batveats). The key to this issue is the space preceding the equal sign. The Batch interpreter is as literal as difficult teenagers, too smart and unforgiving for their own good. The variable name starts with the first nonspace character after the set command and ends with the character just before the assignment operator or equal sign—no matter what that character is. Therefore, the variable being set here is two characters in length, an X followed by a space:

```
set X = Hello
```

The %X% resolved to nothing, but %X % does have a value, and that value is Hello, correct? Not quite; this is our second batveat. The value of the variable is the string of characters after the equal sign extending to the end of the statement. Therefore, the assigned value is the space after the equal sign followed by the five characters in the word Hello.

Let's modify the echo command from Listing 2-4 like so:

```
set X = Hello
> con echo The value of X-space is "%X %".
```

Resolving the variable with the trailing space now reveals its value, which contains a leading space:

```
The value of X-space is " Hello".
```

This works, but typically a variable name with a trailing space is an accident waiting to happen. We even can embed spaces in the middle of a variable name, but there's a big difference between being able to do something and it being a good idea. This in no way should be construed as an invitation to create cryptic code; it's more of a warning about spaces around the equal sign in a set command.

Taking one last pass of Listing 2-4, let's remove the spaces before and after the equal sign and go back to the original echo command:

```
set X=Hello
> con echo The value of X is "%X%".
```

Finally, we get the desired result written to the console:

```
The value of X is "Hello".
```

An even easier mistake to make is to add an unintentional space or two to the end of a line trailing the value. Because it won't be obvious just looking at the text in the editor, it's quite easy to miss. (In Notepad++, go to **View ▸ Show Symbol ▸ Show Space and Tab** to represent spaces as faint dots. Other good editors will have a similar feature.)

There are valid reasons to prepend or append a variable's value with spaces, as you'll learn later in this book, but be careful not to do it by accident. However, I'm hard-pressed to come up with an example of a variable's name legitimately being appended with one or more spaces. Ensure that there's no space between the variable name and the equal sign when using a basic set command.

The Command Separator

The ampersand is a special character that functions as a command separator; it's not treated like simple text. For instance, you can string the three lines of code from Listing 2-3 together into a single line, with each command separated by the & character:

```
set ;=semicolon& set @=at& set #=hashtag
```

This is functionally equivalent to the three commands on three distinct lines.

On occasion this technique is useful for consolidating simple and similar commands, but using it excessively can make the code difficult to read. However, I've found two very handy uses for the command separator.

Appending Remarks to a Command

One use of the command separator is to add text at the end of a line so that it's treated as a comment. The rem command creates a *remark* out of the text that follows it. Typically, we place a rem command on the line (or lines) preceding some interesting code as a comment, but we also can attach it to a specific command with the command separator. For instance, the following two lines perform the same logic:

```
set myMood=reflective
set myMood=reflective& rem This is a thoughtful and contemplative mood.
```

The second line, however, provides a little more information to anyone reading the code.

Terminating a Command

The second use of the command separator is to terminate a command definitively so the coder can clearly delineate the existence or nonexistence of any trailing spaces. Is the following command setting the variable to null, a space, or multiple spaces?

```
set myMood=
```

As written, it is impossible to tell (unless you make your editor display spaces as visible characters).

If you hadn't read the earlier discussion, the following command might appear to be setting the variable to an ampersand:

```
set myMood=&
```

But this command unequivocally tells the reader that the variable is being set to null because the statement is terminated by the ampersand immediately after the equality operator.

Likewise, there are instances when the coder might want a variable to be a certain length (you'll see a great application of this when formatting reports in Chapter 22). The following sets the variable to a 10-byte left-justified value containing the text pensive followed by three spaces:

```
set myMood=pensive    &
```

Without the ampersand it would be quite difficult to determine how many spaces come after the text, if any. Technically, the ampersand isn't separating two commands, but it definitely is terminating the one command.

Displaying Variable Information

The set command has one more interesting use. When used without an equal sign, it writes out the value of the variable, so if the myMood variable is already defined, you can enter this command in a bat file:

```
set myMood
```

The resulting output written to the console might be as follows:

```
myMood=hopeful
```

If only the first part of the variable name is typed after the set command, all variables that start with that text will be displayed. Thus, the following command might output more than the value of the `myMood` variable:

```
set myM
```

Maybe, just maybe, it might output this:

```
Mymar=A Genus of Fairyflies
myMood=hopeful
```

It's unlikely that such a variable would've been set, but if it does exist and if these were the only two variables set on the machine starting with `mym`, that would've been the output. Note that the command finds all variables, regardless of case. Also notice the example of a variable value containing embedded spaces.

After seeing this technique work with complete variable names and then partial variable names, we can extend it to no variable name at all:

```
set
```

This command without arguments generates a list of all active variables, those loaded when the bat file started, along with any additions and modifications to the list from the bat file itself.

Persistently Setting a Variable

The set command is ephemeral in nature. It defines variables in a particular Batch stream until the variable is reassigned or the script terminates, at which point all variables set via the set command vanish into the ether. But at times we'll want a variable to be accessible to other processes or other bat files on the computer—and for long after the original bat file has terminated, even after the computer is shut down and rebooted. What we want is an extreme set command, or a *set Xtreme* command. Aptly named, we have the setx command just for this purpose. (Truthfully, I have no idea where the name of the command originated, but it's a story I tell at parties. In the Introduction you were warned about inviting my ilk to parties.)

It would be logical to assume that the syntax of the set and setx commands would be the same. What else would you expect other than a variable, an equal sign, and a value? It's a bit puzzling why, but this isn't the case. The setx command doesn't call for an equal sign. Instead, the variable name and value are delimited (or separated) by a space or spaces like so:

```
setx myMood puzzled
```

While discussing the set command, it became clear that variable names and values can indeed contain spaces. That obviously presents a predicament when a space is the delimiter in the command that sets the variable. But encasing the variable name and/or value in double quotes makes quick work of the issue. This command creates a variable with a two-word name and assigns it a two-word value:

```
setx "my mood"  "cautiously optimistic"
```

To test this, first execute the previous statement in one bat file, and then execute the following command in another bat file or even at the command prompt:

```
set my m
```

To see the effect, you must start the second bat file or open the command prompt *after* the setx command completes, because the interpreter loads a session with the computer's existing variables when that session begins.

All variables starting with my m (case-insensitive and inclusive of the embedded space) will be displayed, including the variable my mood. Unless this variable is reassigned by some other process, such as a future setx command, it'll exist with this value for as long as the computer is operable.

The setx command is a great tool to aid in the development of compiled code. When a particular program being developed eventually runs in production, it'll obviously be running on a different machine with its own environment variables. While animating that program, some IDEs have a good mechanism of simulating those environment variables and the setting of file connectors; others sadly do not. I've seen a few inelegant solutions to get around this shortcoming, but a great solution is to actually set all the needed values on your development machine before animating.

For each program developed in certain languages, I'll create a bat file with a series of setx commands, one for each variable that needs to be set persistently. After executing the bat file, I can animate the program, and it'll find all the environment variables that I expect it to find when it'll later execute in its production environment. If I want to animate a different program, I can first run the bat file associated with it, quickly and easily, and if I feel a need to restore some variables to their prior state when I'm done, I can create a bat file for that as well. (Some IDEs store all variables from the environment just once when it opens. If your IDE behaves this way, ensure that you run the bat file before opening the IDE.)

Command Line Help

The last Batch command that I'll introduce in this chapter is the command that documents the ones I've already discussed along with all of the many others to come. The help command accepts another command as its argument and returns a wealth of information about the command, starting with a brief description of its function and its general syntax.

I'll demonstrate with the set command simply because it's been so central to this chapter. To invoke the help command, enter it into a command prompt (type **CMD** into the Windows Start menu and press ENTER).

Then, to receive more details on the set command in particular, enter the following:

```
help set
```

The interpreter produces far too much information about the set command to display here in its entirety, but here are the first few lines:

```
Displays, sets, or removes cmd.exe environment variables.

SET [variable=[string]]

  variable  Specifies the environment-variable name.
  string    Specifies a series of characters to assign to the variable.
```

The command's brief description is followed immediately by its general syntax, which obviously starts with the command name itself. All text inside of square brackets (also called hard brackets) is optional. The square brackets surrounding the text, [variable=[string]], indicate that the command can work with or without the text inside. Remember that the set command used without an argument returns a list of all active variables. The nested square brackets take it a step further, indicating that string is also optional—that is, variable can be set to nothing at all.

The help for some commands gives examples of the command's use along with additional notes and a list of available options. An *option* is a setting or tweak assigned to a command to turn on or off some additional functionality. They're also called *switches*; in fact, the help command frustratingly uses the two terms interchangeably. For consistency, I'll use only the more popular term *option*, but if someone mentions a Batch command switch, they're referring to an option.

Options are usually defined with a forward slash followed by a single letter, but you'll eventually encounter some that are more complex. Scroll down in the command prompt displaying the help for the set command to see two interesting and useful options. The /A option allows for the command to perform arithmetic (Chapter 6). The /P or prompt option is used to set a variable with user-entered data (Chapter 15).

In Chapter 1, what was possibly your first bat file contained a command to copy some files. I won't cover the details of the xcopy command until Chapter 7, but in the previous chapter it used three options (/F, /S, and /Y). What those do exactly isn't important—yet. What's important is that they turn some functionality on or off and that they're documented with the help command.

Some commands have many options, others just a few, and others still none. As I introduce commands, I'll detail options that I find important and useful, but you'll want to use the help command to find a more complete list. Some undocumented options, however, aren't found with the help command, and to uncover those gems, go to *https://ss64.com/nt/* or some other resource.

I recommend using help when you first work with a particular command or as a reminder of available options. Try using it for any of the other commands mentioned in this chapter, even the help command itself. Yes, entering this at the command prompt

```
help help
```

displays documentation about the help command.

NOTE *Following any Batch command with* **/?** *retrieves the same information. That is, entering* **set /?** *works the same way as* **help set***.*

Summary

Batch coding can be complex, and even something as seemingly simple as setting variables can have some nuances. In this chapter, I detailed the set command and its quirks as well as compared it to the setx command, which sets variables persistently. You also learned how to resolve variables and display them on the console. You can now add remarks to your bat files, use the command separator for multiple purposes, and, most important, quickly access documentation for any command.

In the next chapter, we'll delve further into variables, specifically the scope of variables. We'll examine how to define where and when variables possess certain values and how to enable the powerful feature of delayed expansion. As a preview, I'll let you in on a secret: one variable's value can be the name of a second variable with its own value.

3

SCOPE AND DELAYED EXPANSION

In the prior chapter, you learned about variables, how to set them, and how to resolve their values. In this chapter, I'll focus on the `setlocal` command, which is central to some significant and disparate features of Batch and alters when, where, and how you can handle variables. First, it defines *scope*: where and when those variables can be accessed and manipulated. Second, it enables a feature called *delayed expansion*, which alters how variables are resolved, one upshot of which allows you to store one variable inside another variable.

All languages handle scope in some fashion, but delayed expansion, or something similar, is far less common, and you'll see some surprising uses for it. Finally, the `setlocal` command enables *command extensions*, an awkward term for a mass of additional functionality that's turned on for many other Batch commands.

Scope

Scope defines the life span of a variable. A *global variable* can be set, resolved, deleted, and modified anywhere, and that works fine for most simple bat files. A *local variable* is created with a limited shelf life, meant to be accessible in a single section of code where it's *in scope*. Where those modifications aren't recognized, the variable is *out of scope*.

In Batch, the setlocal command starts a section of code where variables are in scope, and the endlocal command ends that section, making those variables out of scope. Everything defined or manipulated between the two commands is active in that space, but after execution of the endlocal command, those variables revert to their prior state.

To demonstrate, the following code writes the state of three variables to the console both in and out of scope of the setlocal command. One is defined only inside the scope of the setlocal, one only outside, and one both inside and outside. To the right of the echo commands, I've included remarks showing the results, in particular the resolved variables, written to the console:

```
❶ set inAndOut=OUT
   set outer=OUT

❷ setlocal

❸ set inAndOut=IN
   set inner=IN

❹ > con echo Inside Scope:              &rem Inside Scope:
   > con echo    Outer Variable = %outer%    &rem    Outer Variable = OUT
   > con echo    Inner Variable = %inner%    &rem    Inner Variable = IN
   > con echo  In/Out Variable = %inAndOut%  &rem  In/Out Variable = IN

❺ endlocal

❻ > con echo Outside Scope:             &rem Outside Scope:
   > con echo    Outer Variable = %outer%    &rem    Outer Variable = OUT
   > con echo    Inner Variable = %inner%    &rem    Inner Variable =
   > con echo  In/Out Variable = %inAndOut%  &rem  In/Out Variable = OUT
```

There's a lot to unpack here. Let's take the first variable defined: inAndOut is set to OUT ❶ before the setlocal ❷ is executed, meaning that it was set out of scope of the command. After the setlocal executes, the same variable is set to IN ❸ where it's in scope. When inAndOut is first interrogated, it resolves to IN ❹ because it's in scope. But after the endlocal ❺ executes, it's out of scope and reverts to its prior state, which is OUT ❻. (As a side note, IN-N-OUT is always set to delicious.)

Now consider the inner variable, which is defined just once, when it's in scope. That is, after the setlocal ❷ executes, it's set to IN ❸. The variable then resolves to the value of IN ❹ before the endlocal ❺ is executed, but here's where it gets interesting; after the endlocal ❺, it reverts to its prior state of not being defined at all—that is, null or empty ❻.

The final variable is outer, and it's also defined just one time, but when it's out of scope. It's set to OUT ❶ before the setlocal ❷ executes. As you might expect, the variable is still OUT ❻ after the endlocal ❺ executes when it's out of scope. But as you might not expect, its value is also available while in scope of the setlocal ❷, as its value also is OUT ❹ before the endlocal ❺ executes.

This example shows that the setlocal command doesn't inhibit us from using variables already in scope. Everything existing up to that point is still available. What it does is this: *a snapshot is taken of the environment at the moment that the setlocal executes, to which it returns when the endlocal executes.*

Defining scope with the setlocal and endlocal commands has just one use, but it's an important one: to hide or section off variables in a portion of code to prevent conflicts. By default, Batch variables are global; a variable set in one bat file can be resolved or reset in a called bat file and even in a called internal routine. By default, many other languages use the opposite methodology, limiting the scope of variables used inside called programs and routines. Sometimes global variables are perfectly fine, but in other instances, limiting the scope is the better option. The ability to define scope gives you the power to use what's best for your application.

If you're coding a utility bat file that'll be called by many other processes, you may have no idea what variables the calling process is using. Placing a setlocal at the top of your bat file and an endlocal at or near the end defines and limits scope. The upshot is that if you happened to use a variable name in common with the calling bat file, you won't step on its variable, which allows the caller to invoke your bat file with the assurance that there'll be no ill side effects. The same is often done with called internal routines. (In Chapter 10, we'll look at calling internal routines and other bat files.)

Defining scope raises an interesting question. If a utility bat file is called to perform a specific task, there's a good chance that at least part of that task is to set and return a certain variable. There's a means for allowing a variable or variables to survive an endlocal command, and I'll share that in Chapter 16.

Delayed Expansion

The setlocal command is a multipronged tool. In addition to defining scope, it also enables delayed expansion when used with a very descriptive argument:

```
setlocal EnableDelayedExpansion
```

Fittingly, the argument is spelled out without any semblance of abbreviation.

Delayed expansion implements two rounds of variable resolution: the initial resolution and a delayed resolution or expansion. When the interpreter executes a bat file, it processes each line of code one by one, first reading in or parsing a line and then executing that line. The initial resolution happens as the interpreter parses the line, and the delayed expansion happens as it executes the line.

This feature allows for some interesting behavior that isn't available in most languages. For instance, you can treat the value of a variable as a variable itself—or its value can be treated as a portion of another variable name. In Listing 3-1, Toyota is a variable name as well as a value; that's not a coincidence.

```
setlocal EnableDelayedExpansion
set Car=Toyota
set Toyota=Prius
```

Listing 3-1: Setting Car and Toyota with delayed expansion enabled

First, we need the setlocal command with the argument to enable delayed expansion. Next, we set Car to the make of a car, which is a Toyota in this case. But Toyota produces several models, and if we want to capture a particular model, we can set the variable defined as Toyota to the value Prius.

Values and Variables

As I mentioned previously, Toyota is both a value and a variable. It's the value of the Car variable and also a variable containing the Prius value. Now we can execute three statements to write three variables to the console, as shown in Listing 3-2.

```
> con echo                 Car = %Car%
> con echo           Car Again = !Car!
> con echo    Delayed Expansion = !%Car%!
```

Listing 3-2: Resolving Car by three different means

Here's the output Listing 3-2 generates:

```
              Car = Toyota
        Car Again = Toyota
 Delayed Expansion = Prius
```

The first resolution of Car is quite pedestrian by now. Surrounding the variable with percent signs (%) resolves it to its value of Toyota. The second command introduces something new: exclamation marks (!) are used as delimiters to resolve a variable, !Car!, instead of percent signs. The variable surrounded with exclamation marks also resolves to Toyota, but why have two different characters that perform the same function? The answer will present itself after we examine the final command.

The third resolution truly shows the power of delayed expansion. The variable is surrounded by percent signs, and that's surrounded by exclamation marks. The interpreter first resolves %Car% to be Toyota. Make sure that you are seated for this next part: that value is now surrounded by exclamation marks, which causes it to be resolved yet again, so !Toyota! becomes Prius. Putting it all together, the variable is resolved like so:

!%Car%! → !Toyota! → Prius

To answer the question about two different characters performing the same function, the interpreter needs both to perform this resolution since we now have two rounds of it: percent signs do the inner resolution, and exclamation marks do the outer resolution. (Can't we just encase the variable with two sets of double percent signs? No, the syntax for the for command has a specific purpose for the double percent signs, which you'll learn about in Chapter 17.)

The best way to demonstrate exactly how delayed expansion affects the code is to run the same code without it enabled. If we remove the setlocal from Listing 3-1, the results of Listing 3-2 are:

```
              Car = Toyota
        Car Again = !Car!
Delayed Expansion = !Toyota!
```

Without delayed expansion, the exclamation marks are treated as simple text and are of no significance to Batch. The !Car! variable isn't resolved at all; the interpreter doesn't even consider those three letters to be a variable. The !%Car%! variable experiences one round of variable resolution, but again, the exclamation marks are simply along for the ride.

In Chapter 2, I adeptly sidestepped an issue by mentioning that a variable name shouldn't start with a number. Technically, you can set such a variable, but you won't be able to resolve it with percent signs; you can do it only with exclamation marks and with delayed expansion enabled. The best way to deal with this little oddity is never to start variable names with numbers.

Now we have a variable that can be resolved to a value that's resolved a second time to be yet another value. That's not typically easily done, or even done at all, in those fancy modern compiled languages. To be honest, as cool as an entire word being both a variable and a value may be, it's not used often in the real world, but partial variable names have many applications.

Partial Variable Names

This technique becomes even more interesting and useful when the resolved value is used as just a portion of a variable name. To demonstrate, consider these set commands defining the signature culinary masterpieces of five cities:

```
set foodNash=Hot Chicken
set foodNYC=Thin Crust Pizza
set foodChic=Deep Dish Pizza
```

```
set foodNO=Muffuletta Sandwich
set foodSTL=Frozen Custard
```

Each variable name, which is the concatenation of food and a common abbreviation for a city, is set to the dish for which that city is famous. Only five variables are shown, but you could define any number.

The following set of variables has the same abbreviations for the five cities, where each is appended with Full and assigned the full name of the city:

```
set NashFull=Nashville
set NYCFull=New York City
set ChicFull=Chicago
set NOFull=New Orleans
set STLFull=St Louis
```

Now consider this echo command with two examples of delayed expansion:

```
> con echo The best !food%city%! can be found only in !%city%Full!.
```

If city is set to NO and delayed expansion is enabled, this command writes the following to the console:

```
The best Muffuletta Sandwich can be found only in New Orleans.
```

To understand how this worked, let's first take a look at the !food%city%! variable. The inner variable, city, and its encasing percent signs is resolved to NO, revealing the foodNO variable. Next the exclamation mark delimiters resolve it to the most delicious sandwich ever created; no, it's not a glorified ham and cheese sandwich. To summarize:

!food%city%! → !foodNO! → Muffuletta Sandwich

Similarly, the full name of the city is also resolved in two steps. The only difference here is that the hardcoded portion of the variable name comes after the portion to be resolved:

!%city%Full! → !NOFull! → New Orleans

The echo command behaves differently for different values of city, which is important to note. It writes the following four sentences to the console when the variable is set to NYC, Nash, Chic, and STL, respectively:

```
The best Thin Crust Pizza can be found only in New York City.
The best Hot Chicken can be found only in Nashville.
The best Deep Dish Pizza can be found only in Chicago.
The best Frozen Custard can be found only in St Louis.
```

I opened this section by suggesting that having a resolved value as just a portion of a variable name is more useful. This example is pedagogical, but you can easily extend the technique to something more practical. In the professional realm, instead of the realm of city-centric cuisines, you could create a set of variables to define the paths for the transmission of files to different facilities based on their location, say pathNYC, pathNash, and pathSTL. Then a single command to copy a file can use the same delayed expansion technique to transmit the file to one of many destinations. (I'll use this technique again in Chapter 5 when discussing substringing.)

Creative coders can make a seemingly unlimited use of delayed expansion, and we'll get into some of those uses when we explore arrays and hash tables in Chapter 29. The for command in Part II will rely greatly on delayed expansion, and possibly its most interesting application will come in Chapter 16 where a variable will be able to hold two values simultaneously.

Command Extensions

The setlocal command also accepts an argument that turns on command extensions. Unlike delayed expansion, command extensions should be active by default, but you can turn them on explicitly with the following command:

```
setlocal EnableExtensions
```

Enabling command extensions unlocks a great deal of additional functionality and available options for several Batch commands. For instance, the for command is indispensable for any Batch coder. We haven't discussed it yet, but Batch has one variant of the for command when command extensions are disabled. With command extensions enabled, however, it becomes a turbocharged workhorse with at least 10 forms. Even the set command discussed in Chapter 2 (not often considered a dynamic or interesting command) has additional functionality and available options with this setting. The specific features vary from command to command, and you can retrieve their details at the command prompt via the help command (also covered in Chapter 2).

To demonstrate the additional functionality unlocked for just one command by enabling command extensions, return to the command prompt and enter the same command from the prior chapter to retrieve documentation on the set command:

```
help set
```

After a short few lines of text detailing what the command does when command extensions aren't enabled, the interpreter displays the following line:

```
If Command Extensions are enabled SET changes as follows:
```

What follows is all of the expanded functionality that has been unlocked. There's far too much information to show it all, but in this small sample two previously unavailable options are shared:

Two new switches have been added to the SET command:

```
SET /A expression
SET /P variable=[promptString]
```

I mentioned these options in Chapter 2, but I didn't mention that command extensions turn them on. The help command gives you several times the amount of information about the set command's functionality with command extensions enabled than it does when disabled, and the same is true for many other commands. As I introduce more commands, I encourage you to investigate them further with the help command to see a larger list of uses and options and to see what's turned on with command extensions.

Final Thoughts on setlocal and endlocal

After two decades of coding bat files, I have some strong opinions on the use of the setlocal and endlocal commands, and I'm not shy about sharing them. Every high-level bat file that I write has this command at or near the very first line of code:

```
setlocal EnableExtensions EnableDelayedExpansion
```

I'm defining a high-level bat file as a bat file that isn't called from another bat file. I've rarely come across an instance where I didn't want command extensions and delayed expansion enabled. There's virtually no cost for all the extra features. It's as if you could turn your Toyota into a Lamborghini with none of the disadvantages such as cost and gas mileage. But in that rare instance, you can disable these features with the DisableExtensions and DisableDelayedExpansion arguments.

Additionally, whenever I code some logic that might adversely affect other code, I precede that logic with a simple setlocal command with no arguments and terminate it with a corresponding endlocal command. Don't fret; delayed expansion is still enabled from the original setlocal command. You can even nest multiple setlocal and endlocal commands, creating subsections of code with a defined scope within subsections, but not more than 32 levels deep. I have never come close to this limitation, but if you do, you can nest further in a called routine or another bat file. (I'll get to how those calls are performed in Chapter 10.)

For the sake of completeness, it's good form for that original setlocal to have a corresponding endlocal at the end of the bat file, but if omitted, the interpreter executes an implied endlocal before exiting the high-level bat file.

Crucially, this book is written with the assumption that command extensions and delayed expansion are enabled. In general, I won't bore you with what functionality is unlocked with these settings and what isn't. If an example from this book isn't working in your testing, make sure that you've run this command with both of its enabling arguments.

NOTE *I have just one exception to the rule about starting all high-level bat files with the particular* setlocal *command mentioned previously, and it's in this book. In later chapters I'll provide some examples of very short bat files, maybe just two or three lines. These simple examples might not require this command, and its use might pull the focus away from the topic at hand. In those instances, I won't include the command, but understand that it could and should be there.*

Summary

The main focus of this chapter was the setlocal command, which defines scope and enables command extensions. Most important, it enables delayed expansion, opening vast possibilities for defining and using variables.

With delayed expansion enabled, you saw how you can write out one of five sentences based on the value of a variable defining a city with just a single command. But if delayed expansion had been disabled, you may have resorted to interrogating that variable with five if commands. In the example laid out in this chapter, that would've been an inelegant solution, but in general, the if command is an important workhorse in any language, and Batch is no different. In the next chapter, I'll discuss it in detail—and since this is Batch—its idiosyncrasies.

4

CONDITIONAL EXECUTION

The if command, which is quite likely common to all programming languages, causes one or more lines of code to be executed only when a condition is true, and a different section of code can be executed only when that condition is false.

The basics are straightforward, but in Batch the *conditional clause,* or the entity that evaluates to true or false, is quite different from similar clauses in other languages. Most of the compare operators are unique to Batch, and in this chapter you'll learn the syntax to determine whether a path or file exists and whether a variable is populated. It's also important to understand the different techniques for evaluating the return code.

In addition, you'll learn how to efficiently manage instances where multiple conditions need to be evaluated as well as some common stumbling blocks to avoid. It's disturbingly easy to write an if command that works most of the time but either aborts or fails to execute as intended under certain data conditions.

The Basic if Command

In its most basic incarnation, the `if` command executes one or more lines of code if a condition is true. I'll show how you can expand this command to execute a different bit of code if that same condition is false, but let's start with its basic structure.

Nearly every Batch command implementation starts with the command name itself and is often followed by arguments and/or options. For instance, the `set` command always starts with those three letters. Usually, it's followed by an argument consisting of a variable name, an equal sign, and a value, but in Chapter 2 you learned that it works with no arguments or options at all. (Such a command writes out a list of active variables.)

The `if` command is unique. It also starts with its command name, but the similarities end there; it can span multiple lines and has two major components. Here's the general form where you'd replace the italicized text with code:

```
if conditional clause (
   true code block
)
```

The *conditional clause* is an expression that evaluates to true or false. If it's true, the interpreter executes the command or commands inside the *true code block*, and if it's false, this code doesn't execute. In Chapter 16, I'll discuss code blocks in more depth, but for now, a code block is simply one or more lines of code set between parentheses.

With this syntax, the open parenthesis must not only follow the conditional clause; it also must be on the same line. Other languages allow (or even encourage) you to put the open parenthesis on the next line and line it up with the close parenthesis, but this is verboten in Batch. However, good form dictates that the close parenthesis should line up with the beginning of the `if` command with the intervening commands indented. My convention calls for three spaces of indentation, but any amount will do. Here's a functioning example:

```
if "%today%" equ "07/04/2026" (
   set event=sestercentennial
)
```

The conditional clause, `"%today%" equ "07/04/2026"`, is looking for equality between a resolved variable and some hardcoded text. This conditional clause is fairly straightforward, but I'll soon demonstrate far more impressive ones using different compare operators, keywords, and even an option. Many coding languages put the conditional clause inside parentheses; for better or worse, the clause stands on its own in Batch, and the parentheses are used to enclose the upcoming code block.

If the conditional clause is true, the command in the code block (in this example, the `set` command) is executed, resulting in event being set to the term for a quarter-millennium celebration.

The following more compact format fitting on a single line is functionally equivalent to the previous example:

```
if "%today%" equ "07/04/2026"  (set event=sestercentennial)
```

You no longer need the parentheses when using a single line. The following is functionally equivalent to both prior examples:

```
if "%today%" equ "07/04/2026"  set event=sestercentennial
```

Technically, because of the lack of parentheses, the set command is no longer in a code block. In lieu of a concise term, it's now just the command that executes when the conditional clause is true.

In both of the prior examples, I've left two spaces after the conditional clause, and I often leave more than two. Syntactically this isn't needed, but since nothing clearly delineates the conditional clause from what comes after it, readability is enhanced with a little separation.

You can even execute multiple commands on a single line with the & command separator, as discussed in Chapter 2:

```
if "%today%" equ "07/04/2026"  set event=sestercentennial& set code=ugly
```

If the conditional clause is true, an additional set command, which happens to be self-critiquing of the code, is executed. I've seen this technique used on occasion, usually when setting an error code and error message, but in instances such as this, using a single line just makes the code inscrutable.

If there's anything remotely interesting in the logic being performed, use multiple lines of code:

```
if "%today%" equ "07/04/2026" (
    set event=sestercentennial
    set code=elegant
)
```

Elegant is undoubtedly a gross overstatement here, but I hope you agree that this technique makes the code far more readable. With just a glance, the reader knows that if the condition is true, two variables are set.

The Conditional Clause

The examples in the previous section all use a straightforward conditional clause, but the clause can be far more dynamic, taking on many other forms and using different operators and keywords.

Compare Operators

A *compare operator*, unsurprising enough, compares two operands for equality or for one being greater than the other. You may have guessed that the equ operator in the previous examples represents equality, and you'd be right.

Here's the complete list of Batch compare operators:

equ or ==   Equal

neq   Not equal

lss   Less than

leq   Less than or equal

gtr   Greater than

geq   Greater than or equal

You can choose between two functionally equivalent alternatives for the equality operator. To differentiate from the single equal sign used for assignment, such as in a set command, Batch uses double equal signs for the compare operator. My preferred syntax is the equ operator because it looks similar to the others, but some coders prefer the == operator for the opposite reason.

The neq operator evaluates the conditional clause to true if the two operands being compared are *not* equal. The last four operators determine which operand is greater or less than the other. For example, assuming that age is set to a numeric value, the following one-line code block executes only if the variable is set to a value greater than 12:

```
if %age% gtr 12 (
    > con echo Adult Movie Theater Ticket Required
)
```

You might be tempted to try %age% > 12 as the conditional clause, but the greater-than sign already has a defined purpose in Batch; in fact, it's being used in this code block to write a short message to the console. For this reason, you must use the three-character alpha code of gtr as the operator. Similarly, the operators listed in this section are needed for greater-than or equal, less-than, and less-than or equal compares.

Less intuitively, these operators also work on alphanumeric values. All numbers are less than all letters; a is less than A; A is less than b; b is less than B; and so on. This'll do nothing to end the larger debate, but at least in the Batch universe, Picard is greater than Kirk.

Conditional Clause Keywords

You'll find the following indispensable keywords in the help for the if command, but make no mistake; these keywords are specific to the conditional clause:

exist   The exist keyword checks for the existence of either a path or a file and returns true if found. You can hardcode the path or file, or for flexibility, you can use a variable containing the potential path or file:

```
if exist C:\Batch\myFile.txt      set do=something
if exist %pathAndFileName%        set do=something
```

You can also string multiple variables together to build the path or filename.

defined   The following conditional clause using the defined keyword checks whether a variable is defined—that is, does it resolve to anything, even a space? A common mistake is to use percent signs around the variable, but here's the correct syntax using this keyword:

```
if defined varThatMayBeEmpty     set do=something
```

This is functionally equivalent to the following with percent signs resolving the variable:

```
if "%varThatMayBeEmpty%" neq ""    set do=something
```

This keyword is often used to validate expected input variables. If one or more is not defined, you can take appropriate action, possibly initiating an abort.

not   The not keyword negates any conditional clause when used at the very beginning of the clause. This is extremely useful in setting defaults for variables in the event that they've not yet been set by someone or something else. For instance, the following ensures that skyColor is set to its usual color:

```
if not defined skyColor        set skyColor=Blue
```

You can couple the not keyword with the exist keyword to determine whether a specific file doesn't exist. Armed with that knowledge, you can then create a file, initiate an abort, or do whatever makes sense for your application. Some coders use the not keyword with the equ operator, but I find this iffy at best and much prefer the neq operator alone. Logically there's no difference, but whatever your preference, be consistent.

WARNING   *After two decades of Batch coding I still try to add s to the end of the exist keyword more often than I care to admit. Notepad++ faithfully alerts me every time because it emboldens keywords; that spurious character drops the bold font for the entire word, making it stand out. Code without an editor like this at your own peril.*

The Case-Insensitive Option

The if command has exactly one option, and much like the keywords we've looked at so far, it applies to the conditional clause. The /i option makes the equality (and inequality) operator in the conditional clause case-insensitive.

To demonstrate, the conditional clause without the option in the following if command evaluates to true only if myMood resolves exactly to happy—the hardcoded value on the right side of the inequality:

```
if "%myMood%" equ "happy"        set do=something
```

Here's the same code with the addition of the /i option:

```
if /i "%myMood%" equ "happy"     set do=something
```

The conditional clause now evaluates to true if the variable resolves to HAPPY, Happy, happy, or any of the other 29 possible permutations on the capitalization of the word.

NOTE   *The /i option probably looks a bit different from others that I've mentioned already and ones yet to come. As mentioned previously, I use lowercase for Batch commands even though the case doesn't matter to the interpreter. Options also work regardless of the case. Even so, since options are usually just a forward slash followed by a single character, I typically capitalize them for emphasis. But depending on the font, the capital I often looks like a lowercase L, so I depart from my personal convention for the /i option, used most often with the if command. And yes, the irony that this is the option concerned with case-insensitivity has not been lost on me.*

The errorlevel Variable

After calling an executable or performing many Batch commands, a return code is stored in the errorlevel pseudo-environment variable. (The command in Chapter 1 that copied a file is one example of many to come that will set this variable.) You'll learn more about pseudo-environment variables in Chapter 21, but for now, consider errorlevel to be a variable containing a return code that you shouldn't set with the set command. (If you do, you'll just break the errorlevel variable.) The errorlevel variable can be evaluated like any other in Batch as part of an if command. For example, the following recognizes a return code of 1 or greater as a failure:

```
if %errorlevel% geq 1     set msg=FAILURE
```

Batch also supports an archaic syntax that works only for this unique variable, where the percent signs and the equality operator are removed. The following is functionally equivalent to the previous example:

```
if errorlevel 1          set msg=FAILURE
```

At first this may seem simplified and appealing because content has been dropped with nothing added, but the syntax disguises a surprising batveat. Many Batch coders mistakenly interpret this conditional clause as looking for equality between the return code and 1. After all, testing it with a return code of 0 correctly returns false, and testing it with a return code of 1 correctly returns true. But the conditional clause errorlevel 1 is equivalent to both %errorlevel% geq 1 and %errorlevel% gtr 0. It evaluates to true for all positive integers.

Couple this syntax with the not keyword for something truly opaque:

```
if not errorlevel 0      set msg=The Return Code is NEGATIVE
```

Doesn't this look like a conditional clause that would evaluate to true when the return code isn't equal to 0? It's really the negation of the return code being greater than or equal to 0. The %errorlevel% lss 0 conditional clause is functionally equivalent and far more readable.

Another problem with the syntax lacking a compare operator is that more often than not, 0 represents a good return code, and all others, including negative values, indicate a problem of some sort.

The neq operator results in this conditional clause being true for all nonzero values:

```
if %errorlevel% neq 0    set msg=FAILURE
```

You may run across the arcane syntax, so it's important to understand how it works, but it's more important to not propagate it. Always use percent signs (or exclamation marks) and a compare operator to evaluate the errorlevel pseudo-environment variable.

The if...else Construct

One of the unwritten rules of coding languages is that an if command must come with the possibility of an else keyword. The keywords I mentioned earlier are associated with the conditional clause, but this one is tied to the if command itself. Here's the general form of the if...else construct, where once again the italicized text must be replaced with code:

```
if conditional clause (
    true code block
) else (
    false code block
)
```

The first two lines and the close parenthesis starting the third are identical to the general form I showed at the beginning of this chapter. The else keyword follows, and it in turn is followed by the *false code block*, set between a second set of parentheses. This represents the code that executes when the *conditional clause* evaluates to false.

Here's a simple example of an if...else construct:

```
if %fahrenheit% gtr 70 (
    set pants=shorts
) else (
    set pants=jeans
)
```

If the fahrenheit variable is greater than 70, the pants variable is set to shorts. Otherwise, the pants variable is set to jeans. One or the other code block will always execute.

You can condense this construct into a single line of code:

```
if %fahrenheit% gtr 70 (set pants=shorts) else (set pants=jeans)
```

The parentheses surrounding the code in the *false code block* are technically optional, but they should be included for readability.

Unless you have contempt for those that'll be reading your code, the one-line if...else construct is usually bad practice, although you might make exceptions for the simplest of tasks.

Unlike in other languages, in Batch the else keyword can't be coded on a line of its own; it can't even start or end a line. To clearly demarcate the two code blocks, it's best to code the keyword sandwiched between the close and open parentheses on a single line.

The else if Construct

The if...else construct is great when there are exactly two branches in the logical flow, one for true and one for false. When there are more than two branches, the else if construct allows for multiple conditional clauses. Listing 4-1 has three clauses and four branches, one branch for each conditional clause and a default branch that executes when none of the clauses evaluates to true.

```
if %fahrenheit% gtr 80 (
    set pants=shorts
) else if %fahrenheit% gtr 60 (
    set pants=light khakis
) else if %fahrenheit% gtr 32 (
    set pants=jeans
) else (
    set pants=lined jeans
)
```

Listing 4-1: An else if construct with four logical branches

This logic assumes that fahrenheit is set to an integer describing the temperature. If it's greater than 80 degrees, the first set command executes. If it's greater than 60, which is to say between 61 and 80, inclusive, the second set command executes. If the first two conditional clauses are false and the mercury registers as above freezing, the third set command executes. If all three clauses are false, the temperature is 32 degrees or below, so the fourth and final set command assigns a very warm pair of pants.

There's no open parenthesis immediately after the first else keyword. Instead, it's followed by another if command with a conditional clause of its own and only then by the open parenthesis.

Listing 4-1 contains two else if clauses, but you can code any number depending on the need. The interpreter executes the code block corresponding to the first conditional clause that evaluates to true; afterward, control jumps to the end of the entire construct without evaluating the other clauses.

Many times, you'll want a final code block executed if none of the conditional clauses is true—that is, a default code block. For instance, if Listing 4-1 fails to set a certain variable, someone is in danger of leaving the house without the proper attire. The final else keyword is not followed by an if command, so its code block, the default code block, executes if none of the three conditional clauses prior to it evaluated to true.

In Listing 4-1, fahrenheit is being interrogated to determine in which of four ranges it falls. This is a popular use of else if conditional clauses, but they don't have to be so closely linked. Each conditional clause can interrogate completely different variables or make use of the three keywords covered earlier. For example, here's a reimagining of Listing 4-1 with only the three conditional clauses changed:

```
if /i "%season%" equ "Summer" (
    set pants=shorts
) else if exist C:\Batch\Spring.txt (
    set pants=light khakis
) else if %celsius% gtr 0 (
    set pants=jeans
) else (
    set pants=lined jeans
)
```

The first conditional clause performs a case-insensitive compare for equality of a resolved variable and hardcoded text. The second clause is looking for the existence of a file, and the third is looking to see whether the value of the celsius variable is above the freezing point. Once again, due to the default code block, this code is guaranteed to set the variable to one of the four values.

Enhanced Equality Determination Techniques

I would be remiss if I didn't mention an important batveat associated with these conditional clauses. In some of the examples in this chapter I've surrounded each side of the equality with double quotes in a conditional clause, but without them the commands would still work—most of the time. The following two if commands are very similar but *not* functionally equivalent:

```
if /i "%myMood%" equ "happy"    set do=something
if /i %myMood% equ happy        set do=something
```

If myMood is set to happy, the clause evaluates to true, and if it's set to sad, the result is false. Either way, it works for both commands.

That's great, but now imagine that the variable hasn't been set or that it's been set to null or some number of spaces. The command without the double quotes will crash, but it hints at the issue with the following cryptic message (assuming you haven't used the echo off command mentioned in Chapter 2):

```
happy was unexpected at this time.

C:\Batch> if /i  equ happy          set do=something
```

The first line here is the error message, and it's followed by what has confused the interpreter. To understand the error, we must think like the interpreter. Once it sees the if command start the line, it expects one out of a finite list of items to come next (maybe not, exist, defined, or /i), with anything unrecognizable assumed to be the left side of a conditional clause. Obviously, it finds /i. Assuming that one of the three keywords doesn't come next, the interpreter is now expecting exactly three items in a specific order: some text; an operator such as equ, neq, or ==; and some more text. If the value of myMood is pretty much anything, it will resolve to be the first text field. The interpreter will then be pleased to find the equ operator, and knowing that it's dealing with an equality, it'll interpret the hardcoded happy as being the right side of that equality. *Success.*

This all blows up when the variable resolves to nothing or any number of spaces. The interpreter sees if /i to start the statement, so it doesn't expect to see equ next. The not keyword would've made sense, but not equ. As a result, it incorrectly considers equ to be the left side of what might be an equality and what comes next to be the operator. But what comes next is the happy text, and the list of operators clearly doesn't contain this word. As the message states, the interpreter doesn't expect to see happy at this time. *Failure.*

Fortunately, there are two methods of evaluating variables that might resolve to nothing.

The Preceding Dot Technique

One common technique to get around this issue is to prefix each side of the equality with a dot, or almost any character as long as it's applied consistently, so that the interpreter will definitely find something on both sides of the equality:

```
if /i .%myMood% equ .happy          set do=something
```

The preceding dot technique works nicely when the variable is set to null, as the command resolves to if /i . equ .happy. The dot isn't equal to the dot followed by the word, so it evaluates to false, and we move on. If the variable had been set to happy, the command would've been resolved to if /i .happy equ .happy, and equality would've been found. *Success.*

But I'm not a fan of this technique because it's susceptible to yet another batveat. Now imagine that the variable is set to a two-word mood, such as irritably depressed—not good on many levels having nothing to do with the Batch code. Again, it blows up:

```
depressed was unexpected at this time.
C:\Batch> if /i .irritably depressed equ .happy        set do=something
```

Don't get down. The interpreter is fooled by the embedded space. Don't tell anyone, but it really isn't that bright. It thinks that .irritably is the left side of the clause and finds depressed to be a completely unexpected operator. *Failure.* But there's another technique.

The Double Quotes Technique

Coming full circle, this brings us back to the example with the double quotes around each side of the equality:

```
if /i "%myMood%" equ "happy"        set do=something
```

The double quotes here provide something on either side of the equality just as the dot did, but that's not all.

The interpreter considers everything inside the double quotes to be one entity. When the variable with the embedded space is resolved, the interpreter sees this:

```
if /i "irritably depressed" equ "happy"
```

Despite the embedded space, the interpreter treats "irritably depressed" as one entity, or in this case the left side of the equality, with the right side being "happy". The upshot is that Batch correctly recognizes these two entities as not being equal. *Success.*

If there's a chance that the alphanumeric variable being interrogated might not be set or that it might contain embedded spaces, I almost always encase each side of the clause with double quotes. However, you may have noticed that I don't have double quotes encasing %errorlevel% when used in a conditional clause. That variable will always be set to a number, so there's no need for the quotes. Even more important, when the interpreter sees numbers being compared without quotes, it does a numeric compare, meaning that 000 is equivalent to 0. Adding the quotes results in a text compare, and "000" isn't equal to "0".

Preceding Dot vs. Double Quotes

When comparing alphanumeric values, I *usually* encase each side of the equality with double quotes. It works when a value is null; it works when a value is one or more spaces; it works when a value has embedded spaces; and it works for more typical non-null spaceless values. However, I'm using the nondefinitive qualifier *usually* because of an extremely fine point.

Consider the case of a variable containing a value with a trailing space. Perhaps the value sad is padded with a trailing space to make a four-character value. Is that equal to the three-character value sad? In the purest and most accurate sense, no, they aren't equal—and using the double quote method correctly finds them to be different. But in a less strict scenario you might consider these values to be equivalent.

Using the dot method will find equality between the two values because the trailing space becomes just another space between the left side of the equality and the operator. In this narrow instance of trailing spaces, the dot method is better, but it'll work only if the variables don't have any embedded spaces.

In the final analysis, the double quote technique is far superior to the dot method, with one very distinctive case when it isn't. Get into the habit of using double quotes for almost all non-numeric compares.

NOTE *Batch provides an interesting and compact alternative to the if command, although it does behave differently. It's not a command, it doesn't have any keywords, and it doesn't even support a conditional clause. In Chapter 28, I'll return to the topic of conditional execution and provide more details about what it is than what it isn't.*

Summary

The if command is instrumental in virtually all, if not all, coding languages, and Batch is no different. In this chapter you learned about the conditional clause, including its valid operators for comparing two operands and its keywords for proving out the existence of a variable, path, or file, and what happens when the clause evaluates to true and false. You also learned how to evaluate multiple clauses so as to execute multiple branches of logic conditionally.

As is often the case, Batch gives you a little more to consider, so I detailed useful techniques to enhance your conditional clauses comparing both alphanumeric and numeric values. But what makes a value alphanumeric or numeric? I'll answer that question in the next two chapters concerning data types.

5

STRING AND BOOLEAN DATA TYPES

The first thing to learn about assigning data types in Batch is that Batch doesn't allow for the assignment of data types.

There's no underlying egalitarian ethos at play, but all Batch variables are created equal. Intrinsically, there's no difference between a variable holding a number, text, or even a boolean. However, a variable set to a number can be treated as numeric, and I'll focus on those data types in the next chapter.

In this chapter, after an overview of all Batch data types, you'll learn about string and character variables. You'll also explore strings further with methods for substringing and text replacement. Booleans were not devised by the creators of Batch, but I'll show you how to build and use this useful data type.

Common Data Types

Many if not most programming languages not only allow but also require every variable to be declared as a specific data type before it can be assigned a value or used in any fashion. There are variations from language to language, but here's a general list of data types:

Character   Single alphanumeric character

String   Zero to many alphanumeric characters

Integer   Positive and negative whole numbers

Floating-point   Numbers with a decimal place

Boolean   True or false

For better or worse, Batch variables aren't declared. One comes into being ex nihilo the first time the interpreter discovers a new variable name. This practice does allow for a great deal of flexibility, but it can be tricky and dangerous. One misspelled instance of a variable name used a dozen times is considered to be an entirely different variable by the interpreter, and the mistake will not be caught by the guiding hand of a compiler. Instead, it's treated as a new variable that'll likely resolve to nothing.

A variable can be assigned an integer, and arithmetic can be performed on it. That same variable can then be assigned text and treated like a string. That also means that arithmetic can inadvertently be performed on a variable containing a string, but on the upside, a number can easily be treated as a string without any type of conversion when written to the console or a report. It's pure digital anarchy, a coding language for nihilists, and somehow it works.

Even though you can't assign data types, you can create variables and treat them as one of the types, but—and I cannot stress this enough—the underlying structure of every Batch variable is really just a few nondescript bytes of memory.

Characters

A character is merely a single byte of text; in the world of Batch, think of it as a very short string, as it's treated exactly like any other single-character string. I'll keep this section short and move on to strings.

Strings

A string is text of any length, containing alphabetic characters, numbers, and/or special characters. The following command sets the aString variable to a five-word string:

```
set aString=Awesome Batch Code Dares Excellence
```

Including embedded spaces, its length totals 35 characters or, in the parlance of coders, bytes.

Many special characters, such as the dollar and pound signs, can be explicitly included in the string, but others, such as the percent sign, cannot, because they have specific uses in Batch. In Chapter 14, I'll address how escaping allows for the inclusion of all characters in a string, but for now, understand that the interpreter won't abort when it comes upon an exclamation mark in a string, but you might not see your expected result. For instance, the last character in the value being assigned to this variable is an exclamation mark:

```
set aString=Awesome Batch Code Dares Excellence!
> con echo A String is "%aString%"
```

Here's the result of the echo command:

```
A String is "Awesome Batch Code Dares Excellence"
```

The punctuation mark isn't written to the console because it wasn't included in the string variable.

NOTE *As mentioned in Chapter 3, I'm assuming that delayed expansion is enabled throughout this book. This example is a great case in point, because if delayed expansion had been disabled, the exclamation mark would've been just another character, not a delimiter used to resolve a variable. The character would've been included as part of the value and would've been written to the console with the rest of the text. Being able to treat an exclamation mark as simple text might be the only advantage of disabling delayed expansion. This trivial advantage pales in comparison to the functionality afforded by delayed expansion, which is why I recommend its universal use.*

In later chapters, I'll discuss how to write strings and other data types to files, but here I'll explain how to build, concatenate, substring, and manipulate strings.

Build and Concatenate

The previous example used a single set command to assign the value Awesome Batch Code Dares Excellence to a variable. The following six lines perform the same task:

```
set a=Awesome
set b=Batch &
set c=Code
set d=Dares
set e= Excellence
set aString=%a% %b%%c% %d%%e%
```

In practice, this method would be horribly inefficient for building a string, but it nicely demonstrates the principle of concatenation.

The variables defined by the first five letters of the alphabet are each set to a single word. Then on the last line all five variables are resolved and concatenated together to create aString. Take note of the four embedded spaces in the result. One is from the trailing space after Batch, another is from the leading space before Excellence, and the other two are embedded in the last set command.

The previous example shows how to create a string by concatenating other strings, but you can also append or prepend an existing string with other text:

```
set longText=This field contains a brutal run-on sentence and if its prose
set longText=%longText% were to be typed into a single line the reader would
set longText=%longText% be forced to scroll way over to the right to read what
set longText=%longText% you are reading now and then scroll way back to the
set longText=%longText% left after mercifully getting to this period.
```

Here a string is being appended with additional text four times to create a very long string.

This method is my preference for creating long string variables, but you can do the same task with the "continuation character" or caret (^). When the interpreter comes to a caret at the end of a line, it appends to that line the next line:

```
 set longText=This field contains a brutal run-on sentence and if its prose ^
were to be typed into a single line the reader would be forced to scroll way^
 over to the right to read what you are reading now and then scroll way back ^
to the left after mercifully getting to this period.
```

In this example, three carets are used to make a four-line set command. The first and third lines have a space in front of the caret, and their following lines start in the first byte, resulting in a space between the words. To demonstrate a different means of doing the same thing, the second caret immediately follows the word way, and the next line has a space prior to the next word, over. The upshot is a long string of words, all separated by a single space.

I am not a fan of this technique for the simple reason that it plays havoc with my indentation scheme. I indent most commands two or more spaces, as the first line of the set command shows, but any spaces at the beginning of the subsequent line are considered part of the appended text. This effectively means that these lines must be left-justified. I'll delve into indenting schemes further in Chapter 9. For now, just understand that it works—but it's ugly.

NOTE   *I put "continuation character" in quotes because this is a gross simplification. The caret is really an escape character. In Chapter 14, I'll explain why that matters, but many Batch coders simply refer to it as the* continuation character.

Substrings

Any language worth its salt will support a substringing function that retrieves a portion of a string, and Batch is up to the task. For the next few examples, let's consider the aString variable being set just as it was earlier:

```
set aString=Awesome Batch Code Dares Excellence
```

A *substringing function* needs two numbers, the offset or starting position and the length of the desired text. Surprisingly, Batch uses the zero-offset that predominates more modern languages and not the one-offset more common of 20th-century languages. This means the first byte is position 0 (not 1), the second byte is position 1, the 100th byte is position 99, and so on.

The syntax to substring is a bit clunky. The variable is resolved with percent signs as is typical, but the closing percent sign is preceded with a colon, a tilde, the offset, a comma, and ultimately the length. Hence, the following syntax returns the first three characters of the aString variable:

```
set subString=%aString:~0,3%
```

The offset of 0 tells the interpreter to start with the first byte and the length is defined as 3, resulting in the text Awe bcing assigned to subString.

The following extracts the text some out of the first word of the same string:

```
set subString=%aString:~3,4%
```

We need to start in the fourth byte, which is a zero-offset of 3. If you find the zero-offset confusing, think of the offset as the number of bytes *before* the substring. More obviously, the length is 4.

Here are two substrings put together with a hardcoded to and a couple spaces:

```
set phrase=%aString:~15,3% to %aString:~8,5%
```

The 15th byte is the capital C in Code, so the first substring is the remaining three bytes of the word. The eighth byte is the space before Batch, so the next five bytes encompass that entire word. The result is an apt, if not corny, reinterpretation of the original string: ode to Batch.

If the length isn't defined, the interpreter returns the remainder of the string. To demonstrate, the following substring has no length and no preceding comma. The offset corresponds to the 25 bytes preceding the last word in the 35-byte variable:

```
set subString=%aString:~25%
```

The upshot is that subString is assigned the string Excellence, the last 10 bytes of the original string.

Negative Offsets

Notice the negative offset in the following example. Interestingly, this also assigns Excellence to the variable:

```
set subString=%aString:~-10%
```

A *negative offset* indicates that the starting position is relative to the end of the string, not the beginning, which means -10 tells the interpreter that the substring is to start 10 bytes from the end of the string. Since no length is given, it returns the remainder of the text. As long as the variable is populated, %aString:~-1% is an easy way to inspect its last byte.

Both of these commands result in the same ode substring:

```
set subString=%aString:~15,3%
set subString=%aString:~-20,3%
```

The first command's offset is 15 bytes from the start of the original string, while the second command finds the same position by counting 20 bytes from the end of the 35-byte variable.

Negative Lengths

A negative length works in a similar fashion. Don't think of it as a *length*; think of it as the number of bytes at the end of the string *not* in the substring. For instance, the following returns a string with the first and last bytes stripped off:

```
set subString=%aString:~1,-1%
```

You can even use negative offsets with negative lengths. The following extracts the penultimate byte of the string:

```
set subString=%aString:~-2,-1%
```

The offset of -2 tells the interpreter to start with the second to last byte, and the length of -1 indicates that the last byte is dropped.

Substring in Practice

One nice feature of retrieving a substring in Batch is that a null is simply returned if calling for a substring beyond the length of the string. Thus, the interpreter won't crash when it comes upon %aString:~99,1% for the 35-byte string, nor will it return a space. Instead, it returns only an empty string. It's a handy way of determining the length of a string with no fear of the null pointer exceptions prevalent in compiled code. If the 36th byte equals null (that is, "%aString:~35,1%" equ "") but the 35th byte is populated, the string is exactly 35 bytes in length.

However, this syntax works only when substringing a populated string. As I just mentioned, the resolution of %aString:~35,1% is null if the string is between 1 and 35 bytes in length, and of course, it resolves to the 36th byte if the string is 36 bytes or longer. But if the string is empty or set to null, `%aString:~35,1%` resolves to `~35,1`, or everything between the colon and trailing delimiter. Likewise due to this batveat, when trying to inspect the last byte of an empty string, `%aString:~-1%` resolves to `~-1`, not the null you may have expected.

You now know how to extract any portion of a string from another string, but all of the offsets and lengths are hardcoded in the earlier examples. Often, if not most of the time, those two numbers will be variables. In the following example, the offset and length are defined as obviously named variables and used in the third command:

```
set offset=15
set length=3
set subString=!aString:~%offset%,%length%!
```

The percent signs encasing `offset` and `length` first resolve these variables to their numeric values. Then the exclamation marks kick in so that `!aString:~15,3!` resolves to our familiar `ode`, which is yet another victory for enabling delayed expansion.

After finishing the next chapter, where I discuss arithmetic, you'll be able to calculate variables holding integer values to be used as offsets and lengths to find a substring.

Text Replacement

Batch also has a handy mechanism for replacing all or part of a string with other text. For example, assume that the following variable contains this awkward filename:

```
set filNm=File_Name_With_Underscores.docx
```

If you aren't fond of this filename, you could change the underscores to dashes. In Chapter 7, I'll introduce the ideal command for renaming a file, but here I'll discuss how to build a variable containing the new filename.

The text replacement syntax is similar to what was used for substringing. The variable and a colon are surrounded by percent signs as before, but now there's no tilde. Instead, after the colon comes the text to search for and change, followed by an equal sign delimiter, and finally the replacement text:

```
set newFilNm=%filNm:_=-%
```

Each and every underscore character (_), not just the first one encountered, is changed to a dash (-), resulting in `File-Name-With-Underscores.docx`. Be careful not to change more text than you intend.

Looking at this filename, it also would make sense to change the word `Underscores` to `Dashes`. Fortunately, Batch doesn't require that the target and replacement text be the same length, so this additional command further updates the value of this variable to File-Name-With-Dashes.docx:

```
set newFilNm=%newFilNm:underscor=Dash%
```

Since both words end in es, I'm using the singular Dash as the replacement text, and the target text is underscor, which isn't even a real word. Also, notice that Underscores is capitalized in the variable's value, but underscor is lower-case in the replace syntax. Very important, Batch does a case-insensitive replacement. The target text can be whichever case or even mixed case with no effect on the outcome, but the replacement text will be used exactly as it is entered in the command. Hence, %newFilNm:UNDERscor=Dash% is functionally identical to the variable resolution in the previous command, but %newFilNm:underscor=DASH% would result in a new filename of File-Name-With -DASHes.docx.

It's subtle, but the prior two commands show two distinct methods of assignment. The first assigns the modified value of filNm to newFilNm, leaving filNm unchanged. The second command reassigns newFilNm to itself so that its ultimate value reflects both text replacements. These two methods give you the flexibility to either alter a variable's value in place or maintain two variables, one with the old and one with the new text.

You can also use delayed expansion to turn the target text, targ, and the replacement text, repl, into variables. Here's an example:

```
set targ=Love
set repl=Hate
set aString=I Love Broccoli
set aString=!aString:%targ%=%repl%!
```

The result is the far more honest string I Hate Broccoli.

A text search is one wonderful application of the text replacement syntax. In Chapter 24, I'll compare and contrast two methods of determining whether one string is part of another string. The findstr command works well, but the method based on the previous syntax executes in a fraction of the time. Spoiler alert: the text search logic replaces the searched for text with null, and the result is compared to the original text. If they differ, the text was found.

Booleans

Booleans are ever-present in compiled languages having two, and *only* two, possible states: true or false. Once set, you can use them alone as the conditional clause in an if command to be evaluated as true or false, thus determining whether a block of code should be executed. Batch doesn't support booleans explicitly, but with a little ingenuity, you can create them.

Much ink has been spilled exploring the question, "Does God exist?" This isn't one of those books, but we can answer a far easier question, "Does

God.txt exist?" In Chapter 4, I showed how to use an if command to determine the existence or nonexistence of a text file:

```
if exist C:\Batch\God.txt (
    set god=Found
) else (
    set god=NotFound
)
```

A variable is being set to Found or NotFound based on the status of the file at a certain instant in time. The god variable can then be interrogated in the future to determine whether *God.txt* existed at that earlier time. It works, but it's a bit clunky; a boolean would provide a more elegant solution. You could then easily reference the boolean as many times as is necessary throughout the code and maybe even reset it.

Setting and Evaluating Booleans

In Batch, a boolean, like all variables, is really just some text, but text that can be evaluated as true or false. As a convention, I always prefix boolean variable names with a lowercase b followed by an uppercase character to make it stand out as a boolean. (A more verbose and descriptive option is to lead with the bool text.) Let's duplicate the logic in the previous example with the only difference being that the clunky variable god is replaced with the boolean, bGod, which gets set to true if *God.txt* is found and false if it isn't:

```
if exist C:\Batch\God.txt (
    set bGod=true==true
) else (
    set bGod=false==x
)
```

In other languages, a boolean is explicitly set to true or false. For instance, a valid Java command is bGod = true;. But the previous set commands for the Batch boolean look a bit different; in particular, each has three equal signs. The first is simply for the assignment; the other two are a portion of the assigned value. When the conditional clause of the if command is true, we set bGod to true==true; if not, false==x is the value. That certainly looks odd, but now the variable, while still technically nothing but text, can be evaluated as the conditional clause of another if command like so:

```
if %bGod%  > con echo Let us pray.
```

But how? If bGod had been set to what we consider true, the interpreter resolves if %bGod% to if true == true. The variable contains an equality operator, double equal signs, with identical values on either side. (Don't ask about the spaces around the operator, but this is what the interpreter sees.) Put all of this after an if command, and it evaluates to true.

If the variable had been set to what we consider false, however, the command would've been resolved to if false == x, which compares two values that clearly differ, resulting in the code after the if command not to be executed.

The if command with a boolean can also be used with the not clause:

```
if not %bGod%  > con echo Live every day to the fullest.
```

If the text, if not %bGod%, resolves to if not true == true, the result of the evaluation is *not true* or false. But when the text resolves to the double negative if not false == x, it evaluates to *not false* or true, and the text is written to the console.

Converting Booleans to Strings

I've chosen true==true as the value for true, but x==x or 0 == 0 would've worked and required fewer keystrokes. Even false==false would evaluate to true, but let's not be difficult. Likewise, false==x could've contained any two differing strings, but I chose these values so that either the text true or false is at the forefront of the boolean value. The structure of the boolean variable allows you to mimic another feature of booleans in compiled code—the conversion of the boolean to a string.

As structured, you can convert Batch booleans to the string true or false by simply stripping off everything after and including the two equal signs. When we get to the for command in Chapter 19, I'll show exactly how that works, but for now, the following line of code truncates the extraneous text:

```
for /F "delims==" %%b in ("%bGod%") do  set bStrGod=%%b
```

After this executes against a valid boolean, the *boolean string* variable named bStrGod will contain either true or false.

(If boolean variables are prefixed with b, it might make sense to prefix boolean string variables with bs, but the convention that I've settled on heads off accusations of my code being full of BS.)

Summary

Strings are ubiquitous in Batch, and in this chapter, I detailed how to build and concatenate them. Substringing and text replacement are two powerful and useful tools that all Batch coders should master, despite their esoteric syntaxes. Booleans are not so ubiquitous, but I hope that I demonstrated the usefulness of this underused data type.

In the next chapter, I'll continue the discussion on data types, delving into the numeric data types. I'll detail integers of three different bases and floating-point numbers, providing a great opportunity to explore how arithmetic is tackled in Batch.

6

INTEGER AND FLOAT DATA TYPES

In Chapter 5, I detailed string and boolean data types. In this chapter, I'll pivot to numeric data types, specifically the integer and floating-point data types, investigating them in great detail. Batch handles integers with ease, whether they be of the decimal, hexadecimal, or octal variants.

However, floating-point numbers are similar to booleans in that Batch doesn't actually support them explicitly as a data type. But once again, that limitation affords the imaginative Batch coder with an opportunity to be inventive, and that's exactly what we'll do before this chapter is done.

An Octals Case Study

August 1, some year in the aughts: I can't remember the exact year, but of the month and date I am quite certain, for reasons that will be clear by the end of this chapter.

I was still relatively new to Batch, but I knew more than many, so a co-worker came to me with a task with which he had been struggling. In the Batch code he needed to determine the prior day's date given only the current date. That's pretty straightforward for most days of the year, but it becomes complicated when today's date is the first of the month. Months have different lengths; New Year's Day poses a unique challenge; leap years happen every four years, except for when they don't.

This initial event occurred in February, maybe March, and it was an interesting little exercise that I coded up and tested. Like any good coder, I tested the first day of the year and the last. I also tested the first day of a handful of months, particularly the extremes, like January and December. I tested March 1 for several different years, not because I was coding this around February but because of the peculiarities of leap years. In short order, I handed over the code and moved on to other projects.

The code worked great for about six months. Then on August 1 it suddenly didn't. I don't remember the downstream consequence, but my co-worker spent a good chunk of time tracking down the root cause. He eventually zeroed in on my bat file but couldn't figure out why it stopped working on that day. His boss would hear none of it—code doesn't work for half of a year and then just blow up. My co-worker must have made some sort of change that broke the process, and he was challenged to find it.

That search ended up wasting half of his workday, but after much due diligence he finally brought the failure to me. I opened the execution log, found the results of the logic that attempted to find the date before 08/01, and . . .

I looked skyward, raised my hands, and with Shatnerian melodrama screamed, "OCTAL!" I am embellishing, slightly—the moment was not as dramatic as Khan stranding Captain Kirk (played by William Shatner with Shakespearean flair) in the center of a dead planet in *Star Trek II: The Wrath of Khan*, but for me at least it was quite memorable.

What in the execution log upset me so? Let's find out, but before delving into octals, I'll start with integers.

Integers

We have already used the set command for alphanumeric values, but it's also used for arithmetic with the /A option. Recall what happens with a statement such as this:

```
set x=4+5
```

The variable denoted by x is set to the text 4+5.

Using the /A option turns it into an *arithmetic* set command, so the following results in the x variable being set to the number 9:

```
set /A x=4+5
```

The /A option transforms the set command into a means to perform addition and other arithmetic operations. Those previous values are obviously hardcoded as numeric.

A slightly more interesting example involves setting variables to numeric values and then adding them via the set /A command, as shown in Listing 6-1.

```
set nbr1=4
set nbr2=5
set /A sum = nbr1 + nbr2
> con echo The sum is %sum%.
```

Listing 6-1: Adding two numeric variables via the set /A command

The console output is The sum is 9., and Listing 6-1 demonstrates that the /A option has altered the set command significantly—three times. First and most obviously, arithmetic is unlocked. Second, there are spaces around the equal sign, and in Chapter 2 I made a rather large point of the danger of doing that. To demonstrate, this command lacking the /A option

```
set myVar = X
```

does not set myVar to X. It sets a variable with a six-character name, myVar with a trailing space, to the two-character value of a space followed by X. By comparison, the /A option makes the set command behave more like an assignment operator of a modern language in that spaces in the command are not treated as parts of variable names or values; refreshingly, they are just spaces.

These three commands are all functionally equivalent; each sets myVar to 7:

```
set myVar=7
set /A myVar=7
set /A myVar = 7
```

To get the desired result without the /A option, spaces cannot exist around the equal sign. However, with the /A option they can exist, but they also aren't required, which is the second significant difference unlocked with the /A option.

The third difference in Listing 6-1 is that the variables nbr1 and nbr2 are not surrounded by percent signs. Hence, the /A option allows you to resolve variables without the ubiquitous delimiters. In a nod to flexibility, you still can use the percent signs and embedded spaces, or not, so these four statements are logically equivalent:

```
set /A result = nbr1 + nbr2
set /A result = %nbr1% + %nbr2%
set /A result=nbr1+nbr2
set /A result=%nbr1%+%nbr2%
```

The spaces make the code much more readable, so I advise against the last two options in the previous code. The first option is the cleanest, but some people are so used to having percent signs surround variables that the second option might provide comforting consistency.

Let's take one more pass at the set /A command from Listing 6-1, but this time, executed at the very beginning of a bat file:

```
set /A sum = nbr1 + nbr2
> con echo The sum is %sum%.
```

The resulting value of sum written to the console will be 0. Because nbr1 and nbr2 are not yet defined, unset variables used in the numeric context are considered to be zero, unlike unset variables used in the alphanumeric context, which default to null. Since neither is set, the arithmetic 0 + 0 results in 0.

WARNING   *The range of permissible integers includes the values −2,147,483,648 through 2,147,483,647, inclusive. Batch stores numbers as 32-bit signed fields, so any integer will take on one of these 2^{32} values. This rarely poses a problem, but because the code is not compiled, take care to ensure that the data being processed conforms to the limitation. The code won't abort, nor will it hang; it'll simply fail to calculate the correct value. Batch is not the preferred language for macroeconomics.*

Batch Arithmetic

Batch arithmetic does more than simple addition. The following listing shows the five primary arithmetic operations (addition, subtraction, multiplication, division, and modulo division) and their syntaxes:

```
set /A sum = nbr1 + nbr2
set /A difference = nbr1 - nbr2
set /A product = nbr1 * nbr2
set /A quotient = nbr1 / nbr2
set /A modulo = nbr1 %% nbr2
```

The operators are similar to those in other programming languages, but note the double percent sign for modulo division. The help command shows a single percent sign, but the correct Batch syntax requires two. (In reality, the modulo character is just a single percent sign, but the first percent sign is actually *escaping* the second. If this doesn't make much sense right now, hold that thought for Chapter 14, but use two characters for now.)

Now let's execute these arithmetic commands, but first we'll define the two operands, nbr1 and nbr2. The results are shown to the right of each statement as a comment (as mentioned previously, the ampersand separates two commands, and the second one can be a rem command):

```
set nbr1=7
set nbr2=2
```

```
set /A sum = nbr1 + nbr2          &rem sum=9
set /A difference = nbr1 - nbr2   &rem difference=5
set /A product = nbr1 * nbr2      &rem product=14
set /A quotient = nbr1 / nbr2     &rem quotient=3
set /A modulo = nbr1 %% nbr2      &rem modulo=1
```

The addition, subtraction, and multiplication operations produce no surprises, but dividing 7 by 2 returns 3 rather than 3.5, because Batch arithmetic handles only integers and truncates the decimal portion of the result. Dividing 19 by 10 doesn't yield 1.9, and it won't even return the rounded value of 2. The intermediate result of 1.9 is truncated to 1.

Modulo is a useful operator that returns the remainder. Modulo n returns the values 0 through $n - 1$, so the modulo 2 operation returns 0 for even numbers because 2/2, 4/2, 6/2, and so on are integers and do not produce a remainder. Odd numbers return 1, because 3/2, 5/2, 7/2, and so on all have a remainder of 1.

Oddly, Batch doesn't support the exponential or power function, which is a source of frustration for some but an impetus for creativity for others. You can create a routine that takes in a base and an exponent and returns the exponential result (and I'll do just that in Chapter 18).

Augmented Assignment Operators

Augmented assignment operators can streamline the code when you want to add a number to a variable and store the result in that same variable. The most obvious example is a simple counter where you might want to increment a variable by one for each execution of the set command, for example:

```
set /A veryVerboseTallyVariable = veryVerboseTallyVariable + 1
```

I intentionally chose a verbose and cumbersome variable name because try as we coders might, they sometimes become nearly unavoidable.

The following syntax is logically identical, condensed, and easier to comprehend:

```
set /A veryVerboseTallyVariable += 1
```

The next command adds 17 to a far more succinctly named variable:

```
set /A nbr += 17
```

Likewise, the following set commands subtract 2, multiply by 2, divide by 2, and perform modulo 2 division, respectively:

```
set /A nbr -= 2
set /A nbr *= 2
set /A nbr /= 2
set /A nbr %%= 2
```

Again, note the double percent signs for the modulo division. Many experienced Batch coders don't know that the augmented assignment operators are available in Batch, wrongly assuming that they exist only in more modern languages, but they do exist, and you should use them when appropriate.

Order of Operation

You can do more complex arithmetic with the order of operation rules from mathematics. You might have learned the PEMDAS acronym in a pre-algebra class (or "Please Excuse My Dear Aunt Sally" as a mnemonic) for "parentheses, exponents, multiplication and division, and addition and subtraction." For Batch we have PMDAS, which is a whole lot harder to pronounce, but as mentioned, exponents aren't supported (maybe the mnemonic "Please Make Dessert Aunt Sally" will catch on). Let's take this example:

```
set /A nbr = 3 * (1 + 2) / 4 - 5
```

First, the 1 and the 2 are added to make 3 because they are in parentheses, even though addition and subtraction are last in the order of operation. Multiplication and division share the same hierarchy, so the interpreter performs them from left to right. The 3 leading the expression is multiplied by the 3 from the addition, giving us 9, and 9 is then divided by 4, resulting in 2.25. Actually, that's truncated, so it's simply 2. Finally, subtract 5, and -3 is the result.

This example is pedagogical only, because it would be far simpler just to set nbr to -3. In practice, a mix of hardcoded numbers and variables will be used. For example:

```
set /A nbr = ((nbr1 + nbr2) * -10) / 4
```

The outer parentheses here are unnecessary by the rules of PMDAS, but they make the statement more readable.

Augmented assignment operators can also work with more complex expressions. These two statements are logically identical:

```
set /A nbr = nbr + (2 * (4 + nbr) - -5)
set /A nbr += 2 * (4 + nbr) - -5
```

In both commands the variable nbr is being incremented by a mathematical expression also containing nbr, with the only difference being that the second command uses the augmented assignment operator. Based on the order of operations, both add 4 to the variable, double it, and subtract –5. (Subtracting –5 is equivalent to adding 5.) Ultimately, the result of this expression is the amount by which nbr is incremented.

Octal and Hexadecimal Arithmetic

Batch supports both octal and hexadecimal arithmetic. Both number systems are more similar to the way a computer *thinks* than base 10, so it's useful for a coder to understand them and be able to use them.

The decimal number system is base 10 and uses the digits 0 to 9. There is no digit for 10; instead, there are two digits: a new place value starts with 1, while the ones place restarts at 0, hence 10. In contrast, the *octal number system* is base 8, using the digits 0 to 7. Adding 1 to the octal 7 does not produce 8, because 8 (and 9) are meaningless characters in the octal number system. Instead, the octal number 10 (pronounced "one-zero" because it is not "ten") is equivalent to the decimal number 8. Likewise, the octal 11 is equal to the decimal 9, and so on.

The *hexadecimal number system* is base 16, so it has the opposite problem of octal: it needs 16 unique digits, more than the 10 used in most human number systems on account of our having evolved to possess five digits on each of two hands. After counting from 0 to 9, we have the "numbers" A, B, C, D, E, and F. The hexadecimal number B is equal to the decimal number 11, the hexadecimal F is equal to the decimal 15, and the hexadecimal 10 is equal to the decimal 16.

Batch can perform arithmetic with octal, hexadecimal, and/or decimal inputs, while always returning the answer as a decimal. Hexadecimal numbers are preceded with 0x, and octal numbers are preceded with 0 alone. Hence, these two variables are assigned octal and hexadecimal values, respectively:

```
set octalNbr=012
set hexadecimalNbr=0xB
```

Regardless of the base of the operands—decimal, octal, or hexadecimal—Batch always stores the result as a decimal. To demonstrate, first take this example:

```
set decimal7=7
set decimal1=1
set octal7=07
set octal1=01

set /A decimal = decimal7 + decimal1
set /A octal = octal7 + octal1
```

The numerals 7 and 1 are being added as decimals and octals. The decimal result is obviously 8. The sum of the two octal numbers is octal 10 ("one-zero," not decimal 10), but the interpreter immediately stores the value as a decimal 8. In this example, decimals and octals behave the same way, but that's not always true.

Now take this example:

```
set decimal11=11
set decimal2=2
set octal11=011
set octal2=02

set /A decimal = decimal11 + decimal2
set /A octal = octal11 + octal2
> con echo The decimal sum is %decimal%.
> con echo The octal sum is %octal%.
```

The decimal addition yields decimal 13, while the octal addition yields octal 13 ("one-three," not decimal 13). Remember, the octal number system has no 8 or 9. Octal 10 is decimal 8, and in this example octal 13 is decimal 11. Therefore, in Batch, 11 + 2 = 13, but 011 + 02 = 013 = 11, so the following result is displayed:

```
The decimal sum is 13.
The octal sum is 11.
```

The interpreter can even handle arithmetic with a mixture of decimal and octal values. The decimal addition of 10 + 10 is 20, and the octal addition of 010 + 010 is 16. When adding a decimal and an octal, say 10 + 010, Batch gives the correct result of 18. Usually, this type of arithmetic is done by accident, but sometimes savvy coders will use this to their advantage, and it's good to know that it's possible.

In a similar fashion, these values are treated as hexadecimals:

```
set /A hexadecimalNbr = 0xA * 0x14
```

With this multiplication, 0xA is equal to decimal 10, and 0x14 is four more than 16 when converted to decimal. After this statement executes, the variable is equal to 200, the product of 10 and 20.

Octals and hexadecimals can be powerful tools; however, be careful to ensure that there are no leading zeros if you are intending to do decimal arithmetic. Since hexadecimals start with 0x, accidentally performing hexadecimal arithmetic is far more difficult, but unknowingly performing octal arithmetic because of a seemingly innocuous leading zero is exceedingly easy.

NOTE *Because math is all around us, you'll find boxes containing various examples of bat file arithmetic in Chapters 16, 18, and 21. Batch also has arithmetic operators for bit manipulation: bitwise and, bitwise or, bitwise exclusive or, logical shift left, and logical shift right. I'll wait until Chapter 30 to explore them because these operators use some special characters that have other uses and because many experienced coders have never manipulated a bit in compiled code, much less Batch.*

Floating-Point Numbers

Batch doesn't explicitly handle floating-point numbers—that is, non-integer rational numbers. In fact, if extensive processing is to be done on such numbers, there are better tools to use than Batch. It would be analogous to digging a foundation for a house with a spade shovel. It can be done, but only by the most austere ascetic. If the task is big enough, write some compiled code and call it from the bat file, but when some lightweight floating-point arithmetic needs to be done, Batch can handle it, just as you can use the spade shovel to plant a couple tulip bulbs in the front yard.

Keep in mind that all Batch variables are really just glorified strings. We can easily assign a couple of variables floating-point values—that is, some numbers with a period for the decimal point. Here are two amounts in dollars and cents:

```
set amt1=1.99
set amt2=2.50
```

If these were integers, we could simply add them with the set /A command. Let's try it and see what happens:

```
set /A sum = amt1 + amt2
```

The result is the value 3 being stored in the sum, not the hoped-for 4.49. The decimal part of each number is completely ignored, resulting in the sum of the integers 1 and 2.

We need to remove the decimal place, do the arithmetic, and restore the decimal place. Multiplying each amount by 100 would do the trick, but again, Batch isn't going to allow that. Since the floating-point value is just a disguised string, however, we can remove the decimal point with the syntax described in the previous chapter:

```
set amt1=%amt1:.=%
set amt2=%amt2:.=%
```

Now the amounts are 199 and 250. This set /A command results in 449:

```
set /A sum = amt1 + amt2
```

To restore the decimal, we can't simply divide by 100—once again, that works only for integers—but we can use more of the string-parsing logic from the previous chapter. Using substringing, the following set command resets the variable to a concatenation of three items: everything but the last two bytes of the number, a hardcoded decimal place (or a dot), and the last two bytes of the number:

```
set sum=%sum:~0,-2%.%sum:~-2%
> con echo The sum is %sum%.
```

Finally, the variable written to the console has been set to 4.49.

Multiplication works the same way. If you buy that new computer for $499 with no payments for the first year and an interest rate of 19 percent, how much will you owe a year from now? The interest rate translates to a factor of 1.19, but again we must remove the decimal place. After finding the product of two integers, we restore the decimal place by inserting it before the last two bytes, as shown in Listing 6-2.

```
set amt=499
set factor=1.19
set factor=%factor:.=%
set /A product = amt * factor
set product=%product:~0,-2%.%product:~-2%
> con echo The product is %product%.
```

Listing 6-2: Multiplication of an integer and a floating-point number

The product of 593.81 might make you reconsider the financing plan.

The goal of every coder should be to write "bullet-proof" code. Unfortunately, the previous offering is more of a cotton mesh than Kevlar, and there are a number of batveats to discuss. We've made several assumptions, and if any one of them is violated, the code will break. The addition assumes that both numbers have two decimal places; 1.9 instead of 1.90 will throw off the result by a factor of 10. A non-numeric character, other than the decimal place, will cause issues, and a leading zero on the value will trigger octal arithmetic. The multiplication is even more complicated. Listing 6-2 contains an integer amount, but if amt had been expressed in dollars and cents, the product would have resulted in four decimal places, not two. To represent the result as dollars and cents, the last two bytes should be truncated—or better yet, rounded.

I won't go into these nuances here for the simple reason that if the inputs are not consistent and data validation is required, Batch floating-point arithmetic may not be the optimal solution. Coding for all possible situations would be tedious at best. What's important is that the coder understands the options at hand. If all the values have a consistent number of decimal places, one can do the arithmetic with just a few lines of code. On the rare instance when I have resorted to using the floating-point data type in Batch, it has been for a very specific task involving consistent data. Break out that spade shovel, but only when appropriate.

An Octals Case Study, Continued

So, what exactly did I find in that execution log on that first day of August of a year early in the millennium? In the bat file, today's date was formatted as CCYYMMDD, for instance 20050801, which was broken down into three discrete fields:

```
todaysYear = 2005
todaysMonth = 08
todaysDay = 01
```

If todaysDay is anything other than 01, we simply subtract 1 from the eight-digit number and move on. But when it is 01, we need to do some additional arithmetic. Considering just the month logic (and understanding that there'll be some special logic for January), we must subtract 1 to determine the prior month:

```
set /A month = todaysMonth - 1
```

When todaysMonth is 03, the month is 2; when todaysMonth is 07, the month is 6. But when todaysMonth is 08 as it is on August 1, the month in the previous arithmetic resolves to the value of -1.

The interpreter sees the leading 0 and treats the arithmetic as octal arithmetic. Octal understands only the digits 0 through 7, so when the interpreter sees 8, it considers the character to be as foreign as "ohkuh" (the numeral corresponding to eight in the Vulcan language) and simply ignores it. Ultimately, the set /A command assigns the mathematical result of what remains of the expression, which is -1, to the month variable. This value ends up breaking the date logic, and we fail to get the desired date of July 31.

"OCTAL!"

Using substringing and the if command, I inserted this one-line fix to strip the leading zero, if present, off the value of the todaysMonth variable:

```
if %todaysMonth:~0,1% equ 0  set todaysMonth=%todaysMonth:~1%
```

The code worked fine for years to come, even on the firsts of August and September. If the original code hadn't been run on August 1, it would have failed if run on September 1, since September is denoted by 09. But what if the code hadn't been run on either of those days? When would it fail next? On October 1, the month would be denoted as 10. The interpreter would have treated that like a decimal, and the code would have performed as expected. So, the firsts of August and September are the only dates capable of breaking the code.

Be very aware of octal.

Summary

In this chapter, I discussed numeric data types and how they are treated in Batch. Unlike most other languages, Batch variables are not defined as a certain data type. Intrinsically, all variables are simple strings, but when that string contains a number, it can be treated as numeric.

Addition, subtraction, multiplication, division, and even modulo division work on decimal integers with relative ease, using the order of operation rules you likely learned in school. Octal and hexadecimal integers are also supported, although octal arithmetic can all too easily be invoked in error. Take it from my personal experience and ensure that your decimal integers are not prefixed with any zeros. Augmented assignment operators offer a handy and underutilized tool for incrementing integers.

The floating-point numeric data type isn't supported in Batch, but you've learned that with a little work, you can perform some lightweight arithmetic on numbers with a decimal point.

Changing gears, I'll discuss file movements in the next chapter. An immensely useful feature of Batch is the creating, copying, moving, renaming, and deleting of files and directories.

7

WORKING WITH FILES

If you were to ask a coder only tangentially acquainted with Batch for its primary use, their response would likely mention moving files around. Batch can do much more, but without a doubt one of its primary uses is file movements. In this chapter, we'll explore the different commands and techniques available. You'll also learn about creating empty files, along with methods for merging, moving, renaming, and deleting files. I'll introduce file masks and wildcards, allowing you to execute the commands you're about to learn on many similarly named files instead of just one.

Commands for Copying Files

Batch has three commands for copying files: copy, xcopy, and robocopy. In this section, I'll compare them and give recommendations on when to use each one, because they have their respective niches. Are you copying many small files or a few large files? Is the network stable? Is speed a consideration? Do you want a straightforward return code or one that's more nuanced? How important is the logging to you? You'll need to answer many questions before deciding on the optimal command and options for any particular copy.

copy

The copy command offers a quick and easy way to create empty files:

```
copy nul C:\Target\EmptyFile.dat
```

In Batch, the word nul represents a perpetually null or empty file (apparently, someone felt the need to abbreviate *null*). Here we're making a copy of the nul file to produce an empty file with a path and name of our choosing (in Chapter 12, I'll demonstrate how to dispose of unwanted output by sending it to this file where it disappears). A fun fact: Windows won't let you create a file named nul in any folder, regardless of the extension or the lack of an extension, even manually. Go ahead and try.

The only other use I've ever had for the copy command is to merge two or more relatively small files. The /B option performs a *binary* file copy, which means that every byte, even special characters such as the carriage return and line feed, are copied without alteration, resulting in a true concatenation of the files. The source files are separated by the plus sign, followed by the merged file:

```
copy /B C:\Source\Header.txt + C:\Source\Details.txt C:\Target\MergedFile.txt
```

We're concatenating two files here, but we can merge more with more plus sign delimiters.

You may have noticed that I've mentioned only two uses for the copy command, neither of which involve the copying of actual files. You can use the command to copy files, but I never use it for this purpose because it's primitive and has a paucity of options. These shortcomings were apparent shortly after the first release of Batch, and it was soon largely replaced by the far more useful and configurable xcopy command.

xcopy

The basic syntax for the xcopy command has two arguments—the source file and the destination path:

```
xcopy C:\Source\File2Copy.txt C:\Target\
```

One huge advantage of the xcopy command is that it'll create the target directory if it doesn't yet exist. In contrast, the copy command wouldn't find the path and would fail.

In the previous example only a target path is given, which means the copied file will have the same name as the source file. But we can rename the destination file as part of the xcopy command by simply giving it a filename:

```
xcopy C:\Source\File2Copy.txt C:\Target\RenamedFile.dat
```

This command sometimes fails because the interpreter isn't sure whether the destination is a directory or a file (in Chapter 12, I'll discuss how to make that work all of the time).

The xcopy command has two options that I use nearly every time I invoke the command. The /Y option suppresses the prompt to confirm overwriting a destination file. Although it might make sense to ask for confirmation when running via a command prompt or even interactively, in most other situations it does nothing more than halt processing and create a hang, so it's best to turn it off.

The other option I can't do without is /F. It displays the full source and destination paths and filenames of every file copied, which leaves a useful audit trail when the wildcard is used to copy multiple files. Without the /F option, only the source file or files are shown along with a total file count. At the other extreme, if you're not interested in all of this information, you can use the /Q option (for *quiet* mode) to turn off the display altogether.

Using these two indispensable options, the following command suppresses the prompts and supplies detailed logging:

```
xcopy C:\Source\File2Copy.txt C:\Target\ /Y /F
```

This command has too many available options to reasonably go over here; use the help command for a full list. As a small sampling, however, the /U option copies only files that already exist at the destination; the /S option copies folders and subfolders; and the /J option uses unbuffered I/O, which is optimal for very large files.

Although copy has been deprecated in favor of xcopy, Microsoft technically considers xcopy itself deprecated in favor of the even newer robocopy command. Even so, the wide use of the xcopy command means it'll still be available in foreseeable operating systems, and as I'll detail shortly, it's still the better choice in many instances. I even used this command in what may have been your very first bat file in Chapter 1.

robocopy

Removing the last character from the name of the command reveals the title of an old science-fiction film, but robocopy really stands for *robust copy*, which isn't hyperbole. Although xcopy has many useful options, robocopy provides some impressive logging and a mind-boggling array of options.

Even though the robocopy command is far more powerful than xcopy, it's also quite easy to use. The arguments are a bit different: first provide the source directory sans the filename, then the destination directory, and finally the file, files, or file mask to be copied:

```
robocopy C:\Source\ C:\Target\ File2Copy.txt
```

This example is functionally equivalent to the xcopy command from the previous section and reproduced here:

```
xcopy C:\Source\File2Copy.txt C:\Target\
```

Because the first two arguments of the robocopy command are known to be paths, you can leave off the trailing slash, which is a great advantage over xcopy where a missed slash can turn a destination directory into a filename.

robocopy Logging

To get an idea of how robust robocopy really is, look no further than its logging capability. If you are an xcopy aficionado, be seated before glancing ahead. Verbose is the only word that comes to mind, and even that isn't adequate. Besides the list of files copied, logs include a fancy header, the start and end times, file sizes, copy speed statistics, source and destination paths, total counts of the files and directories copied and skipped, along with any failed copies, a list of the command line options used, and much more. It's even formatted nicely with plenty of whitespace for readability.

The simple robocopy command shown previously to copy a single file generates the following log:

```
-------------------------------------------------------------------------------
   ROBOCOPY     ::     Robust File Copy for Windows
-------------------------------------------------------------------------------

  Started : Tuesday, January 30, 2007 12:18:44 PM
   Source : C:\Source\
     Dest : C:\Target\

    Files : File2Copy.txt

  Options : /DCOPY:DA /COPY:DAT /R:1000000 /W:30

------------------------------------------------------------------------------

      New Dir          1 C:\Source\
         New File          83146 File2Copy.txt
100%

------------------------------------------------------------------------------
```

	Total	Copied	Skipped	Mismatch	FAILED	Extras
Dirs :	1	1	0	0	0	0
Files :	1	1	0	0	0	0
Bytes :	81.1 k	81.1 k	0	0	0	0
Times :	0:00:00	0:00:00			0:00:00	0:00:00

```
Speed :              20786500 Bytes/sec.
Speed :              1189.413 MegaBytes/min.
Ended : Tuesday, January 30, 2007 12:18:44 PM
```

Some of the results are self-explanatory such as Total, Copied, and FAILED, but others are not. If a file to be copied is already in the destination path and is identical, robocopy is smart enough to not waste time overlaying it and instead considers it justifiably Skipped. A Mismatch occurs when a copy is thwarted because a source file and a destination folder (or a source folder and a destination file) have the same name. Extras are files and directories not at the source but already at the destination. Obviously, the files weren't copied, but the interpreter feels obligated to note their existence. For this task of copying one small file, the logging may be overkill. A more interesting task might go on for pages, but for that more interesting task, the logging may be invaluable.

By default, all this information is written to the console (in Chapter 12, I'll discuss how to instead redirect logging from any command or even an entire bat file to a logfile). But the robocopy command is unique in that you can easily create a logfile with an option. The path and name of the logfile simply follows the appropriately named /LOG option, delimited by a colon.

This may be the first instance you've seen where an option has more than one character after the slash, and this command has plenty more. Adding the plus sign to the option, /LOG+, results in the information being appended to the logfile if it already exists. To demonstrate, consider the following:

```
set roboLog=C:\Batch\Robocopy.log
robocopy C:\Source\ C:\Target\ File2Copy.txt /LOG:%roboLog% /NP
robocopy C:\Source\ C:\Target\ AnotherFile2Copy.txt /LOG+:%roboLog% /NP
```

After defining roboLog as the path and name of the logfile, it's used in two robocopy commands. The first creates the logfile with information from its copy, overwriting an existing file if present, and the second robocopy command appends to that logfile with the results of its copy.

Both of the last two commands use the /NP option, which stands for *no progress*, because I consider it a necessity when creating a logfile. If the information is being written to the console, the progress of each copy is shown in real time as a percentage, updated multiple times a second. Relatively large files might display several dozens of values before 100% is finally shown. That status is great when viewed on the console, but in a logfile, each update becomes a new record. It doesn't take many large files to turn the log into a complete mess. Even small files can result in a few extra unneeded records in the logfile. The /NP option cleans that up very nicely, updating the log only after each copy completes.

Useful robocopy Options

There are many robocopy options, so I'll quickly go over the most useful ones. But first, here's a command to serve as the canvas for the options:

```
robocopy C:\Source\ C:\Target\
```

This simple command (lacking the third argument of a file) copies all files in the source directory to the target directory.

The command automatically performs retries of failed copies, which is fabulous, but the default is a staggering one million attempts, each separated by a 30-second wait. This can result in a hang of several months for a fatally flawed attempted copy. The /R and /W options override the default number of *retries* and the *wait* time in seconds, respectively:

```
robocopy C:\Source\ C:\Target\ /R:20 /W:5
```

With these options, the interpreter will retry the failed copy up to 20 times, with 5 seconds between each attempt, before initiating an abort. Choose values that make sense to you and your hardware, but the defaults must not stand.

If you add the /S option, it also will copy all the *subdirectories*, except for empty subdirectories:

```
robocopy C:\Source\ C:\Target\ /S
```

The /E option copies all of the subdirectories, *empty* and nonempty alike:

```
robocopy C:\Source\ C:\Target\ /E
```

You can refine this option to copy only the files in the source directory (*C:\Source*) and its immediate subdirectories, but not lower levels of subdirectories. The /LEV option defines the number of *levels*, including the root, as 2, to handle that:

```
robocopy C:\Source\ C:\Target\ /E /LEV:2
```

Unbuffered I/O is more efficient for very large files and is invoked oddly enough with the /J option. (This option is borrowed from the xcopy command, where the /U option was already spoken for.) The /MIN and /MAX options set *minimum* and *maximum* byte limits for the files to be copied. The following two commands copy all files in a folder, using unbuffered I/O for only the files of at least 1GB:

```
robocopy C:\Source\ C:\Target\ /MIN:1000000000 /J
robocopy C:\Source\ C:\Target\ /MAX:999999999 /MT
```

I snuck the /MT option, which stands for *multithreading*, into the command for the smaller files. By default, the robocopy command copies files serially, but this option copies eight files in parallel. You can even define the number of threads; /MT:128 is the maximum, but in my experience, this isn't appreciably faster than the option default of eight. We can debate the threshold, but unbuffered I/O for large files and multithreading for smaller files will optimize any copy.

The /MINAGE and /MAXAGE options (*minimum* and *maximum ages*) define what's to be copied based on the last modified date. You can use them individually or together to create a date range. The following command copies only files touched since Microsoft's disastrous release of Windows Me on September 14, 2000, excluding anything that was changed in the last seven days:

```
robocopy C:\Source\ C:\Target /MAXAGE:20000914 /MINAGE:7
```

You can define the value of both options as either a date (formatted as CCYYMMDD) or a number of days. The interpreter is smart enough to know that the eight-byte number represents a date and not a timespan of more than 50,000 years. Batch may not be a new language, but it was used by neither the Denisovans nor our hunter-gatherer forebearers. Any number less than 1,900 is considered by the interpreter to be a number of days.

The /PURGE option deletes extra files and directories at the destination, which you obviously should use with caution, but it's a very handy tool for creating backups. If you back up a folder one day, change the name of a file in the source directory the next, and then back up the folder again, you'll end up with an extraneous file in the backup unless you use the /PURGE option. Even better is the /MIR option that *mirrors* a directory tree. The /MIR option essentially does what the /PURGE option does, but it includes subdirectories.

The /XF option *excludes* one or more *files* from the copy, while /XD similarly *excludes* one or more *directories*. The /L option doesn't copy anything; it produces a *list* of everything that would've been copied if the option hadn't been used.

You can also use the robocopy command to move files (see "Moving Files" on page 80). As always, use the help command for a complete list of available options.

The robocopy Return Code

The xcopy command is like most Batch commands in that a successful execution returns an errorlevel of 0, while a failure returns a number other than 0. In contrast, robocopy is unique—a uniqueness that if not understood can breed much bewilderment. A return code of 0 means that nothing was copied, but if at least one file was copied successfully, the interpreter returns an odd number between 1 and 15, inclusive, but even some of those codes aren't exactly *good* return codes. Here are the six basic return codes the robocopy command generates:

0 No error, but no file(s) was copied; in other words, all files were skipped.

1 One or more files copied successfully.

2 One or more extra files or directories were found; none were copied.

4 One or more mismatches were found; none were copied.

8 Some files or directories could not be copied.

16 Nothing was copied; there was a serious error.

Oh, the elegance of the *powers of two*; a mathematician must've come up with these return codes. Wouldn't it have been easier to use codes 0 through 5? No, the four codes in the middle aren't mutually exclusive; that is, it's possible for more than one of them (even all four) to be true at the same time. The interpreter adds up all of the codes that are true and returns the sum as the errorlevel.

As an example, envision a robocopy command of all files in a source folder to a destination folder where some files are copied successfully, but the destination also has extra copies. Return codes 1 and 2 are both true; hence, 3, their sum, is returned as the errorlevel. It's also possible that when files were copied, extras were found along with a mismatch, and another file failed to copy because it was held open by someone or some process. Do the math (1 + 2 + 4 + 8), and the interpreter returns 15.

These return codes give the savvy coder the opportunity to fine-tune the error handling. Return codes of 1 and 3 are clearly good, and I often consider 3 or less to also be good. Anything from 4 to 7 involves a mismatch, and anything above that has at least one explicit failure. Depending on the circumstances, mismatches might be completely acceptable so that only a return code of 8 or greater would be considered bad.

To explicitly verify that at least one file was copied, we need to look only for an odd-numbered return code, which we can do with the modulo function from Chapter 6.

xcopy vs. robocopy

Despite the subjective nature of the word, most Batch coders agree that robocopy is *better* than xcopy because of its myriad of options, multithreading, automated retries, impressive logging, and everything behind the scenes that makes it more efficient. But there's one major batveat. When trying to copy a single file, the xcopy error handling is *better* by far. Both of these commands are attempting to copy a named file that doesn't exist:

```
xcopy C:\Source\NonExistentFile.txt C:\Target\
robocopy C:\Source\ C:\Target\ NonExistentFile.txt
```

The xcopy command reports that no files were copied and returns an errorlevel of 4, but the robocopy command simply returns 0, stating that there were no errors and no files copied. I contend that this should be an error. When attempting to copy multiple files, both commands return 0 when there are no source files—that makes sense, but both of these commands are calling for an explicit file to be copied, and the robocopy return code doesn't distinguish between the file not being found and being skipped because it already exists at the target directory. The skipping of nonupdated files is a great feature of robocopy, but it's something quite different from a file not being found. The robust logging makes this clear, but the return code does not.

This failure of the return code to report why a file wasn't copied (not found or skipped) is a deficiency, but we can overcome it. When copying one specific file with the robocopy command, you can perform an if exist on the target file when errorlevel is 0. If it exists, the file was properly skipped; if not, there was an error. Or, do as I do and just use xcopy in this situation.

There are other instances when the complex return code of the robocopy command is more than what's needed. You might not care whether there are extra or mismatched files and instead just want a simple result of good or bad, zero or nonzero. There's nothing wrong with that, and if I'm being honest, I sometimes still use it in new code out of habit and ease of use.

That said, the robocopy command is, as its name suggests, much more robust. It's far more configurable, faster, and less prone to fail. If copying very large files, a large number of files, or files that might fail due to a connectivity issue, robocopy is the obvious choice, and that complex return code is a major boon at times. Also, the xcopy command has a 254-byte limitation on the length of a path and filename. I've never come close to exceeding this limitation, but if you ever do, robocopy can handle it.

The most definitive statement I'll make on this topic is that you should never use the copy command to copy a file, but keep it in your toolbox for creating an empty file or merging files.

File Masks and Wildcards

All of the previous xcopy examples copied a single file, and the robocopy examples copied either a single file or all of the files in a directory. But with file masks and wildcards, you can create far more targeted commands that copy only some of the files in a directory; in fact, they might copy a different number of files every time they execute. A *file mask* replaces the filename in both of these commands and consists of one or more *wildcard* characters, possibly with some hardcoded text or resolved variables. Then when it executes, the command copies all of the files that satisfy or fit the file mask.

File masks are not unique to commands that copy files. Upcoming commands in this chapter for moving, deleting, and even renaming files also accept file masks in lieu of filenames, allowing you to move, delete, and rename multiple files at once. The for command makes great use of file masks, and I'll demonstrate how in Part II. Any command that performs some action on a file probably works with wildcards; experiment if in doubt.

Batch recognizes two characters as wildcards, the asterisk (*) and the question mark (?). They behave quite differently, and I'll detail both with the xcopy command, but first let's take a look at a set of files to copy. A meticulously organized person might maintain spreadsheets with budget information, one file for each month of a year. For this demonstration, the *C:\Budget* folder contains spreadsheets with a naming convention noting the year and month. Here are just three:

```
Budget.January2008.xlsx
Budget.February2008.xlsx
Budget.March2008.xlsx
```

These files are from the year of the financial crisis and the start of the Great Recession, and the folder contains similarly named files from the year before and after, along with other types of files.

The Asterisk Wildcard Character

The asterisk is the most common Batch wildcard character and is a stand-in for zero to many characters. To demonstrate, the following xcopy command copies all of the files, and only the files, from 2008, or more specifically, the files residing in *C:\Budget* that satisfy the Budget.*2008.xlsx mask:

```
xcopy C:\Budget\Budget.*2008.xlsx C:\Target /F /Y
```

The asterisk is the wildcard, meaning that this command copies every file with a name that starts with Budget. and ends with 2008.xlsx, with something, or even nothing, in between. If a file named *Budget.2008.xlsx* happens to be in the folder, it also satisfies the mask and is one of the copied files.

By the end of the year, a dozen such files should satisfy this mask, one for each month, resulting in the command copying all 12. But the command won't copy files from 2007 or 2009, nor will it copy a Word document with the same name but a different extension, such as *Budget.June2008 .docx*. If you were to remove the first dot from the name of one of the files, *BudgetAugust2008.xlsx*, the interpreter won't copy it either because it doesn't satisfy the mask.

The following very subtle change of inserting the letter J before the wildcard results in the command copying only three files, the ones for January, June, and July:

```
xcopy C:\Budget\Budget.J*2008.xlsx C:\Target /F /Y
```

Add one more character before the wildcard, and the Budget.Ju*2008.xlsx mask excludes the January file.

You aren't limited to a single wildcard in a mask. Here's an example that uses two asterisks, where the last one is a stand-in for the extension:

```
xcopy C:\Budget\Budget.*2008.* C:\Target /F /Y
```

The aforementioned Word document, *Budget.June2008.docx*, now gets caught up in the dragnet.

You now know that the asterisk wildcard can represent any text of any length, including no text at all, but there are times that you may want to be more restrictive. Batch has a lesser known and much lesser understood wildcard character for this purpose.

The Question Mark Wildcard Character

While the asterisk is a wildcard for zero to many characters, the question mark is a wildcard for exactly one character, *usually*. (Yes, the italics mean that a batveat is on the way.) To copy files only with four-character months, I'll use four question marks where there once was an asterisk:

```
xcopy C:\Budget\Budget.????2008.xlsx C:\Target /F /Y
```

This command copies the files for June and July, but not the files for March, April, May, and all the other months, which happen to be more verbose.

That seems straightforward, but I promised you a batveat. If a set of one or more question mark wildcards comes at the end of a file mask or if those question marks immediately precede a dot, Batch also considers a null to be a valid replacement value for each of the question marks.

To illustrate, I'll make a tweak to the file naming convention by inserting a period between the month and year, resulting in filenames such as these:

```
Budget.April.2008.xlsx
Budget.May.2008.xlsx
Budget.June.2008.xlsx
Budget.July.2008.xlsx
```

Next, I'll insert the period into the file mask between the four question marks and the year like so:

```
xcopy C:\Budget\Budget.????.2008.xlsx C:\Target /F /Y
```

Even some experienced Batch coders might expect the files for June and July only to satisfy this mask. They would be correct in that files for March, April, and all the other months denoted with more than four letters won't be copied, but the file for May will also satisfy the mask. The first three wildcards match on each of the three letters in May, but the fourth question mark matches on a null or nonexistent character. Even the oddly named *Budget..2008.xlsx* satisfies this mask.

The upshot is that when *n* question mark wildcards come at the end of a file mask or are followed by a dot, the mask is satisfied with zero to *n* characters. Otherwise, *n* question mark wildcards are satisfied with exactly *n* characters. It's a very subtle oddity, and understanding it might save you hours of grief.

To put a fine point on the difference between the two Batch wildcard characters, shot, shoot, shut, shunt, shallot, and even sht all satisfy the sh*t file mask. Of these words (and one nonword), only shot and shut satisfy the sh?t file mask.

SHORT FILENAMES AND FILE MASKS

As an even more subtle batveat, sometimes filenames that don't appear to satisfy a file mask end up satisfying the mask. What we think of as the filename is really the long filename. By default, Windows also assigns a short filename for every file on your computer. It's a little-used legacy of older operating systems, but it still exists, and when the interpreter compares a file to a mask, it looks for matches against *either* the long or short filename.

The short filename is at most eight bytes long with no more than a three-byte extension. The aptly named *NineBytes.Long* might have a short filename of *NINEBY~1.LON*. If you try to copy all files with an extension of no more than three bytes with the *.??? file mask, the interpreter copies the file with the four-byte extension because its short filename satisfies the mask. This issue doesn't come up often, but if you're getting an unexpected hit on a file, check out its short filename. (You'll learn how in Chapter 17.)

Moving Files

Moving a file is similar to copying a file; the only difference is that after a file is copied, it exists in two places, while after a file is moved, the original file is no more. The move command performs this task easily. It simply takes the source and the target as arguments, and you'll usually see it with the /Y option to suppress the confirmation prompt for overwriting the target:

```
move C:\Source\File2Move.txt C:\Target\ /Y
```

Plenty of old code still contains the move command, but it has been largely deprecated in favor of the robocopy command. The following command with the /MOV option is functionally equivalent to the previous move command:

```
robocopy C:\Source\ C:\Target\ File2Move.txt /MOV
```

Removing the filename from this robocopy command moves all the files in the source folder, but nothing from the subfolders.

Adding the /S option results in moving all of the contents in all the subfolders, even if the target subfolders need to be created:

```
robocopy C:\Source\ C:\Target\ /MOV /S
```

This command moves all of the files. They are no longer at the source, but the source folder structure remains. Now this is where it gets a bit weird, worthy of a batveat. We've been discussing the /MOV option, which is obviously short for *move*, but a similarly named option called /MOVE stands for . . . I guess *move with an E*. These two options are subtly different. The robocopy command with the /MOVE option truly moves files and directories.

The addition of the E to the option deletes the source directory structure after copying all of the files to the destination:

```
robocopy C:\Source\ C:\Target\ /MOVE /S
```

What we have is a /MOV option that moves files while copying subdirectories and a /MOVE option that moves both files and subdirectories. It isn't particularly intuitive.

When considering which command to use for a particular move, the robocopy command is the most efficient choice for all the same reasons mentioned in "xcopy vs. robocopy" on page 76. But like the xcopy command, the move command has the more straightforward return code and still has a place in the Batch ecosystem.

Deleting Files

When files are no longer needed, it just makes sense to clean them up. The del command easily deletes one or more files. The /Q option, which again stands for *quiet* mode, prevents the interpreter from asking permission to delete the file. The command accepts multiple arguments of files to be deleted where you can use both explicit filenames and file masks. The following command deletes one specific file named *Junk.txt* and all files in the folder with the *.OLD* extension:

```
del /Q C:\Source\Junk.txt C:\Source\*.OLD
```

Use the /A option to select files for deletion based on their attributes. For example, delete only hidden files using the /AH option. Negating the logic, the /A-H option deletes only files that are *not* hidden. As always, use the help command for a complete list of options.

Delete all the files in a folder by simply using the directory as the argument to the del command, but the directory itself will still exist. You'll need a different command for that, and I'll share it in Chapter 13.

Renaming Files

The ren and rename commands are Batch synonyms; that is, they are the same command. The first argument is the file to be renamed, and the second argument is the new filename:

```
ren C:\Batch\File2Rename.txt NewFileName.txt
```

If the destination file already exists, the interpreter returns an errorlevel of 1. If there's the possibility that a file with the same name is already there, I'll quietly delete it prior to the rename:

```
del C:\Batch\NewFileName.txt /Q
ren C:\Batch\File2Rename.txt NewFileName.txt
```

Wildcards are supported even for this command, but I've used the ren command only for explicit filenames, primarily because the command doesn't write a list of renamed files to the console. (If I have more than one file to rename, I'll use a dir command as input into a for command and do the renames one by one. We'll explore these commands further in Chapters 13 and 17, respectively.)

The ren command isn't complicated, but I've seen one common batveat far too often. It's easy to use the path on both arguments, but when you reflect on this for a moment, the interpreter already knows the path from the first argument. The file isn't being moved or copied anywhere; by the nature of this command, it's being renamed in place. If the first argument doesn't have a path, the current directory is assumed (more on that in the next chapter), but the second argument is the new filename only and should never have a path associated with it.

Summary

This chapter likely will become one that you reference most in this book. Batch would be nothing without the ability to create, copy, move, merge, and delete files, and I introduced a bevy of commands for those tasks here. Some of the commands I discussed are straightforward, but I covered more than one batveat along with solutions for mitigating them. You also learned how to execute these commands on multiple files at a time with the use of file masks and wildcards.

Copying a file might sound like a simple task, but I detailed the many techniques available and considerations at play. I hope that I showed you how powerful and useful the robocopy command really is, while also instilling in you an appreciation for the simplicity and usefulness of the xcopy command.

In the next chapter I'll describe how to execute a program compiled in another language, which will involve a deeper discussion about how the interpreter finds the program to execute when you don't provide a path.

8

EXECUTING COMPILED PROGRAMS

This chapter is ostensibly about a bat file executing or calling a program written and compiled in another language. In truth, the syntax to do that is pretty straightforward. The most interesting facet of this chapter is that sometimes the program being executed doesn't have a defined path in the bat file. How does the bat file find the executable?

The main focus of this chapter will be on two highly important mechanisms for finding such a program, the *current directory* and the path variable. This topic goes well past the executing of programs. You'll use it when calling other bat files, and it impacts many other instances when a resource isn't defined with a path. For instance, in Chapter 7, I discussed many commands for copying, moving, deleting, and renaming files. All of those commands will work perfectly well in your bat files when the file or files in each command aren't defined with a path in the bat file, but only if you understand these concepts. And of course, you'll also learn different ways to invoke programs and pass them arguments.

Calling an Executable

Often a bat file is little more than a vehicle or a wrapper for calling a compiled program, also known as an *executable*. The bat file will simply set some variables needed by the program, call the executable, and perform some error handling on the backend. More sophisticated bat files might call dozens of different programs, maybe even employing conditional logic on some calls. Simple or complex, a feature of Batch is the ability to call executables written in other languages.

The call command accepts the executable as its first, and possibly only, argument. The following command calls or executes the program *MyProg .exe* located in the *C:\Executables* directory:

```
call C:\Executables\MyProg.exe
```

The call command calls a program; that should surprise no one, but it's about to get weird. This is the only command in Batch, and possibly all other languages, that works perfectly well when the command name itself is omitted. The following command, while not technically a call command, performs the same function as the call command in the prior example:

```
C:\Executables\MyProg.exe
```

Think about this for a moment. The command set x=1 sets a variable, but the statement x=1 will do nothing more than confuse the interpreter. If the text robocopy is left off the beginning of a robocopy command, no one in their right mind would expect the remaining text to copy a file. (If this isn't weird enough, the presence or lack of the call command gets a little weirder when calling other bat files in Chapter 10.)

It almost seems like magic, but consider it from the interpreter's perspective. When it interprets a new line, it usually expects the first item to be a command. When it finds set, it then anticipates a variable, an equal sign, and a value; when it finds robocopy, it next looks for a different set of arguments. When it finds something completely unexpected, the interpreter doesn't balk; it gives you, the coder, the benefit of the doubt, assumes that whatever it is can be executed, and executes it—just as the call command would.

Some Batch coders use the call command for executables; some do not. I'm in the latter camp, preferring the clean look of the executable alone or just a resolved variable on a single line of code, but I've no qualms with those who explicitly spell out the command. More important, consistency is key; stick with your convention of choice.

I also prefer to keep the program name in a variable with a fully qualified path, setting it only when it isn't already defined. This ensures that the desired program is stored in the variable by default, while also allowing others to set it to an alternate program for the sake of flexibility:

```
if not defined pgmMyProg  set pgmMyProg=C:\Executables\MyProg.exe
```

Then when it comes time to execute the program, this simple command, if I can call it a command, will *call* the desired program:

```
%pgmMyProg%
```

This variable contains the path of the executable, but let's return to the concept of a line of code consisting of nothing more than a hardcoded path and filename.

You can shorten it by removing the path, leaving just the name of the program and maybe the extension:

```
myProg.exe
```

This looks even simpler, but when you stop to ponder where on the machine or even on a network the interpreter is to find the program, the complexity grows. Before delving into those details, I'll need a digression about two commands/variables.

The cd Command and Variable

The cd command is also a variable, a special variable that's one of a few Batch pseudo-environment variables. In Chapter 21, I'll have much more to say about these variables. For now, just consider them to be variables originally set by the interpreter that have some unique features.

The variable stands for *current directory.* The command is a bit more ambiguous, as it can also mean *change directory* because it's used to . . . well, change the current directory.

When you double-click or open a bat file, the current directory is the directory or folder where the bat file resides. If the same bat file is called from a different process, the current directory is inherited from that process. Simply calling a bat file or executable in a different directory doesn't change the current directory, but the cd command does.

The first and last lines shown next use the cd variable to display the current directory. The meat of this sandwich is the cd command that adeptly changes the current directory to its argument, assuming the directory exists:

```
> con echo Current Directory is: %cd%
cd C:\NewDir\
> con echo Current Directory is: %cd%
```

If a bat file with these three lines resides in *C:\Batch*, executing it displays both the original current directory and the newly assigned current directory to the console:

```
Current Directory is: C:\Batch
Current Directory is: C:\NewDir
```

You can also set the current directory relative to the existing current directory. A single dot represents its existing value, so this assigns the cd variable to a subdirectory:

```
cd .\Child\
```

Two dots represent the existing current directory's parent, so the following moves the current directory up one level:

```
cd ..
```

(The ..\.. argument finds the grandparent directory.)

You can even reassign the cd variable to a sibling directory by first going up one level with the two dots:

```
cd ..\Sibling\
```

I'm hesitant to even mention this, but chdir is a Batch synonym for the cd command. That is, the command in the prior example is functionally equivalent to chdir ..\Sibling\. However, the cd variable has no synonym, so you can use either chdir or cd to change the current directory, but you need to use cd when resolving the current directory. I find it easiest to always use cd for both purposes.

Before I get into the purpose of the current directory, I need to introduce another command that's also a variable.

The path Command and Variable

Much like cd, path also is both a command and a pseudo-environment variable. The variable is predefined on Windows machines with a semicolon-delimited list of directories needed by the computer, such as paths for Java and Windows executables. (To see the path variable currently set on any Windows machine, open a command prompt, and using what we learned in Chapter 2 enter the command **set path**.)

Just as the cd command sets the current directory, the path command sets the path variable. In the following line of code, the existing value is being prepended and appended with two other directories; notice the semicolons inserted at the end of each additional directory as a delimiter:

```
path C:\PrependDir\;%path%C:\AppendDir\;
```

You can completely reassign the path variable—or even wipe it out entirely if the argument is solely a semicolon. The various directories in this variable exist for a purpose, probably allowing for some necessary processes to run. Be extremely cautious about changing the variable persistently on your machine, such as with the setx command, but the path command shown previously changes only the path for the execution of the bat file. At worst you might break your bat file, but you won't break anything else on your computer. In the next section, I'll explain why you might want to change the path variable.

WARNING *The set command offers an alternative means of resetting both the cd and path variables, but out of consistency, I resist this method because some other pseudo-environment variables can't or shouldn't be reset with this command—and it requires a few more keystrokes.*

Finding an Executable

Let's get back to executing a program simply by invoking nothing but its name and extension like so:

```
myProg.exe
```

Where does the interpreter find the executable? The first place it looks is in the current directory. If found there, that's the file executed. Otherwise, the interpreter will look for it sequentially in each directory defined in the path variable and execute the first one it finds. If it can't find an executable with this name in any of those directories, the interpreter does nothing more than set errorlevel to the value of 9009. (Oddly, the bad return code is 1 if the call command precedes the name of the executable.)

Let's execute the same line of code, assuming that *myProg.exe* lives in *C:\Executables*. If this directory is the current directory, the program will be found and executed. Otherwise, if this directory is in the path variable, the program will likely be found and executed. This assumes that the program isn't superseded with a different program of the same name and extension residing in the current directory or higher in the path variable hierarchy.

If none of this is true, the program won't be found, but there are different methods to make sure that the interpreter finds the executable. First, we can use the cd command to change the current directory prior to executing the program:

```
cd C:\Executables\
```

Alternatively, we can alter the path variable to contain the directory in one of two ways. Here I'm prepending the path:

```
path C:\Executables\;%path%
```

And here I'm appending the path:

```
path %path%C:\Executables\;
```

If the directory is appended and if another file named *myProg.exe* exists in a directory defined earlier in the path variable, that other program will be the one executed. Prepending the directory ensures that my executable is picked up before any other, but this isn't without its own dangers. It might be introducing something into the path variable that'll override a resource used by some other process.

This is in no way a bad technique; in fact, it's quite useful when managed wisely. One great use of finding an executable using the current directory or path variable is to make the code portable. You can keep a bat file in a single folder or a more complex folder structure with other bat files, as well as any number of executables, configuration files, and other resources. You then can copy that folder to other machines and networks with different root directory structures. Since the current directory essentially follows the high-level bat file around, it'll work in those various locations if the current directory is used to find its other components.

You can house a default executable in the same folder as your bat file. If run on its own, it'll use this executable. If called from another bat file with a different current directory, it may find a different program, allowing others to use your bat file to invoke their own executable. In short, you can create a hierarchy of same-named programs with different ones executed in different instances.

To take this one step further, I hinted earlier that the extension isn't even required to invoke a program. That is, if *myProg.exe* resides in the current directory, it'll *probably* be invoked with this line of code:

```
myProg
```

The interpreter finds an executable given no extension with the aid of another pseudo-environment variable, pathext, which contains a hierarchy of semicolon-delimited extensions in much the same way that the path variable contains a hierarchy of directories. The interpreter still looks for the executable in the current directory, followed by the directories in the path variable, but in each folder, it now looks for the first executable it can find with the *myProg* filename and an extension listed in the given hierarchy.

If the pathext variable hasn't been altered by someone or something else, it will likely contain about a dozen file extensions, starting with *.com, .exe, .bat,* and *.cmd*—in that order. Thus, the only entity that would prevent the previous command from executing *myProg.exe* from the current directory would be *myProg.com* in the current directory. (If you ever have to reset this variable, use the set command. The pathext variable is only a variable, not a command.)

Pushing and Popping the Current Directory

The `cd` command does quite a nice job of changing the current directory, but the prior current directory is lost into the ether, never to be known again. Often that's perfectly fine, but in other instances, you may want to change the current directory temporarily before reverting it to its prior state. Perhaps a utility bat file is written to be callable from many other bat files. In short order, I'll discuss exactly how to call one bat file from another, but for now, we only need to understand the perspective of the called bat file.

The called bat file may create or use resources in a certain folder, so changing the current directory at the bat file's onset makes sense. However, when the called bat file completes and turns control back to the calling bat file, the prior current directory should be restored. It's simple courtesy because the calling bat file may be working in a different directory and changing its current directory might very well cause it problems. A more self-serving motivation is that the called bat file wants to keep its directory to itself. If the called bat file doesn't restore the current directory, the calling bat file might drop unwanted files in what's now the current directory. The called bat file can hide its directory from the unwashed masses while also presenting itself as being courteous.

To solve this issue, you could store the prior current directory in a variable just before the `cd` command is executed, and then you could execute another `cd` command at the end of the bat file to set it back. But Batch provides two commands that together will do this far more elegantly, namely, the `pushd` and `popd` commands.

The `pushd` command changes the current directory just like the `cd` command, but it also *pushes* the prior current directory onto a stack to be used later. It's sometimes referred to as the *push directory* command, although for the sake of brevity it's usually pronounced as it's written, that is, the "push-d" command. Near the beginning of the bat file this command will succinctly perform both tasks:

```
pushd C:\NewDir\
```

At or near the close of the bat file, the following short command will remove *C:\NewDir* as the current directory and retrieve or *pop* the prior current directory off the stack, using it to restore the current directory:

```
popd
```

This is sometimes called the *pop directory* command, but more commonly, the "pop-d" command.

Notice that there's no argument; `popd` is the rare command that accepts no arguments at all, ever. As multiple `pushd` commands execute, each one pushes another prior current directory onto the stack, and each subsequent `popd` command will restore the one most recently added.

Also of note, if the argument passed to the pushd command is a network path, the highest unused drive letter is assigned to that path, and the popd command will unassign it. Lastly, the pushd command with no argument displays the full list of directories on the stack starting with the most recently added.

WARNING *It's very important that pushd and popd commands be balanced. If a pushd assigns a network path, a corresponding popd should always execute, even if an error is handled. If not, any mapped drive letters will remain mapped, even after the bat file finishes up. If that happens often enough, the computer will run out of usable drive letters.*

Finding Other Resources with the Current Directory

The current directory is used for far more than finding programs to execute. For any resource, such as a file, if the path isn't defined, the current directory is assumed to be its path. For instance, in Chapter 7, this command deleted an explicit file and everything ending in a particular extension:

```
del /Q C:\Source\Junk.txt C:\Source\*.OLD
```

The following command performs the same task with far fewer keystrokes *if*—the *if* being a critical qualifier—the current directory is *C:\Source*, which is the path twice removed from the prior command:

```
del /Q Junk.txt *.OLD
```

The same is true for the source argument of an xcopy command and any other command that accepts a path and filename as an argument. I usually prefer to use explicit paths to avoid any ambiguity, but this technique grants the same type of flexibility described throughout this chapter for a great number of commands. Flip through Chapter 7 again, imagining all of the commands for copying, moving, and renaming files without explicit paths. They'd all be good commands if the interpreter finds the particular file or files in whatever happened to be the current directory at that time.

Passing Arguments to an Executable

At the beginning of this chapter, I demonstrated how to call a compiled program. Before moving on, I have one last observation to share about this syntax.

Executables often accept one to many parameters at execution time. Those parameters are passed to the program as arguments by simply listing them after the program. For readability, I've put the three arguments into variables:

```
set inFile=C:\Batch\Input.dat
set outFile=C:\Batch\Output.dat
set logFile=C:\Batch\Log.dat

%pgmMyProg% %inFile% %outFile% %logFile%
```

The input file is the first argument passed to the program; in many languages, that would be considered args[0] inside the program. Likewise, the output file is the second argument, args[1], and the log is the third, args[2]. You can also use hardcoded values, and the arguments can be anything you like; they don't have to be files.

Summary

Executing a compiled program appears pretty basic at first. After all, you don't even need a command. But you can't truly understand how it works without knowing the details about the current directory and the path variable that I've detailed here. You've learned how the interpreter uses them to find executables, files, and any other resources, along with multiple means of managing the content of these important variables.

Executing another bat file is similar to but not the same as executing a compiled program, and you'll learn about those differences in Chapter 10. But before I delve into that, you'll learn about labels and their many important uses in the very next chapter, primarily their impact on when commands are executed and how often.

9

LABELS AND NONSEQUENTIAL EXECUTION

In politics, labels have gotten a bad reputation, but at the most basic level, a *label* is an identifier that concisely defines a product or an object in as few words as possible. Commerce would grind to a halt if we didn't have labels; grocery stores would contain shelves and shelves of mysterious canned products. What's for dinner? It might be beans or pumpkin pie mix; we won't know until we open it.

Without labels Batch wouldn't be thrown into quite this level of disarray, but an important tool for creating more complex bat files would be missing from your coder's toolbox. Up until now every bat file, snippet, and listing in this book has executed sequentially. The interpreter interprets each line, one by one, executing the first command first, followed by the second. This continues until one of two things happens: either the final command of the bat file is interpreted, or a syntax error crashes the bat file. Labels allow you to execute Batch commands in a nonsequential manner. In this chapter, I'll introduce the concept of branching forward and backward in the code, repeating some section of code based on a data condition and even creating a couple commands not intrinsic to Batch.

Labels will also afford me a great opportunity to discuss a topic that's exceedingly important: coding conventions, in particular, indentation.

Labels

A *label* in Batch is what you might expect it to be, a tag defining a block of code. More specifically, a certain spot or location in the bat file is *labeled*. A label isn't a command, and although it's never executed, you'll soon see that it's critical to the execution flow.

Labels can contain letters, numbers, and some special characters, and, most important, they must start with a colon. Oddly, the name of the label can contain additional colons, but never in the second position. For example, here's some code being defined or labeled for exactly what it does, checking the state of a specific variable:

```
:CheckStatus
 if /i "%status%" equ "fail"  > con echo Failure
 if /i "%status%" equ "good"  > con echo Success
```

Similarly, this bit of code handles a very rudimentary abort process and is labeled as such:

```
:Abort
 echo The Process is aborting
 exit /B 1
```

I'll discuss the exit command in Chapter 10. For now, it's simply being used to get out of the bat file.

Defining a label is straightforward, but before getting into the impactfulness of labels and how to use them, allow me a digression, maybe even a rant, on coding conventions.

Indentation

Many Batch coders refuse to indent their code. I'm not sure why, as every other language I'm familiar with has some sort of a convention, if not a hard requirement, on indentation. My best guess is that at its core is a fundamental disrespect of the language, considering Batch a utilitarian nuisance that must be dispatched with as quickly as possible with no regard for readability, much less aesthetics. For your Batch code to garner the respect it merits, I recommend starting all commands with an indentation of two spaces. Indent all logic inside the code blocks of if commands (and similar structures yet to be discussed) another three spaces, with nested structures indented even more.

This topic might seem like a non sequitur in a chapter about labels, but in reality, it's the ideal location. Labels should stand out a bit, or even more than a bit. A well-formatted document of any kind has parts, chapters, sections, and/or subsections, where each often has some sort of a header or cue—or dare I say *label*—that visually stands out from the rest of the text with a different font, font size, emboldening, underlining, colorization, or a combination of some or all of the above. These options are unavailable when writing a bat file. Our arsenal for the task has been reduced to one significant item, indentation, with a nod to capitalization and whitespace.

Since the first character of a label is always a colon, I always place that colon in the second byte of the line, reducing my typical indentation to one character. Therefore, when anyone, including myself, views a bat file that I've written, all the labels stand out. I reserve the first character of a line for the start of a `rem` command. For instance, here's a rudimentary remark, label, and two simple commands:

```
rem - This code does something.
 :DoSomething
  set do=something
  set doMore=somethingElse
```

The uppercase character after the colon in the label also adds to its prominence.

I hope I'm not coming across as the Stalin of Batch coding conventions. This is just one coder's opinion, and other well-thought-out conventions exist that are different from mine. What's important is that the code should be easy to read. There are many ways to accomplish this, but a complete lack of indenting most certainly fails the test, even if this topic brings out my autocratic side.

The goto Command

Now that we have a label defining a snippet of code, what good is it? Some coders actually use labels as makeshift remarks (which is fine, I guess), but the true function of a label is to direct the process flow to the code under the label. This is where the goto command comes into play, and it does what it sounds like it would do. It instructs the interpreter to skip to (or go to) a location in the code defined by a label. Consider these two commands:

```
goto :Abort
goto :DoSomething
```

The goto commands are sending control to the `:Abort` and `:DoSomething` labels defined previously in this chapter.

Well, that's not entirely true; the first command sends the execution to the abort routine, and the second goto command never executes. In a bat file, a label itself can come before or after the goto command that branches to it, but what's important to understand is that the execution never returns to the command immediately after the goto command. Once the goto is executed, we are totally at the mercy of the code under the label.

To go to a label defined as `:Abort`, you can also do so with this command:

```
goto ABORT
```

Two things are going on here. First, the colon has been dropped from the label name in the `goto` command. I suspect that this is an early bug that Microsoft won't fix to maintain backward compatibility. Second, the actual label has only the `A` capitalized, but the `goto` command shows the entire label name capitalized.

This example demonstrates that the label name is case-insensitive, as Batch is in general, and that the colon is optional in the `goto` command. While the interpreter makes this permissible, I see no reason for the two label names to differ in any way as it can only breed confusion. Consistency is key.

The `call` command introduced in Chapter 8 is also used in conjunction with labels, but its behavior is quite distinct from the `goto` command. I'll come back to the `call` command and those differences in Chapter 10.

Branching Forward

The `goto` command sends control or the process flow in one of two directions; one is to branch forward over code. Three `echo` commands write text to the console in this example, but only the first and third are executed:

```
> con echo Before GOTO
goto :MyLabel
> con echo After GOTO
:MyLabel
> con echo After LABEL
```

It's not hard to imagine more complex code using this technique. A `goto` command might be done conditionally based on the results of an `if` command, and instead of branching over a single `echo` command, it might be skipping a far larger section of code. For instance, you can skip the execution of one or more programs if a certain file is present or not present, or if a failure is detected, you can jump to the code that will abort the bat file's execution, skipping everything else.

The `goto` can also be a tool to break out of a loop. Unfortunately, I haven't discussed loops yet; in Part II, I'll discuss the `for` command and loops extensively. But for now, to understand this logic you need to know only that this loop will execute once for each name listed in the `listOfNames` variable, regardless of how many names it contains:

```
for %%n in (%listOfNames%) do (
    if /i "%%n" equ "Waldo"  goto :FoundName
)
> con echo ** Name Not Found **
:FoundName
```

The if command is searching for a particular name. If and when it's found, the goto command breaks out of the loop, jumping down to the label on the last line.

This is important for two reasons. One, it's efficient—if the name is found near the beginning of the list, CPU cycles aren't wasted pointlessly searching the rest of the list. More important, the echo command is never executed if the name is found. Notice that the logic not only breaks out of the loop prematurely but also branches over the writing of the message that indicates that the name wasn't found.

Branching Backward

The examples in the previous section use a goto command to skip forward in the code. Next, I'll look at examples of a goto command going in the reverse direction. But first, I've already discussed how we can build certain components of more modern languages that aren't explicitly part of Batch (think booleans and floats), but many others are yet to come. Batch doesn't have a while command, nor does it support a do...while command. In other languages, a while command executes a block of code zero to multiple times until a condition is met. A do...while command is very similar; the only difference is that the code block will execute once before the condition is evaluated. Let's create both of these in Batch.

The while "Command"

To demonstrate the usefulness of a Batch while command, we'll write some code that'll strip all leading zeros off a value, a necessity for any coder not wanting to perform octal arithmetic accidentally (long story on that in Chapter 6 if you missed it). The while command might execute a bit of code as long as—or *while*—the first byte is 0, and that code will do nothing more than strip off one leading byte.

The following code performs the task perfectly:

```
:StripLead0s
 if "%nbr:~0,1%" equ "0" (
    if "%nbr:~1,2%" neq "" (
       set nbr=%nbr:~1%
       goto :StripLead0s
) )
```

The interpreter essentially ignores the label when it's first encountered and interrogates the first character of nbr. If it's zero, the code next verifies that there's a second byte—that is, that the 0 is in fact leading something. If both are true, the code block is entered, where it strips off the leading 0 before the goto command sends control back to the label just prior to the if command.

Let's step through the code with three different numbers to really get a feel for the logic. If the variable has no leading 0, the code block is never executed. If it has one leading 0, the code block is executed once. Then the leading byte is checked again, and since it's no longer 0, the execution flow proceeds to whatever comes next. If nbr has 17 leading 0s, the code block removing a 0 executes 17 times, and after the leading byte is checked an 18th time, the execution moves on.

The word *while* doesn't appear in that listing, but it does everything a proper while command would. As far as I'm concerned, it's a Batch while command.

> **NOTE** *The previous snippet is the first example I've shown of one if command nested inside another, but you'll see many more nested commands in the chapters ahead. As another note on coding conventions, I've stacked the two trailing close parentheses on a single line in that listing. This makes the code more compact, especially when nesting multiple levels deep, and it keeps the focus on the interesting logic, but I concede that I'm in the minority. Most Batch coders line up each close parenthesis with its respective if command. This requires more lines of code, but the following is functionally equivalent to my previous code:*

```
:StripLead0s
 if "%nbr:~0,1%" equ "0" (
    if "%nbr:~1,2%" neq "" (
       set nbr=%nbr:~1%
       goto :StripLead0s
    )
 )
```

Do what feels right to you and do it consistently. Also, notice that the label name contains a numeric value. As mentioned previously, we aren't restricted to letters of the alphabet. And by the way, doesn't that indentation look nice?

The do...while "Command"

A Batch do...while command looks quite similar; the only difference is that the main logic must be executed at least once. In languages with a built-in do...while command, the conditional clause usually comes at the tail end of the structure (understandably after the main logic is executed once), and Batch is no different. Compared to the while command, the main logic is moved from inside the if command code block to just after the label and prior to the if command.

To demonstrate, let's take an example where the textStr variable is to be right-padded with at least one space to build it out to a minimum of 25 bytes in length. If the original string is less than 25 bytes long, the result will be 25 bytes; if it's originally at least 25 bytes long, a single space will be appended to the result. (The string might be part of some concatenated text to be displayed on the console, where the space-padding will line up the columns. But of course, we'll want a space between it and whatever comes next, even if it requires an extra byte.)

The fact that the right padding must be done at least once lends itself to the do...while command:

```
:PadRight
set textStr=%textStr% &
if "%textStr:~24,1%" equ ""  goto :PadRight
```

As with the `while` command, the label precedes the bulk of the code, but the core logic immediately follows it, which in this case is a single `set` command padding the string with one space. Then the 25th byte is examined. (Remember, it's zero-offset.) If it doesn't exist, the `goto` command sends the execution back to the label so that another space can be appended to the string. This repeats until that 25th byte is populated, ensuring that the string is at least 25 bytes long and also that at least one space has been added regardless of the length.

In Chapter 26, I'll detail how to perform automatic restarts of a failed process that might work if tried again with little more than a label and a `goto` command—also known as the `do...while` command.

The :eof Label

One special label not created by the coder but intrinsic to all bat files is `:eof`, which stands for *end of file*. When the following `goto :eof` command executes in the main logic of a called bat file, control is returned to the calling bat file:

```
> con echo We are about to exit the bat file.
goto :eof
> con echo This command will never be executed.
```

Executing the same command in the high-level bat file will cease the process entirely even though no label defined as `:eof` exists in the bat file.

If you're of the contrarian nature and decide to define your own `:eof` label, the interpreter will simply ignore it as if it were a nonsensical remark. In Chapter 10, I'll explore this unique label further, in particular, how the interpreter handles the `goto :eof` command when inside a callable routine.

Variable Labels

Working in a language that doesn't have a compiler has some definite downsides, but I've already shown you some silver linings (delayed expansion, for example). One more is the ability to define the label name in a `goto` command at the time of execution, although the label itself must be hard-coded. To set that up, envision a different label for each month of the year. The first three are shown here without their respective month-centric code beneath them:

```
:MonthJanuary
:MonthFebruary
:MonthMarch
```

Obviously, the following command will send the execution to one particular label in the previous snippet:

```
goto :MonthFebruary
```

But that's old news by now. More interesting, if the variable month is set to the value February, the following command will call the same label:

```
goto :Month%month%
```

The argument to this goto command is the concatenation of the hardcoded :Month and the value of the month variable. After the variable is resolved, the command directs the execution to the label :MonthFebruary. The same goes for the other valid months, meaning that the same line of code also goes to :MonthMarch if month is set to the value of March.

But that does raise the question of what happens when the resulting label name doesn't exist in the bat file, for instance, if month is set to Erele (February in the Yoruba language). The interpreter writes the following message to the console:

```
The system cannot find the batch label specified - MonthErele
```

Unfortunately, you'll never see this message because the process will immediately crash.

In Chapter 10, you'll see that Batch handles a bad label name better when used with a call command, but if you use this technique with a goto command, ensure that the argument resolves to a valid label.

A BRIEF HISTORY OF THE GOTO COMMAND

I fear that I must address the elephant, maybe even the herd of pachyderms, in the room. For my first job as a coder, I was in a COBOL bootcamp for nine weeks. Bob Cook, our masterful instructor, demonstrated the COBOL goto command, explaining that we might run across it in some archaic code written while I was still in diapers. We needed to understand what the code was doing, but he immediately followed this up with something along the lines of "Never, under any circumstance, code a goto command. Never. Period. Did I mention not to do this . . . ever?"

Ill-advised use of goto commands can produce *spaghetti code*, where control jumps from place to place making it nearly impossible to follow. Not long after the bootcamp, I had to make a small change to what should've been a simple program. It was so riddled with goto commands that my simple change resulted in a cascade of unintended consequences. After wasting three days attempting to understand the program enough to make the minor tweak, I finally gave up and took another three days to rewrite it from scratch. Far more recently, I was giving some Batch pointers to a co-worker who was aghast that I used a goto command, and I certainly understood their dismay. The DNA of all coders is rapidly and indelibly being hardwired with an aversion to the goto in all instances.

Without a doubt, the goto has a bad reputation, and I agree completely with the ostracization of the command to the scrap heap of coding history—in compiled code. But in Batch, when done correctly, the command is quite useful, even necessary. It's the best way to code around the lack of a true while command and the lack of a break command to break out of a loop. (In actuality, Batch does have a break command, but it doesn't break out of anything or behave like synonymous commands in other languages. It's a *no operation* or *no-op* command. Don't ask.) The goto command provides a very nice means to these ends, and I'll demonstrate even more uses in the next chapter. Don't be afraid of the goto, but use it cautiously and wisely.

Summary

In this chapter, I introduced the concept of labels and how to navigate to them via the goto command. You learned how to create labels, explored tips on their use, and saw how instrumental they are in the building of the while and do...while commands. I also introduced the indispensable :eof label.

But you can navigate to labels in two distinct ways. Much of the next chapter will also focus on labels and how you can use them to create callable routines inside a bat file. I'll also detail how to call one bat file from another, a crucial topic as you begin creating projects too complex for a single bat file.

10

CALLING ROUTINES AND
BAT FILES

In the previous chapter, I introduced labels and nonsequential execution, both of which also play a major part in this chapter. I'll soon introduce a new twist on an already discussed command, allowing you to create and call a routine defined by a label. Instead of simply handing control over to the code just after the label, control is returned to the place from where it was called after the routine executes. As you write more complex and interesting bat files, you'll want a full understanding of routines.

In Chapter 8, I introduced the concept of calling executables compiled in other languages. I'll expand on that discussion here, describing different techniques for one bat file calling another bat file. You'll obviously learn about the most typical type of call, one that returns control to the calling bat file. But you'll also learn techniques for relinquishing control to the called bat file and how to spawn a second parallel Batch process. In addition, you'll explore different ways to exit from a routine or bat file gracefully, with or without a return code.

The call Command, Revisited

Before you can create callable internal routines, you must understand the similarities and differences between two commands that work with labels. One is the call command first introduced in Chapter 8, where we used it to call programs compiled in other languages. The other is the goto command, introduced in Chapter 9 for altering the execution flow of a bat file.

To compare and contrast the two commands, recall this code from Chapter 9:

```
> con echo Before GOTO
goto :MyLabel
> con echo After GOTO
:MyLabel
> con echo After LABEL
```

The goto command skipped the middle echo command, resulting in this output:

```
Before GOTO
After LABEL
```

To demonstrate the contrast, Listing 10-1 changes every instance of goto in that code to call, including both the goto command and the text in the echo commands, while leaving everything else identical in this very concise bat file.

```
> con echo Before CALL
call :MyLabel
> con echo After CALL
:MyLabel
> con echo After LABEL
```

Listing 10-1: A short bat file demonstrating the call command

Execute the bat file from Listing 10-1, and you'll get the four lines shown in Listing 10-2 written to the console, not the three some may have expected.

```
Before CALL
After LABEL
After CALL
After LABEL
```

Listing 10-2: The results written to the console when executing Listing 10-1

The display of Before CALL obviously executes right off the bat (pun intended). The call command temporarily hands control to the code just after the label, resulting in After LABEL being displayed. When this was a goto command, that was it; the bat file ended after that display. But with the call command, after everything between :MyLabel and the end of the bat file executes, control returns to the command immediately after the call command. Hence, After CALL is displayed.

Some might expect the execution to be completed at this point, but the interpreter next encounters :MyLabel again. We aren't calling it or going to it; instead, it's just the next line of code. Notice that I didn't call it a command or even a statement. It's just a line of code, a placeholder, and in this context, little more than a very subtle speed bump on the path to the next command. The interpreter moves on to the last line in the bat file, and the text After LABEL is displayed a second time. The interpreter finds no other command to interpret, and the bat file is done.

While the goto command relinquishes control, the call command remembers from where it came and returns to that spot when its business is done. We now have the makings of a callable internal routine, and we'll be calling that routine with the call command.

Calling Internal Routines

As your Batch code gets more interesting, you'll want to execute a bit of code multiple times from various locations in a bat file. For instance, you might want to call an executable more than once, or you might want to periodically check a directory for some files in need of copying. When we get to interactive Batch, you might want to ask the user a question and get a response several times.

Faced with a need for multiple invocations of a section of code, a novice coder might resort to cutting and pasting—a loathsome and odious option in my exceedingly judgmental (but accurate) opinion. A far better solution is to create an internal routine and call it from those multiple locations. You can even place some code that's called only once into a routine just to better organize your bat file. Sometimes it's perfectly fine to run right through a label, but more times than not, you'll want to create a routine that can be invoked only by calling it.

For the following exercise, I'll take Listing 10-1 and reconfigure it so that the label defines a callable routine. That is, the execution flow will call the routine, return from it, and exit the bat file before falling through to that routine again. To this end, I'll need a way to terminate both the routine and bat file. The final display of After LABEL that appears in Listing 10-2 will be no more. Instead, we'll expect these three lines of output:

```
Before CALL
After LABEL
After CALL
```

The following code, which looks quite a bit different, does exactly that:

```
  > con echo Before CALL
❶ call :MyLabel
  > con echo After CALL
❷ goto :eof & rem End of TestCall.bat

❸ :MyLabel
  > con echo After LABEL
❹ goto :eof & rem End of :MyLabel

❺ :AnotherLabel
  > con echo This is Never Executed
❻ goto :eof & rem End of :AnotherLabel
```

Before stepping through the code, notice the three goto :eof commands. As you might expect, the first one ❷ jumps to the *end of file*, ceasing the bat file. The other two ❹ ❻ are something quite different—something new.

After the initial echo command, the call command ❶ invokes the routine that :MyLabel ❸ defines, which contains just two commands. The first is the familiar echo of After LABEL to the console, and the second is a goto :eof command ❹. Because this command is being executed after a label is called, it ends not the file but the routine, and control returns to the command just after the call command ❶, writing After CALL to the console. Finally, the main goto :eof command ❷ exits the bat file, because the interpreter knows that it isn't in a routine.

When inside the :MyLabel ❸ routine, going to :eof (or *end of file*) is a misnomer; it's really more of an *end of routine*, but let's not quibble over semantics. If you remove this goto :eof command ❹, control would've continued through to the code under :AnotherLabel ❺ before returning to the mainline logic. But with this command ❹, the code under :AnotherLabel never executes.

Since the goto :eof command has two distinct uses, I usually follow such commands with a remark defining exactly what it's terminating, either the name of the routine or the bat file itself. I'm simply placing the rem command after an ampersand, which separates the two commands on a single line of code. Programmatically, it's not necessary, but this practice very much enhances the code's readability, especially when the routines become longer and more complex than the previous examples.

Calling Bat Files

Short or repetitive bits of code are great candidates for internal routines; you can add one or more routines to the end of a bat file to create a well-organized module of which you can be proud. But sometimes those short bits of code aren't so short, or they are so useful that you would like to make them available to other bat files written by you and maybe even others. Instead of a routine, this scenario calls for one bat file calling another bat file. For instance, you might create a single bat file to handle logging and call it from multiple other bat files.

Executing one bat file from another works a bit differently than executing an internal routine. But first, let's return to how a compiled program is executed from Chapter 8. When the interpreter comes across a line of code that's simply the name of an executable, it invokes the executable. Hence, this "command" executes the program:

```
C:\Executables\CompiledProg.exe
```

After the program completes its task, control returns to the bat file. You might expect the calling of a bat file to work the same way, but alas, it does not. However, the following line of code indeed executes the called bat file, but with an enormous batveat:

```
C:\Batch\CalledBat.bat
```

That batveat is simple: control never returns to the calling bat file. The entire process ends when the called bat file ends. The vast majority of the time you'll want control returned; otherwise, there wouldn't be much point in coding anything after the invocation of the called bat file. To see control returned, you can insert the call command just before the called bat file:

```
call C:\Batch\CalledBat.bat
```

To sum up, whether calling bat files or compiled executables of another language, you can use the call command or omit it, but there's a difference. When calling an executable, both techniques are virtually identical. When calling a fellow bat file, the call command ensures that control is returned to the caller. Without the command, control never returns.

Since I've never found a use for a non-returning bat file invocation, my preference always is to omit the call command for executables and use it for bat files. One advantage is that at a glance, it's obvious what type of file is being called.

Early in my career, I learned about the need for the call command vis-à-vis bat files the hard way when I couldn't figure out why my bat file just stopped executing. There was no hang or abort message; it just stopped. Complicating matters, my troubleshooting was understandably focused on the called bat file. It took quite a while before I noticed the missing call command and, more important, understood its significance. But that isn't the only idiosyncrasy concerning the call command.

Notes on Calling a Label

In the previous chapter, I mentioned that it's possible to leave the colon off the label name in the argument of the goto command, although including it is highly encouraged. With the call command, the colon is always required when calling a label defining an internal routine.

This apparent incongruity might not make sense until you consider that the goto command is concerned only with going to labels inside its bat file, while the call command calls entities inside and outside of its bat file. The upshot is that something very unexpected happens when an attempt to call :MyLabel is invoked without the colon:

```
call MyLabel
```

A colon would've told the interpreter to call an internal routine, but instead the interpreter tries to call an external file. First it looks for an executable, such as *MyLabel.com* or *MyLabel.exe*, in the current directory. Then it looks for *MyLabel.bat* and a few other types of executables with this filename, also in the current directory. Then it goes through all the directories in the path variable desperately looking for anything named MyLabel that it can execute. If no such file is found, the interpreter won't look for a label of that name, even if :MyLabel is a valid label in the bat file; instead, it generates an error.

When navigating to a label with either the goto or call command, always use the colon, for consistency's sake if nothing else.

NOTE *In Chapter 9, I mentioned that the goto command aborts a process when the label isn't found. The call command is a little more forgiving. They both write out an error message when its argument is an invalid label, but the call command also sets errorlevel to 1. If you choose not to interrogate the return code, the process continues on cavalierly as if nothing is amiss. (See Chapter 28 for more details on how to handle a failed call command.)*

Launching Bat Files

Sometimes you might want to launch or spawn a bat file as a new process. That is, you may wish to kick off another bat file but don't want the interpreter to wait around for it to finish up before continuing. For instance, you can execute multiple processes in parallel to speed up overall processing time. You can spin off a noncritical but time-consuming task, perhaps a logging process, to execute on its own time. In Chapter 26, I'll discuss how to automatically kill and restart a process that's hung. To make this happen, I'll spawn the process susceptible to hanging as an independent bat file and monitor it from the main bat file.

To launch or spawn a bat file, simply use the start command in lieu of the call command:

```
start C:\Batch\LaunchedBat.bat
```

This command creates a second command or DOS window where the file *LaunchedBat.bat* executes simultaneously with the bat file that started it.

The exit Command

The exit command, as you might imagine, exits routines, bat files, or entire executions, and it can even set a return code. It overlaps in functionality with the goto :eof command, but I'll soon show a significant distinction.

The exit command with no arguments abruptly ends the entire process. Sadly, the second echo command won't be executed:

```
> con echo The Meaning of Life is...
exit
> con echo ... %meaningOfLife%
```

The first echo command writes its message to the console, but the exit command closes the window before you can read it. This happens regardless of where the exit command is invoked—in the high-level bat file, in a called bat file, or even in a routine in either type of bat file. This variant of the command is analogous to a sledgehammer.

However, the /B option turns the exit command into more of a jewelry mallet. The documentation is unclear as to what B represents, but for me it stands for *break* in that the following command breaks out of just the code being invoked, whether it's a called bat file or a routine inside a bat file:

```
exit /B
```

This command exits the entire process only if invoked in the main logic of the high-level bat file. It doesn't change errorlevel and is logically equivalent to goto :eof. Both commands are valid, and the usage usually comes down to personal preference. Mine is the goto :eof command, but only in those instances when I don't need the return code.

At the beginning of Chapter 9, I referenced the rudimentary abort logic reproduced in Listing 10-3 but left its explanation for later, which is now.

```
:Abort
 echo The Process is aborting
 exit /B 1
```

Listing 10-3: An abort routine labeled as :Abort

This exit command behaves just like exit /B with one exception. When control is returned to where the code was called, the command's numerical argument following the option becomes the new value contained in errorlevel. In short, the command breaks out of a bat file or routine and returns an exit or return code. In the prior example, the return code is 1. But if no errors are detected, the main logic of a bat file might end by setting the return code to 0:

```
exit /B 0
```

If a fatal error is detected, a goto :Abort command from the mainline logic will direct the interpreter to the abort logic shown in Listing 10-3. The goto command must be used because a call command would treat the abort logic like a called routine; the errorlevel would be set, but control would be returned to the spot of the fatal error. But when navigating to the label with the goto command, a routine isn't invoked; it's still considered to be in the mainline logic, and the exit command ends the bat file instead of a routine.

To make this more flexible, you can create a variable for the exit code, setting it to different values for different failures:

```
:Abort
 echo The Process is Aborting
 exit /B %exitCode%
```

Then this logic can be accessed via multiple goto commands in the bat file.

(A real-world abort routine will be far more interesting than this simple echo command. The error message could be multiple lines and have variable content, all written to a logfile as well as the console, but I've simplified it here to keep the focus on the exit command.)

Summary

In this chapter, I've detailed the different methods of calling internal routines and other bat files. You've learned how to return from those calls with or without a return code, or how to simply end the entire process abruptly from anywhere. You also learned how to launch or spawn another bat file, which is entirely independent of the first bat file. Above all else, you now understand the significant and subtle differences between the goto and call commands. In a nutshell, the call returns control and can reach outside of its bat file, while the goto does neither.

One large piece remains in this puzzle. A calling bat file can pass multiple arguments to a called bat file, and that called bat file can even set and pass back parameters in return. There's more to this than one might expect, and I'll detail all of the nuances in the very next chapter.

11

PARAMETERS AND ARGUMENTS

In the previous chapter, I demonstrated how a bat file can call both internal routines and other bat files, but I didn't discuss how to pass data back and forth between the calling and called logic. By default, all variables set in the calling code are exposed to the called code, and vice versa. If the code is closely coupled, there's technically no need to pass arguments and accept parameters, but to make that work, both sets of code must agree on and use the same set of variables.

That's adequate if you're creating a second bat file simply to break up a large project and the called bat file will never be called from elsewhere, but to make more generic code that's reusable by other processes and coders, the act of parameterizing the data going in and out of bat files and routines is critical.

In this chapter, I'll detail everything you need to know about arguments and parameters, including the esoteric syntax unique to Batch. You'll learn how to pass arguments to a bat file or routine and how to accept returned parameters. You'll even learn about the hidden parameter, how and why to shift parameters, and how to pass arguments to a bat file with just a few mouse clicks.

Passing Arguments

To demonstrate how to pass arguments and accept parameters, I'll write a short bat file that builds a simple example of Mad Libs, the game that made long car trips tolerable for kids before the ubiquity of handheld electronic devices. The bat file accepts three ordered parameters (an adjective, a verb, and a noun) and inserts them into the following text before displaying the result to the user:

> Bats are _____ (adjective) mammals. They _____ (verb)
> around in caves, but if you stand under them, you might get hit
> with _____ (noun).

I'm not sharing the called bat file with you just yet, because I'll first concentrate on how to call *MadLibs.bat* while passing it the three arguments. After all, the calling bat file really doesn't care how the sausage is made; it just wants a grinder. The calling bat file needs to know only the arguments to pass and the expected results. That's it. (In the next section, I'll look at this from the perspective of the called bat file, *MadLibs.bat*.)

In Chapter 10, I demonstrated how the call command invokes another bat file. That's exactly what the next command is doing, but now three arguments follow the name of the bat file representing an adjective, a verb, and a noun, precisely in that order, all delimited by spaces:

```
call C:\Batch\MadLibs.bat adorable fly guano
```

Someone is obviously cheating because the result written to the console makes far too much sense for this game:

```
Bats are adorable mammals. They fly around in caves,
but if you stand under them, you might get hit with guano.
```

More typically, if an 11-year-old boy were to play this game, he might come up with the following set of words representing an adjective, verb, and noun:

```
call C:\Batch\MadLibs.bat stinky fart poop
```

The result is

```
Bats are stinky mammals. They fart around in caves,
but if you stand under them, you might get hit with poop.
```

which somehow still works—at least for a preteen boy.

Argument Delimiters

The passed arguments in the previous example are delimited from each other and the name of the called bat file by spaces. The space is by far the most common delimiter, with the comma a definitive second, but the semicolon, equal sign, and tab character also work. Consider these two call commands:

```
call C:\Batch\MadLibs.bat adorable fly guano
call C:\Batch\MadLibs.bat,adorable;fly=guano
```

Both commands are functionally equivalent, but the second looks to be an exercise in obfuscations.

Comma-delimited data is fairly common (for instance, the contents of a *.csv* file). Because the comma is in the set of Batch argument delimiters, you can store comma-delimited data in a variable and then resolve that variable as part of a call command like so:

```
set myArgs=adorable,fly,guano
call C:\Batch\MadLibs.bat %myArgs%
```

The interpreter treats each piece of text separated by a comma as a unique argument (assuming other delimiters aren't in the data). This might look like a single argument, but in reality, the command is passing three arguments.

Argument Encasing

Looking at the list of permissible argument delimiters does raise an interesting question: Is it possible to pass spaces and the other delimiters as actual argument data? Yes, it's very possible, but first consider the problem posed by these (three?) arguments:

```
call C:\Batch\MadLibs.bat ad hominem took off ice cream
```

Someone is clearly being very difficult, using two-word versions of the three arguments. (And anyone who uses ad hominem as a Mad Libs adjective is being more pretentious than difficult. He's probably a certain guy in the office correcting everyone's use of parameter and argument.) The result is six arguments, not three, for the interpreter to handle.

Since a space is one of the characters for delimiting arguments, the interpreter considered ad to be the adjective argument, while the verb argument is hominem, and the noun argument is took. This results in a nonsensical word salad, even by the standard of Mad Libs. The remainder of the command, `off ice cream`, becomes the fourth, fifth, and sixth arguments to a bat file that accepts only three; they are duly ignored with no further harm done.

The solution to this issue is to encase each argument in double quotes, which also provides the side benefit of being far more readable:

```
call C:\Batch\MadLibs.bat "ad hominem" "took off" "ice cream"
```

The called bat file needs to do something to work with arguments that may or may not be double quoted, and I'll get to that shortly.

With all of this in place, the output at least makes grammatical sense, mostly:

```
Bats are ad hominem mammals. They took off around in caves,
but if you stand under them, you might get hit with ice cream.
```

The encasing double quotes provide another great advantage; they'll hold the place of any missing arguments or those set to spaces. For instance, just to be contrarian, someone might refuse to supply the first argument. (After all, dropping an adjective will still make grammatical sense, but omitting a noun or verb will surely break the sentence structure.) Without the double quotes in the following example, the second argument would skew to become the first, and the third would become the second. Instead, three arguments are being passed, even if the first is null:

```
call C:\Batch\MadLibs.bat "" "hop" "fudge"
```

The `hop` and `fudge` arguments correctly map to the verb and noun, respectively, and there's no adjective, resulting in the following output:

```
Bats are  mammals. They hop around in caves,
but if you stand under them, you might get hit with fudge.
```

The encasing double quotes also allow you to the use commas, semicolons, equal signs, and even tab characters as arguments or as part of arguments.

Argument Variables

Up to this point I've shown only hardcoded arguments, but more often than not, arguments are variables, and if you can't be absolutely certain that there are no (and never will be) embedded spaces, I suggest adding double quotes to the resolved variables:

```
call C:\Batch\MadLibs.bat "%arg0%" "%arg1%" "%arg2%"
```

When the `call` command executes, the three argument variables are resolved and passed to the called bat file, each encased in double quotes.

NOTE *The "parameter versus argument" argument: there's some debate about the difference between these two terms. I've seen different definitions, but I'm writing with the distinction that* arguments *are passed from the* calling *code, and* parameters *are accepted by the* called *code. But there's a gray area, and it's commonplace to hear coders talking about "passing parameters" and "receiving arguments." We all know what's meant. I don't want to be that pedantic jerk in the office correcting everyone, but I'll try to use these words consistently.*

Accepting Parameters

Let's change our perspective by 180 degrees and look at Listing 11-1 where the called bat file accepts the three parameters, which means finally sharing the entirety of *MadLibs.bat*, which produced multiple rounds of output in the previous examples.

```
set adjective=%~1
set verb=%~2
set noun=%~3

> con echo.
> con echo Bats are %adjective% mammals. They %verb% around in caves,
> con echo but if you stand under them, you might get hit with %noun%.
goto :eof
```

Listing 11-1: The MadLibs.bat bat file accepts three parameters and displays a Mad Lib.

Any bat file that accepts parameters should begin in one of two ways. It should have remarks detailing the parameters that the bat file accepts, or it should define the parameters at the top of the file with set commands using unambiguously named variables. For this bat file, I chose the latter approach.

The first parameter is descriptively named adjective, and %~1 is the best syntax for resolving the first argument passed into a bat file. Incrementing the integer gives us the value of the second argument, %~2, which is assigned to verb. Finally, another unambiguously named variable, noun, is assigned to the third argument, %~3.

Resolving Parameters with a Tilde

This next point is as important as it is subtle; if you remove the tilde from the first line of the bat file, %1 resolves to the first parameter exactly as it's received, with or without double quotes. However, %~1 resolves to the first parameter with its encasing double quotes removed—and if there are no double quotes to remove, the resolved parameter is unchanged, so the tilde causes no harm. The same holds for the other parameters: %~2 resolves to the second parameter with any double quotes removed, and %2 resolves to that parameter as it was passed.

The inclusion of the tilde is exactly what I was referring to in the prior section when I mentioned that the called bat file would need to do something in order to work with arguments that may or may not be encased in double quotes in the `call` command. The *MadLibs.bat* file clearly has the syntax with the tilde allowing it to work both ways, thus providing a courtesy to the coder of the calling bat file.

The *only* time that I wouldn't use a tilde to resolve a parameter is when I explicitly want to maintain the double quotes, and such instances are rare at best. Using the tilde gives the calling bat file the flexibility to use double quotes or not. Consider these functionally equivalent commands:

```
call C:\Batch\MadLibs.bat ugly running "cell phone"
call C:\Batch\MadLibs.bat "ugly" "running" "cell phone"
```

The calling bat file must use the double quotes for arguments with any embedded spaces, such as the third one above; otherwise, the double quotes aren't required, but they won't hurt. I mentioned that these two commands are functionally equivalent, but that wouldn't be true if *MadLibs.bat* hadn't used the tildes in the first three commands.

If you think the syntax for resolving a parameter looks odd, you aren't alone. Variables are typically resolved with two percent signs, but here a single percent sign is followed by a one-digit number (or a tilde and a number) and nothing else. Variables named with a leading number can't be resolved with percent signs, so when the interpreter sees a percent sign followed by a number (with maybe a tilde between them) a parameter is assumed. Once understood, it does offer a very concise syntax for resolving parameters.

Resolving the Entire Parameter List

You can resolve an entire parameter list, regardless of the number of values, simply with a percent sign followed by an asterisk, which is very handy when a called bat file wants to call another bat file or a routine passing along the same parameter list. Consider this command inside a called bat file, particularly the trailing %* characters:

```
call C:\Batch\SecondCalledBat.bat "%arg0%" %*
```

This command is passing an argument list consisting of a simple variable, followed by the parameter list coming into the bat file or routine. I've encased the first argument, the `arg0` variable, in double quotes just in case it contains any embedded delimiter characters, such as a space; this ensures that the interpreter treats the variable as a single argument, not multiple arguments. The rest of the arguments are the complete set of parameters passed into the called bat file, regardless of how many. Ultimately, the first parameter into the bat file is the second argument in the call, and so on. (Spoiler alert: we'll use this technique extensively when we get to object-oriented design in Chapter 32.)

Internal Routine Parameters

To this point I've discussed parameters only in reference to the calling of another bat file. Fortunately, there really is no difference when calling a routine inside a bat file. We can easily rewrite the complete bat file from Listing 11-1 as an internal routine. Notice in Listing 11-2 that the only difference is the addition of the label.

```
:MadLibs
 set adjective=%~1
 set verb=%~2
 set noun=%~3

 > con echo.
 > con echo Bats are %adjective% mammals. They %verb% around in caves,
 > con echo but if you stand under them, you might get hit with %noun%.
 goto :eof
```

Listing 11-2: The :MadLibs routine accepts three parameters and displays a Mad Lib.

The call command to invoke the routine has the same arguments, and the double quotes are handled the same way:

```
call :MadLibs "ad hominem" "took off" "ice cream"
```

The only difference is that a label is called instead of another bat file. Everything else works exactly the same.

The Hidden Parameter

Many modern languages treat the incoming parameter list as an array, in particular a zero-offset array. Coupling that with the fact that Batch surprisingly uses a zero-offset for substringing, many coders have looked for a parameter in %~0 (yours truly included). The result can be befuddling, as adding the following echo command at the top of the routine from Listing 11-2 demonstrates:

```
:MadLibs
 > con echo Parm 0 is %~0
 set adjective=%~1
```

The text written to the console contains the name of the routine being executed:

```
Parm 0 is :MadLibs
```

Before I explain what exactly is going on, earlier in the chapter, the Mad Libs logic was in an external file and called like so:

```
call C:\Batch\MadLibs.bat "adorable" "fly" "guano"
```

Take the same `echo` command added to the previous `:MadLibs` routine, and add it to the called bat file from Listing 11-1, and the result is the following:

```
Parm 0 is C:\Batch\MadLibs.bat
```

I hesitate to call %0 the first parameter. It's more of a hidden parameter coming just prior to the first parameter. From this example, it's obvious that the hidden parameter is the name of the routine or bat file being executed, but where's it coming from?

A bat file is often the first argument of the `call` command, and that argument is passed into the called bat file itself as %0. In fact, %0 matches the capitalization of the path and filename (or label name) in the `call` command, not the capitalization of the actual path and filename. If the path isn't part of the argument, it isn't part of %0. Furthermore, if the `call` command has double quotes around the path and filename, so will %0. For that reason, it's usually best to resolve it with the tilde, %~0, just like the other parameters.

The hidden parameter is omnipresent in all bat files, not just called bat files or called routines. Even a high-level bat file, the one that you may have started with a double mouse click, has its path and filename in the hidden parameter. We don't often think about what's going on when we open a bat file, but it isn't magic. Windows executes a `call` command, with the bat file as its only argument, for you. The result is %0 being resolved to the path and the name of the bat file encased in double quotes.

This hidden parameter has many uses. For error handling, it offers an easy means of logging the routine in which the error occurred. If the bat file is moved to a different directory, computer, or domain, the hidden parameter allows the bat file to know its location. When we get to the `for` command, there's a relatively straightforward means of retrieving just the path from a variable holding a path and filename. You can then use it in any number of ways. For instance, you can drop output files into a subfolder under the bat file, or the bat file can perform different actions based on where it resides. It's a very useful, and hidden, feature of Batch.

Shifting Parameters

If the first parameter is resolved with %~1 and the ninth parameter is resolved with %~9, it might make sense that the 10th parameter would be resolved with %~10. Alas no, the interpreter recognizes only parameters 0 through 9, or single-digit ordinal numbers. It would be nice if a compiler could gently remind you that %~10 isn't a valid parameter, but again no, this is Batch. To demonstrate what can go wrong when this parameter is resolved, consider the example of a double-digit parameter list shown in Listing 11-3. The first half of the alphabet is being passed to a routine that's attempting to write five selected letters to the console.

```
call :Alphabet A B C D E F G H I J K L M
goto :eof

:Alphabet
> con echo Parm 1 is "%~1"
> con echo Parm 2 is "%~2"
> con echo Parm 9 is "%~9"
> con echo Parm 10 is "%~10"
> con echo Parm 13 is "%~13"
goto :eof
```

Listing 11-3: A first pass at the routine :Alphabet to display five parameters

The first three look fine, but parameters 10 and 13 look to be junk:

```
Parm 1 is "A"
Parm 2 is "B"
Parm 9 is "I"
Parm 10 is "A0"
Parm 13 is "A3"
```

When we humans ponder %~13, we see the number 13 and might expect the 13th parameter, M, to be resolved. But the interpreter has never been confused with artificial intelligence, much less human intelligence. When it encounters %~13, it sees the first parameter, %~1, which is resolved to A, followed by the hardcoded value 3. The result is A3. Similarly, %~10 resolves to the first parameter, but it's appended with a zero, resulting in A0.

Batch, however, isn't limited to only nine parameters. In fact, I've seen dozens passed as there's no practical limit (other than the limit of 8,191 characters in any command). To access the 10th parameter and beyond, you need the shift command. To demonstrate, let's fix the :Alphabet routine from Listing 11-3:

```
:Alphabet
> con echo Parm 1 is "%~1"
> con echo Parm 2 is "%~2"
> con echo Parm 9 is "%~9"
shift
> con echo Parm 10 is "%~9"
shift & shift & shift
> con echo Parm 13 is "%~9"
goto :eof
```

The resolutions of parameters 1, 2, and 9 are unchanged before the shift command executes, which shifts each parameter one position to the left. The second becomes the first, the third becomes the second, and the 10th parameter becomes the ninth. It may be counterintuitive, but after a shift command, %~9 resolves to parameter 10. Then after three more shift commands, %~9 resolves to M, the 13th parameter, producing the desired output:

```
Parm 1 is "A"
Parm 2 is "B"
Parm 9 is "I"
Parm 10 is "J"
Parm 13 is "M"
```

When introducing the command separator (&) in Chapter 2, I mentioned you should use it sparingly. In other situations, it can make a mess of the code, but shift is such a simple and succinct command, putting three on one line actually cleans up the code.

Note that the shift command doesn't impact the resolution of %*. This funky syntax still resolves to the complete and original parameter list regardless of how many shift commands execute.

Shifting the parameters raises an interesting question. What happens to the path and filename resolved with %0 after the shift command executes? The short answer is that it gets wiped out and replaced with the first parameter, at least by default. But the shift command has a lone option, and that option defines which parameter gets dropped with the shift; all parameters prior to it are maintained. It's formatted differently from the options we've described to this point. The /n option drops the *n*th parameter, so that the following command drops the first and preserves %0:

```
shift /1
```

Parameter 0, or the hidden parameter, is unchanged. Parameter 1 is discarded while parameter 2 slides over to become parameter 1. The third parameter becomes the second, and so on. With a small change, the following command preserves the first four parameters (and the hidden parameter), while discarding the fifth:

```
shift /5
```

Parameter 6 is shifted to parameter 5, and the rest are shifted accordingly.

This option accepts parameters 0 through 8—although there's no need to use /0 as that's the default behavior. For some unknown reason, /9 is invalid. Don't ask.

Returning Parameters

You now know how to pass arguments to routines and other bat files and write the received parameters to the console, but in the real coding world many routines accept some parameters and pass others back to the caller. Because Batch variables in a called process are globally available, some coders simply set a hardcoded variable name in a routine and use it elsewhere. Such Philistines! A far more elegant and flexible solution is to allow the caller to define the name of the variable returned.

NOTE *I'm using* Philistines *as a pejorative, but not without pause. Today the term is concise shorthand for brutish individuals indifferent to aesthetics and artistry, and that's exactly how I'm using it. But we wouldn't slur an entire people if they had modern day representation. Even the gypsy moth is being renamed, rightly, so as not to offend a group of people, although the moth can still be slandered with impunity. I'm sure that there were both good and bad Philistines, but because they were completely wiped out over two and half millennia ago and viewed unfavorably in the texts of three major world religions, their name is taken in vain with little or no remorse. In recent decades even our more distant cousin, the Neanderthals, have enjoyed a more rehabilitated image than the Philistines.*

The following example contains three parameters; the first two are numbers to be added and the third is the result of the addition. This routine may be short, but due to its complexity, a comment is really needed:

```
rem - Parm 3 is the sum of Parms 1 and 2
:Add
  set /A %~3 = %~1 + %~2
  goto :eof
```

To the right of the equal sign in the set /A command, the first two parameters are being resolved and added together. To the left of the equal sign—that is, what's being set—is the cryptic text %~3. A variable name in this area may have been expected, but instead the third parameter is being resolved. The set /A command is in fact setting a named variable to the sum of the two numbers. Most important, that variable name is the third parameter passed into this routine. This technique isn't difficult, but it's unintuitive, and it isn't common in other languages. I've seen it flummox many a coder.

An example of a call to the routine should clarify what's happening. The following call command passes two numbers and a variable name, where the double quotes are optional:

```
call :Add "7" "8" "sum"
```

After this call, the sum variable contains the value of 15. I can't stress enough that with this technique, the calling code defines the name of the variable to be returned. To further make this point, the three calls in this example are done to the same :Add routine:

```
call :Add "5" "8" "sum1"
call :Add "9" "11" "sum2"
call :Add "%sum1%" "%sum2%" "sum4Nbrs"
> con echo The sum of all four numbers is %sum4Nbrs%.
```

The first two have hardcoded numbers, returning the sum1 and sum2 variables, respectively. Both of those variables are resolved and passed as arguments in the third call, returning sum4Nbrs.

Notice that sum1 and sum2 don't have delimiting percent signs in the first two calls because the variable name is being passed. But in the third call, I'm resolving them because their values are being passed—the same values that were assigned during the first two calls. Finally, the echo command writes this to the console:

```
The sum of all four numbers is 33.
```

The same variable used as the output for one call is the input for another, but can the variable be used for both purposes in a single call?

One Variable as Input and Output

A single variable can simultaneously be an input to and an output of a routine or bat file. To set this up, imagine a routine that squares an integer. The first parameter is the input, and the second parameter is the output—simply the input multiplied by itself:

```
:Square
set /A %~2 = %~1 * %~1
goto :eof
```

The routine doesn't show much that we haven't already discussed, although the input of %~1 is used twice. The calling code defines the output variable, which is resolved as %~2 in the routine.

The calling code could use two different variables for the input and output. But suppose that you want to replace a variable's value with its square. To accomplish this, you could pass its value as the first argument—notice the percent signs encasing it—and pass the name of the variable as the second argument, not encased with percent signs:

```
call :Square %nbr% nbr
```

If nbr was set to 5 before the call, it'll be set to 25 afterward. The :Square routine offers some real flexibility, usable with two different variables or the same one.

Let's make one more tweak to this code and write a routine with a single parameter that's both the input and output. The parameter is a variable containing a number as its value, and the routine replaces that value with its square, which makes calling the routine even easier:

```
call :SquareMe nbr
> con echo The squared number is %nbr%.
goto :eof

:SquareMe
set /A %~1 = !%~1! * !%~1!
goto :eof
```

First, notice the new routine (or label) name. More important, notice that the routine accepts a single argument, the unresolved variable name of an integer—not the integer value.

Comparing :SquareMe to the :Square routine, the set /A command has two critical updates. First, instead of multiplying %~1 by itself, !%~1! is now each operand. In the prior example, a value was being accepted, but now a variable name is the input, so %~1 resolves to the variable name, and with the use of delayed expansion, the exclamation marks resolve that name to the integer value. (Have I yet mentioned the true awesomeness of delayed expansion? The applications are limited only by your imagination.)

The second change is that the product is being assigned to the first parameter, %~1, and not the second, %~2. Remember that in :SquareMe the sole parameter is now the variable name. The result is that a call to this routine changes the value of the variable even though that variable isn't explicitly mentioned in the routine.

NOTE *I've demonstrated return parameters with routines, but returning a parameter from a called bat file works virtually the same way. Actually, it works exactly the same way if the called bat file is not limiting scope via the setlocal and endlocal commands. If it is limiting scope, there's a special technique that allows one or more variables to survive the endlocal, and I'll detail it in Chapter 16.*

Input Parameter Lists of Varying Lengths

Let's build more of a real-world routine that uses what we've learned so far in this chapter. The following routine accepts a list of one-to-many numbers (no reasonable limit) and returns two variables, one populated with the sum of the inputs and the other populated with the product of the inputs:

```
rem - Parm 1 = Sum of multiple numbers, returned parm
rem - Parm 2 = Product of multiple numbers, returned parm
rem - Parms 3+ = Set of numbers to add and multiply
 :Arithmetic
  set %~1=0
  set %~2=1
 :NextParm
  set /A %~1 += %~3
  set /A %~2 *= %~3
  shift /3
  if "%~3" neq ""  goto :NextParm
  goto :eof
```

Since we don't know how many input parameters to expect for a given call, we put those at the end of the parameter list, with the output parameters occupying the first two positions. (No one said inputs must come before outputs.) Due to its complexity, the :Arithmetic routine includes much needed comments defining the parameter list.

The sum, represented as %~1 because it doesn't yet have an actual variable name, is initialized to 0. Likewise, the product, %~2, is initialized to 1. (For my fellow math geeks, that's what we respectively call additive and multiplicative unity.) Ignore the second label, :NextParm, for a moment and focus on the two set /A commands that follow. The first command sets the first parameter, the sum, to itself plus the first input number on the list, %~3, which is the third parameter. Similarly, the next command sets the second parameter, the product, to itself multiplied by the first number on the list, again %~3.

The shift command that comes next is crucial. The number of input parameters is unknown, so we want to discard the just used third parameter and shift the parameters that come after it to the left without disturbing the first two, which are also the return parameters in this instance. The /3 option accomplishes that seamlessly. Next, we look at the newly minted third parameter to see whether it's populated. Keep in mind that this was the second input number on the original list or the fourth overall parameter before the shift. If it's populated, we'll go back to the :NextParm label that we ignored earlier. Now those two set /A commands add and multiply the second input parameter to the sum and product, respectively.

This process repeats until the list of numbers, regardless of its length, is exhausted, at which point the conditional clause of the if command is false, allowing control to fall to the trailing goto :eof command and the routine passes back the first two parameters.

The following code tests the new routine:

```
call :Arithmetic sum product 5 8 9 11
> con echo The sum is %sum%.
> con echo The product is %product%.
```

The resulting text is written to the console:

```
The sum is 33.
The product is 3960.
```

By the way, if this construct looks familiar, that's because it's an example of a Batch do...while command from Chapter 9. At least one input parameter is assumed, and the routine performs the arithmetic as long as, or *while*, more parameters exist.

Drag-and-Drop Parameters

With a few mouse clicks, you can pass the path and name of any file, or multiple files, into a bat file. It's something that dumbfounded multiple people, including me when I was learning Batch. Simply right-click on any file and select **Copy**; then right-click on the bat file to execute and select **Paste**. The bat file executes, with the sole parameter being the path and filename of the copied file (encased in double quotes if the path or filename has embedded spaces). Alternatively, you can select the file, drag, and drop it onto the bat file with the same result.

This technique works for any number of files. If you copy *n* files onto your bat file, *n* space-delimited parameters are passed—each one being a path and filename. The same is true if you drag and drop *n* files onto your bat file, and it even works for directories.

At first, the dragging and dropping of files onto a bat file might seem like little more than a Batch parlor trick, but its uses are manifold. You can design a wrapper bat file that processes a single file. Maybe a program is being executed with a file as input; the program might convert the file to a different format or add a trailer record. Maybe the Batch code will simply rename the file or add an extension to the existing filename. What's important is that the bat file is performing some action on an input file.

One possible action is to simply copy the input file to another directory. Consider the following two commands that make up the entirety of *BackUpOneFile.bat*:

```
xcopy %1 D:\Some\Deep\Hard\To\Reach\Folder\ /F /Y
pause
```

The first argument to the xcopy command, which is %1, resolves to the bat file's first parameter, which will be the path and filename of any file dragged and dropped onto *BackUpOneFile.bat*. The command copies the input file to the desired target path, some deep hard to reach folder on the *D:* drive. (I'm intentionally retaining any encasing double quotes with the %1 syntax, instead of %~1, because the xcopy command requires the double quotes if the path or filename have any embedded spaces.) Finally, the pause command simply holds the window open for the user to see the result of the copy.

Ultimately, if you place *BackUpOneFile.bat* on the Windows desktop, you can quickly drag and drop any one file onto it, and the bat file will copy the input file to the desired directory without your needing to navigate to that directory.

In order to pass an argument to a bat file without this drag-and-drop technique, you must enter a call command (into another bat file or at the command prompt) with the input file keyed in as the argument. But with this technique, any user, even noncoders, can easily run the bat file without any input from the keyboard. You can create a Windows shortcut for the bat file located anywhere on the network so as to hide the source Batch code, making it more difficult for a user to accidentally delete or modify it.

When a path and filename is passed to a bat file as a parameter, Batch offers an easy way to get quite a bit of information about the file, such as the last modified date and time, size, attributes, path, extension, filename, and more. I'll discuss this in detail after exploring the for command in

Chapter 17. The for command will also unlock loops, so that if we drag and drop *n* files onto a bat file, each can be processed sequentially.

Summary

This chapter along with Chapters 8 through 10 have hopefully opened up your Batch universe to far more than a single routineless sequentially executed bat file. In the not-so-distant past, your bat files couldn't call executables or other bat files, and the interpreter executed each command just once and in order until it found the end of the bat file. But now you have the tools to start building interesting and complex bat files.

In this chapter, you learned how to pass arguments to bat files and routines and receive them as parameters in the called bat file. I detailed how to delimit the arguments and even how to pass the delimiters themselves as arguments. You also got a glimpse of the hidden parameter, the Yeti of the Batch universe. I demonstrated how to pass back caller-defined variables containing a return value. You may have even learned how to play Mad Libs.

In the next chapter, I'll expand that universe even more by introducing various outputs, created by both the interpreter and you. I'll show you how to capture the output of Batch commands and how to create files of your own.

12

OUTPUTS, REDIRECTION, AND PIPING

You can now do quite a bit with Batch, such as setting, resetting, and interrogating variables of various data types, calling routines and other bat files, and performing arithmetic; however, most of what you've learned will have no lasting effect (except for file movements and the ability to set variables persistently). At the end of a bat file's ephemeral execution, all of the bits and bytes that've been manipulated may vanish into the ether, and it'll be as if the bat file had never existed.

I'll leave the metaphysics of Batch for another time, but whenever code of any type is executed, the intent is to effect some sort of change. Some coders will use Batch simply as a wrapper, setting a few variables before calling an executable that'll bring about that change, but Batch can do much more. In this chapter, I'll discuss two general types of output: output from the interpreter (stdout and stderr) and output from you, the coder. After learning the distinction, you'll be able to write the different types of output to the console, new files, and existing files. In this way, you can store the product of all those variables, calls, and arithmetic on your computer.

The discussion about the two types of output will lead to a couple of related and interesting topics. One is the redirection of the output of any Batch command to a file, and the other is piping, the technique of sending output from one command into another command. Maybe most important, you'll learn what exactly is scrolling by so quickly on the console and how to manage it—that is, either save or suppress it.

Interpreter-Generated vs. Coder-Generated Output

When you open or execute a bat file, it creates two general types of outputs: interpreter-generated and coder-generated. To be perfectly clear, the interpreter technically creates all of the output, but some of that output is the result of commands entered by you, the coder, to write something to the console or a file. That's *coder-generated output*. As a byproduct of the run, the interpreter is also creating output that you didn't explicitly request. That's *interpreter-generated output*.

All Batch commands create interpreter-generated output; a few also create coder-generated output. By default, Batch writes both types of output to the console, and if the bat file is even moderately complex, the text scrolls by in a jumble that's too fast to read.

The echo command is a great example of one that generates both general types of output, and in its simplest manifestation, it writes all of its arguments to the console. Consider this command:

```
echo Greetings, Earthlings.
```

The execution of this command writes the output shown in Listing 12-1 to the console.

```
C:\Batch>echo Greetings, Earthlings.
Greetings, Earthlings.
```

Listing 12-1: Output generated by the interpreter and the coder

The desired text, Greetings, Earthlings., is output, but it isn't alone and appears twice, with the current directory prepended to the first line for some reason. (I'll assume that the current directory is *C:\Batch* throughout this chapter.)

The two lines in Listing 12-1 represent entirely different types of outputs. The second line is from the coder—a message written to the console with the echo command. The interpreter generates the first line. It isn't the output of the echo command; it's a *report of the execution* of the echo command.

The distinction is as subtle as it is important. The interpreter, at a minimum, logs the execution of every command by writing it, prepended with the prompt. By default, the prompt is the current directory followed by a greater-than sign. Many commands produce additional interpreter-generated output, such as the xcopy command, which often produces a list of the files copied.

Clearly, the intermingled output is a mess, and if this example doesn't look like a mess, that's because I'm showing the output from only a single command. Before long, I'll show you how to clean up the console by sending these distinct outputs to different destinations, but first you'll need to better understand the interpreter-generated output, which itself is actually two different outputs.

stdout and stderr

Batch writes every bit of interpreter-generated output to one of two data streams. A *data stream* is a transmission of information from a source—in this case, the interpreter—to a destination, which by default is the console. A file descriptor represents each data stream, and the most voluminous by far is the stream described as *stdout*, pronounced *standard out* (or less frequently, *standard output*). In fact, the only interpreter-generated output not found in stdout are error messages, which are written to the file descriptor *stderr*, pronounced *standard error*.

The stdout data stream can become dense and cryptic, but it's often invaluable to help you determine what exactly transpired during a bat file's execution. You can often see the results of if commands, what files were created, and much more. To demonstrate, the following del command deletes a file and is followed by a set command that captures errorlevel as the return code:

```
del C:\Batch\DeleteMe.txt
set rc=%errorlevel%
```

Nothing here creates coder-generated output; all output comes from the interpreter.

If the *DeleteMe.txt* file exists, the previous code deletes it and writes the following to stdout:

```
C:\Batch>del C:\Batch\DeleteMe.txt

C:\Batch>set rc=0
```

Most variables are resolved in stdout, such as errorlevel being resolved to 0 in this example. (Frustratingly, the interpreter fails to resolve variables fully in certain situations, such as when using delayed expansion. See Chapter 31 for more details.)

Interspersed with stdout can be the second type of interpreter-generated output, the output written to the stderr data stream, but only if there are any errors, of course. If, for instance, the file in the del command doesn't exist, the interpreter outputs the following:

```
C:\Batch>del C:\Batch\DeleteMe.txt
Could Not Find C:\Batch\DeleteMe.txt

C:\Batch>set rc=0
```

The first and last lines are written to stdout, but the middle line stating that the file couldn't be found is written to stderr. It's important to understand that error messages are written to stderr, while all other interpreter-generated output goes to stdout. Both are needed to get a full picture of what happened during a bat file's execution, and unless we do something to intervene, both are written to the console.

(By the way, let's not quibble over why the return code is 0 even if an error message is generated. But if we must, the file doesn't exist after the del command completes, so in a certain prosaic sense, it was successful, or it's a bug.)

Writing Files

Creating, writing to, and appending to files are basic functions of most coding languages, and Batch allows you to build files with both coder- and interpreter-generated output. Up until now, all of the output that you have seen has been written to the console, and when the bat file completes, the window closes.

Often, you'll want to create files that persist beyond the life of the bat file's execution. You can write data to a file to use as input to an executable or even another bat file. If I want a record of how often others run one of my bat files, I'll set it up to write one record to a central logfile with information about when and on what server it ran. You can even build reports, and capturing the interpreter-generated output into a file provides you with a great audit trail of exactly what transpired during the bat file's execution.

From Coder-Generated Output

I've shown that we can write text to the console with the > con syntax. With a similar syntax, we can write to a file with two commands: the familiar echo command writes a record, and the not-so-familiar type command writes an entire file to another file.

Writing a Record to a File

Let's return to the extraterrestrials. Instead of greeting us via the console, they might want to enter their greeting into a simple text file, and they can accomplish this with a single line of code:

```
echo Greetings, Earthlings.> C:\Batch\ET.txt
```

This line of code has four distinct elements. The first is the `echo` command, and the second is the command's argument: the `Greetings, Earthlings.` text. The third element is the greater-than sign (>), or redirection character. This character redirects the output of the command preceding it to the target, which is the fourth element: the *C:\Batch\ET.txt* file. Putting it all together, the previous statement writes the one line of greeting to the text file.

The following alternative syntax performs the identical task, but it's easier to read because the message no longer abuts the greater-than sign as it did in the previous example. I've moved the redirection character to the fore, again followed by the target:

```
> C:\Batch\ET.txt  echo Greetings, Earthlings.
```

If you replace the path and filename in this example with `con`, you'll recognize the familiar syntax for writing to the console.

The following example demonstrates the appeal of this syntax. If the aliens have more than one line to communicate, they can set the target file path and name to a variable and use it in successive `echo` commands. This syntax allows for multiple usages of the redirection, target, and echo command to be lined up in an orderly fashion, making it easier to read what's being written to the file:

```
set alienFile=C:\Batch\ET.txt
>   %alienFile%  echo Greetings, Earthlings.
>>  %alienFile%  echo.
>>  %alienFile%  echo Take us to your leader.
```

Before we move on, I snuck a couple of subtle yet important features into the previous code. The first `echo` command has a single greater-than sign for the redirection, while the subsequent commands each use two greater-than signs. The single character operator creates a new file with its text, deleting the current file of that name if it exists. The two-character operator appends to an existing file. A rookie mistake is to use a single greater-than sign for multiple commands, leaving the novice Batch coder wondering why only the last of several commands worked, when they all actually worked, each wiping out the existing file and writing a single line of text.

The other important feature is the `echo` command followed immediately by a dot; it'll write a blank line, not a dot. After this code executes, the complete contents of *ET.txt* contain these three lines:

```
Greetings, Earthlings.

Take us to your leader.
```

If you ever need to write a single dot on a line, leave a space between echo and the dot.

Writing a File to a File

Another useful command that you can couple with redirection is the type command. Used alone, the command writes out, or types, the complete contents of a file to stdout and the console. With redirection, it can insert the full contents of that file into another file. The following example writes the contents of *DetailRecs.txt* to *OutFile.txt*, prepended with a header record and appended with a trailer record via a couple echo commands:

```
set outFil=C:\Batch\OutFile.txt
>  %outFil%  echo This is a Header Record
>> %outFil%  type C:\Batch\DetailRecs.txt
>> %outFil%  echo This is a Trailer Record
```

Notice that only the first echo command has the single character redirection operator, thus ensuring that it's truly a header record.

From Interpreter-Generated Output

You now know that the mess scrolling by on the console is mostly stdout with the possibility of some stderr and coder-generated output. You can also control the destination (console or file) of the coder-generated output. The missing piece is what to do about the interpreter-generated output. By default, it's sent to the console, but with a modicum of effort, you can write everything the interpreter generates to a file, commonly called a *trace file*.

In the previous section, you learned how to redirect the output of the echo and type commands to a file, but you can redirect the output of any command, in particular the call command. In Chapter 10, I introduced the concept of calling routines within a bat file, so you can create a routine containing the bat file's main logic and call it at the top of the file. What's new here is the redirection operator and the trace file appended to the first line in the following example:

```
@call :GetTrace > C:\Batch\Trace.txt
pause
goto :eof

:GetTrace
> con echo Greetings, Earthlings.
> con echo.
> con echo Take us to your leader.
goto :eof
```

This is a complete bat file that writes the greeting to the console and captures the trace file.

The at symbol (@) prefixing the first command suppresses the call command itself from the console, but not the call command's output. Critically, the output from the call command is the stdout coming out of the called routine, and that output is redirected via the greater-than sign in the first line away from the console and to the trace file. Notice that the greeting itself at the bottom of the file is explicitly being sent to the console with > con prefixing each of the three echo commands. Without the redirection, the greeting would've been written to the trace file with the rest of stdout.

Each data stream has a reference or numerical handle so that you can refer to one or the other with minimal keystrokes. The reference for stdout is 1, and placing that reference number before the redirection character explicitly diverts stdout to the trace file. But stdout is redirected by default with the greater-than sign alone, so the following two commands are functionally equivalent:

```
@call :GetTrace > C:\Batch\Trace.txt
@call :GetTrace 1> C:\Batch\Trace.txt
```

In both commands, stdout alone is written to the trace file, and any error messages from stderr will end up being displayed on the console.

The stderr data stream is referenced by 2, so you can redirect these error messages instead with this one-byte modification prior to the redirection symbol:

```
@call :GetTrace 2> C:\Batch\Trace.txt
```

You can even redirect each data stream, stdout and stderr, to entirely different files at once:

```
@call :GetTrace 1> C:\Batch\stdout.txt 2> C:\Batch\stderr.txt
```

In practice, separating the data streams is rarely useful as any error messages won't be tied to the commands that generated them.

A far superior solution, shown in Listing 12-2, is to write both outputs to the trace file, and that's accomplished with this particularly esoteric syntax at the end of the command including 2 and 1, for stderr and stdout, respectively.

```
@call :GetTrace > C:\Batch\Trace.txt 2>&1
```

Listing 12-2: The ideal technique to redirect stdout and stderr to a trace file

As you are aware, the ampersand (&) is the command separator used to execute two commands coded on a single line. But used in the manner shown in Listing 12-2, the interpreter treats the ampersand simply as part of the redirection syntax. Just chalk this up as another batveat and don't ask why, but it's the best technique for capturing a trace file.

Suppressing stdout and stderr

You can watch stdout and stderr scroll by on the console, or you can save both data streams to a trace file. In other situations, this data simply isn't needed at all. It might not be worth the disk space to create a log of every execution of a stable and frequently run process, and you might not even want stdout and stderr written to the console because you want it uncluttered for any coder-generated output. In such cases, you'll want to outright suppress the interpreter-generated output. Two techniques work; one is simple but works only on stdout, while the slightly more complex technique also works on stderr.

The @echo off Technique

The simple technique to suppress stdout is with the `@echo off` command. Based on what you've learned about the echo command, you might expect this particular command to write `off` to stdout. Afterall, `echo Hello` writes `Hello` to stdout. Usually, echo writes out its arguments, but there are two exceptions.

The `off` argument instructs the interpreter to suppress (or turn off) stdout, and the `on` argument turns it back on, with one catch. The echo command to suppress stdout is itself written to stdout. Fortunately, Batch allows for the suppression of any single command's contribution to stdout simply by prepending it with the at symbol (@). Hence, the command to suppress stdout that is itself suppressed is `@echo off`. I quietly introduced this technique in Chapter 2 to clean up the console but sidestepped a deeper explanation for later (which is now).

If the extraterrestrials were to communicate with us via the console, this simple bat file would do the trick:

```
@echo off
echo Greetings, Earthlings.
echo.
pause
```

The first echo suppresses stdout so as to keep the console uncluttered and readable. Try this bat file without that first line to see the difference. It's ugly; each echo command generates both general types of output to the console. With this command in place, the second echo command writes only its arguments to the console. The echo command followed immediately by a dot writes a blank line. Finally, the pause command keeps the window open so that it doesn't disappear in a flash. The result is:

```
Greetings, Earthlings.

Press any key to continue . . .
```

Press any key, and the pause command allows the bat file to continue, closing the window. In Chapter 3, I mentioned that I start every high-level bat file with a `setlocal` command that enables command extensions and delayed expansion. This echo command is the only command that might come before that `setlocal`, thus keeping the console pristine. However, you also can prepend the `setlocal` command itself with an at symbol to suppress its execution from stdout.

As a side note, every novice Batch coder will likely try to write a blank line with nothing but spaces following the echo command, even if only by accident. But that command simply writes out the state of the echo, which is either on or off. For instance, executing the following two lines at the beginning of a bat file writes ECHO is off. to the console:

```
echo off
> con echo
```

Likewise, replacing the first line with echo on activates stdout, resulting in ECHO is on. as the output.

The @echo off technique has one more catch. While stdout is suppressed, stderr is unaffected, which means that any unredirected error messages will appear on the console with little or no context.

The Redirection to nul Technique

The best technique for suppressing all interpreter-generated output is to redirect stdout and stderr to the *nul* file introduced in Chapter 7. This file is always empty, regardless of what's written to it, making it something of a Batch trash receptacle. For instance, reworking the call command from Listing 12-2 to send stdout and stderr to *nul* instead of a trace file effectively suppresses all interpreter-generated output:

```
@call :GetTrace > nul 2>&1
```

However, the name of the routine is now a misnomer. (Rename the label :SuppressTrace if you must.)

This technique does require that you create a routine for the main-line logic, but it's very effective, it's relatively simple, and you can use it to suppress all the interpreter-generated output of called bat files as well as routines. The leading at sign even suppresses the call command itself from stdout.

You can use this technique to suppress the output of any command. For instance, the following executes the compiled program, while simply discarding its command line output:

```
> nul SomeProgramWithUnwantedOutput.exe
```

Prepending (or even appending) the program execution with a redirection to the *nul* file resolves the issue nicely.

Remarks in stdout

I've one last remark about stdout. In Chapter 2, I introduced the rem command as a simple means of entering a remark or comment into the code. An alternative syntax exists and has ramifications for stdout.

Remarks generated with the rem command are written to stdout. However, any line in the code preceded with two colons (::) is also treated as a remark, but it's a hidden remark suppressed from stdout. Consider these two valid remarks:

```
rem This is a Remark shared to stdout.
::This is a Top Secret Remark not meant for the Hoi Polloi.
```

You'll find only the first remark in stdout. Also notice that the dual colons don't require a space before the remark text. In Chapter 9, I mentioned that labels must start with a colon, but the second character must be a different character. This is because the double colons signify a hidden remark.

There's nothing nefarious about a hidden remark. Remarks that explain the code can be useful in stdout, but others might muddy it up. This is a great technique for coders to keep notes for themselves in the code, and only in the code. For instance, it's always good to maintain a detailed history of revisions in the source code, but those details might just make a mess of the trace file. If so, use double colons for such remarks.

Redirection of Any Command

I've shown that redirection of the echo, type, and call commands can write output to a file, but those are just three examples. You can redirect the output of any Batch command. To take just one example, you can send output of the following xcopy command to a logfile:

```
set copyLog=C:\Batch\Copy.log
>> %copyLog% xcopy C:\Batch\*.dat D:\Backup\ /Y /F
```

The .dat files are copied to *D:\Backup* with or without the redirection, but the interpreter now appends the resulting text that lists all of the files just copied along with a total count to the *Copy.log* file. It's appended because of the two greater-than signs; the single character operator would have created a new file with the output.

Although you can perform redirection for any command, many don't have output or have drab output not worth capturing. In the next chapter, I'll introduce the dir command, which writes details about all the files and subfolders in a directory to stdout. That's the type of information that's easily and often redirected to a file. Command line output from a compiled program is another example of data often worth capturing.

Piping

Redirection typically sends output to a file, but piping sends output to an entirely different destination. *Piping* is the concept of joining two distinct commands. The interpreter sends the output of the first command to the second command as input via some sort of a tube, hose, duct, conduit, or . . . there's a better metaphor for a physical conveyance, oh . . . a pipe.

The character used to make this connection is, appropriately enough, the pipe character, also called the vertical bar or upright slash. On most keyboards, it's above ENTER, and you press SHIFT-\ to access it.

To this point you've seen the results of the echo command redirected to the console, stdout, or a particular file, but you also can pipe those results to other Batch commands. Recall the xcopy command from Chapter 7 that, as part of the copy, gave the destination file a different name from the source file. At the time, I warned that such a command sometimes fails, and I promised a solution in this chapter, and that solution is piping. The following command certainly appears to be a straightforward copy with a renamed destination file:

```
xcopy C:\Batch\OldName.txt C:\Target\NewName.txt /Y /F
```

If the *NewName.txt* file exists at the target path, this command simply overlays the file and moves on. But due to the vagaries of Batch (or less diplomatically, a possible bug), if *NewName.txt* doesn't exist, the interpreter gets a bit confused. The source file is clearly *OldName.txt*, but is *NewName.txt* the name of the destination file or the destination folder? The *.txt* extension should make it obvious to the interpreter, but directory names can include dots. (But shame on anyone who would give a folder name a typical file extension.) When the interpreter gets confused, it does what a lost human should do; it asks directions:

```
C:\Batch>xcopy C:\Batch\OldName.txt C:\Target\NewName.txt /Y /F
Does C:\Target\NewName.txt specify a file name
or directory name on the target
(F = file, D = directory)?
```

If you had typed the xcopy command into a command prompt and seen that message written to the console, undoubtedly you would've simply entered F and been done with it. The same would've been true if the stdout of a bat file had gone to the console, but when this command is in a bat file with a redirected stdout, the interpreter essentially asks the trace file for a response and waits in perpetuity. At some point someone will investigate the long-running execution, scroll down to the bottom of the trace file, and find the text in the previous example. This is what coders call a *hang*; it's worse than an abort because the execution never ends. The cause can be an endless loop, but in this case, the cause is the interpreter asking for a response from an entity that cannot respond. The only human response is to kill the command window, find and correct the issue, and rerun.

The only way to respond programmatically with an answer in real time is to anticipate the question and code for it before the bat file ever executes. To this end, I'll precede the xcopy command with a response from an echo command. The following echo F command is simply writing F, the response for file, and that response is piped as input to the xcopy command:

```
echo F | xcopy C:\Batch\OldName.txt C:\Target\NewName.txt /Y /F
```

Now stdout shows F being entered as the answer to the question even though the response wasn't from a human:

```
C:\Batch>echo F   | xcopy C:\Batch\OldName.txt C:\Target\NewName.txt /Y /F
Does C:\Target\NewName.txt specify a file name
or directory name on the target
(F = file, D = directory)? F
C:\Batch\OldName.txt -> C:\Target\NewName.txt
1 File(s) copied
```

(Yes, the interpreter and stdout took some liberties with the spacing before the pipe.)

Finally, the interpreter copies the file to the destination folder using the new name. If echo D had preceded the pipe, the target file would've been *C:\Target\NewName.txt\OldName.txt*. That's clearly not the intention here, but in a different situation you could define the destination as a directory with the piping technique.

To make this more generic, you could set a variable to either F or D, depending on the format of the target. If the target ends in a period and extension, you can assume it's a file; if not, it's a directory. Then you can pipe the resolved variable into the xcopy command with an echo command.

But what effect does this technique have when the xcopy command doesn't ask for a response? It's synonymous with trying to impart wisdom to someone, perhaps a teenager, who doesn't want to listen. Just as a parent's words are lost into the void, the information piped to the xcopy command is completely ignored if a question wasn't asked. It's as if the echo command never executed. So, if a response is requested, the piping will give it, and if a response isn't requested, it's harmless.

There are many applications of piping. In Chapter 24, you'll learn how to perform some fairly complex text searches by piping both echo and type commands into a findstr command, allowing you to find specific text in a string or to find all the records in a file with that text. You can even sort the output of any command by piping it into the yet to be discussed sort command.

stdin

Even though this is a chapter about outputs, any discussion of stdout and stderr wouldn't be complete without a mention of the input data stream *stdin*, pronounced *standard in* (or less frequently, *standard input*) and referenced by 0, which is input from the console. But little more than a mention is needed. In most literature on the subject, all three are mentioned together as if they were of equal importance, but while stdout and stderr are ubiquitous, stdin is used only occasionally.

In the following example, the first command redirects a message to the console via echo. The second command is quite new, something of a reversal on the first command:

```
@> con echo Enter some data to be saved in a file:
@type con > C:\Batch\FromTheConsole.txt
```

The stdin data stream is the input from the keyboard or the console and is denoted in this context with the reserved word, con. Up until now, I've used con only as output, in particular output to the console. Ultimately, the type command redirects stdin into a text file.

This command temporarily halts processing. The user can type a line of text and press ENTER to write that line of text to the file. The file can accept multiple lines of text until the user terminates the command by pressing CTRL-Z, followed by ENTER when the cursor is at the beginning of a line. (I never said it was user-friendly.)

Many times, you may request a basic response of the user at the console—often a simple yes or no—and I'll discuss how such interactive bat files work in Chapter 15. In those rare instances when you request more involved input from the user, redirecting stdin saves that data to a file for later use.

Summary

In this chapter, I covered three related topics: outputs, redirection, and piping. The stdout and stderr data streams are important and useful interpreter-generated outputs, giving you detailed information about a bat file's execution. These are distinct from coder-generated output, the output that you explicitly create. You learned how redirection creates new files and appends to existing files. I showed how to capture the interpreter-generated output in a trace file or suppress it altogether. Individual commands also have output and you learned how to redirect it to a file and pipe it to other commands.

Later in this book I'll discuss many applications of these new tools. In Chapter 22, formatting simple reports with Batch will make great use of redirection. I already mentioned the use of piping for text searches and redirection with the dir command. In the next chapter, I'll discuss this extremely useful command and everything else you need to know about directories.

13

WORKING WITH DIRECTORIES

Batch is an ideal tool for interrogating Windows directories. What files or types of files are in a directory? Are some directories filling up? Where's a lost file? You can answer such questions and many more with some Batch code.

In this chapter, you'll learn how to create directories, delete directories, and retrieve a plethora of information about existing directories. Before long, you'll be able to quickly generate a report detailing the contents of a directory, including filenames, subdirectories, and all the contents of any subdirectories. The information can include the size, last modified date, and attributes of all files, or even just select files. Eventually, you'll learn how to process these files and directories one by one in a bat file, but I'll start by sharing how to retrieve this useful data. I'll also explore how to easily determine the existence of a specific file or file mask.

Finally, you'll learn how to map local and network directories to drive letters. Nearly anyone who works on a Windows computer can alleviate some day-to-day drudgery and become more efficient with a few tips from this chapter coded into a simple bat file.

Directory Basics

A *directory* is a mapped location on a computer's disk drive that can house files and other directories or subdirectories. On a Windows computer, a directory is represented by a folder; in fact, the terms *directory* and *folder* are often used interchangeably. In Windows Explorer, you can create and delete subdirectories and files in a directory with just a few mouse clicks. You can do the same with a bat file, maybe more easily.

Creating Directories

To create a directory, Batch uses the md and mkdir commands. Both stand for *make directory*, and they're actually the same command (Batch synonyms).

The md command accepts no options, and its only argument is the directory to be created:

```
md C:\Batch\MakeMe\
```

This useful yet simple command accepts multiple directories to be created, but when you use a single command for each directory, the return code of each command clearly tells you which directories were and were not successfully created. The md command works with or without the trailing slash, but I recommend using it, for no other reason than its presence makes the argument look like a directory.

Deleting Directories

The counterpart to the md command is the rd command, for *remove directory*, which deletes a directory and any files that might be in it. It also has a Batch synonym, rmdir, and it has only two options, both of which I always use: /Q invokes *quiet* mode, and /S deletes any *subdirectories* and their contents:

```
rd /Q /S C:\DeleteMe\
```

This command also accepts one-to-many directories as arguments, with or without a trailing slash. If there are no subdirectories, the command works with or without the /S option, but if there's one or more subdirectories, nothing at all is deleted without the option. I haven't yet been able to conceptualize what it means to delete a directory but not its subdirectories, so I always use the /S option.

Retrieving Directory Information

Batch has two commands for retrieving detailed information about directories and the files they contain, one far more useful than the other. I'll start with the indispensable one.

The dir Command

One immensely helpful tool is the dir command, which is short for *directory*. Many will use it at the command prompt to display information to the console. When used alone in a bat file, that information is simply dumped to stdout, which usually means it's subsumed by everything else contained in stdout, so it isn't all that useful. However, you'll typically use the dir in one of two fashions.

First, with what you learned in Chapter 12, you can redirect the output of the command to a file to be read by a program, a human, or eventually a bat file. Second, and even more impressive, I'll show how to feed the dir command into a for command, skipping the step of creating the file. That'll come in Part II, but before you use dir in a for command, you need to understand the complexities of the dir command itself.

Without Options

The simplest dir command accepts a single argument: a directory or folder. The double quotes are optional if the path has no embedded spaces:

```
dir "C:\Important Stuff\"
```

For the purpose of demonstration, assume that this directory holds electronic copies of some important personal documents and a couple of subdirectories with other important stuff. The result of the command might be the nicely formatted report written to stdout shown in Listing 13-1.

```
 Volume in drive C is OS
 Volume Serial Number is 2E7D-DB30

 Directory of C:\Important Stuff

07/25/2020  05:19 PM    <DIR>          .
07/25/2020  05:19 PM    <DIR>          ..
10/05/2019  06:44 PM           280,643 Birth Certificate.jpg
04/01/2014  08:28 PM           120,542 Car Title.pdf
07/25/2020  05:18 PM            61,124 Passport.png
07/25/2020  05:20 PM    <DIR>          Retirement
07/25/2020  10:51 PM            64,760 SSI Card.png
07/18/2020  02:26 PM    <DIR>          Taxes
               4 File(s)        527,069 bytes
               4 Dir(s)  173,275,090,944 bytes free
```

Listing 13-1: Sample output of an optionless dir command

After three header lines, the first two <DIR> entries signify that this is a subdirectory and not a root folder associated with a drive letter; these two lines don't appear for the dir C:\ command. More interesting, all of the files in this folder are clearly shown, each with its last modified date and time along with the file size. Subdirectories are also clearly delineated.

Notice that the files and subdirectories are intermingled, sorted alphabetically by default, but as you'll soon see, this command is extremely customizable with its options, giving you much control over this output.

You can even list multiple directories in a single command:

```
dir "C:\Important Stuff\" C:\Batch\
```

This command displays all the files and subdirectories under the first folder, followed by similar information for the second folders under another heading: Directory of C:\Batch.

Some Useful Options

The dir command has no shortage of useful options; a couple options even have options of their own. I'll discuss the ones I've used often, but as always, find the full list in the help, dir /?.

The /O option controls the sort *order*, but it works a little differently from most options you've seen at this point. Additional characters define the sort order. For instance, /OG groups the directories before the files, and a dash reverses the sort order so that /O-G groups the files before the directories. (Painfully, G represents *group directories first*.) The option /OEN orders by *extension* and then by *name*, while /O-E-N reverses the order. Some may find it *odious*, but /ODS sorts by modified date and time followed by file size:

```
dir "C:\Important Stuff\" /ODS
```

The *attributes* option, /A, limits what's displayed. The /AH option lists only hidden files, while /A-H omits hidden files from the list; /AD shows only directories, while /A-D doesn't display directories. There really should be an option for files only, but the no directories option accomplishes the task as only Batch can.

By default, the file sizes are displayed with commas, which is great for readability (for humans), but if we want to do any arithmetic on these numbers, the /-C option removes the commas. Quite often, the coder wants to produce a simple list of filenames without any clutter. The /B option, which stands for *bare*, does the job nicely.

Putting a few of these options together, the following command skips the directories (/A-D), orders by size from smallest to largest (/OS), and shows only the filenames sans their respective paths (/B):

```
dir "C:\Important Stuff\" /B /A-D /OS
```

This command without any options produced the report in Listing 13-1. With these options, the result is far more succinct, just a simple list of filenames:

```
Passport.png
SSI Card.png
Car Title.pdf
Birth Certificate.jpg
```

Notice from Listing 13-1 that the passport is the smallest file and the birth certificate is the largest, thus showing that the files are still ordered by size even though their byte counts aren't displayed. The succinct output might look like a downgrade; true, it isn't as informative for humans, but in Part II this will be ideal data to feed into a for command that'll process one file at a time.

Another useful option is /S, which stands for *subdirectory*. It essentially runs a dir command on a directory, and then it runs it again on all of its subdirectories, returning a well-formatted report with subheadings for each. The dir C:\ /S command provides a report on every folder on your computer, but it won't be quick, and the result will likely be longer than this book. When used in conjunction with /B, each bare filename is prepended with its path—which might seem like a contradiction but not after you consider that each file could be in any number of directories.

Default Set of Options

If you're planning to run multiple dir commands, all with the same options, those options don't need to be repeated for every command. Instead, you can load one or more options into the dircmd pseudo-environment variable. Once it's set, all subsequent dir commands will use the options in the dircmd variable by default.

For example, the following code executes both dir commands showing bare filenames (/B), no directories (/A-D), and sorted by extension (/OE):

```
set dircmd=/B /A-D /OE
dir "C:\Important Stuff\"
dir "C:\Some Other Folder\"
```

You can override one or more of the options in the dircmd variable for a particular dir command. Assume that the next dir command follows the previous code where dircmd was set:

```
dir "C:\Important Stuff\" /O-E
```

This still uses the options for the bare format of files only, but the sort order is reversed.

At any point, you can turn this feature off by setting dircmd to null or nothing at all.

The where Command

The where command is similar to the dir command; it searches one or more directories to find *where* a file exists. If you're shrugging your shoulders as you read this asking, "Doesn't the `dir` command do that and a whole lot more?" my answer would most definitely be in the affirmative. Most anything you can do with `where`, you can do with `dir`, only better.

However, the `where` command performs one task far more efficiently than the `dir` command ever could. With the /Q option, the `where` command returns an exit code indicating success or failure in lieu of a list of files found, making it easy to determine whether a particular file exists or whether at least one file matching a file mask is present. (The /Q option stands for *quiet* mode like some others you've seen, but quiet for this command means something slightly different. For the others, a prompt is suppressed, but here the output is suppressed.)

The following command looks for at least one file starting with the text FindMe, case-insensitive, in the folder *C:\Batch* and sets `errorlevel` based on the result:

```
where /Q C:\Batch\:FindMe*
```

The return code will be 0 if at least one file fits the mask, 1 if not, or 2 if the syntax is incorrect.

If you look closely, there appears to be a problem with the path and file mask; there's what looks to be an extraneous colon between the two. The `dir` command rightly accepts a path and filename (or mask) together as one argument. The `where` command treats them as separate arguments delimited by a colon. This does allow you to enter multiple semicolon-delimited paths with a single filename or mask, but that's of little consolation. To make matters even more confusing, the colon is dropped in favor of a space when using the /R option—which stands for *recursive*, meaning that it also searches subdirectories:

```
where /Q /R C:\Batch\ FindMe*
```

I'm begrudgingly including this command. The syntax is just plain wrong, but it does have one worthwhile function. Think of it as an `if exist` command with a return code. Use it for this narrow task, but otherwise stick with the `dir`.

Mapping Drive Letters

Batch has two very useful commands for mapping drive letters. One maps local paths to drive letters, and the other maps network paths and shares to drive letters. If you're a noncoder—first off, I'm giving you a slow clap, congrats on getting to the 13th chapter—but more to the point, if this sounds like something that only coders can use, that isn't the case.

Mapping paths is a great tool if you often work in various specific paths on your computer or network throughout the day. Navigating to them might take some time, especially if these paths are several folders deep. Another challenge, especially if you work from home, is that you probably won't be able to see the network paths until you connect to a virtual private network (VPN). To make all of this easier, write a short bat file and run it each morning, perhaps after connecting to the network, and you can access these paths with ease throughout the day. After the mapping is done, access each path by clicking a drive letter in Windows Explorer.

The subst Command

The subst command maps a local directory, or any folder on your Windows computer, to a drive letter. The command name is short for *substitute* because after using it, you can substitute a drive letter for a directory. (No, it isn't used for substringing.) The following command maps *Z:* to the path shown, although it'll fail if the path doesn't exist or if the drive letter is already mapped to another path:

```
subst Z: C:\ParentFolder\ChildFolder\GrandchildFolder\
```

After this command executes, you'll find *Z:* in Windows Explorer as an alias of the *C:\ParentFolder\ChildFolder\GrandchildFolder* path. Now the bat file can access anything in that path by invoking only the drive letter. For example, after the previous command executes, the following command creates an empty file in the *GrandchildFolder* directory, with an economy of typing:

```
copy nul Z:\EmptyFile.txt
```

The subst command with neither arguments nor options displays all folders currently mapped by earlier subst commands. If a certain other folder had already been mapped prior to the earlier subst command, the succinct command

```
subst
```

might generate the following output:

```
Y:\: => C:\Certain\Other\Folder\
Z:\: => C:\ParentFolder\ChildFolder\GrandchildFolder\
```

The mapping of *Z:* will now be in effect on the machine, even to other processes (bats and humans alike) until the machine is logged off or unless the following command is run to *delete* or disconnect the mapping via the /D option:

```
subst Z: /D
```

This command maps only local directories; it doesn't map directories on other computers, but there's another command for that.

The net use Command

The `net use` command maps network directories and shares as the `subst` command maps local directories. The following command maps *Y:* to a share on a remote server:

```
net use Y: \\RemoteServer\ShareName\
```

You can now use the drive letter *Y:* to access this path on another machine, again by both bats and humans, until the mapping is deleted or the machine is shut down. Like the `subst` command, `net use` has an option to disconnect or delete the mapping, but it's more verbose:

```
net use Y: /DELETE
```

The creators of the `/D` and `/DELETE` options were at least subconsciously honoring the famous quote, "a foolish consistency is the hobgoblin of little minds." Ralph Waldo Emerson might disapprove, but in a nod to foolish consistency, I've capitalized the verbose option as I have the others because that's my convention, but not without reservations. My primary driver behind this convention is to minimize capitalizations, but when an option, which is usually a single character, grows to six characters, it begs to be lowercase. Do what feels right to you.

Much like the `subst` command, the command with no additional arguments, `net use`, produces the complete list of directories and drives mapped by earlier `net use` commands.

NOTE   *I need to head off some hate mail here. This is actually the `net` command with `use` being its first argument. The command has more than a dozen other first arguments—for instance, `share` creates a file share. But due to the popularity of use, coders commonly refer to the `net use` command. In fact, the help, `net use /?`, details information on it like any other command.*

Summary

In this chapter, you learned how to create and delete directories. I detailed the all-important `dir` command, which you'll see again before long, and the `where` command, which you'll not see again in this book because of reasons stated earlier. You now can pull up an incredible amount of information on a directory and all of its contents, and in Part II, I'll demonstrate how to enumerate through this data so that you can perform a task on each file or directory. You also learned how to map local and network directories, a skill that's incredibly useful for anyone, not just coders, who works often on a Windows computer.

Changing gears, I'll next delve into the concept of escaping. To some this might be the most confusing title in the book; what's escaping, what's being escaped, and what are we trying to escape? Those questions and more will be answered in the next chapter.

14

ESCAPING

This chapter is about a vexing problem and its Batch solution. The problem is that you sometimes want to use a character as simple text but that particular character has a specific function in the coding language. The solution is escaping.

In this chapter, I'll explain all the intricacies surrounding how to escape a character in Batch. A certain syntax is used the majority of the time, except for when it isn't. You'll learn about multiple rounds of escaping, the syntax, and why you might want to escape a character more than once. I'll also return to the "continuation character," used to continue a command on multiple lines of code, because when you remove its veil, it turns out to be an escape character. However, before getting into how to solve this problem, you must first understand and appreciate the problem.

The Problem Statement

You may want to use a certain character in some code, but what happens if it's a special character with a certain predefined function in the coding language? For instance, say you're attempting to use the special character in a text string. It happens in all languages, but it happens quite frequently in Batch because of the language's uniquely esoteric syntax.

As you've seen repeatedly in this book, percent signs delimit variables; one on either side of a variable resolves the variable to its value. But long before the existence of Batch, the percent sign was used to denote a percentage—that is, a proportion of 100. Hence, a text string in Batch can't simply refer to 50% without the percent sign being interpreted as a delimiter. The insidious aspect of this issue is that there's no compiler to catch the problem and the interpreter might not even fail to execute the code, instead producing unexpected results.

To demonstrate, consider this command writing what appears to be a simple statement to the console:

```
> con echo Between 60% and 80% of Americans don't understand percents!
```

The interpreter treats everything between the two percent signs—that is, the space followed by and 80—as a variable. Assuming that such a variable isn't set, which is a virtual certainty, it (along with the percent signs) resolves to null. The result is this nonsensical statement written to the console:

```
Between 60 of Americans don't understand percents
```

And if this command had used only one percent sign, it alone would've been dropped from the output. By the way, what happened to the exclamation mark at the end? Hold that thought.

The solution to this quandary is escaping any special characters. Escape characters can be tricky, but they are very useful and indispensable in many situations. Before long, I'll come back to the previous echo command to show you how to make it write the desired text.

The Caret Escape Character

The primary Batch escape character is the caret (^). In other contexts, it's called a hat or used to indicate an exponential, but in the Batch realm, it's a caret. On most keyboards, you can type it using SHIFT-6. The upshot is that the interpreter treats the vast majority of characters following the caret as simple text.

The following echo command is attempting to write to the console some trite pablum one might expect to find on a bad motivational poster at an office run by people who don't understand that *Office Space* was a comedy, but the cringeworthy content is only part of the problem. It simply doesn't work:

```
> con echo Together We Are > You & Me Alone
```

The interpreter treats the second greater-than sign as a second redirection character, creating an extensionless file named You in the current directory, and the ampersand ends one command and starts another. Obviously, the Me command with the Alone argument fails outright.

The command is clearly a mess, but it's fixable with carets. I'm inserting the primary Batch escape character just prior to the two characters that thwarted us before:

```
> con echo Together We Are ^> You ^& Me Alone
```

You can think of each caret in this command as a special messenger. The escape character is giving the interpreter this clear message upon its discovery:

> The very next character following me is to be treated as simple text. Don't interpret it as you normally would. Oh, and by the way, promptly discard me for I am but a digital Pheidippides, a simple messenger who expires after the completion of his task.

The result is this maybe inspirational and motivational message written to the console:

```
Together We Are > You & Me Alone
```

Another way to get the interpreter to treat the special characters as text is to enclose the string in double quotes:

```
> con echo "Together We Are > You & Me Alone"
```

It's important to note that while this command doesn't have escape characters, it also writes out the double quotes to the console.

I'll soon reveal some exceptions, but the caret is the most commonly used Batch escape character, and you can use it to escape the less-than symbol (<), pipe (|), and parentheses (()), among other special characters. But Batch doesn't treat all characters equally.

Escaping the Caret

Since the interpreter treats the caret as an escape character and throws it away, you might ponder the plight of a caret wanting to be treated simply as text itself. For example, if you were to write the Pythagorean theorem to the console, I hope you aren't surprised to learn that Batch doesn't support superscripts: $A^2 + B^2 = C^2$. Instead, carets indicating exponentiation will suffice if we can make it work: A^2 + B^2 = C^2. (The Pythagorean theorem assumes that A and B are the sides of a right triangle adjacent to the right angle and that C is the hypotenuse.) This might be a first attempt at a solution:

```
> con echo The Pythagorean Theorem:  A^2 + B^2 = C^2
```

Unfortunately, each caret tells the interpreter to treat the following character, a 2 in each instance, as simple text, which it would've done anyway:

```
The Pythagorean Theorem:  A2 + B2 = C2
```

The interpreter simply throws away the carets as if they were never there.

The solution rests in the fact that the caret is self-escaping; a caret is escaped with another caret. I've replaced each caret in the following code with double carets. In each instance, the first caret is the escape character, followed by the text caret:

```
> con echo The Pythagorean Theorem:  A^^2 + B^^2 = C^^2
```

Now you'll get the desired result:

```
The Pythagorean Theorem:  A^2 + B^2 = C^2
```

We still can't manage a superscript, but the result written to the console is the next best thing and much to a mathematician's liking.

Escaping Percent Signs and Exclamation Marks

After studying the Pythagorean theorem, you might ace the math test, but this celebratory Batch command fails to produce the desired result as the two special characters are dropped from the text written to the console:

```
> con echo I Scored 100% on my Math Test!
```

D'oh! We forgot the carets. You can be forgiven for thinking this quick fix will show the percent sign and the exclamation mark:

```
> con echo I Scored 100^% on my Math Test^!
```

But the output is unchanged. Unfortunately, as is often the case with Batch, there are batveats. The caret doesn't work as the escape character for the percent sign or the exclamation mark.

The escape character for the percent sign is another percent sign, and the escape character—actually the escape characters, plural—for the exclamation mark is two carets. If this doesn't make any sense to you, you are not alone. I've never found a good justification for this anomaly, but the following command writes I Scored 100% on my Math Test! to the console:

```
> con echo I Scored 100%% on my Math Test^^!
```

Reflect on this a moment; in comparison to the Pythagorean theorem example, there seems to be a contradiction in how Batch handles double carets. The text ^^2 resolves to ^2, but in relation to the math test, the text ^^! resolves to !, leaving nary a caret in sight. Yes, that's how it works. The interpreter handles double carets one way if followed by an exclamation mark and another way if followed by anything else. Consider it a batveat of a batveat (or a meta-batveat).

Getting back to the problem statement from the beginning of the chapter, this command writes the desired text:

```
> con echo Between 60%% and 80%% of Americans don't understand percents^^!
```

The interpreter writes the appropriate text to the console thanks to each set of double percent signs and the two carets preceding the exclamation mark.

NOTE *As noted in Chapter 3, I've written this book with the assumption that delayed expansion is always enabled, but if it's disabled, Batch treats the exclamation mark like any other character with no particular significance in Batch and with no need of being escaped.*

Multilevel Escaping

The previous examples demonstrate how to write hardcoded text to the console with single-level escaping, and the same techniques successfully set a simple variable, but there's a catch. For instance, the following set command resolves the two escape characters and stores Together We Are > You & Me Alone into the variable:

```
set pureDrivel=Together We Are ^> You ^& Me Alone
```

Unfortunately, the uses for this variable are severely limited. The variable does in fact contain the two special characters, but if you tried writing it to the console or a file or tried piping it to another command, it would fail to work as intended. Because the escape characters were removed from the text as it was assigned to the variable, when that variable is later resolved, the characters that have special meaning to the interpreter pose the same problem that escaping initially solved.

The solution is to escape the escape character—yes, double-level escaping. The following two lines of code write the desired text to the console, and by desired text I mean that it contains a greater-than sign and an ampersand with no escape characters:

```
set pureDrivel=Together We Are ^^^> You ^^^& Me Alone
> con echo %pureDrivel%
```

To see what's happening, let's focus on ^^^&. The first caret is the escape character for the second caret, and the third caret is the escape character for the ampersand. When resolved, the set command stores ^& as part of the variable's value. When the echo command resolves the variable, the remaining caret—the one that was treated as text just a moment ago—is now the escape character for the ampersand, resulting in just the ampersand surviving to be written to the console.

Let's look at the entire text string. The first command sets pureDrivel to the value Together We Are ^> You ^& Me Alone; then the second command writes the text Together We Are > You & Me Alone to the console.

Multilevel escaping can get a bit more complicated. For instance, if you're concatenating two variables into a larger variable before writing that second variable to a file, you'll need three levels of escaping.

As for the mechanics of triple-level escaping, consider this: because of the four escape characters in ^^^^^^^& (that's seven carets), it resolves to ^^^&. A second round of escaping sees this resolve to ^&, which ultimately resolves to & on the third round. The number of escape characters is $2^n - 1$, where n is the number of escapes. I said it was tricky, but it's also pretty cool.

The Continuation Character

On more than one occasion, I've heard coders refer to the caret as the Batch *continuation character*, and I even introduced it as such in Chapter 5 with an example that used it in a set command spanning four lines of code. Technically, that's incorrect, but in practice, it does perform this function. Allow me to explain.

It should be the goal of every coder to write code that does not force the reader to scroll right and left. (It should also be efficient, well-documented, well-organized, and even elegant, but maybe that's just my opinion, so I digress.) In most compiled languages when a command gets too long to easily read, you simply press ENTER and continue typing on the next line. The compiler is smart enough to know that the command encompasses two, three, or even more, lines.

The Batch interpreter isn't that forgiving (or smart), but when you append a caret to the *very end* of a line of code, the statement continues on the following line. Even when a line isn't particularly long, I sometimes use this technique to line up the arguments I'm passing to an executable for readability:

```
C:\Batch\SomeExecutable.exe %Arg1% ^
                            %Arg2% ^
                            %AnotherArg% ^
                            %YetAnotherArg% ^
                            %AndAnother%
```

At the end of most lines in a text file, two bytes represent the *carriage return line feed*. In hex, the bytes are x'0D' x'0A', and together they are often referred to as the CRLF, but they are not usually visible in the text editor.

(If using Notepad++, select **View ▸ Show Symbol ▸ Show End of Line** to make the CRLFs visible. Other editors have a similar feature.)

In reality, the caret is still just an escape character, and it's escaping the CRLF. In keeping with what an escape character does, when the interpreter sees the caret, it doesn't treat the CRLF following as it normally would—that is, as the end of a line. Instead, it just treats the CRLF as any other whitespace and ignores it, essentially wrapping the line. In this way, the caret is the "continuation character." (But I still cringe.)

A common mistake that invalidates this text wrapping is to append the line apparently ending in a caret with a space or two after the caret. Since the caret escapes the very next character, this does nothing more than escape a space, which is pretty close to doing nothing at all and leaves the CRLF undisturbed. This oversight can be very difficult to troubleshoot for those who simply think of the caret as a continuation character instead of as an escape character for the CRLF. Knowledge is power.

You've learned that single characters are escaped by a single escape character, except for the exclamation mark, which requires two escape characters. The CRLF is yet another exception, but for the opposite reason. The CRLF is actually two characters, the carriage return character and the line feed character, and it's the only example in Batch of two characters escaped by a lone character.

Summary

In this chapter, you learned the many ways to use the caret, and sometimes the percent sign, to escape special characters, but the discussion is just beginning. This technique is an indispensable tool, and you'll see more than one application of it later in this book.

If nothing else, I hope this chapter has demonstrated how very tricky escaping can be. When I was a novice Batch coder, I received some simple, yet sage, advice about escaping from a more experienced co-worker. The advice was to test diligently; test all possible characters that the code might reasonably encounter in the data. With so many caveats, batveats, and exceptions, you shouldn't assume that escaping will work in all contexts after seeing it work in one particular context. In your test plan, pepper the code doing the escaping with all of the special characters that could possibly come its way.

For something completely different, the next chapter will discuss how a bat file can work interactively with a human, asking questions, getting responses, and performing conditional logic based on those answers.

15

INTERACTIVE BATCH

Let me be the one to break it to you if there was any doubt in your mind. Batch doesn't have a graphical user interface (GUI), but it does have a functional user interface (UI). In this chapter, I'll discuss different means of getting input from the user into a bat file as it executes, such as selecting one option from a list or typing in a response to a question. I'll also describe how to alter the visual display or look and feel of the console including clearing the screen, changing colors, and updating the title. Finally, I'll bring everything together to build a fully operational Batch UI (BUI) ready to execute.

UIs, GUIs, and BUIs

A user interface at its core is a means for the user to communicate with a computer, passing information in and getting something back. Every time you make an online purchase, you're using a graphical user interface, which is a more sophisticated user interface with graphics allowing user input from more than just a keyboard. A video game is a glorified UI, and every time you touch an icon on your smartphone to open an app, you're using a user interface. Commander Data of *Star Trek: The Next Generation* was (or will be) an android, possessing an incredibly advanced UI able to interact with humans with use of all five senses.

Sticking with the science-fiction theme, the Batch UI is more along the lines of the 1983 movie *War Games.* There are no panels, drop-downs, icons, menus, or radio buttons, and certainly no touchscreen or voice commands in the Batch UI, or BUI (pronounced boo-ē). Be warned, if you use this term with coders, you'll likely receive some blank stares and raised eyebrows. I've tried but so far failed to add BUI to the coding lexicon, but I hold out hope that it'll still catch on.

The BUI isn't sexy, but it can ask questions of the user, who can then respond by entering a string of text or selecting an option from a list by pressing a single key. A coder would be a sadist to use Batch to build a complex UI for a large number of users, not to mention soon-to-be unemployed. But there are many instances when a bat file needs a piece of data or two from the user, especially if the user is also the coder. I've coded a number of BUIs, but for each one I can count on one hand the number of people who've ever used it.

The possible needs for a BUI are plentiful. Your bat file might be copying files to or from a server, where you ask the user to specify the server. As another example, you might want to create a report but be able to generate it from test or production data depending on the user's preference. Or you might ask the user to enter a date range of files to be backed up.

Choosing a Selection from a List

Two commands allow the user to input data into a BUI. One asks for the user to choose one out of multiple possible selections, and the other asks for a typed freeform response. The first one is the choice command, and as the name suggests, it allows the user to make a *choice* from a list of two or more selections.

To get started, let's ask the user a question—Do you want a Joke, Pun, or Riddle?—and allow them to enter J, P, or R for one of the three selections, respectively. The following choice command does just this:

```
choice /C:JPR /M:"Do you want a Joke, Pun, or Riddle"
```

The /C option lists the *choices*, /C:JPR, and the text encased in double quotes associated with the /M option is the *message* presented to the user. Both of these options also work without the colon delimiter. That is, /C JPR is functionally equivalent to /C:JPR, but I much prefer the colon because it nicely ties the option to its values or its message, much like a valued rug ties a room together. Also, notice the lack of the question mark at the end of the question. The interpreter adds the punctuation after giving the user the list of possible selections.

The previous command displays the following to the user on the console:

```
Do you want a Joke, Pun, or Riddle [J,P,R]?
```

The execution of the bat file suspends at the choice command until the user presses one of the three keys (or exits the command window). If the user presses a key not on the list, the computer beeps and continues to wait, but what happens when the user selects one of the choices?

Up until this point errorlevel has merely been a return code, usually 0 for the successful execution of a command and something greater than 0 for a failure. But after a choice command executes, it sets errorlevel to the user's selection; more specifically, it's set to the integer value corresponding to the position of the user's selection in the list. More simply, if the choices are defined by /C:JPR, selecting J returns 1, P returns 2, and R returns 3.

I find it a bit misleading that the variable returning the valid selection contains the word *error* in its name, but after getting over the issue of semantics and the fact that this reserved word is doing double duty, it's not difficult to interrogate the variable to determine the user's selection and which logic to execute next.

Here's another example of a choice command that also appears to be missing something (other than a question mark):

```
choice /M:"Do you want to try again"
```

The /C option is missing, but this is a yes or no question, and when that option is omitted, the implied default is /C:YN, returning 1 for Y and 2 for N.

Two additional options always go hand in hand with each other. The /T option sets the *timeout*, or the number of seconds given before the command times out and the interpreter chooses the *default* selection defined by the /D option. The following command gives the user 20 seconds, /T:20, to make a selection before a pun, /D:P, is inflicted upon them:

```
choice /C:JPR /M:"Do you want a Joke, Pun, or Riddle" /T:20 /D:P
```

Sometimes it doesn't make sense to list the selections. For instance, when asking the user to rate something on a scale from 1 to 5, it might instead be preferable to explain the rating system with some text. Assume that you want to pose the following to the user requesting a response:

```
Rate your agreement to the statement on a scale of 1 to 5.
I love bat comedy.  1 (Agree) to 5 (Disagree)
```

Together, the following echo command and choice command produce the desired text and wait for a response:

```
echo Rate your agreement to the statement on a scale of 1 to 5.
choice /C:12345 /M:"I love bat comedy.  1 (Agree) to 5 (Disagree)" /N
```

You'll need the /C:12345 option so that the interpreter has the list of possible selections, but you don't want [1,2,3,4,5]? displayed because it'll compete with the instructions on the prior line. The /N option (*no choice keys*) suppresses the display of choices, showing only the desired message to the user. The question mark is also suppressed with the /N option, but you can include it in the message string if the message is posed as a question.

If a bat file is to perform a task on a selected server, a series of echo commands could list any number of servers along with their associated keyboard keys as a prelude to a choice command. That would work great for a predefined list of servers, but if the list is particularly long or unknown at coding time, you can instead ask the user to key in any server name with the next command.

Freeform User Input

The other command allowing the user to input data is the set command (from Chapter 2) when used with the /P or *prompt string* option. Much like its optionless counterpart, the set /P command assigns a value to a variable, where that value can be a string of any reasonable length or even null. The difference is that the text after the equal sign isn't the value assigned; it's the prompt string displayed to the user. Whatever the user enters is assigned to the variable once they press ENTER.

To demonstrate, the question after the equal sign is displayed to the console:

```
set /P yourAns=How are bats like false teeth?  &
```

The execution is put on hold until the user responds, at which point the interpreter assigns that response to the yourAns variable.

Forget to use the /P option, and the variable is assigned to the text after the equal sign without prompting of the user. Notice three minor yet important details. First, this command doesn't append the question mark to the message string, so I added it. Second, I added a couple of spaces after that question mark to move the start of the response away from the question. Finally, I terminated the line with an ampersand to make those spaces obvious at a glance. These subtle tweaks will be equally appreciated by your users and any readers of your code.

Every joke needs a punchline, and it's displayed to the user on the second line of the following code after they have had a chance to ponder the question and enter a guess:

```
set /P yourAns=How are bats like false teeth?  &
echo ** They both come out at night.
echo ** You said: "%yourAns%"
```

The third and final line displays the user's answer encased in double quotes. It's a joke. I didn't say it was a good joke.

Altering the UI Look and Feel

Batch provides three more commands that alter the look and feel of the console, and a couple of them have additional applications:

Updating the Title

When a bat file executes, a command window opens, and the title in the white bar across its top is likely to be *C:\WINDOWS\system32\cmd.exe*, the program that runs a bat file. The title command resets that title to something a little more identifiable and far less generic. The following changes the title to the text that follows it:

```
title Batch Improv Theater
```

The embedded spaces in the argument list aren't an issue, and if you encase the text in double quotes, they'll also be part of the title.

Use of this command isn't limited to interactive bat files where its value is obvious. Any bat file that runs on a machine where other bat files might also be running can only be enhanced by a title. If one of those bat files is hung or otherwise trapped in an endless loop, which one should be killed? If none of them has a title, they may all look identical, leaving you no way of knowing. The title command solves this problem. In fact, I'll use this command in Chapter 26, where I'll title a process susceptible to hanging so that another bat file can find it and kill it, if it does indeed hang. You can even reset the title multiple times during a run, perhaps showing the status or the step being executed.

Clearing the Screen

The cls command is a severe abbreviation of *clear screen*. When this optionless command executes, the screen or console is cleared, revealing a blank (and for now black) canvas. To cut through the noise, you can execute this command before posing a question to the user.

Changing Colors

Opening or executing a bat file brings up a command window with white text on a black background, which is the exact opposite of how humans have been reading since the advent of papyrus and ink. Contemplate for a moment the text you're currently reading as if it were white on jet-black paper. It seems anachronistic now, but it must have been avant-garde in the early days of Batch.

The `color` command provides 16 different colors from which to choose for both the foreground text and background, for a total of 240 permutations, although certain combinations are virtually unreadable and even painful to the eye.

Go to the help menu, `color /?`, to get the full list of colors denoted by the hexadecimal digits 0 to F, but the set of popular colors includes black (0), blue (1), red (4), and white (7). The `color` command accepts a two-character color attribute as its argument, where the first character represents the background color and the second represents the foreground or text color. By the way, the interpreter is smart enough to reject a command that assigns the same color to both.

A black background supporting white text is the default Batch color scheme, which you can call for explicitly with this command: `color 07`. Flipping the attribute around to `70` creates a white background supporting black text, but black text on a bright white (F) background is more appealing:

```
color F0
```

My preference for readability is bright white on a blue background, `color 1F`, but aesthetics aside, the greatest use of this command is to flag problems. You may run certain bat files daily to perform mundane or repetitive tasks. You may run such a bat file upon logon each morning and then ignore it, but on the rare instance when a file can't be copied or a process aborts, the `color` command offers a great means of throwing up a red flag (literally) to alert the user. If using the default color settings, after writing an error message to the console, this line immediately changes the screen from black to red (4), brightens the white text a tad (F), and holds the window open:

```
@color 4F & pause
```

That should get the user's attention even if they've moved on to other tasks and the command window is off to the side. If it doesn't, you can also use the `cls` command to clear the screen before writing an error message. To heighten the contrast, you can make the background green with `color 2F`, when the process completes successfully.

The `cls` and `color` commands are nonfunctional if stdout has been redirected to either a trace file or the nul file. If you need to clear the screen only once, execute the `cls` command just before redirecting stdout to the trace; otherwise, `echo off` is the only realistic option for keeping stdout off the console. Likewise, you can execute the `color` command prior to or after the redirection. Do it early, and the color will be set for the duration of the redirection. You also can turn the screen red for an abort at the end of the execution after returning from the redirection. The `title` command is the favorite child of the bunch, as it works anywhere in a bat file, regardless of redirection.

Fully Functional Batch UI

Let's put all of this together into a fully functional bat file that can interactively share a joke, a pun, or a riddle, repeatedly. The next two code snippets contain the entire bat file. Here's the first portion of *BatchImprov.bat*:

```
❶ @setlocal EnableExtensions EnableDelayedExpansion
  @echo off
  color 1F
  title Batch Improv Theater

❷ :Again
  cls
  > con echo.
❸ > con choice /C:JPR /M:"Do you want a Joke, Pun, or Riddle"
  > con echo.
❹ if %errorlevel% equ 1 (
      call :Joke
  ) else if %errorlevel% equ 2 (
      call :Pun
  ) else if %errorlevel% equ 3 (
      call :Riddle
  )
  > con echo.
❺ > con choice /M:"Do you want to try again"
  if %errorlevel% equ 1  goto :Again
  goto :eof
```

After the setlocal command ❶ (my ubiquitous opening command), the echo off command suppresses stdout so that only my coder-generated output gets to the console. Notice that neither command is written to the console thanks to the leading at sign (@). The color command then sets the background to blue and the text to bright white, for no other reason than readability. Next, the title command defines the title of the command window. After the :Again label ❷, the cls command clears the screen to complete the setup.

Three echo. commands are strategically placed in the code to display blank lines for readability. The same choice command ❸ from earlier asks the user for their jocular liking. Since there are three selections from which to choose, an if command with an else if construct interrogates errorlevel ❹. Depending on the user's response, different call commands are invoked for a joke, pun, or riddle, based on the values of 1, 2, or 3, respectively.

A second choice command ❺ then asks the user if they want more of this humor, using the implied default choices of Y and N. If the user selects Y, the interpreter returns 1 and we go back to the :Again label ❷, where we clear the screen and begin again. A selection of N indicates that the user has had enough, and we exit the bat file.

The three routines called in the previous listing are defined here in the final portion of *BatchImprov.bat*:

```
:Joke
> con echo Please give an answer to the joke:
> con set /P yourAns=How are bats like false teeth?  &
> con echo ** They both come out at night.
> con echo ** You said: "%yourAns%"
goto :eof

:Pun
> con echo We hope you find this punny:
> con echo Crossing a vampire bat with a computer means love at first byte.
goto :eof

:Riddle
> con echo Please give an answer to the riddle:
> con set /P yourAns=This type of bat is silly.  &
> con echo ** A Dingbat.
> con echo ** You said: "%yourAns%"
goto :eof
```

The :Joke and :Riddle routines are similarly structured. A set /P command asks for a response before revealing the punchline and the user's answer. The :Pun routine simply writes out the witty pun with no input from the user.

This bat file doesn't capture stdout and stderr, because doing so wouldn't allow for the use of the cls command between each selection. If that were to cause a problem during development, you could temporarily comment out the echo off command, but be prepared for a messy console impeding your testing.

Each choice and set /P command in *BatchImprov.bat* is a little different from the ones shown earlier in this chapter. Along with the echo commands, each one is using redirection to explicitly write its prompt or message to the console via the > con syntax. This addition would have been required if stdout had been redirected to a trace file; otherwise, it would have written unanswerable prompt strings to the trace. But since stdout is simply being suppressed, the redirection to the console is redundant in this case. I didn't include the redirection earlier in the chapter because I wanted to focus on the new commands alone, but in practice it's best to always define the destination explicitly as I've done here, even if it isn't required.

The *BatchImprov.bat* bat file is now fully functional. Run it and you can answer questions and see the results until you answer N to the Do you want to try again? prompt. Undoubtedly, you'll soon get bored due to the limited content, but we still have many enhancements to discuss. In Appendix A, you'll find a far more dynamic version of this bat file capable of reading files containing libraries of jokes, puns, and riddles; storing them in arrays; and randomly accessing the arrays to get unique material multiple times during a single execution.

Summary

In this chapter, I created the most substantial bat file yet, and I did it to demonstrate how to communicate interactively with users. You learned how to provide users with a list from which to choose a selection and how to store a typed freeform user response of any length into a variable. I also introduced useful commands for clearing the screen, updating the title, and changing background and text colors, including other noninteractive uses for these commands.

In the next chapter, the last of Part I, I'll discuss code blocks, which is an integral topic as you move forward. A code block isn't simply a "block of code." I'll explain what it is, why it's important, and how it's useful in the next few pages.

16

CODE BLOCKS

A *code block* can sometimes be a rather generic term, referring to some amorphous section of a program or a few lines of code. In Batch, it's a well-defined entity: one or more commands in between a set of open and close parentheses. A prominent example is the code often executed when an `if` command is true.

That seems simple enough, but it's far more difficult to use a code block properly and wisely than it is to define it. A very powerful feature of Batch is that delayed expansion allows you to resolve variables in two distinct ways inside a code block, but the uninitiated often misinterpret that functionality as a bug. In this chapter, I'll detail all the intricacies involved, and you'll also learn how code blocks, specifically naked code blocks, provide an interesting technique for allowing a variable to survive code of limited scope. If that doesn't yet sound impressive, I'm confident that it will soon.

Resolving Variables in a Code Block

I discussed in detail the process of setting and resolving a variable in Chapter 2, but those rules change inside of a code block. As I'll soon demonstrate, this is a great feature of Batch, but it's often misunderstood and can result in a perplexed and cranky coder. Even after many years of Batch coding, it's still easy to stumble into this particular issue from time to time. While I usually find and fix the issue relatively quickly (after letting out an audible "D'oh!"), it can lead to hours of frustration for more novice coders. This batveat is best described with an example.

On many occasions, co-workers have presented me with an apparently simple code snippet such as the one in Listing 16-1.

```
set price=$450
if %bSale% (
    set price=$350
    > con echo The sale price of a 50-inch TV is %price%.
)
```

Listing 16-1: A variable set and resolved in a code block . . . and a mystery

The code block is accompanied by an exasperated query:

> A variable has an initial setting, but I'm resetting it to something else and it doesn't seem to "take." I'm setting the price of a 50-inch TV to $450, and I know that the bSale boolean is true because the echo to the console happens, but the variable's not being reset to $350. The echo command writes out $450. It's as if the first command inside the code block doesn't execute while the second one does. Crazy, huh? To test this theory, I moved only the echo command from inside the if command code block to just after it. Suddenly, I get the sale price to display like I wanted, but that's not a solution because I want to execute the command only if there's a sale. I even tried not setting the variable prior to the if command, but then it resolved to nothing at all. Ugh! This makes no sense. What's going on?

The quick and much too brief reply is, "Replace the percent signs with exclamation marks." The only change needed to Listing 16-1 is the resolution of price at the end of the echo command:

```
set price=$450
if %bSale% (
    set price=$350
    > con echo The sale price of a 50-inch TV is !price!.
)
```

The result is what the confounded coder had expected all along:

```
The sale price of a 50-inch TV is $350.
```

After the coder incredulously tries and sees the exclamation marks work, they typically return more peeved than relieved and with the combination of another query and a new complaint: "Sometimes you use percent signs to resolve a variable, and at other times, you use exclamation marks. What kind of a programmatical sadist would dream this up? Isn't Batch esoteric enough? When I set a variable, I expect it to be set. Period. What possible use could this have?" The only variations in this diatribe are in its intensity and level of vulgarity. These comments are from a very subdued and pious co-worker. Before addressing the question of this feature's use, I owe you a far better explanation of what's going on with the `price` variable.

The coexistence of two values of a variable is another application of delayed expansion, first introduced in Chapter 3, which allows for the resolution of variables at either parse time or execution time. When a variable is set inside a code block, you can think of it as having two values at one time. One is the current value to which it was set in the code block, resolved at execution time. The other is the value assigned to it as it entered the code block, resolved at parse time.

If a variable simultaneously has two distinct values, we need two different means of resolving the variable. To that end, *percent signs are the delimiter for revealing its value as it entered the code block*, and *exclamation marks are the delimiter for retrieving its current value inside of the code block*. The code can reset a variable multiple times in the code block, and percent sign delimiters will still resolve it to its state before entering the code block.

The upshot is that at the time of the `echo` command in Listing 16-1, `%price%` resolves to $450, and `!price!` resolves to $350.

Despite my co-worker's protestation, this isn't sadistic at all; it actually represents a fascinating feature that's lacking in most programming languages. The ability for a single variable to hold two values may be hard to grasp, but once understood, it offers many possibilities. To demonstrate, I'll alter the message written to the console in Listing 16-1. Instead of just giving the sale price, it would be easier to see the savings by showing both the original and sale prices. I'm using the same `price` variable for both values in Listing 16-2—once resolved with percent signs and once with exclamation marks.

```
set price=$450
if %bSale% (
    set price=$350
    > con echo A 50-inch TV has been marked down from %price% to !price!.
)
```

Listing 16-2: A variable resolved to two distinct values

This makes a great deal of sense intrinsically because both values are in fact a *price*; one is the original price, and the other is the sale price. You could have used two different variables, perhaps `origPrice` and `salePrice`, but coders with a discerning eye might describe Listing 16-2 as elegant, the greatest of all possible praises of its author, especially after seeing the output:

```
A 50-inch TV has been marked down from $450 to $350.
```

This feature allows the imaginative coder many possibilities. You might have a counter or a variable tallying up numbers, both updated inside of a loop. (In the next few chapters, I'll finally get to the for command and looping.) While inside that loop, you might want access to the original counter or tally value for comparison. A data condition in some iterations of the loop might alert you to the fact that the loop shouldn't have been processed. Without this feature, you'll need to execute the loop once for validation and another time for the core logic. With delayed expansion, you'll need only one loop, and at any point you can restore all variables to their original values and abandon the loop.

This does beg the question as to what happens in nested code blocks. Are there three active values for a variable defined inside an if command code block nested inside another if command code block? No. There are exactly two values; one is its value before entering the outermost code block, and the other is its current value inside the code blocks, regardless of the level of nesting.

F. Scott Fitzgerald famously wrote, "The test of a first-rate intelligence is the ability to hold two opposing ideas in mind at the same time and still retain the ability to function." I've insulted the interpreter's intelligence in past chapters, but Batch's ability to function in this duality does suggest that I may have been too harsh. Maybe the interpreter can handle advanced topics, even theoretical physics. The SchrodingersCat variable can simultaneously hold two values: alive and dead.

The Naked Code Block

In the prior examples, I dealt only with variables inside the code block of an if command, but everything previously discussed in this chapter applies to any code block. Remember that a code block is really just one or more commands inside a set of parentheses.

Another example of a code block is the code that comes after the else keyword of an if command. I've already hinted that the for command uses code blocks, and those code blocks can become very complex with nesting and with multiple variables being assigned and reassigned often. That's why this chapter is the final prerequisite to the upcoming discussion on the most significant Batch command. But code blocks don't have to be associated with a command at all.

A *naked code block* is created as its own entity and not associated with a command such as the if or for. For instance, we can rewrite the if command from Listing 16-2 without the if and the conditional clause. The naked code block in Listing 16-3 looks a bit odd at first, but notice that everything is identical except that I have removed the text if %bSale%.

```
set price=$450
(
    set price=$350
    > con echo A 50-inch TV has been marked down from %price% to !price!.
)
```

Listing 16-3: A naked code block where price has two values

This code is still setting the price variable to the original price before entering the code block, where we reset the variable to the sale price.

In the output we see the same text including both prices, with the only difference being that the code always writes the following to the console, because what was conditional logic now executes unconditionally:

```
A 50-inch TV has been marked down from $450 to $350.
```

To truly demonstrate the power of these parentheses, simply remove them and examine the effect. That's exactly what I've done here, and I didn't even realign the indenting, although doing so would have absolutely no effect on the result. Compare this to Listing 16-3:

```
set price=$450
    set price=$350
    > con echo A 50-inch TV has been marked down from %price% to !price!.
```

In practice, this code makes no sense. The fact that we're setting the variable on one line and resetting it on the very next completely obviates the first set command, which might as well be commented out or deleted. The price variable now has a single value, and percent signs and exclamation marks both resolve the variable to its sole value of $350, resulting in the nonsensical output:

```
A 50-inch TV has been marked down from $350 to $350.
```

The set of parentheses had a marked effect on the code listing. They created a naked code block, allowing the variable to have two values, each accessible with different delimiters. Without the parentheses, the code is junk.

When using a naked code block, it's good form to always line up the open and close parentheses in the same column on unadulterated lines with the code in the code block indented as if it followed an if command. You could rewrite Listing 16-3 with the second set command on the same line as the open parenthesis and the close parenthesis trailing the echo command, but doing so would make the code very difficult to read. (I don't even want to show it.) If you're coding a naked code block, there's probably a good reason for it, and if you hide its existence, an elegant solution suddenly turns cryptic.

One good reason for using a naked code block is to swap the values of two variables without an intermediate variable. This code turns fact into fiction and fiction into fact better than any politician:

```
(
    set fact=%fiction%
    set fiction=%fact%
)
```

The first set command is simply resetting the fact variable, but the second set command isn't using this updated value when it resets fiction. Instead, the percent signs resolve fact to its value before entering the naked code block. The interpreter reads and parses both set commands—and resolves both variables—before setting either variable. If you were to remove the parentheses, both variables would take on the value initially defined as fiction, completely defeating the value swap.

Surviving an endlocal Command

Any code block, but specifically the naked code block, has another very useful purpose: allowing a variable to survive an endlocal command. In Chapter 3, you learned that all variables between a setlocal command and an endlocal command will revert to their prior state once the endlocal executes. This wonderful Batch feature ensures that a called routine doesn't step on variables that might be used by the caller, but it raises a very pertinent question. How can that called routine return a result if nothing can survive its endlocal command?

The "Problem" with the endlocal Command

To demonstrate the problem, the routine shown in Listing 16-4 accepts a monetary amount as dollars and cents as its first parameter and attempts to pass back that amount with a 6 percent sales tax added as its second parameter.

```
:AddTax
 setlocal
 set factor=106
 set inAmt=%~1
 set amtNoDec=%inAmt:.=%
 set /A wTaxNoDec = amtNoDec * factor + 50
 set wTaxDec=%wTaxNoDec:~0,-4%.%wTaxNoDec:~-4,2%
❶ set %2=%wTaxDec%
❷ endlocal
 goto :eof
```

Listing 16-4: Some good math wasted

For now, don't get bogged down in the math. (See the "An Arithmetic Digression for My Fellow Math Geeks" box for those details.) Pertinent to this discussion, the :AddTax routine starts with a setlocal command, followed by six set commands. The last set command ❶ assigns the result of the arithmetic to the second parameter, but the endlocal command ❷ immediately wipes it out. Nothing's returned. I'm trying to protect or hide changes to the first five variables from being seen by the code outside of the routine, but I also want to let this last variable through. As of yet, I'm unsuccessful.

After some contemplation, it might make sense to reverse the commands before the goto :eof:

```
endlocal
set %2=%wTaxDec%
goto :eof
```

But alas, that doesn't work either. Now, the wTaxDec variable doesn't survive the endlocal, so this logic most likely sets the return parameter to nothing at all (or whatever value wTaxDec was set to prior to the routine). It's a different manifestation of the same issue; nothing set between the setlocal and the endlocal survives.

AN ARITHMETIC DIGRESSION FOR MY
FELLOW MATH GEEKS

The best way to add 6 percent to an amount is to multiply it by 1.06, but since Batch doesn't intrinsically support floating-point numbers or decimals, I'll ultimately multiply the amount by a factor of 106 and then deal with the skewed place value.

To start, I set the "amount with no decimal point" (amtNoDec) to the input amount (inAmt) with its decimal removed. The set /A command multiplies the two integers to produce the "with tax amount with no decimal" (wTaxNoDec) while adding 50 to the product solely for the sake of rounding. Since both numbers have in essence been multiplied by 100, the product is 10,000 times the actual amount, so adding 50 amounts to adding a mere half cent.

To get the final result of wTaxDec, or the "with tax amount with a decimal," we must essentially divide the prior number by 10,000. Two substrings, one with a length of -4 and the other with an offset of -4, break up the number into two values, four bytes from its end. I then insert a decimal point between the two substrings, while also truncating the last two bytes off the second with a length of 2, thus leaving the result as dollars and cents. If this doesn't look familiar, refer to Chapter 6.

This code assumes the input is formatted just so, and it isn't bullet-proof. The dollar amount must contain exactly two numbers after the decimal denoting the cents, and there mustn't be a leading zero, so 0.99 and anything less than 10 cents won't work. OCTAL!

The Naked Code Block Solution

The simple addition of two parentheses (and some indentation for readability) creates a code block starting with an `endlocal` command—and solves the problem. Compare this to Listing 16-4:

```
:AddTax
 setlocal
 set factor=106
 set inAmt=%~1
 set amtNoDec=%inAmt:.=%
 set /A wTaxNoDec = amtNoDec * factor + 50
 set wTaxDec=%wTaxNoDec:~0,-4%.%wTaxNoDec:~-4,2%
 (
    endlocal
    set %2=%wTaxDec%
 )
 goto :eof
```

The open parenthesis starts the code block. The `endlocal` command wipes out the *current* state of the five variables, returning them to their pre-`setlocal` states. Now it gets interesting. Exclamation marks resolve a variable to its current state inside the code block, but percent signs resolve a variable to its state at the beginning of the code block before the `endlocal` executed. Hence, `!wTaxDec!` resolves to nothing (or junk), but `%wTaxDec%` resolves to the value to which it was assigned just before the code block, and that's the value I'm assigning to the second parameter just before getting out of the routine.

The upshot is that there's a narrow window inside the naked code block—between the `endlocal` and the close parenthesis—where we can resolve these five variables with percent signs. I've capitalized on this window by using percent signs to resolve the only one that I want, assigning its value to the return parameter.

Now we just need to call the routine to see it work:

```
call :AddTax 25.75 result
> con echo The amount with tax is $%result%.
```

The following output shows the 6 percent sales tax successfully added to the original amount:

```
The amount with tax is $27.30.
```

This example sets a parameter being returned by a routine, but a routine isn't a requirement of this technique. At any point in a bat file, you can hide variables by invoking a `setlocal` command. In the following example, two variables, survive and persist, survive the `endlocal` in the code block, but extinct does not:

```
setlocal
set survive=This variable will survive the endlocal
set persist=Multiple variables can survive and persist past the endlocal
set extinct=Time is very short for this variable
(
    endlocal
    set survive=%survive%
    set persist=%persist%
)
```

This code block is similar to the prior example, but there are two pertinent differences. First, it's preserving multiple variables. Second, the set commands look redundant—each variable is being set to its own resolved value. The current value of each variable is null after the endlocal, but the last two set commands are restoring the variable's own values from just before the code block.

This technique is simple yet unintuitive. An endlocal command starts a naked code block, followed by one or more set commands assigning variables, often to themselves. The world outside of the naked code block can now use the shared variables, but not any unshared variables. If you want to do this assignment conditionally, simply place an if command with the conditional clause of your choosing around the set command inside the naked code block.

I must admit that there's an alternative solution for this task not involving the naked code block. Part of me regrets even sharing it, but I will because you might just run across it someday. You can also make these two variables survive an endlocal by replacing the prior naked code block with these three commands on this one very ugly line of code:

```
endlocal&set survive=%survive%&set persist=%persist%
```

Adding a space or two after each command separator (&) might make this a bit more readable, but not nearly enough. Use the naked code block.

Summary

In this chapter, you learned exactly how variables are resolved in code blocks. The next time you hear someone say, "Use exclamation marks inside and percent signs outside of a code block," I hope that you'll have the knowledge to add a little more depth to the conversation. Now that you've learned the nuances concerning delayed expansion and variable resolution in a code block, you won't just manage to make something work; you'll be able to use both values contained in a variable where appropriate. I also introduced the naked code block and demonstrated its crucial role in allowing variables to survive an endlocal command.

Next up is the long-awaited for command. We now have everything in place to explore this greatly important Batch command in Part II.

PART II

THE FOR COMMAND

The for command is easily the most indispensable and cardinal command in all of the Batch coding universe. Loops would be nearly impossible without it, and it comes in a number of forms with many options and keywords to perform varying and diverse tasks. This command commands its very own section of the book that you're now holding.

If the for command had no options at all, it would still be the most powerful command in Batch, and I'll detail this optionless variant in Chapter 17. But the command also sports four incredibly impressive options. In Chapter 18, I'll introduce the options that handle directories, recursion, and iterative loops. In Chapter 19, you'll learn about the file reading option, which is actually a misnomer because it unlocks an awesome amount of functionality far beyond the reading of files. We'll finish up with a discussion on advanced techniques concerning the for command in Chapter 20.

17

FUNDAMENTALS OF THE FOR COMMAND

In this chapter, I'll introduce the for command, in particular, the for command used without any options, which just touches on its overall power. This optionless command creates loops, where the input is zero to many values, either simple text values or filenames. Some call this the *basic* for command, but I chafe at the modifier because there's nothing basic about the for command, even without the options (which I'll discuss in upcoming chapters).

Speaking of modifiers in a totally different context, the syntax for this command allows for several *modifiers*, and you'll learn how to use these modifiers to extract a wealth of information about any file, such as its size, last modified date and time, attributes, and portions of the path and filename. You'll also see a couple detailed real-world applications of the optionless for command as a small demonstration of its power, and I'll start with suggestions on how to build personalized documentation about this important command.

Creating Personalized Documentation

Before getting started in earnest, I highly recommend dumping the help documentation for the for command into a text file for future reference. As you learned in Chapter 12, you can redirect the output for any command to a file, and this is true for the help command:

```
for /? > %userprofile%\OneDrive\Desktop\ForCommand.txt
```

With the use of this path, the command creates the *ForCommand.txt* file on my Windows desktop. You can try it with the *OneDrive* node removed or write it to the folder of your choosing, but the desktop is a handy place for this file. (You'll learn about the userprofile pseudo-environment variable in Chapter 21.)

I haven't suggested that you do this for any other command, and you'll always be able to find the help information at the command prompt, so you might be curious why I'm suggesting it here. It'll eventually become more *self*-documentation (like a digital notebook) than *help*-documentation, as you explore and experiment more with the for command. Some of the documentation isn't the clearest and, as you'll soon see, could really use some annotating. With this file, you can add your own comments and amend the stated syntax so that it makes more sense to you. You can also add examples of the different forms the command can take and include templates that you can retrieve and use later.

Subtle changes in the syntax of the for command will greatly impact its functionality or possibly render it inoperable. As a result, all too often coders will take a stab at a for command. If that doesn't work, they'll take another stab or several, adding a certain keyword, using double quotes around the input, or maybe trying single quotes. They'll eventually find something that works or appears to work. A better way is to understand the intricacies of the command's many forms. Create this personalized documentation and you'll have everything you need to know about the command in one place (other than this book, of course).

The Optionless for Command

Let's start with the optionless for command. The for command can be used with (appropriately enough) four options, and I'll delve into those in the next two chapters, but even when used without options, it's a heavy lifter. The following isn't an actual command but is the general syntax used to execute a loop zero to many times, and it's loosely based on what you'll find in the help documentation:

```
for %%variable in (input) do command
```

The words for, in, and do are reserved words and will appear just as shown here in your for commands. The parentheses also will appear as shown, but what's inside them is one of the three main components of an optionless for. Those components are the for variable (*%%variable*), the input you are feeding into the command (*input*), and the core logic executed in the loop (*command*).

The for Variable

The for variable is central to this command. If the loop executes multiple times, its value changes with each pass. You define the for variable as two percent signs followed by a singular character. Numbers and many special characters are valid, but most coders use letters of the alphabet pretty much universally. Typically, %%i is the variable of choice, where i represents *index*.

Some coders use %%i exclusively as if it was the only allowed for variable, but don't limit yourself. A one-character variable name doesn't allow for a great deal of descriptive potential, but use what's at your disposal. I often use %%f for a *file*, %%c for a *count*, and %%n for a *name* or *number*, although %%# also works for *number*. As with other variable names, many coders use uppercase, but I use lowercase. Do what makes sense to you, and do it consistently.

The Input

The second component of the for command is the input found inside the parentheses or the input you're feeding into the command. It can be a set of filenames, a single filename, a file mask, multiple file masks, hardcoded text, or resolved variables. It'll be a while before I can show you all of those, so for now, just consider it to be the input, starting with a single file. (The help documentation uses set instead of input, as in a *set* of files, but that term is incomplete and easily confused with the command of the same name.)

The Command

Finally, the command is the core logic that executes for each pass of the loop, which can be zero to many times. It can be a single command or many commands spanning several lines of code, and anywhere in that logic you can resolve the for variable to its current value, but this variable is quite different from variables you've seen up to this point. Typically, you resolve variables with percent signs, front and back, but you resolve the for variable as it's defined: prefixed with two percent signs. More plainly, if you define the for variable as %%n, you can resolve it with %%n as part of the command.

Similar to the way Batch accepts parameters, a strategically placed tilde removes any double quotes encasing the variable. With for variables, the tilde comes after the second percent sign and before the variable name—for example, %%~n. As with parameters, if there are no double quotes, the tilde has no effect on the resolution.

In a very surprising twist, the for variable is case-sensitive, which is a notable oddity in the world of Batch. Therefore, %%i isn't the same entity as %%I. In yet another twist, in Chapter 14 you learned to escape a percent sign with another percent sign. This variable also sports double percent signs, but the interpreter is smart enough to differentiate. For instance, if %%i turns out to be a for variable, the interpreter resolves it to its value; if not, the interpreter treats the first character as an escape character and resolves it to the text, %i. Let's put this all together into some examples we can actually execute.

The following for command writes the path and filename to the console:

```
for %%f in (C:\Batch\MyInputFile.txt) do  > con echo Filename is %%f
```

For its three components, I'm choosing %%f for the for variable as shorthand for *file* because the input is a file, *C:\Batch\MyInputFile.txt.* The command component is a single echo command that writes text to the console.

Before long you'll see how the for command can create a loop executing multiple times, but this example executes exactly once, with the variable set to the path and filename inside the parentheses. Moving to the command after the do reserved word, the %%f in the echo command resolves to the input text, which writes the following to the console:

```
Filename is C:\Batch\MyInputFile.txt
```

Notice the two instances of %%f in the line of code, one close to the beginning and a second at the very end. The first defines the for variable, and the second instance uses the variable; that is, the command component resolves it and uses its value.

It's a bit easier to follow if you add parentheses around the echo command, which is also legitimate syntax:

```
for %%f in (C:\Batch\MyInputFile.txt) do  (> con echo Filename is %%f)
```

If the command component contains logic that's at all complex, it's best to rewrite it on multiple lines for the sake of readability.

The following example is functionally equivalent to the two previous examples, but the echo command is now on its own line. With multiple line syntax, the parentheses are required:

```
for %%f in (C:\Batch\MyInputFile.txt) do (
   > con echo Filename is %%f
)
```

The open parenthesis must follow the do reserved word on the same line. That's an important stipulation because other languages allow, and even encourage, the open parenthesis to be on its own line, lined up with the close parenthesis.

This next example demonstrates three additional points about the optionless for command:

```
for %%F in ("C:\Program Files (x86)\Notepad++\notepad++.exe") do (
    > con echo Filename is %%F
    > con echo Filename is %%~F
)
```

First, notice that multiple commands are more than possible in the code block of a for command. Second, I changed the for variable to %%F, just to show that I can make it pretty much any character that I desire, as long as I consistently use %%F or %%~F in the code block (although you won't see me use a capital for this type of variable again). Third, I've encased the input path and filename in double quotes. Embedded spaces, parentheses, and even plus signs are in the path and name of the Notepad++ 32-bit executable, but the interpreter is unfazed because of those double quotes.

To demonstrate that the tilde works as it does with parameters, notice that the double quotes are present in the output from the first echo command using %%F, but not the second using %%~F:

```
Filename is "C:\Program Files (x86)\Notepad++\notepad++.exe"
Filename is C:\Program Files (x86)\Notepad++\notepad++.exe
```

This for command might seem like overkill for a single filename as input because it most definitely is overkill. You could've written these two lines of text to the console far more easily with nothing more than two echo commands. The real benefit of this logic becomes apparent when you use filesets and file masks to execute the loop multiple times, once for each file.

> **NOTE** *The terms for command and for loop are largely interchangeable, but there's a subtle difference. Technically, loops can execute zero to many times, but I often use the term loop when, because of the nature of the input, I'm confident that it will execute multiple times. Conversely, I use command when I know that the logic in the code block will execute exactly once, as in all of the previous examples, but I also use it if there's ambiguity since it's the more general and inclusive term.*

Filesets, File Masks, and Loops

A *fileset* is, as you might expect, a set of files, and the for command accepts a fileset as input as easily as it accepts a single file. Two files delimited by a comma and a space are in the input fileset here, but you can include any realistic number of files:

```
for %%f in (C:\Batch\MyInputFile.txt, C:\AnotherFolder\AnotherFile.dat) do (
    > con echo Filename is %%f
)
```

A comma without the space would also delimit the two files, as would a space without the comma, but both make the code more readable.

Here's the output:

```
Filename is C:\Batch\MyInputFile.txt
Filename is C:\AnotherFolder\AnotherFile.dat
```

This is the first example of a for command transformed into something that executes more than once—that is, something more often called a for loop. The interpreter executes the code block twice because the fileset contains exactly two files. A third file in the fileset would have produced a third line of output.

In Chapter 7, I introduced file masks using wildcards in the context of the xcopy and robocopy commands, and the same rules (and batveats) apply when you create a file mask as the input to a for command. The asterisk stands in for any number of characters, even no characters at all, and the question mark usually represents exactly one character. However, question marks coming at the end of the mask or followed by a dot, can also represent no character at all.

To demonstrate, I'll start with a familiar for command, replacing the filename with the simplest of all masks, a lone asterisk:

```
for %%f in (C:\Batch\*) do (
    > con echo Filename is %%f
)
```

Instead of writing a single filename to the console, the interpreter now outputs every file in the folder, one by one, because every file satisfies the mask. If there are 17 files in *C:\Batch*, all 17 fit the mask, and the interpreter writes a message to the console for all 17. The echo command executes just once if only one file exists in the folder, and it doesn't execute at all if no files exist.

Writing filenames to the console isn't very satisfying, but you can perform far more interesting tasks with file masks. You might rename every file that satisfies a mask, or you might call a compiled program once for each file. Whatever the task, the basic structure of the for loop won't change, and if the logic is going to be at all complex, it's best to set it up in an internal routine. Here's a call command invoking just such a routine for each file, passing the path and filename of each file as the sole argument:

```
for %%f in (C:\Batch\*) do (
    call :SomeComplexTask "%%~f"
)
```

If a dozen files fit this mask, the call command invokes the routine 12 times, once for each file.

Batch even accepts a comma-delimited list of file masks as input to a for command. That is, you can create a fileset containing multiple files and/or file masks.

Simple Text as Input

Another intriguing use of the optionless for command isn't found in the help. You can process a list of values one by one by entering them inside the parentheses as the input. The same set of characters that Batch uses for delimiting passed arguments also delimits this list, so you can use commas, semicolons, equal signs, and tab characters, but a space-delimited list is the norm. The syntax is similar to several previous examples, but with the delimited text replacing the filename or mask. For example, this for loop sequentially passes each of the five words in the parentheses to the code block:

```
for %%i in (Individual line for each word) do (
    > con echo %%i
)
```

The result sees each word written to the console on individual lines:

```
Individual
line
for
each
word
```

Notice that Batch treats the for inside the parentheses as simple text and not as the reserved word that starts the command. I've taken some shots at the interpreter, but it's smart enough to recognize the difference contextually.

The prior input list is space-delimited, but the interpreter treats anything encased in double quotes as a single value, meaning that the following for command executes its code block exactly twice:

```
for %%i in ("Just two lines for" "these seven words") do (
    > con echo %%~i
)
```

The result is these two lines of output to the console, not seven:

```
Just two lines for
these seven words
```

Notice that the use of a tilde when resolving the for variable, %%~i, removes the double quotes from each string.

These simple examples belie the immense usefulness of the technique. To illustrate, I'll start with a bat file that accepts a single parameter for some sort of processing. The process isn't important here; maybe the passed value is added to a data structure, or maybe it's a filename passed to a called executable. Whatever the process, the point is that if I have 17 items to process, I must call the bat file 17 times. But with this technique of using a list as input to a for command, I can enhance the bat file so that it'll accept any number of these parameters and process them one by one in a single execution.

I'll start by putting the logic for processing a single parameter into a callable routine defined by the `:ProcessParm` label. Now I can call that routine zero to many times with this code at the top of my bat file:

```
for %%i in (%*) do (
   call :ProcessParm %%i
)
goto :eof
```

I've entered `%*` into the parentheses as the input of the for command. (Remember from Chapter 11 that these two bytes expand to the entire parameter list as received by the bat file.)

If there are 99 parameters, all 99 values become the input to the for command, and the interpreter executes the body of the loop 99 times. In its first pass, `%%i` resolves to the first parameter in the list and is the argument passed to the routine in the call command. After the first pass completes, the second parameter becomes the argument for the second pass, and so on, until the interpreter processes all 99 parameters.

Other uses for this technique abound. For instance, you can easily sum up a space-delimited list of numbers. I haven't introduced arrays yet, but this offers a great means of adding multiple values to an array.

Retrieving File Information

The optionless for command has one more awesome feature. It can retrieve copious amounts of information and data about a file, such as its size, last modified date/time, and much more. Earlier in this chapter, I discussed using the technique of passing a filename into a for loop for the unimpressive purpose of simply writing the path and filename to the console. For example:

```
for %%f in ("C:\Program Files (x86)\Notepad++\notepad++.exe") do (
   > con echo Filename is %%~f
)
```

Let's turn that into something impressive. Instead of just regurgitating a path and filename, the code will retrieve and write out an abundance of information about the file. If the file has something to hide, we'll expose it. The only changes I'll eventually make to the code in the previous example is to the code block associated with the for command, but first I must introduce modifiers.

Modifiers

The tools for extracting this bevy of useful data about a file are called *modifiers*, and 9 out of 10 of them are a single alpha character strategically inserted into the for variable as it's being resolved. (I'll get to the 10th one soon.)

To use a modifier, start with a for variable such as %%f. Then insert a tilde and the modifier character after the two percent signs and before the one-character variable name. For instance, X is the modifier for retrieving a file's extension, meaning that for the for variable, %%f, the interpreter resolves %%~Xf to the extension.

The following code block now has 11 echo commands. The first two are nothing new; they both display the path and filename, the first with the double quotes in place and the second with them removed. The nine other echo commands use a specific modifier to, understandably enough, modify the %%f variable:

```
for %%f in ("C:\Program Files (x86)\Notepad++\notepad++.exe") do (
    > con echo                    Filename = %%f
    > con echo      Filename Without Quotes = %%~f
    > con echo Fully Qualified Path Name = %%~Ff
    > con echo            Drive Letter Only = %%~Df
    > con echo                   Path Only = %%~Pf
    > con echo               Filename Only = %%~Nf
    > con ccho          File Extension Only = %%~Xf
    > con echo              Short Name Only = %%~Sf
    > con echo              File Attributes = %%~Af
    > con echo          File Date and Time = %%~Tf
    > con echo                   File Size = %%~Zf
)
```

I've documented each of the nine modifiers in the code itself.

Executing this code might write the following text to the console. Carefully examine the impact of each modifier on the output:

```
                Filename = "C:\Program Files (x86)\Notcpad++\notepad++.exe"
 Filename Without Quotes = C:\Program Files (x86)\Notepad++\notepad++.exe
Fully Qualified Path Name = C:\Program Files (x86)\Notepad++\notepad++.exe
       Drive Letter Only = C:
               Path Only = \Program Files (x86)\Notepad++\
           Filename Only = notepad++
     File Extension Only = .exe
         Short Name Only = C:\PROGRA~2\NOTEPA~1\NOTEPA~1.EXE
         File Attributes = --a--------
     File Date and Time = 03/11/2010 01:23 PM
               File Size = 2958480
```

That's quite a bit of data. Starting with the third line, the F modifier gives us the fully qualified pathname. Often, %%~Ff resolves to the same value as %%~f as it does here, but not always. If the input consists of a filename and extension without a path and if the interpreter finds the file in the current directory, then %%~f mimics the input without the path, but %%~Ff resolves to the full path and filename.

Next, you can see the individual components of this fully qualified pathname in the next four modifiers: D (drive letter with the colon), P (path or directory without the drive letter), N (bare filename—that is, without the extension), and the aforementioned X (file extension, including the preceding dot).

The S modifier generates the short filename defined by the operating system (I promised I'd show you how to find this in Chapter 7), while the A modifier generates a list of file attributes. A file has 11 possible attributes, and if the file doesn't have a particular attribute, the corresponding byte is a dash. The only attribute that pops in this list is a, meaning that the file is archived, but the lack of other values indicates that the file isn't hidden, compressed, read only, or characterized by any of the other possible attributes. (I'll discuss attributes more in Chapter 30.)

Finally, the T modifier provides the date and time when the file was last modified, and the Z modifier returns the file size in bytes. (Remember that S is taken.) The lack of commas makes it hard to read, but you can see from the output that the file is nearly 3MB.

NOTE   *Unless you've jumped directly to this portion of the book, you know that I'm not a fan of the overuse of capitalization, but everything has its place. The modifiers are case-insensitive, but I use uppercase to make them stand out. The lowercase for variable, which in this case is f for file, terminates what's to be resolved, but I know that I'm in the minority. Be aware that most coders do just the opposite, so you're more likely to see %%~zI to get the file size of %%I than my %%~Zf used to get the size of %%f.*

The applications of modifiers are boundless, but one simple use is to execute some sort of complex task for a file, but only if the file has data in it. Say the Batch code is to process a data file coming from another source. Even if the source has no data to report, it's best for it to create an empty file, because no file at all would leave the specter of a failed process. To make this work, the bat file needs to determine whether the file is empty or populated. Consider this:

```
for %%f in ("C:\Batch\IntermediateFile.dat") do (
    if %%~Zf gtr 0  call :SomeComplexTask "%%~Ff"
)
```

The if command inside the for command efficiently (and maybe even elegantly) verifies that the size of an intermediate data file, %%~Zf, is greater than 0 bytes before calling a routine and passing it the path and name of the file.

The path Modifier

I owe you a 10th modifier, and just in case you haven't found this syntax convoluted enough, the syntax for the path modifier is completely different from the other nine. But that's not a problem, because its function is also completely different. I'll explain what it does momentarily, but first understand that this modifier is actually an oddly delimited variable. While the other modifiers are each a single character, the path modifier is a variable name preceded by a dollar sign and trailed by a colon.

To set this up, and for reasons that will soon become obvious, let's use the path variable in the modifier (the same variable containing a concatenation of semicolon-delimited directories introduced in Chapter 8). The variable should already be set on your machine, but you can append and prepend additional directories to it:

```
path C:\Batch\SubDir\;C:\Batch\;%path%C:\Budget\;
```

To see this modifier in action, let's modify the %%f variable with the %%~$path:f syntax. Notice the path variable, sandwiched between the $ and : characters; all three pieces make up the modifier. Now we can use it in a for command:

```
for %%f in (FourBrits.txt) do (
    > con echo File Found: %%~$path:f
)
```

What's this modifier's actual function? It instructs the interpreter to traverse the path variable, starting from its first listed directory, looking for the first, and only the first, file named *FourBrits.txt*. If the file exists in the second directory in our path variable, but not the first, the resulting output contains the fully qualified path and filename:

```
File Found: C:\Batch\FourBrits.txt
```

If the interpreter can't find a file named *FourBrits.txt* in any of the directories defined in the path variable, it simply resolves %%~$path:f to null.

This functionality was clearly designed for the path variable, and the help documentation explicitly uses the path variable in its example; only near the bottom does it mention that you can replace it with any valid variable, meaning any variable containing a list of directories. Even so, this is usually referred to simply as the *path* modifier and used nearly exclusively with the path variable.

Stacked Modifiers

Used individually the modifiers are very helpful, but their real power becomes apparent when you stack multiple modifiers—that is, when used together to resolve more than one file characteristic at a time. For instance, you can resolve the filename and extension separately and then concatenate them as %%~Nf%%~Xf, but that's a tad bit messy. Instead, %%~NXf sublimely produces the identical result more elegantly. Here are three typical examples:

```
for %%f in ("C:\Batch\FourBrits.txt") do (
    > con echo  Drive Letter and Path = %%~DPf
    > con echo Filename and Extension = %%~NXf
    > con echo     File Date/Time/Size = %%~TZf bytes
)
```

This code might write the following to the console:

```
Drive Letter and Path = C:\Batch\
Filename and Extension = FourBrits.txt
    File Date/Time/Size = 04/20/2018 01:14 PM 518 bytes
```

With stacked modifiers you can easily retrieve the full path of a file without the filename, or just the filename and extension without the path. The last example might look good on a report with the hardcoded text, bytes, at the end.

Stacked modifiers even work with the path modifier:

```
for %%f in (FourBrits.txt) do (
    > con echo Path Found: %%~DP$path:f
)
```

This code writes out the full path, sans the filename and extension, of the first file found in the path hierarchy named *FourBrits.txt*.

Parameters with Modifiers

Before getting into a couple of real-world examples, I'll return to a discussion on parameters from Chapter 11. It turns out that the modifiers that extract file information in the context of for commands work equally well on parameters.

I had mentioned that you can pass filenames, with or without their paths, as arguments to a bat file and that the called bat file can resolve them with %~1, %~2, and so on. Also, you can resolve %~0 to the full path and filename of the bat file being executed. Well, the same modifiers (and stacked modifiers) just discussed also apply to any parameter that represents a file. Assume that the following code receives the names of two files as its first two parameters:

```
> con echo          Size of File #1 = %~Z1
> con echo  Date and Time of File #2 = %~T2
```

The first command writes out the size in bytes of the first file, and the second command writes out the last modified date and time of the second file.

Attach two specific stacked modifiers to the hidden parameter, and %~DP0 resolves to the drive letter and path of the bat file being executed. With this information, you can create a subdirectory, deposit other files in this or sibling directories, or update a logfile associated with the bat file, and you can do this without knowing where the bat file will eventually be installed. Maybe it will live on multiple servers.

Modifiers allow you to retrieve a great deal of file information with minimal keystrokes.

Real-World Applications

Let's put all of the useful tools that you've just learned in this chapter to use in two real-world examples.

Renaming Files on a Backup

With the use of a file mask, the optionless for command can generate a list of files, and the modifiers can extract the individual components of the path and filename of each. Combining both of those features, you can copy a set of files to a mirror folder structure on another drive, all while tweaking the target filenames.

Assume that I have a folder called *C:\Budget* that unsurprisingly contains budget information. The name certainly suggests a directory that should be backed up, perhaps to an external *D:* drive, but with the exact same folder structure so that the files are easy to find and compare. To complicate matters, I'd like to prepend the name of every file with Bkup_, because when both folders are open, it's far too easy to work in the wrong one, but not if every file in the backup directory starts with this unique and descriptive text. One way to accomplish this task is with a single command inside a for loop (although in the real-real-world, you'll want some error handling):

```
for %%f in ("C:\Budget\*.*") do (
    echo f | xcopy "%%~Ff" "D:%%~PfBkup_%%~NXf" /Y /F
)
```

I've encased both the source and destination in double quotes to accommodate the possibility of embedded spaces in a filename. The source is the fully qualified path and filename, %%~Ff, but the destination is a bit more esoteric. While it might look like random keystrokes, it's really a concatenation of four items that become more readable when I bolded the two for variables using modifiers in contrast to the constants:

```
D:%%~PfBkup_%%~NXf
```

The destination path starts with the hardcoded drive letter and a colon, D:, followed by the path of the source file variable without the drive letter, %%~Pf; this mimics the source folder from the original drive. The path starts and ends with a backslash, so what comes next, Bkup_, is the start of the filename. To complete the target filename, the interpreter finds a second for variable, %%~NXf, this one having stacked modifiers for the source filename (N) and file extension (X).

Putting it all together, if the interpreter finds a file named *C:\Budget\ Budget.January2023.xlsx*, the resulting destination string is:

```
D:\Budget\Bkup_Budget.January2023.xlsx
```

Where the variable names start and end can be confusing if you're used to Batch variables that are delimited by percent signs. When the compiler sees %%~, it knows that it's about to resolve a for variable—that's the start. Because the variable defined by this for command is %%f, the interpreter terminates the variable when it finds a lowercase f—that's the end. In between the start and end, the interpreter looks for zero to a few valid modifiers. Anything after its termination could be constants, a single percent sign starting the resolution of a more traditional Batch variable, or another for variable.

Each and every file in the source directory matching the mask is copied to the backup path on the *D:* drive with the name of the destination file tweaked. This tool is very powerful with a lot going on inside an apparently modest for command, but to harness that power, a deep understanding of the syntax is a must.

Processing a Variable Number of Files

At the end of Chapter 11, I introduced the concept of a *wrapper* bat file— that is, a bat file that does little more than execute a program designed to process a single input file. The bat file is a wrapper around the executable. Also in that chapter, I demonstrated how to drag and drop multiple files onto a bat file, resulting in one execution of the bat file with multiple arguments. As impressive as that is, it's of little use without a bat file that not only can handle all of those parameters but can do so for a variable number of parameters.

In this chapter, I've discussed two important concepts that are applicable to building such a wrapper bat file. One is the immensely useful technique of using modifiers on a parameter to extract file information, and the other is the for command's ability to process a list of values.

Now, for the setup. I've created a compiled program to convert Java code to C# code, and it accepts two arguments: the input file followed by the output file. Code conversion programs can help minimize the pain of updating old code to a newer language. A module of one language is the input to the program that converts much of the original syntax to another language, outputting a file of the same name but with a different extension in the same folder. From the perspective of the bat file, it accepts one to many *.java* files as parameters, determines the path and filename of the corresponding *.cs* output files, and invokes the compiled code with those two arguments—and the *.java* files can be in any folder.

The following bat file, stripped of all error handling and comments, does everything desired. The for command accepts the entire list of parameters as %*, passing them one by one into the code block as %%f, which in turn is the sole argument passed to the :ConvOneFile routine:

```
for %%f in (%*) do (
    call :ConvOneFile %%f
)
goto :eof
```

```
:ConvOneFile
ConvJava2CS.exe   %~F1   %~DPN1.cs
goto :eof
```

When invoking *ConvJava2CS.exe*, this Batch code passes it two arguments, the input and output files, respectively. I'm retrieving the fully qualified name of the input file with %~F1, which is the first parameter with the F modifier. The output path and filename, %~DPN1.cs, is more complex. I'm using the same parameter, namely, %~1, but with the modifiers for the drive (D), path (P), and filename (N)—that is, %~F1 without the extension denoted by the X modifier. Then I tack on the new extension with the hardcoded .cs to create the output filename. Notice that a single percent sign, not two, is leading these variables, because these are parameters, not for variables; I'm calling the executable from inside a routine, not inside the for command.

A critic (or maybe someone not versed in Batch) might balk at this, arguing that it's better or easier to accept a single parameter into the compiled code and do the manipulation of the filename in the program. But this approach is inflexible; if someone else wanted to run this process on scores or even hundreds of files, they might want the output dropped into a subfolder, or even a folder on another server. By manipulating the filenames in the Batch code, dropping the output into a subdirectory doesn't require a change to the compiled code; instead, simply change %~DPN1.cs to %~DP1%subDir%\%~N1.cs. You could define a hardcoded subdirectory, but here I'm using subDir as the variable for the subdirectory node. You can even execute an md command with %~DP1%subDir%\ as its argument to create the subdirectory if it doesn't already exist.

There's always overhead with changes to compiled code, even simple ones. You have to run the compiler and take care to keep the source and executable in sync. Whenever possible, coders should make simple changes, such as deriving file connectors or filenames, in the Batch code, in my humble opinion at least.

You can now use this bat file to process multiple files or a single file or even no files. If no arguments are passed, the for command has no input, and the code block never executes. Once again, just a few lines of code are doing much more than first meets the eye.

Resolving Variables in Code Blocks

Before moving forward with all of the functionality and power that you can unlock from the for command with options, I must mention that up to this point I've resolved variables for a single use inside of a code block associated with a for command, but this is hopelessly simplistic and naive. It's far more common to assign a piece of data to a variable and then use it, and maybe even modify it, all inside a complex code block. This is the same type of code block detailed in Chapter 16, and the same rules concerning how to resolve variables apply.

For example, you might want two distinct fields for a file's date and time, but the T modifier resolves them as a single value, and that isn't an issue at all with this code:

```
for %%f in ("C:\Program Files (x86)\Notepad++\notepad++.exe") do (
    set filDtTm=%%~Tf
    > con echo                    File Date = !filDtTm:~0,10!
    > con echo                    File Time = !filDtTm:~11!
)
```

At the top of the code block, I assign the entire string to the filDtTm variable and then substring out the date and time on the next two lines, respectively. This is a fine yet crucial point: I'm using exclamation marks and delayed expansion to resolve the variable just set inside the code block. Percent sign delimiters would've resolved this to the value of filDtTm prior to the code block, and since it's unlikely to have been set at all, the results probably would've been garbage (~0,10 and ~11).

Ultimately, if you assign a value to a variable inside a code block, you must use exclamation marks to retrieve its current value. If the logic gets overly complex, there are other techniques, and in Chapter 20, I'll demonstrate how to make full use of delayed expansion inside these more complex code blocks. But as a rule, understand that these variables have two possible values and do your best to not overcomplicate the code.

Summary

In this chapter, I detailed the optionless for command, its components, how it works with filesets and file masks, and how to retrieve a great deal of file information with modifiers. You learned that this command usually accepts a file or files as input, but it can also accept a string of text. I hope you found the real-world applications interesting and informative and that they encouraged you to think about other pertinent uses for this important command. I also included some pointers on how to resolve variables defined in the code block of the for command.

The remaining chapters of Part II will reveal much more, all of which will be needed to appreciate the panorama of the for command. In the next chapter, I'll discuss some functionality that's opened up with options; one enumerates directories instead of files, one traverses subdirectories looking for files, and the last implements a crucial bit of functionality: an iterative loop.

18

DIRECTORIES, RECURSION, AND ITERATIVE LOOPS

Many Batch commands have options, but most offer a slightly different flavor or tweak on the command. The options of the for command are a completely different story. The four available options impact the for command in four distinct ways. In this chapter, I'll detail three of them, and the fourth will follow in the next, requiring its very own chapter.

One option changes the focus of the command from files to directories, and another uses recursion to traverse subdirectories looking for files. You'll also learn how those two options used together can traverse a directory tree looking for subdirectories.

The last option in this chapter morphs the for command into something unlike anything that I've yet discussed. Its functionality has little in common with the optionless for command or the command with its other options. It creates an iterative loop, executing logic as it increments or decrements an index or counter by a fixed amount from one number to another. This tool is nothing less than an absolute necessity for any coder.

The Directory Option

Not all of the option letters are descriptive of their function, but the /D option stands for *directory*. While the optionless for command enumerates through a list of filenames, the /D option allows the command to enumerate through a list of directories or folders. The general syntax shows that other than the insertion of the option, it's unchanged from its optionless cousin:

```
for /D %%variable in (input) do command
```

Before using the option, here is an example reminiscent of the prior chapter, an optionless for command sporting a sole wildcard character for the filename after a path:

```
for %%f in (C:\Budget\*) do (
   > con echo Filename is %%f
)
```

The resulting output includes the path and filename of every file in the folder written to the console.

In the following example, I'm making two tweaks to the optionless for loop: one important and one cosmetic. The important addition is the insertion of the /D option before the for variable. Notice that the rest of the for command itself is completely unchanged. The cosmetic tweak is that I'm replacing the word File with Directory in the echo command:

```
for /D %%f in (C:\Budget\*) do (
   > con echo Directory Name is %%f
)
```

Another possible change to this code could include the replacement of %%f with %%d for *directory* (but I'm trying not to complicate this example).

The files in this folder that were displayed without the /D option are no longer part of the output. Now the interpreter writes every directory immediately under *C:\Budget* to the console, perhaps:

```
Directory Name is C:\Budget\BankStatements
Directory Name is C:\Budget\CreditCardStatements
```

This output assumes that these are the only two subdirectories, but any subdirectories of those subdirectories aren't listed in the output.

The Recursion Option

Another useful option is /R, which conveniently stands for *recursion*. This option empowers the for command to search recursively through a directory and all its subdirectories (and their subdirectories, and so on) for files fitting a mask. Compared to the syntax of the optionless command, its generic syntax differs by more than the option itself:

```
for /R [[drive:]path] %%variable in (input) do command
```

The most significant difference is that the path to be searched now comes before the for variable. The interpreter is unfazed if you omit the trailing slash, but it's good form to include it to make clear that it's a path. The path can be as little as a drive letter followed by a colon, and you'll need encasing double quotes for any embedded spaces. Inside the parentheses, the input will be one or more space- or comma-delimited masks of filenames without paths. For example, the following searches the *C:\Budget* directory and all of its subdirectories for Word documents, writing all that are found to the console:

```
for /R C:\Budget\ %%w in (*.docx) do (
    > con echo Word Document Name is %%w
)
```

The following for command finds those misplaced photos from your trip to Italy, or at least any file with a *.jpg* or *.bmp* extension, and a filename starting with *Italy*. Because of the /R option, the command looks not just in the root *C:* folder but everywhere on your *C:* drive as well:

```
for /R C:\ %%p in (Italy*.jpg, Italy*.bmp) do (
    > con echo Photo from the Italy Trip is %%p
)
```

(Multiple file masks work in all for commands, regardless of the options or lack of options.)

The for /R command has a couple other variants. The hard brackets surrounding the drive and path in the general syntax mean that they are optional, and if omitted, the current directory is assumed. Hence, the previous command is functionally equivalent to the following since *C:* is the current directory:

```
cd C:\
for /R %%p in (Italy*.jpg, Italy*.bmp) do (
    > con echo Photo from the Italy Trip is %%p
)
```

In both examples, %%p resolves to the fully qualified path and filename for each found photo.

In an odd and subtle batveat, all inputs to a for /R command must contain at least one wildcard character. If you use an explicit filename (or any text without an asterisk or question mark) as input in the prior command, it returns *C:* and all of its subdirectories followed by your filename, even if the file doesn't exist in the directories. To find an explicit filename, you must add a wildcard character somewhere in the filename input. I recommend a trailing asterisk because it usually runs the least risk of accidentally capturing additional files.

NOTE *For better or worse, the interpreter handles the recursion itself, or the stepping into each subfolder, hiding it from you. In Chapter 23, I'll return to recursion and explain how to define the actual recursive call, opening up many possibilities.*

Directory Recursion

If the /D option allows for directory searches and the /R option allows for recursive file searches, you might expect that they can be used together for recursive directory searches, and you would be correct. The format follows the general syntax of the /R form of the command with /D coming before /R and with nothing but an asterisk for the input in the parentheses:

```
for /D /R C:\Budget\ %%d in (*) do (
    > con echo Directory is %%d
)
```

Running this code displays all subdirectories of *C:\Budget* and all of their subdirectories, and so on. For instance, assuming that two particular subdirectories and one sub-subdirectory exist, this is the output:

```
Directory is C:\Budget\SubDir
Directory is C:\Budget\Taxes
Directory is C:\Budget\SubDir\SubSubDir
```

In a curious oddity, the for /R command alone can perform this same functionality without the /D option, or at least something really similar. To demonstrate, I've taken the previous for command and made two small tweaks. I've removed the /D option and changed the input from an asterisk to a dot:

```
for /R C:\Budget\ %%d in (.) do (
    > con echo Directory is %%d
)
```

It's far from intuitive, but the dot inside the parentheses instructs the for /R command to enumerate directories instead of files. (Directory and dot both start with D, if that helps.) This also produces a list of subdirectories, but notice three peculiar differences:

```
Directory is C:\Budget\.
Directory is C:\Budget\SubDir\.
```

```
Directory is C:\Budget\SubDir\SubSubDir\.
Directory is C:\Budget\Taxes\.
```

When you use the /R option with the dot as input, the first difference is that the interpreter now enumerates the root directory, in this instance *C:\Budget*, as well as the subdirectories. Second, it returns each directory with a trailing backslash followed by a dot, and third, it sorts the output differently, processing subdirectories of a directory before processing its sibling directories. Notice that when using the /D and /R options in tandem with an asterisk, the interpreter processed *C:\Budget\Taxes* before *C:\Budget\ SubDir\SubSubDir*, just the opposite of the results with the /R option with the dot.

WARNING *Everything I've detailed about the dot as input to the* for */R command is exactly what the help would have you believe, but it isn't entirely true. The dot at the end of each line of output is just a reproduction of the input. This is another manifestation of the batveat mentioned in the prior section. Any input without a wildcard character tells the command to step through all subdirectories, appending each with that input. The dot nicely terminates each directory in the prior example, but if you instead use a tilde as the input, the resulting directories in the output all end with a tilde, not a dot.*

The differences in the output are subtle and, depending on your application, inconsequential, but they're differences, nonetheless.

The Iterative Loop Option

The /L option turns the for command into an iterative loop, an essential item in any coder's toolkit and possibly the most used variant of the command. The loops I've discussed up to this point have enumerated through a list of files, directories, or text of some sort. However, this option turns the for command into a loop that increments or decrements by some numerical value or step from one number to another with a fixed ending value. Most coding languages implement iterative loops in some fashion. In fact, many also have a command called for specifically for this purpose. Batch is unique in that the for command does so much else.

The general syntax to turn the command into an iterative loop is:

```
for /L %%variable in (start, step, end) do command
```

Other than the addition of the /L option, the only other difference between this and the optionless for command is the data inside of the parentheses, where three comma-delimited numbers now make up the input. The first is the *start*, or beginning index; the second is the *step*, or the amount by which that index increments for each iteration of the loop; and the last is the *end*, or last possible value the index can take.

To demonstrate, this for /L loop starts with the value 1, each iteration steps by 2, and it ends at 3:

```
for /L %%i in (1, 2, 3) do  > con echo Index is %%i
```

This command sets the for variable, %%i, to 1 during the first iteration of the loop; then it increments or steps by 2 so that %%i resolves to 3 the second time through. That matches the ending value, so the loop doesn't execute again. Here's the output to the console:

```
Index is 1
Index is 3
```

The following for command starts with the variable set to 10 and then increments by 1 up to 12:

```
for /L %%i in (10, 1, 12) do  > con echo Index is %%i
```

This iterates through the indices of 10, 11, and 12.

To decrement the index, assign a negative value to the step:

```
for /L %%i in (2, -1, 0) do  > con echo Index is %%i
```

This results in the index descending from 2 to 0:

```
Index is 2
Index is 1
Index is 0
```

All three of the numerical inputs can be negative:

```
for /L %%i in (-1, -3, -7) do  > con echo Index is %%i
```

This for loop executes for these three indices:

```
Index is -1
Index is -4
Index is -7
```

Given the following start and step values, it's clear that the for command generates an increasing sequence of positive multiples of 10, starting with 10:

```
for /L %%i in (10,10,35) do  > con echo Index is %%i
```

What's less clear is exactly where the sequence ends. The end value of 35 isn't a multiple of 10, so it isn't in the sequence, but once the index is greater than 35, the loop ends, so 30 is the last number in the sequence. The command would've been functionally equivalent if the end value had been

30, 39, or any integer in between, but for clarity, 30 would've been the best option. Also, notice that I omitted the spaces after the commas in the `input`. I usually include the spaces for readability, but this example demonstrates that they aren't needed (and easily forgotten).

Power Function Routine

Unfortunately, Batch doesn't support the power function. In Chapter 6, I mentioned that we could write a short routine for the task, and here is the promised routine, which uses an iterative loop. It accepts three parameters: the base of the exponential, the exponent, and the name of the return variable containing the result:

```
:Pow
 set %3=1
 for /L %%i in (1, 1, %2) do   set /A %3 *= %1
 goto :eof
```

(If the return parameter has you bamboozled, return to Chapter 11.)

I'm initializing the return parameter to 1. Then the loop starts at 1, increments by 1, and increases up to the value of the exponent or the second parameter. Hence, the loop executes n times if the exponent is n. The command inside the loop multiplies the return parameter by the base of the exponential or the first parameter. Hence, if the base is b, this for loop multiples together n copies of b. When the loop is done, the return parameter contains b^n, and the routine ends.

To find 5^3, call the routine passing these three arguments:

```
call :Pow 5 3 pow
> con echo Five cubed = %pow%
```

The code multiplies 3 copies of 5 and writes Five cubed = 125 to the console.

A Case Study

As a seven-year-old mathematical prodigy in the late 18th century, the great mathematician Carl Friedrich Gauss received, along with the rest of his class, some busywork from the teacher. The students were to add up all of the numbers from 1 to 100. Moments later, the teacher looked up and saw all of the children busily adding with their chalk and slate, except for one. He approached the young Gauss, preparing a stern reprimand, only to notice the correct answer of 5,050 written on the boy's piece of slate.

Gauss had realized that there were 50 pairs of numbers adding up to 101 ($100 + 1, 99 + 2, \ldots, 51 + 50$). He quickly multiplied 50 by 101, wrote down the answer, and sat back waiting for his peers to finish, probably wondering what was taking them so long.

There are other variations of this story, and it may be apocryphal, but if any of those other students had had access to a Windows computer, they may have been able to complete the task even before the young genius—that is, if they could have quickly typed the following:

```
set sum=0
for /L %%i in (1, 1, 100) do (
    set /A sum += %%i
)
> con echo The sum is %sum%.
```

This loop iterates the %%i index from 1 to 100, where the set /A command tallies up all of the indices. Before the loop, the set command explicitly initializes sum to 0, thus guaranteeing that the final result is the desired value. Gauss's tech-savvy classmates could've then rewritten the output The sum is 5050. on their pieces of slate in a time comparable to Gauss himself.

AN ARITHMETIC DIGRESSION FOR MY
FELLOW MATH GEEKS

As a further mathematical digression, what would have transpired if Gauss had had Batch like his theoretical classmate? He realized that to add the numbers 1 through *n*, he needed to multiply one-half of *n* by one more than *n*. I'm sure that he would have looked for a more generic and efficient solution. With this in mind, would he have used the following code instead of the for loop?

```
set n=100
set /A sum = (n / 2) * (n + 1)
```

Probably not; this arithmetic and code looks straightforward, and this particular example would've worked great—for this particular value of *n*. But in general, for any positive value of *n*, this logic would've worked only half of the time.

The beauty of Gauss' elegant solution is that it works for all positive integers, including odd and even numbers alike. The sum of the numbers 1 through 9 is equal to the product of 4.5 and 10, or 45. Gauss surely would've noticed that the arithmetic in the previous code would've failed for odd numbers because Batch doesn't intrinsically support floating-point arithmetic. The interpreter considers 9/2 to be 4, not 4.5. This truncation of the decimal part essentially rounds down the intermediate arithmetic, resulting in an incorrect result.

Even at such a young age, I'm sure that Gauss was too smart and driven to leave this solution unfinished. (This has absolutely nothing to do with my own compulsion to not leave a solution half-solved.) It isn't elegant, but adding (n %% 2) * (n + 1) / 2 to the prior expression adds back exactly what was lost by the truncation:

```
set /A sum = (n / 2) * (n + 1) + (n %% 2) * (n + 1) / 2
```

The result of the modulo is 1 for odd numbers, thus adding back half of $n + 1$. For even numbers, the modulo is 0, thus not contributing erroneously to the already correct result. This solution works for all positive integers—and all eras.

Summary

In this chapter, you learned about three options of the for command. The /D option allows the command to enumerate through directories instead of files, and the /R option uses recursion to traverse subdirectories. I even demonstrated two methods of recursively enumerating directories.

You also learned how to create an iterative loop with the /L option and all of its facets. I used the for command with this option to create a routine for raising one number to another, and I even got in a quick mathematical history lesson and a little Batch arithmetic.

That leaves one option left, and you'll learn all about it in the next chapter. It allows for the reading of files and much more

19

READING FILES AND OTHER INPUTS

By far the most involved syntax and powerful functionality of the already powerful for command is unleashed with the /F option, which allows for *file reading*. The optionless for command can do quite a bit with a file such as getting its name, path, drive, size, and attributes, pretty much everything concerning a file except its actual contents. Enter the /F option.

After introducing its syntax, I'll demonstrate how to read a file, record by record. You'll learn how to manipulate the input data, place the entire contents of a record into a variable, or break it into what Batch calls tokens. By tokenizing the data, you'll be able to extract just the portions of data you desire.

Although the for /F command ostensibly reads files, the input can take on other forms. This command can treat a string as a single record file, and you can even use the output from another Batch command as its input. All of this will allow you to manipulate and process different forms of information in many different ways.

The for Command with the /F Option

The /F option transforms the for command into a multifaceted tool for reading files. This command with this particular option has multiple forms, but I'll start by considering just one. Here's the general syntax of the form or variant of the for /F command that reads a file or a set of files:

```
for /F ["suboptions"] %%variable in (file-set) do command
```

In comparison to the optionless for command, this syntax is quite different. Most obviously, the /F option is in place. I've also changed the generic *input* placeholder inside the parentheses to the more specific term of *file-set*, but that's little more than nomenclature. In comparison to the optionless version of the command, this variant accepts only a file, a file mask, or multiple files or file masks.

The most significant difference is the addition of the ["suboptions"] clause. The square brackets indicate that these suboptions are themselves optional, but if you include them, encase them in double quotes. Each of the possible *suboptions* is denoted with its own specific keyword. I'll discuss one of them, usebackq, later in this chapter, but the others have a direct impact on how you will read and manipulate the data.

Reading the Contents of a File

The keywords tokens, delims, skip, and eol might not roll easily off the tongue, but they're instrumental elements of the *suboptions* clause, which controls the reading of files. The best way to see what they do is to explore the behavior of the for /F command without options and then add in the clauses associated with these four keywords one by one to demonstrate their usefulness.

Let's return to the introduction of the for command in Chapter 17 where I briefly worked with a file named *FourBrits.txt* but said nothing about its contents. For this demonstration, assume that it's a small file of four records. Each record has five elements, the first being a language and the remainder being four particular male names as they are written in that language. The spaces or tabs delimit the elements, and here are the complete contents of the file:

```
English   John      Paul    George    Richard
Spanish   Juan      Pablo   Jorge     Ricardo
French    Jean      Pol     Georges   Richard
Italian   Giovanni  Paolo   Giorgio   Riccardo
```

Consider this for command:

```
for %%a in (C:\Batch\FourBrits.txt) do (
    > con echo %%a
)
```

The output is exactly what you'd now expect: a single line of data displaying the path and filename of the input file:

```
C:\Batch\FourBrits.txt
```

To demonstrate the new option, I'll add /F to the logic:

```
for /F %%a in (C:\Batch\FourBrits.txt) do (
    > con echo %%a
)
```

And now the output:

```
English
Spanish
French
Italian
```

Such a small change results in a vastly different outcome. Instead of a single write to the console in the form of the filename, the code now outputs the first word of each record inside the file itself. Due to the /F option, the command is opening and reading the contents of the file. There's still much to work out, but the command is actually reading each of the four records in the file, setting %%a to the first word in the record. If the file had contained 64 populated records, the previous logic would have written 64 words to the console on the same number of lines.

This output raises many more questions than it answers. Why isn't this writing the entire record? Can we parse out just parts of the record? Must we read every record? This is where the keywords in the *suboptions* clause from the general syntax come into play.

Tokenizing the Data

A *token* in Batch is an element of a record, and by default each token is delimited by spaces or tabs. Inspecting the first record in the file, it contains exactly five tokens:

```
English    John     Paul     George     Richard
```

By default, Batch sets the number of tokens to 1. This explains why in the previous example, the interpreter resolved %%a to the first word (or token) in each record and dropped the rest of the record.

To change this default, you can use the tokens clause; it's the tokens keyword followed by an equal sign and the setting, which in this case is 2:

```
for /F "tokens=2" %%a in (C:\Batch\FourBrits.txt) do (
    > con echo %%a
)
```

The tokens clause tells the interpreter which token or tokens to pass into the loop as the for variable. Executing this code produces the following output written to the console:

```
John
Juan
Jean
Giovanni
```

Due to the tokens clause, the interpreter now sends the second word or token into the loop, writing John and its translations to the console. Setting it to 5 would have retrieved Richard's name instead. With this clause you can extract a single token with relative ease.

Extracting Multiple Tokens

It's nice to be able to pull out individual tokens, but it's more useful to be able to pull out multiple and select tokens. To extract all five tokens, assign the text 1-5 to the tokens keyword. But this raises an interesting question. How will those five tokens be resolved with only the single variable, %%a, defined?

Additional variables are elegantly implied in simple alphabetical order. If %%a is the variable defined in the for /F command, it resolves to the first token defined in the tokens clause, then %%b resolves to the second, %%c to the third, %%d to the fourth, and, finally, %%e to the fifth. Consider the following:

```
for /F "tokens=1-5" %%a in (C:\Batch\FourBrits.txt) do (
    > con echo %%a:  %%b, %%c, %%d, and %%e
)
```

This code formats the record so that the language is followed by a colon and two spaces. Then in the output, the names are separated by commas and spaces with a conjunction before the last name:

```
English:  John, Paul, George, and Richard
Spanish:  Juan, Pablo, Jorge, and Ricardo
French:   Jean, Pol, Georges, and Richard
Italian:  Giovanni, Paolo, Giorgio, and Riccardo
```

You can also pick and choose which tokens to extract instead of a range. A comma in the tokens clause separates the desired tokens. This code sends only the second and fourth tokens into the loop:

```
for /F "tokens=2,4" %%a in (C:\Batch\FourBrits.txt) do (
   > con echo %%a and %%b played guitar.
)
```

This result is written to the console:

```
John and George played guitar.
Juan and Jorge played guitar.
Jean and Georges played guitar.
Giovanni and Giorgio played guitar.
```

The second token from the data record is now the first token the tokens clause defines, so Batch assigns it to %%a, not %%b. Likewise, %%b now resolves to the fourth token in the record, which is the second token selected. More succinctly, the variable letter mimics the token's position defined by the tokens clause—not its position in the record.

To this point, I've used %%a as the for variable. Regardless of the letter you choose for the variable, the interpreter assigns subsequent tokens to corresponding letters in the alphabet. The previous code is functionally equivalent to the following code:

```
for /F "tokens=2,4" %%x in (C:\Batch\FourBrits.txt) do (
   > con echo %%x and %%y played guitar.
)
```

The only difference is that I've changed %%a to %%x, meaning that %%y now resolves to the second token instead of %%b.

The catch is that choosing %%x as the for variable limits you to just three possible tokens, because there's nothing to assign after %%z (despite the efforts of Dr. Seuss in *On Beyond Zebra!*). You won't see this nearly as often, but numbers also work. For instance, if you extract three tokens and define the for variable as %%7, the interpreter will use %%8 and %%9 for the implied tokens.

The keyword also accepts a combination of numbers, commas, and dashes. For instance, the tokens=1,3-5 clause processes all of the tokens except John, the second token.

Extracting the Remainder of a Record

There's another twist concerning the tokens keyword. An asterisk represents the remainder of the input record as is, including embedded whitespaces. Consider this code using 2* in the tokens clause:

```
for /F "tokens=2*" %%a in (C:\Batch\FourBrits.txt) do (
   > con echo %%a, Rest of the Band: "%%b"
)
```

This command assigns the second token to %%a because of the 2 in the clause; then the interpreter assigns the remainder of the record, the third, fourth, and fifth tokens, including any embedded spaces and tabs, to %%b because of the asterisk (*). The language, the first token in each record, isn't to be found anywhere in the output:

```
John, Rest of the Band: "Paul      George    Richard"
Juan, Rest of the Band: "Pablo     Jorge     Ricardo"
Jean, Rest of the Band: "Pol       Georges   Richard"
Giovanni, Rest of the Band: "Paolo      Giorgio   Riccardo"
```

To bring this discussion full circle, when we simply added the /F option to the for command at the beginning of the chapter, the default tokens clause passed the first token only into the code block. On many occasions you'll want to extract the entire record exactly as it appears in the input file as a single entity. Since the asterisk represents the rest of the input record, assigning it alone to tokens selects the entire record:

```
for /F "tokens=*" %%r in (C:\Batch\FourBrits.txt) do (
   > con echo Entire Record: "%%r"
)
```

Also notice that I changed the variable to %%r. Here's the output:

```
Entire Record: "English   John      Paul    George    Richard"
Entire Record: "Spanish   Juan      Pablo   Jorge     Ricardo"
Entire Record: "French    Jean      Pol     Georges   Richard"
Entire Record: "Italian   Giovanni  Paolo   Giorgio   Riccardo"
```

The prior use of %%a would have worked fine, but I've changed it here for two reasons: first, r stands for *record*, and second, as a simple reminder that any alphabetic character will work.

NOTE *As mentioned in Chapter 17, the for variable is actually case-sensitive, and some nonalphanumeric characters are permitted. This means %%a and %%b resolve only to the first two tokens for the variable defined as %%a; %%A and %%B won't work, unless you change the for variable to %%A. I probably don't need to mention this, but those oddball characters (think %%#) don't lend themselves at all to extracting multiple tokens.*

Defining the Set of Data Delimiters

Being able to break up an input record into tokens defined by delimiters such as spaces and tabs is powerful indeed, but in many instances, you don't have control over the data in the file that you're reading, and a different delimiter, or even a set of delimiters, would be far more applicable. The delims keyword defines one to many *delimiters* used to tokenize the data.

Parsing Comma-Delimited Data

A comma-delimited format is a popular and easy way of storing data. For instance, a *.csv* file contains any number of comma-delimited records, and you can open it and view the data with Excel. Each token is delimited by a comma, and each token can contain spaces. Before demonstrating how Batch reads in CSV data, I'll need some setup.

The *FourBrits.txt* file might contain a name with embedded spaces such as `Richard aka Ringo`. In the space-delimited examples discussed so far, this text constitutes three distinct tokens. I'll now reformat the data and present it in a comma-delimited file called *FourBrits.csv*. The contents of this file will be the same as its like-named *.txt* file except for the delimiters and Richard's alias:

```
English,John,Paul,George,Richard aka Ringo
Spanish,Juan,Pablo,Jorge,Ricardo aka Ringo
French,Jean,Pol,Georges,Richard aka Ringo
Italian,Giovanni,Paolo,Giorgio,Riccardo aka Ringo
```

The next task is to modify the `for /F` command so that it treats the commas as delimiters in lieu of the spaces, and I'll accomplish this with the `delims` keyword. When the keyword isn't present, the interpreter defaults to the set of delimiters containing just the space and tab characters. In the following example, `delims=,` defines the set of delimiters as a single character, the comma:

```
for /F "tokens=1-5 delims=," %%a in (C:\Batch\FourBrits.csv) do (
    > con echo %%a:  %%b, %%c, %%d, and %%e
)
```

When the interpreter now comes to the fifth and final token—a name followed by `aka Ringo`—it writes the text to the console complete with its embedded spaces:

```
English:  John, Paul, George, and Richard aka Ringo
Spanish:  Juan, Pablo, Jorge, and Ricardo aka Ringo
French:   Jean, Pol, Georges, and Richard aka Ringo
Italian:  Giovanni, Paolo, Giorgio, and Riccardo aka Ringo
```

Ringo is nontranslatable.

Pipe-delimited data files are also popular; the `delims=|` clause parses the input data on the pipe so that embedded spaces and commas won't create additional tokens. The equal sign can even be a delimiter with the `delims==` clause. (You'll see an example of that before long.)

Defining Multiple Delimiters

You can even define multiple delimiters with a single `delims` clause. The following code defines the set of delimiters to be the comma and the space. It's subtle, but in comparison to the previous example, the only change is that I've added a space in between `delims=,` and the trailing double quote:

```
for /F "tokens=1-5 delims=, " %%a in (C:\Batch\FourBrits.csv) do (
    > con echo %%a:  %%b, %%c, %%d, and %%e
)
```

The interpreter will now see a new token whenever it encounters a space or a comma. The fifth token will be only the name Richard, in some language, with aka and Ringo relegated to the unassigned sixth and seventh tokens, respectively.

To demonstrate an even larger set of delimiters, I'll use a one-record file named *Alphabets.txt*, containing the uppercase and lowercase Latin alphabets, with one space separating them:

```
ABCDEFGHIJKLMNOPQRSTUVWXYZ abcdefghijklmnopqrstuvwxyz
```

Omitting the delims clause entirely invokes the default delimiter set and results in just two tokens, the uppercase and the lowercase character sets, and nothing more. Instead, in the following code, I'm setting the delims keyword to the Delims text and a trailing space:

```
for /F "tokens=1-8 delims=Delims " %%a in (C:\Batch\Alphabets.txt) do (
    > con echo Token 1 = %%a
    > con echo Token 2 = %%b
    > con echo Token 3 = %%c
    > con echo Token 4 = %%d
    > con echo Token 5 = %%e
    > con echo Token 6 = %%f
    > con echo Token 7 = %%g
    > con echo Token 8 = %%h
)
```

If each of the seven delimiters occurs just once in the data, it seems logical that this logic creates eight tokens. That's not necessarily true, but I've defined that many with the tokens=1-8 clause and added the same number of echo commands. But let's keep an eye on the number of tokens generated. Here's the resulting output:

```
Token 1 = ABC
Token 2 = EFGHIJKLMNOPQRSTUVWXYZ
Token 3 = abcd
Token 4 = fgh
Token 5 = jk
Token 6 = nopqr
Token 7 = tuvwxyz
Token 8 =
```

There is much to point out here, including the fact that the delimiter set is case-sensitive. The uppercase D is one delimiter, but not d. The lowercase letters e, l, i, m, and s, along with a space, round out the set of delimiters. It's a little easier to see the origin of these seven tokens when looking at the original data with the delimiters (other than the space) bolded:

```
ABCDEFGHIJKLMNOPQRSTUVWXYZ abcdefghijklmnopqrstuvwxyz
```

Notice that this data has two of the delimiters (l and m) listed sequentially, and because nothing is between them, you might expect the interpreter to assign null or nothing to the sixth token and bump the text after it, nopqr, to the seventh token. Batch, however, treats the consecutive delimiters (lm) as a single delimiter so that the sixth token is the text nopqr. Thus, tuvwxyz is the seventh token, and since nothing comes after it, the eighth token resolves to nothing.

Be careful to use only tokens that you've defined. If the clause had been tokens=1-7, the final echo command would have resulted in Token 8 = %h, because %%h wouldn't have been the eighth token; it would have been a percent sign escaping another percent sign, followed by a hardcoded character.

When parsing comma-delimited (or pipe-delimited) data, many compiled languages treat consecutive delimiters as two delimiters, honoring the null in between them, which makes perfect sense. Batch, however, typically delimits on spaces, and one look at the original *FourBrits.txt* data with its varying number of spaces between each word makes it clear that it also makes perfectly good sense to treat multiple spaces as a single delimiter.

Unfortunately, this does lead to some frustration when instead of spaces, your data is delimited by commas, but in Chapter 20, I'll show you how to make the for loop honor the nulls between consecutive delimiters. However, if I have control over the input data that's delimited on just a comma, I'll always write a null element to the file as a space in between two commas.

I've listed the space last in the set of delimiters because it has to come last. I hate to disparage the interpreter yet again, but it gets confused if it finds the space anywhere else. For that reason, when including a space in the delimiter set, the delims clause must come at the end of the suboptions, just prior to the trailing double quote.

Skipping Header Records

As you've just seen, the tokens and delims keywords have a great deal of nuance. The next couple are far more straightforward, especially the skip keyword, which lets you skip any number of header records as you read a file.

Let's return to the original *FourBrits.txt* file and add a header record before the unchanged content in the next four records:

```
Four Liverpudlians in Four Languages:
English   John      Paul    George    Richard
Spanish   Juan      Pablo   Jorge     Ricardo
French    Jean      Pol     Georges   Richard
Italian   Giovanni  Paolo   Giorgio   Riccardo
```

Let's run the same for /F loop from the tokens keyword discussion:

```
for /F "tokens=1-5" %%a in (C:\Batch\FourBrits.txt) do (
   > con echo %%a:  %%b, %%c, %%d, and %%e
)
```

It processes the header line as any other, producing the following garbage output, followed by the four lines of good output (only one of which I'm showing):

```
Four:  Liverpudlians, in, Four, and Languages:
English:  John, Paul, George, and Richard
```

Fortunately, the skip keyword defines the number of records to be skipped at the beginning of the file. This will skip the first record and process the data records perfectly:

```
for /F "tokens=1-5 skip=1" %%a in (C:\Batch\FourBrits.txt) do (
  > con echo %%a:  %%b, %%c, %%d, and %%e
)
```

If there had been three header records, the skip=3 clause would have made the for command start at the fourth record.

Suppressing Comment Records

While the skip keyword skips records only at the beginning of a file, the eol keyword, which stands for *end of line* comment character, bypasses all records in the file that start with a defined character. If I were being charitable, I'd say that when the interpreter sees the defined *character* in the first byte of a record, it considers the character to be the *end of line* and treats what remains as a *comment*.

To demonstrate, let's edit the input file again. This time I'm adding a second comment record, and more important, each comment record now starts with a period:

```
.Four Liverpudlian in Four Languages:
English    John     Paul      George    Richard
Spanish    Juan     Pablo     Jorge     Ricardo
French     Jean     Pol       Georges   Richard
.This is a random and annoying mid-file comment with no discernable purpose.
Italian    Giovanni Paolo     Giorgio   Riccardo
```

Adding the eol=. clause to the same for command instructs the interpreter to skip the comment lines, regardless of where they appear in the data, and process only the remaining records:

```
for /F "tokens=1-5 eol=." %%a in (C:\Batch\FourBrits.txt) do (
  > con echo %%a:  %%b, %%c, %%d, and %%e
)
```

Unfortunately, this straightforward keyword has its very own batveat. Given that the delims clause accepts a list of delimiters, you're probably expecting the eol clause to accept one to many characters. But no, it accepts only a single character.

The phrase tokens, delims, skip, and eol doesn't quite roll off the tongue quite like John, Paul, George, and Ringo, but these fabulous four keywords allow for a great deal of flexibility, and there will be more examples of clauses associated with these keywords in this chapter and others.

Defining the Input

You now know how to read a file with the for /F command, but you might not yet know how to read a *file*—there's a distinction. A traditional file is a collection of bytes organized into records stored in a referenceable location on a drive defined by a directory and filename. A *file* is some sort of input readable by the for /F command; it can take different forms and doesn't have to be something that an editor can open.

Other than a traditional file, this command can accept a string as input and also the output of another Batch command. As you'll soon see, subtle difference in the syntax dictates the type of input.

File Input

The *file-set* input is a traditional file or set of files. I've already shown several examples of that form throughout this chapter. Each example contained one file inside the parentheses, and we now know those inputs were files because of the lack of any encasing quotes, single or double. What you've yet to see is a set of files. The following command reads the contents of two files in the order that they are listed in the *file-set*, delimited by a comma or a space, or both for readability:

```
for /F "tokens=1-5" %%a in (FourBrits.txt, MoreBrits.txt) do (
    > con echo %%a:  %%b, %%c, %%d, and %%e
)
```

Assuming that the first file, *FourBrits.txt*, has four records, the for /F command processes each in order, writing four lines to the console. The interpreter then closes that file and opens *MoreBrits.txt*. Each record in this file triggers one execution of the logic inside the code block and writes one more line to the console. I also removed the file paths, so the interpreter will look for these files in the current directory and the directories defined in the path variable.

String Input

Here is the general syntax for the for /F command using a string as input. Take note of the input inside the parentheses:

```
for /F ["suboptions"] %%variable in ("string") do command
```

This form replaces the input text with "string". The double quotes tell the interpreter that they are encasing some sort of text, while a complete lack of quotes tells the interpreter to consider the input to be a file or a set of files. Everything else works exactly the same.

The following `for /F` command is similar to other examples used earlier in this chapter, other than the input:

```
for /F "tokens=1-5" %%a in ("Italian Giovanni Paolo Giorgio Riccardo") do (
   > con echo %%a:  %%b, %%c, %%d, and %%e
)
```

The only difference is that I've taken the last line of text from *FourBrits.txt*, removed some extra spaces for readability, and entered it as the string encased in double quotes.

The `echo` command inside the code block doesn't know the source of the five tokens, whether it's from a hardcoded string or a record read from a file. Here's the familiar result:

```
Italian:  Giovanni, Paolo, Giorgio, and Riccardo
```

In this example, the text inside the parentheses is hardcoded, but you can use a variable containing text, as long as it's encased in double quotes. You can use any string as input, and the interpreter treats it like a single record file.

This feature allows for sophisticated string parsing. I actually used this feature in Chapter 5 with absolutely no explanation of how it worked, promising an explanation later. A `for /F` command converted a boolean to a boolean string, where the `bGod` boolean contained one of two values, `true==true` or `false==x`. At the time I mentioned, while attributing it to little more than a magic trick, that the command strips off the two equal signs and all that follows, giving `bStrGod` the value of `true` or `false`:

```
for /F "delims==" %%b in ("%bGod%") do  set bStrGod=%%b
```

With what you've learned in this chapter, you can now figure out how this works.

The `for /F` command treats the resolved boolean encased in double quotes inside the parentheses as string or text input. The `delims` clause defines the equal sign as the only delimiter, and since I haven't defined the `tokens` keyword, the default clause of `tokens=1` is implied. The result is that the word before the equal signs is the first token, and the interpreter resolves it as `%%b` (for *boolean*, of course), while discarding the second token coming after the equal signs. The `set` command then assigns that first token to the boolean string on its first and only execution.

So, it's not a magic trick at all, instead just a concise means of pulling a single delimited value out of a larger string with a single line of code. Behold the power of the `for /F` command and its multiple inputs.

Command Input

What's inside the parentheses dictates the input of any for /F command. You know that no quotes indicate a file and that double quotes indicate a string. Single quotes indicate that another Batch command is the input, and here's its general syntax:

```
for /F ["suboptions"] %%variable in ('command') do command
```

Any Batch command entered between the single quotes executes first, with its resulting stdout being the input to the for /F command. The interpreter then processes what it considers to be the input, line by line if there's more than one, as if it were a file.

To demonstrate the usefulness of a command as input, consider the dir command introduced in Chapter 13. The following command lists all of the text files in the given directory:

```
dir C:\Batch\*.txt /B
```

The /B option produces a list of filenames and extensions only—no file dates and sizes, and no header and trailer lines. But the command simply writes this information to stdout for your perusal and little more. Many times, you'll want to take this list of files and execute some logic against each one. For example, let's write some code to change the extension on all *.txt* files in a directory to *.bak* to signify that they're backup files.

The single quotes tell the for /F command that the input is a command. The dir command generates a list of filenames, each with an extension and no path:

```
for /F "tokens=*" %%f in ('dir C:\Batch\*.txt /B') do (
    ren "C:\Batch\%%f" "%%~Nf.bak"
)
```

The tokens=* clause ensures that %%f takes on the entire string as its value as it enumerates through the list of files. The default clause would have dropped everything after the first embedded space in the name. The ren command renames the file, using the modifier for the filename (N) and tacking on the hardcoded extension.

I hope that you can appreciate how extremely impressive this is. Three commands are bound up together to perform quite a bit in just a couple lines of code. For those who use this often, it can become commonplace, and for others it might just be overwhelming, but in many languages something like this isn't possible without an intermediate file. With this technique, the dir command isn't just something that can dump information to the console or into a file (although that can also be useful). The unadulterated bare format of the output was clearly designed for this purpose. You can perform many processes, simple or complex, on any number of files. I'll expand on this when I delve into some real-world applications.

Alternative Syntax for Input Types

For some inputs the syntax just discussed simply doesn't work. Sometimes a filename contains embedded spaces, but encasing it in double quotes turns it into string input. If a string contains a double quote, you can't encase it in a pair of those characters. Likewise, commands sometimes contain single quotes. These cases pose a problem requiring a different syntax, and the usebackq keyword, the last of the suboptions available with the for /F command, is the solution.

Before going any further, some Batch abbreviations are obvious; I probably didn't need to tell you that delims is short for *delimiters* and that tokens is short for, well, *tokens*. But there's a good chance that you are puzzled by the cryptic text usebackq. The keyword stands for *use back quote*, which probably doesn't help much, but at least now you'll know how to pronounce it when you see it.

File Input

The best way to show the usefulness of the usebackq keyword is to re-create the type of situation that surely led to its creation. Many examples to this point in the chapter have read a file named *FourBrits.txt*. I rarely embed spaces in filenames, but someone else might have named this file *Four Brits.txt*.

To demonstrate the problem spaces can cause, I've lifted the following for /F command verbatim from earlier, except the filename now contains an embedded space:

```
for /F "tokens=1-5" %%a in (C:\Batch\Four Brits.txt) do (
  > con echo %%a:  %%b, %%c, %%d, and %%e
)
```

Batch considers this to be two files (not one) and will likely fail, not being able to find an extensionless file named *Four*. The obvious solution is to put double quotes around the path and filename, but the for /F command will treat that as a text string instead of a filename, so that won't work.

The solution is to use the usebackq keyword *and* double quotes around the input:

```
for /F "usebackq tokens=1-5" %%a in ("C:\Batch\Four Brits.txt") do (
  > con echo %%a:  %%b, %%c, %%d, and %%e
)
```

This keyword also makes it easier to process paths and filenames containing special characters such as parentheses.

The for /F command successfully reads the file and produces the same output as before. You can even read multiple files, each with embedded spaces in their names:

```
for /F "usebackq tokens=1-5" %%a in ("Four Brits.txt", "More Brits.txt") do (
  > con echo %%a:  %%b, %%c, %%d, and %%e
)
```

Notice that the filenames are delimited by a comma and that a set of double quotes encases each filename.

Here's the general syntax of the command using a *file-set* as input with the usebackq keyword:

```
for /F "usebackq [suboptions]" %%variable in ("file-set") do command
```

This keyword changes the rules. Double quotes can surround each filename, although it still works with the keyword and without any double quotes, assuming the filename has no embedded spaces.

String Input

The usebackq keyword solved one problem but created another. It enables the use of double quotes around a filename, but this seems to disallow the ability to process a string. The solution is to encase the text in a different character and that character is the single quote. Here's the general syntax:

```
for /F "usebackq [suboptions]" %%variable in ('string') do command
```

Therefore, the following two for commands are functionally equivalent:

```
for /F "tokens=1-4" %%a in ("Larry Moe Curly Iggy") do break
for /F "usebackq tokens=1-4" %%a in ('Larry Moe Curly Iggy') do break
```

Without usebackq, I'm encasing the short list of Stooges in double quotes, but single quotes encase the same text when the keyword is present. (I'm also using the break or *no operation* command to make these commands valid while focusing on the keyword and the type of quotes, but these commands produce no output.)

Why does Batch provide two means of performing the same task? To answer this question, I'll use a string of Chicago airports, each encased in parentheses for some unknown reason, as the input. The following two commands are functionally equivalent:

```
for /F "tokens=1-2" %%a in ("(O'Hare) (Midway)") do break
for /F "usebackq tokens=1-2" %%a in ('^(O'Hare^) ^(Midway^)') do break
```

The first example, which doesn't use usebackq, is far more workable. You must escape special characters such as the parentheses when using the keyword, all because of the lack of double quotes. But without the keyword, these characters are just along for the ride inside the double quotes.

But the one character that will never work in a double-quoted string is a solitary double quote itself—even when escaped. Returning to the Stooges, while Iggy Pop was the front man for *The Stooges*, he clearly wasn't a member of *The Three Stooges*, so I might want to put his name in scare quotes, or double quotes, to denote the irony:

```
for /F "usebackq tokens=1-4" %%a in ('Larry Moe Curly "Iggy"') do (
    > con echo The Four Stooges are %%a, %%b, %%c, and %%d.
)
```

(The interpreter is intelligent enough to handle an even number of double quotes inside a set of double quotes, but for clarity I always use the keyword and encase the entire input in single quotes when the string has any double quotes.)

This for /F command writes the following to the console:

```
The Four Stooges are Larry, Moe, Curly, and "Iggy".
```

(Poor Shemp, everyone forgets about Shemp.)

Command Input

You just learned to use single quotes when also using usebackq and string input, so you can no longer use them to encase a command. But this general syntax allows you to use the keyword with a command as input:

```
for /F "usebackq [suboptions]" %%variable in (`command`) do command
```

In some fonts the two characters encasing the command input might look like single quotes, but they're something new.

This brings us back to the cliffhanger concerning the meaning of the text usebackq or *use back quote*. It's named for those crooked single quotes encasing the *command*, which are more properly called back quotes (or back ticks). The keyboard key for the back quote is just above TAB and to the left of the key for the number 1 on most keyboards. This key does double duty, as shifting it gets you the tilde. It's relegated to the nether regions of the keyboard because it's rarely if ever touched by most, but it's an instrumental key for Batch coders.

The following for /F commands are functionally equivalent; the first one mimics a command from the prior section, and the second one uses the keyword and back quotes:

```
for /F "tokens=*" %%f in ('dir C:\Batch\*.txt /B') do break
for /F "usebackq tokens=*" %%f in (`dir C:\Batch\*.txt /B`) do break
```

The first line supports instances where the encased command might contain a back quote, while you'd use the second line—the syntax with the usebackq keyword—when the command might contain a single quote.

When to Use usebackq

You can implement each type of input with or without usebackq, so when should you use the keyword? In a sentence: whenever possible, I use usebackq for file-set and command inputs, and I don't for string input.

Encasing the input in double quotes allows for the most flexibility and should be done whenever possible. It supports embedded spaces in the input and many characters that might otherwise require escaping. Hence, when processing a file-set, I use double quotes and usebackq, and when processing a string, I use double quotes and omit the keyword.

When the input is a command, double quotes don't enter into the calculus. Some may skip the keyword to save a few keystrokes, but I use the usebackq keyword and back quotes around the input for two reasons. First, while both the single quote and back quote are unlikely characters in a command, the back quote is even more unlikely. More important, when you see the single quotes, you immediately ask whether the input is a string or a command; the back quotes remove all ambiguity; it's a command.

If you implement my recommendations, the end result will be that anyone looking at your for /F commands will be able to infer a great deal from the input. If it's encased in back quotes, it's a command; if it's encased in double quotes, focus shifts to usebackq. If it's present, the input is a file-set; if not, it's a string. There are three more forms available in the event of a blue moon, but you'll see an input string containing a double quote or an input command containing a back quote less frequently than you'll see two full moons in a calendar month.

As one final note on the usebackq, if you don't find this keyword cryptic enough, the q is optional. You can replace every instance of usebackq appearing in the code listings in this chapter with its synonym useback. I'm usually in favor of reducing keystrokes, but this puts an additional veil over something that's already inscrutable to many.

Real-World Applications

The ability to read files and to treat strings and the outputs of commands as if they were files has many applications. Truly understanding the different types of inputs possible for a for /F command will allow you to come up with imaginative solutions to problems that may have seemed intractable not long ago.

Process Only Large Files in a Folder

In Chapter 17, I explored an application that passed a number of files into a bat file to be processed one by one. In this example, we'll still process files individually, but instead of a list of arguments, let's process all *.txt* files in a particular folder. To make it a little more interesting, let's process only large files, defined as any file at least 100KB in size.

You can feed the dir command into the for /F command as input with back quotes encasing the command if using the usebackq keyword. The bare format option, /B, produces a clean list of files without headers and is tailor-made for this purpose, but the file size is lost with this option, so let's drop that idea, at least for now.

However, not using the /B option presents other challenges. File dates and times will be present, along with header and trailer records. You'll want to use the size of each file to evaluate whether it's large enough to process, but the pesky commas in the displayed file size will be more than a nuisance.

In Chapter 13, I mentioned that the /-C option of the dir command suppresses the commas, but to figure out how to parse what you want out of its output, you'll want to see a sample. Unless you possess a memory far more detailed than mine, an essential step in building any complex for /F command with an embedded command is to execute that embedded command, the command that will be inside the back quotes, and inspect its output. Here's the command, where workDir is the folder in question:

```
dir %workDir%\*.txt /-C
```

It might generate something like the following:

```
Volume in drive C is OS
Volume Serial Number is 2E6D-DBF0

Directory of C:\Batch

12/25/2011  12:42 PM          538346 Big.txt
11/24/2011  05:22 PM           17234 Little.txt
09/05/2011  10:43 AM              10 Wee Tiny.txt
07/04/2011  07:22 PM         1864408 Wicked Big.txt
               4 File(s)        2419998 bytes
               0 Dir(s)  146181152768 bytes free
```

There's a lot to unpack here, but with this data you can construct the rest of the for /F command. You're interested in the four detail records, but there are five header records, including the empty records, so you'll want to avoid them with the skip=5 clause.

Next, you need to figure out the best way to find the tokens that correspond to the file size and name. The space character is one of the default delimiters, and it'll work great here, but notice that if you had wanted the month, day, year, hour, or minutes out of the data, you would have used a delims clause defining a delimiter set of forward slashes, colons, and spaces. Given that the space is the delimiter, you must now put on your interpreter hat and look for the space-delimited tokens. The date is the first token, and the time comprises the next two tokens; because of the embedded space, the meridiem (AM/PM) becomes the third token. Hence, the fourth token is the file size with the remainder of the data being the filename.

To represent size, you'll use %%s as the for variable, meaning that %%t will be the filename and extension. (If you use %%e as the size, then %%f becomes the file.)

It might be tempting to consider the filename to be the fifth token, but filenames can contain spaces, and any space in the name will delimit yet another token. Fortunately, the filename comes at the end of the data, meaning that the tokens=4* clause assigns two tokens. The fourth token is the file size, and thanks to the asterisk, the rest of the data, which is the filename, becomes the fifth token.

You're not done, but you can put together the main structure of the for /F command. Everything discussed is here, in particular, the dir command inside back quotes:

```
for /F "usebackq tokens=4* skip=5" %%s in (`dir %workDir%\*.txt /-C`) do (
```

Before calling the logic to process a big file, you'll need to navigate two if commands. The first simply verifies that the file size, %%s, is greater than or equal to 100000. The for /F command allows you to skip header records, but trailer records are still in play, so you must get creative. Notice in the dir command output that the fourth token in both trailer records is the text bytes, which surely won't be the case for the detail records you're interested in. Hence, you'll need a second if command to filter out those two unwanted records by inspecting the same %%s variable

Now you can put it all together:

```
for /F "usebackq tokens=4* skip=5" %%s in (`dir %workDir%\*.txt /-C`) do (
   if %%s geq 100000 (
      if /i "%%s" neq "bytes" (
         call :ProcessBigTxtFile "%workDir%\%%t"
) ) )
```

If the workDir variable is populated with the working directory of the text files, this code is ready to process the big text files represented by %%t. Also, it might seem quite odd that %%s is used in both numeric and alpha compares. In Chapter 4, I mentioned that numeric and alpha values are ordered; letters are considered to be greater than numbers, so the bytes geq 100000 conditional clause is always true. If it had always been false, you could have omitted the second if command.

Multiple solutions always exist, and it's great to see a different way to think through an issue. I'm going to take another pass at the /B option of the dir command. I know that it won't provide the file size, but maybe there's another way to get it. I showed how to use modifiers to get the size of a file using the optionless for command in Chapter 17. Maybe two for commands will be better than one.

I'll start with this solution, which implements nested for commands:

```
for /F "usebackq tokens=*" %%f in (`dir %workDir%\*.txt /B`) do (
   for %%g in ("%workDir%\%%f") do (
      if %%~Zg geq 100000 (
         call :ProcessBigTxtFile %%g
) ) )
```

The outer for command has the /F option, along with the usebackq key-word, and it uses %%f as its variable. Its input is a dir command with the /B option encased in back quotes. The tokens=* clause ensures that the code passes each filename, regardless of embedded spaces, into the code block, where I immediately prepend it with the path, put it in double quotes, and use it as the input to the inner for command.

That inner command, which doesn't sport the /F option, uses %%g as its variable, but anything other than %%f would have been good form. I'm deriving the file size with the use of a modifier, %%~Zg; if it's large enough, the call command invokes the routine that processes large files.

Nested for commands don't behave much differently from their non-nested cousins, but an important point is the alpha character chosen for the for variable of each command. I could've used %%f for both commands, but I always use unique values, as it's simply clearer and easier to read. In addi-tion, the outer variable is still available inside the inner command, but only if it hasn't been stepped on by the inner variable.

To prevent a for variable conflict, they should not only be different, but I also recommend staggering them so that any implied variables don't col-lide. For instance, if the outer command is extracting three tokens from the input data and using %%f as its for variable, then %%g and %%h should also be off limits for the inner command.

You've seen two solutions to the same problem. One used a more com-plex command to parse the data, and the other used nested commands. Which way is better is debatable. What isn't debatable is that just as in other languages, multiple possible solutions exist for all problems. Never settle.

Global Text Replacement

Imagine you maintain an old system that runs a number of executables, many of which are housed on an old server. The team is decommissioning the server, \\OldServer, and replacing it with the aptly named \\NewServer. The plan is to move every file on the old box to the new box with the same directory structure.

Fortunately, your team has wisely implemented and adhered to a consis-tent naming convention for the variables that define each program; they all start with _pgm. You control the creation of some of these variables, but not all. You'll never be able to track them all down, but to cut over to the new server successfully, you'll need to tweak all of these variables on the fly—that is, you'll need to change the text for the old server to the new text, and you can't even get a list of all the variable names.

The first problem to solve is retrieving the list of variable names in a given execution. In Chapter 2, you learned that the following command generates a list of all currently active variables that start with the text _pgm:

```
set _pgm
```

If just four such variables were set, the following might be the result of the command:

```
_pgmDBMrge=\\OldServer\Executables\DatabaseMerge.exe
_pgmSTElse=\\NewServer\Executables\SomethingElse.exe
_pgmTtlDiff=\\ThirdServer\Progs\TotallyDifferent.exe
_pgmVldtn=\\OldServer\Executables\Validation.exe
```

The first and last of these need tweaking, the second has already been updated with the new text, and third has a completely different directory structure. You'll need to update two of these without altering the other two. The solution entails the previous set command as the input to a for /F command. The code block will accept the variable name and value and reset the variable to its value with the updated text.

The following for /F command is one solution:

```
for /F "usebackq tokens=1,2 delims==" %%p in (`set _pgm`) do (
    set tempPgm=%%q
    set %%p=!tempPgm:\\OldServer\=\\NewServer\!
)
```

You've placed the command set _pgm between back quotes and used the usebackq keyword in the for /F command. When using the dir command as input, I stressed the importance of understanding its output, and the same holds true for the set command. Looking at the four sample lines of output, the commonality between them is that a variable name is followed by a value, separated by an equal sign. Thus, you're delimiting on the equal sign with the delims== clause and extracting both tokens with the tokens=1,2 clause. The for variable, %%p, is the variable name, implying that %%q is its value.

This code resets the variable in the code block with just two commands. You assign the original value of the input variable, %%q, to tempPgm, a temporary variable. The second command resets the variable name, %%p, to that value with *OldServer*\ replaced with *NewServer*\. Notice that because tempPgm is being set and then used inside of a code block, you must use exclamation marks to resolve the variable to its current value.

This logic updates all variables with this specific prefix while ignoring those without the prefix. There are many other applications based on this principle. You could reset all similarly named variables to null by replacing the code in the code block with one command, set %%p=, and using the default tokens clause.

Notes on the Documentation

I've taken some liberties with the general syntax of the different forms of the for /F command, so I'll compare what you've seen here to what's in the help documentation and explain my reasons. First, this is exactly what you'll find by running for /?:

```
FOR /F ["options"] %variable IN (file-set) DO command [command-parameters]
FOR /F ["options"] %variable IN ("string") DO command [command-parameters]
FOR /F ["options"] %variable IN ('command') DO command [command-parameters]

    or, if usebackq option present:

FOR /F ["options"] %variable IN (file-set) DO command [command-parameters]
FOR /F ["options"] %variable IN ('string') DO command [command-parameters]
FOR /F ["options"] %variable IN (`command`) DO command [command-parameters]
```

I instead list the three forms that I use almost exclusively, followed by the ones I use infrequently:

```
for /F "usebackq [suboptions]" %%variable in ("file-set") do command
for /F ["suboptions"] %%variable in ("string") do command
for /F "usebackq [suboptions]" %%variable in (`command`) do command

for /F ["suboptions"] %%variable in (file-set) do command
for /F "usebackq [suboptions]" %%variable in ('string') do command
for /F ["suboptions"] %%variable in ('command') do command
```

First off, I have more of an affinity for lowercase characters than most coders. Also, I've replaced the ["options"] clause with ["suboptions"]. This for command already has one option, /F, and I see no reason to introduce another type of option, so I've settled on the term *suboptions*, but both of these tweaks are cosmetic.

I've dropped [command-parameters] from the end of each, which just states that the command could have parameters, but that's obvious and unworthy of the extra ink. To truly do it correctly, I could've shown additional optional commands as well as optional parentheses defining a possible code block. To be readable, it has to be a bit vague, so I've decided to also make it succinct.

Another difference is that I've used two percent signs for the for variable, %%variable, as opposed to one. The help shows how you would execute the command from the command prompt, where the only difference is that it calls for a single percent sign. This is a book about bat files, not the command prompt, and the command is usually too complex to be entered at the prompt anyway.

I explicitly show the usebackq keyword in the forms that use it, while the help documentation places them after an odd heading. To accommodate this change, I've also placed the other *suboptions* inside the square brackets because they are still optional.

The final difference is in the first form, and it's the most critical one. When researching this book, I was absolutely flabbergasted to notice that the two forms using the *file-set* as input are identical in the help. Adding the usebackq keyword means that double quotes can now encase the input. Technically, they don't have to be there, but isn't that the whole point of using usebackq? I'm hard-pressed to come up with an instance where I wouldn't want the double quotes while using the keyword, so I'm including them in my documentation, but understand that they are optional.

Use the forms that make sense to you. Better yet, start with one set or the other (I hope mine) and build on it in your own personal documentation about the for command.

Deconstructing Any for Command

The for command, especially when followed by the /F option, can be overwhelming. You can pack quite a bit of logic into just a few lines of code. When you come across one of these constructs, it can be difficult to know exactly where to start your analysis. I've deconstructed many of these commands (a good number being my own) over the years, and whenever I see a command starting with for, I use these questions and steps to figure out what the code is doing:

1. What's the option? Is it optionless, /D, /R, /L, or /F?

2. Based on the option, what type of input is it using? If it's optionless, is the input a file, files, or a list of values? If it's /D, expect a directory as input. If it's /R, expect a recursive process on an input of one or more files. If it's /L, look at the three numbers defining the iterative loop. In all four of these cases, next step through the logic in the code block given the input.

   But if the option is /F, you've only just begun the deconstruction. What type of input is the command using? If there are no quotes, the input is a file-set; if back quotes, a command. If double quotes, usebackq translates to a file-set; otherwise, a string. If single quotes, usebackq translates to a string; otherwise, a command.

3. Determine what the input is contributing. Does the file-set have a wildcard? Roughly how many files are being processed? What type of data is in the file or files? Is the string hardcoded or a variable? What does the command do, and what's its output? Roughly how many lines of output are created? How consistent is the data—that is, will there be header or trailer data?

4. Examine the suboptions and determine how the input is being manipulated. Based on the tokens and delims clauses (or their defaults), how many tokens are created, and how will they be populated from the input? Are any records dropped with skip or eol clauses?

5. Identify the for variable, perhaps %%i, and determine the input data associated with it and its subsequent variables, perhaps %%j and %%k.

6. Examine the code block. Determine how the for variable, and any implied variables, are referenced. Is something being copied, renamed, deleted, or processed in any way?

Maybe these questions and steps seem overwhelming, but to demonstrate how easy they are to use, let's deconstruct some code. Someone you just met online has given you this command telling you that it will back up some files. Just run it:

```
for /F "usebackq tokens=1,3" %%x in (`xcopy * %userprofile%\%random%\`) do (
    if "%%y" neq "copied" > %%x echo This file has been randomly moved.
)
```

But before executing this, you should deconstruct it. Using the prior six steps:

1. The option is /F.
2. Back quotes encase the input, so it's a command.
3. The source argument of the xcopy is an asterisk, meaning that the command copies all files from the current directory to an oddly named folder using two pseudo-environment variables that I've yet to discuss (but will in Chapter 21). If this command copies five files successfully, the output will be a list of the five source files, followed by the trailer record stating: 5 File(s) copied.
4. Based on the tokens clause and the lack of a delims clause, this code extracts the first and third tokens from the space-delimited input. For most of the output, the first token is the full path and name of the source file, assuming that there are no embedded spaces, and the third token is null. For the last line of input, or the trailer record, the first token resolves to the number of files copied, while the third token is the word copied.
5. The %%x is the path and filename up until the last line of output when it becomes the number of files copied. The %%y is nothing at all (again assuming no embedded spaces) before resolving to copied while processing the last line of output. So far, so good.
6. Shifting to the code block, the if command filters out the last record where %%y resolves to the specific text, meaning that for every file that's copied the echo command replaces its entire contents with what looks to be a vague threat.

This looks to be more than a little suspicious. The code is hiding away all files from the current directory, including the bat file itself assuming it's in the current directory, in a randomly named folder. Then it wipes out and replaces the contents of each source file with some text. It's of little consolation that files with embedded spaces in their name may be spared.

Because you now know how to deconstruct a for command, you weren't fooled by this bat file. Without executing the code, you've deduced that it's malicious code—a bat virus.

Summary

In this chapter, you learned about the file reading option of the for command, and you learned that it does much more than read files. The input can be a file, a string, or the output of a command, each with distinct syntaxes. I detailed the syntax for manipulating the input data, creating tokens, and using those tokens in the code block of the command. I also demonstrated much of this functionality with some real-world problems, finishing up with a discussion about how to deconstruct this important command.

In the next chapter, I'll close out Part II with an examination of a few advanced techniques that will either solve a problem associated with using the for command or solve a problem with the use of the for command.

20

ADVANCED FOR TECHNIQUES

The previous three chapters have shown the power of the for command, but they've also demonstrated how tricky it can be to use and even exposed some limitations. In this chapter, I'll explore some advanced topics, including techniques for working around some of those limitations.

In this chapter, I'll explain how to perform the following tasks:

- Make the interpreter honor null values between consecutive delimiter characters in the data interrogated by the for /F command

- Force a string to uppercase (or lowercase) with traditional Batch or by embedding either a PowerShell or Python command into the Batch code, a technique you can extend to other commands, languages, and applications

- Implement two levels of delayed expansion inside the code block of a for command

- Handle escaping in a for command, particularly using the double quote in the delims clause

These techniques will allow you to process more types of data and more complex variables. If you code bat files long enough, at least a couple of these topics will become relevant to you. More important, they should demonstrate a means of problem solving that will spark your imagination when other yet unknown problems arise.

Honoring Nulls

In Chapter 19, I alluded to the fact that when using the delims clause to divvy a string up into individual tokens, the interpreter doesn't honor nulls. Consider the contents of a file named *staff.csv* that contains five items in each employee's record: first, middle, and last names followed by job title and government ID:

```
Amy,Amanda,Andersen,Architect,111-11-1111
Colin,,Clark,Coder,222-22-2222
Mai,Maria,McManus,Manager,333-33-3333
```

The data is well organized, but not very readable. However, the following code displays a rudimentary report to the console with data from the first four tokens, while not displaying the sensitive data at the end of the record—or at least that's the intention:

```
set cnt=0
for /F "usebackq tokens=1-4 delims=," %%a in ("C:\Batch\staff.csv") do (
   set /A cnt += 1
   > con echo Employee !cnt!:
   > con echo    First Name: %%a
   > con echo   Middle Name: %%b
   > con echo     Last Name: %%c
   > con echo     Job Title: %%d
)
```

The first two records generate the following, but notice that there's a major problem:

```
Employee 1:
   First Name: Amy
  Middle Name: Amanda
    Last Name: Andersen
    Job Title: Architect
Employee 2:
   First Name: Colin
  Middle Name: Clark
    Last Name: Coder
    Job Title: 222-22-2222
```

Colin doesn't have a middle name as you can see in the data Colin,,Clark, but the for /F command just skips over the null between the two commas, skewing the later data and exposing Colin's government ID. In many situations, such as when delimiting on any number of spaces, this behavior is exactly what you might want as a coder, but not here. When presented with data like this, you need a means of forcing Batch to honor the null.

This solution inserts a space between consecutive comma delimiters with the use of nested for /F commands:

```
   set cnt=0
❶ for /F "usebackq tokens=*" %%r in ("C:\Batch\staff.csv") do (
      set inRec=%%r
   ❷ for /F "tokens=1-4 delims=," %%a in ("!inRec:,,=, ,!") do (
         set /A cnt += 1
         > con echo Employee !cnt!:
         > con echo     First Name: %%a
      ❸ > con echo    Middle Name: %%b
         > con echo      Last Name: %%c
         > con echo      Job Title: %%d
) )
```

At the beginning of the outer for /F command ❶, I store the entire record in the inRec variable and then use it as text input of the inner for /F command ❷, but take a close look at that input: !inRec:,,=, ,!. First, I resolve inRec with exclamation marks because I've assigned it in the code block. More important, this syntax replaces double commas with two commas separated by a space, which in effect inserts a space. The inner for /F command ❷ passes four comma-delimited tokens into its code block, and when processing Colin's data, that inserted space becomes the second token, %%b, and I write it to the console as the middle name ❸ with the rest of the information.

The report for Amy is unchanged, and Colin's entry looks much better:

```
Employee 2:
   First Name: Colin
  Middle Name:
    Last Name: Clark
    Job Title: Coder
```

His middle name correctly displays as nothing, and his government ID is hidden from sight.

While these nested commands work for this particular data, the logic is far from bulletproof. It doesn't work when a null is the very first token in a record because such a null doesn't present as double commas; the null first token manifests as just a comma leading the record, followed by the second token. It also doesn't catch two consecutive nulls, or triple commas, inserting a space before the second comma, but not after it. Finally, these nested for commands change the null to a space, so it is altered. Depending on how you plan to use the data, that often won't be an issue, but at times you'll want to maintain data integrity.

All of these stipulations might seem to disqualify this approach, but if you know your data, it may be perfectly acceptable. For instance, in this example data, if you're confident that the middle name is the only token that might be missing and you're fine writing an extra space after the tag for the middle name, this syntax works just fine. But there's always room for improvement.

With a few tweaks to the prior solution, the following code corrects for all of the limitations just discussed:

```
set cnt=0
❶ for /F "usebackq tokens=*" %%r in ("C:\Batch\staff.csv") do (
    set inRec=%%r
  ❷ for /F "tokens=1-4 delims=," %%a in ("_!inRec:,=,_!") do (
    ❸ set a=%%a& set b=%%b& set c=%%c& set d=%%d
      set /A cnt += 1
      > con echo Employee !cnt!:
    ❹ > con echo    First Name: !a:~1!
      > con echo   Middle Name: !b:~1!
      > con echo     Last Name: !c:~1!
      > con echo     Job Title: !d:~1!
) )
```

The outer for /F command ❶ is the same. The inner for /F command ❷ is still passing four comma-delimited tokens, but its input (_!inRec:,=,_!) prepends every token with an underscore. This leading underscore prepends the entire record, which in effect prepends just the first token with an underscore. Then the replacement syntax changes every comma to a comma followed by an underscore, which inserts an underscore after every comma, effectively prepending each of the remaining tokens with an underscore. The null token is now an underscore (,_,), so the interpreter honors it.

While this solves one problem, it causes another; we must strip the newly minted leading underscore off each data item or token before using it. I don't often merge multiple commands on a single line of code, but I've done so with four set commands because they're short, simple, and redundant ❸. The first command, set a=%%a, assigns the token %%a to the variable a, allowing me to substring off the first character later in the code block, !a:~1! ❹, leaving only the data after the leading underscore, which is the original content. I then use the same technique for the other three tokens because I'm confident that every token has a leading underscore.

This technique that prepends every token with a character and then strips it off is far more universal.

Forcing a String to Uppercase

If you haven't picked up on this yet, I love Batch coding, but there are times when another coding language offers a different solution, maybe even a better solution, from what I can devise in Batch. For instance, forcing text to uppercase is a trivial exercise in modern languages that have some sort of callable method, such as .toUpper() found in PowerShell or Python's .upper(). Unfortunately, Batch doesn't have a command, or any built-in mechanism, that converts text to uppercase, but I'll show some different means of completing this task.

By now you've seen a few instances of where we've built something from scratch, and for this solution we'll use the case-insensitivity endemic to Batch to create a routine that actually alters the case of text. The following routine accepts a variable name of a string as input and returns the same variable with its contents forced to uppercase:

```
:ToUpper
for %%u in (A B C D E F G H I J K L M N O P Q R S T U V W X Y Z) do (
    set %~1=!%~1:%%u=%%u!
)
goto :eof
```

This optionless for command executes the set command to update the variable with delayed expansion 26 times, once for each character of the alphabet, where each pass resolves %%u to an uppercase character. (Maybe I should've broken with my convention and used %%U here.)

The first pass changes A to A, which looks redundant until you remember that the Batch text replacement syntax is case-insensitive, meaning that this technique changes A and a both to A. Next, we change B to B, C to C, and so on until we exhaust the entire alphabet.

When the for loop completes, it has changed all lowercase letters to their uppercase counterparts without affecting the existing uppercase letters and nonalphabetical characters. The variable passed into this logic as the lone parameter now contains the uppercase text.

You can create a similar routine to force a string to lowercase by changing the input list of values to the set of all lowercase characters. The only other change might be to the label, which you might update to something like :ToLower.

Embedding a PowerShell Command

An alternative solution is to use that PowerShell command mentioned earlier as input to a Batch for /F command. Yes, you read that correctly; you can embed logic from another coding language into Batch code. But before seeing the PowerShell command as part of the for /F command, let's see it run at the command prompt.

If your Windows computer is loaded with PowerShell, you can execute PowerShell commands at the command prompt, and unless you purchased your computer before the first iPhone was released, it's on there, packaged with every Windows operating system since XP SP2 (circa 2006).

Enter this at the command prompt:

```
powershell 'Set this to Upper-Case'.toUpper^(^)
```

The interpreter writes the text between the single quotes to the console, with every alpha character capitalized.

At a glance, this looks like a Batch command named powershell, but there's no such command. Instead, this is the program, *powershell.exe*, and the interpreter should find it as part of the path hierarchy (*C:\Windows\System32\ WindowsPowerShell\v1.0* on most computers). The argument to the program is the PowerShell command that converts text to uppercase, which happens to use dot notation, the antithesis of traditional Batch. The text being forced to uppercase is inside the single quotes, followed by the dot and the appropriate PowerShell method for the task with its parentheses escaped.

You can also put this command into a bat file, and it works great if you're happy seeing SET THIS TO UPPER-CASE written to stdout, but you want this text assigned to a variable. That's where the for /F command comes into play:

```
:ToUpper
for /F "usebackq tokens=*" %%u in (`powershell '!%~1!'.toUpper^(^)`) do (
    set %~1=%%u
)
goto :eof
```

As in the first solution, this routine has one parameter that functions as input and output—that is, the name of the variable containing the text.

The back quotes encasing the input of the for /F command tell the interpreter that a command is the input, in this case an embedded PowerShell command. Notice that this command looks very much like the command that we earlier entered at the command prompt. The only difference is that !%~1! now replaces the hardcoded text. The %~1 parameter resolves to the input variable name; then the exclamation marks and delayed expansion resolve the variable to its value. The output of the PowerShell command is the uppercase version of this text, and the interpreter sends that text into the code block as the variable %%u where we finally reassign it to the same input parameter: %~1.

Embedding a Python Command

There's no need to stop with a PowerShell command. Anything that you can enter at the command prompt can be valid input to a for /F command, including the invocation of any program, not just Batch commands. For this demonstration, I'll invoke the Python runtime, but you can use the runtime for any language as long as you can execute it at the command prompt. You can even execute a program that you've written and compiled in another language and treat its output as input to a for /F command.

Unlike PowerShell, your Windows computer probably didn't come with the Python runtime installed, but you can download it from *https://www .python.org/downloads/*. This isn't a Python book (although No Starch Press does have some great offerings), so I won't delve into the syntax in detail, but with Python installed on your computer, the following routine is functionally equivalent to the previous two that share the same label:

```
:ToUpper
 set subopts=usebackq tokens=*
 for /F "%subopts%" %%u in (`python -c ^"print^('!%~1!'.upper^(^)^)^"`) do (
    set %~1=%%u
 )
 goto :eof
```

I promised not to delve, but very briefly, python is the extensionless executable, or runtime, and -c tells the runtime that a single Python command
comes next. The print() function writes the output generated from what's
inside its parentheses, which is the resolved input variable encased in single
quotes, a dot, and the Python method that converts a string to uppercase.
The Python command is much easier to read when you remove the six
escape characters: "print('!%~1!'.upper())".

The set command in the code block once again assigns the output from
the embedded command to its lone parameter. But also notice that I'm setting a variable to text containing both the usebackq keyword and the tokens
clause, and then I resolve that text as part of the for /F command. There
are two reasons for this. The first and most immediate is that the command
wouldn't have fit on the page otherwise (although it would've been perfectly
valid). Second, this is another opportunity for me to remind you how we
can piece together commands in an uncompiled scripting language.

The actual PowerShell and Python commands themselves are certainly
simple, but the Batch machinations needed to use them do add some complexity. It's usually not the first technique that comes to mind to solve a
problem, but when you can really make use of a command from another
language, the for /F command offers you an effective means of assigning its
output.

NOTE   *In Chapter 19, for the sake of consistency, I recommended getting into the habit of
using usebackq when a command is the input to a for /F command. Part of my ratio-
nale was that while neither the back quote nor the single quote is typically found in
such commands, the single quote is the more likely of the two. For these last two examples, the keyword and encasing back quotes aren't just good practice; they're required
because the embedded PowerShell and Python commands both contain single quotes.*

Two Levels of Delayed Expansion

Delayed expansion is one great feature of Batch that's not available in most
other languages. As you gain experience and start building a more interesting and complex codebase, you'll come upon the fairly common issue
of handling two levels of delayed expansion inside a for command's code
block.

In Chapter 3, I demonstrated delayed expansion by defining variables
containing the culinary delights of five cities. Here are two:

```
set foodNash=Hot Chicken
set foodNYC=Thin Crust Pizza
```

Using the same abbreviations, I also set up variables for the full name of each city:

```
set NashFull=Nashville
set NYCFull=New York City
```

Ultimately, the following echo command contains two examples of delayed expansion that resolve these variables, assuming that city is assigned a valid city abbreviation:

```
> con echo The best !food%city%! can be found only in !%city%Full!.
```

Now let's build on this example to make a list of all 50 states in the United States and assign a culinary capital to each. For instance, while Jefferson City is the capital of Missouri, St. Louis with its frozen custard is considered by many its culinary capital. In the state where I grew up, Connecticut, a long-standing debate still brews between the thin crust pizza unique to New Haven and Middletown's steamed cheeseburger. I've no desire to get into the middle of that rhubarb, but for the sake of this exercise, some authoritative body (me) has been given the power to define the culinary capital of each state, along with that city's, and therefore that state's, dish. Given a list of state postal abbreviation codes, I can define the culinary capital of each like so:

```
set culCapTN=Nash
set culCapNY=NYC
set culCapIL=Chic
set culCapLA=NO
set culCapMO=STL
```

For instance, the culinary capital of TN (Tennessee), culCapTN, is Nash (Nashville). Now we can use the two-digit state codes as input to a for command where delayed expansion resolves the culinary capital variable into city abbreviations. Then a second level of delayed expansion resolves those abbreviations into foods and full city names.

These state codes could be coming from data in a file, but to keep this exercise as simple as possible, I'm using a hardcoded list of state codes as the input to an optionless for command:

```
for %%s in (TN NY IL LA MO) do (
    set city=!culCap%%s!
    > con echo The best !food%city%! can be found only in !%city%Full!.
)
```

The %%s variable resolves to the state code in each of the five passes. In the first pass of the data, !culCap%%s! resolves to !culCapTN!, which then resolves to Nash, which we assign to the city variable. Then the echo command, lifted verbatim from Chapter 3, resolves the two examples of delayed expansion just as it did in the prior chapter, right?

Wrong! If such a scenario had worked, I wouldn't label it an "advanced technique." While the interpreter successfully assigns a city abbreviation to city, when inside a code block such as this one, a variable has two different values: exclamation mark delimiters resolve it to the value it has taken on in the code block, and percent sign delimiters resolve it to its value before the block was ever executed.

Hence, %city% resolves to nothing (or whatever it was set to in prior code), and then !food%city%! resolves to !food!, which in turn most likely resolves to nothing as well. The code doesn't hang or throw an abort—even worse, it just displays an incomplete sentence.

We're in a quandary. Since city was set inside the code block, the only way of resolving it to its current value involves exclamation marks, but delayed expansion demands that we resolve the inner variable with percent signs. (When first faced with this dilemma, most every coder, if not every coder, tries interchanging the delimiters. Try if you must, but it just doesn't work.) In some way, shape, or form, you must make city resolvable via percent signs.

One solution involves a hidden routine. This technique doesn't assign the results of the first delayed expansion resolution to a variable such as city; instead, it passes the value to a routine:

```
for %%s in (TN NY IL LA MO) do (
   call :WriteFoodText "!culCap%%s!"
)
if 0 equ 1 (
  :WriteFoodText
  > con echo The best !food%~1! can be found only in !%~1Full!.
   goto :eof
)
```

The code in the routine then resolves the city as a simple parameter with the %~1 syntax. Since the routine is performing the resolution outside of the for command's code block, the variable !food%~1! resolves nicely to !foodTN!, which resolves again to Hot Chicken.

This technique isn't without issues, however. It's not the type of involved routine that would normally lend itself to being placed at the end of a bat file, and it definitely would not appear in its own bat file. It's really a single command (plus the label and terminating goto :eof command), so it's best kept close to the call command. But if I had placed the label immediately after this for command, the interpreter would execute the routine once for each state and then again one more time when the for command completes and control falls to the next command. To correct for this, I use a clunky conditional clause that can never be true, 0 equ 1, in an if command that acts as the routine's gatekeeper.

This technique can easily confuse anyone reading the code, but it successfully conceals a hidden routine placed near a call command that is the only means of accessing it. It works, and I've used it often, but it's not the kind of logic you'll want to hang up on the fridge next to your kid's artwork.

The far more elegant solution is to nest a second for command inside the first:

```
for %%s in (TN NY IL LA MO) do (
    for /F "tokens=*" %%c in ("!culCap%%s!") do (
        > con echo The best !food%%c! can be found only in !%%cFull!.
) )
```

First, the %%s resolves to the state code; then !culCap%%s!, which resolves to the corresponding city abbreviation, is the string input to the inner for command, where we assign it to %%c. Hence, the inner for command is nothing more than a means of assigning the city to a variable that we can resolve with percent signs. Notice that I've replaced what was being resolved to null in the problem statement, %city%, with the %%c variable. Again, taking Tennessee as the example, %%c resolves to Nash, and then !food%%c! becomes !foodNash!, which in turn resolves to delicious Hot Chicken. Similarly, !%%cFull! resolves to !NashFull!, which resolves to Nashville. Now, that's some fridge-worthy code!

I use the /F option with the inner for command along with double quotes encasing the text input. Setting the tokens keyword to an asterisk ensures that %%c resolves to the entire text string, even if it has embedded spaces, meaning that the code block executes exactly once. (A much simpler optionless for command would have worked as the inner for command for this particular data, but the for /F command is a more universal solution because it handles inputs both with and without embedded spaces.)

Both solutions detailed in this section write the following output to the console:

```
The best Hot Chicken can be found only in Nashville.
The best Thin Crust Pizza can be found only in New York City.
The best Deep Dish Pizza can be found only in Chicago.
The best Muffuletta Sandwich can be found only in New Orleans.
The best Frozen Custard can be found only in St Louis.
```

The problem statement that I've provided may seem a bit contrived, but the need for this technique presents itself often. More realistic examples usually involve a far more complex situation involving files, arrays, hash tables, and more topics I haven't delved into yet. For instance, to retrieve a target path for a robocopy command, you might read the destination city from a file and then look up the city in a hash table to get that path. But every one of those situations boils down to the same issue: you need to use delayed expansion on a variable previously set in a code block. Be on the lookout for similar situations.

Escaping with the for Command

Escaping special characters in a for command is a challenge that can manifest itself in many different ways, and one such example is in the suboptions clause. Input data is often completely outside of our hands as coders. It would be great if all data files were comma- or pipe-delimited, but many times you are forced to use a more complex set of delimiters. The worst possible situation is text delimited by the double quote. If you're trying to extract six tokens, you might consider this suboptions clause, but it's invalid:

```
"tokens=1-6 delims=""
```

While the interpreter sees the first double quote correctly as the start of the clause, the second terminates the clause, and the third is out of context. But this cryptic-looking clause performs the task:

```
tokens^=1-6^ delims^=^"
```

There's no double quote opening the clause, and the double quote at the end doesn't close the clause—it's the sole entry in the set of delimiters. The double quotes encasing the clause are no more. This allows you to include the double quote in the delims clause, as long as you escape it with a preceding caret. But the lack of double quotes encasing the options clause causes other issues. Equal signs and even spaces are no longer protected by the encasing double quotes and are now also in need of escaping.

I've placed a caret before both equal signs. The space in between the two keyword clauses would terminate the larger suboptions clause, so that also needs escaping. That particular caret appears to trail the 6, but it really leads the space. In a less-than-well-documented feature of Batch, you can drop the encasing double quotes as long as you escape special characters and spaces.

Now let's put this all together and test it. Consider the very small file, *UglyData.txt*, with just this one line of data with five double quotes delimiting the six words:

```
This"is"some"messed"up"data
```

This for /F command contains the options clause discussed earlier:

```
for /F tokens^=1-6^ delims^=^" %%a in (C:\Batch\UglyData.txt) do (
   > con echo %%a %%f %%b no longer %%d %%e.
)
```

Here's the output to the console:

```
This data is no longer messed up.
```

In Chapter 19, I mentioned that I usually use usebackq when reading a file. I didn't here because the suboptions are already getting messy, but if you put double quotes around the input file, you would need to add usebackq^ and a space before the tokens clause. (You'll see something similar to this shortly.)

The same principle works when there are multiple delimiters. Let's make *UglyData.txt* even uglier by adding caret, pipe, percent sign, and ampersand delimiters:

```
This^is|some%messed"up&data
```

Now the following suboptions clause makes this work:

```
tokens^=1-6^ delims^=^"^|%%^^^&
```

A caret escapes all of these special characters (even the caret delimiter) except for one; we can only escape the percent sign with another percent sign.

The need for a double quote in the set of delimiters might not come up often, but this technique is indispensable when it does.

We aren't done escaping just yet. In this next example, I'll use the same data and write the same output to the console, but the source of the data will be different. I'll pull the ugly data out of a file and set it to a variable, which will require changes to both the data and the for /F command.

I'll start with the data. In Chapter 14, you learned that when setting a variable, you must escape all special characters, but even this leaves you with a variable containing special characters that can't be resolved later without exposing them. The solution is two levels of escaping:

```
set uglyData=This^^^^is^^^|some%%%%messed^^^"up^^^&data
```

With this set command, all of the double carets resolve to single carets. The interpreter discards all of the other carets because they are escaping other characters; the double percent signs resolve to one, resulting in four becoming two. Finally, the interpreter sets uglyData to the This^^is^|some% %messed^"up^&data text. The next time we resolve this variable, the existing escape characters will be dropped.

There are changes to the for /F command as well:

```
for /F usebackq^ tokens^=1-6^ delims^=^"^|%%^^^& %%a in ('%uglyData%') do (
   > con echo %%a %%f %%b no longer %%d %%e.
)
```

The command contains the more complex delims clause with the set of five delimiters, all of which are escaped. The %uglyData% text input to the for command resolves to This^is|some%messed"up&data, encased in single quotes, and the usebackq keyword is in place with its trailing escape character.

Since a double quote is part of the input, this for /F command must use single quotes around the input string, which necessitates the usebackq keyword. (It's one of those blue moon situations mentioned in Chapter 19.) Notice that Batch more easily handled the double quote when it was inside a file being read; parsing strings is usually more complex than parsing file data. Finally, we see This data is no longer messed up. written to the console.

The biggest takeaway from this discussion is that you should always figure out how many levels of escaping to expect and make sure that the code can support all expected special characters in the input.

Summary

In this chapter, I presented some advanced techniques that I've come across in my career as a Batch coder. It's not an exhaustive list of interesting for command conundrums, but it's representative of many. To tap into the full power of Batch, you must understand the for command, and that requires experimentation and exploration. Don't be intimidated. If you code in Batch long enough, you'll encounter something not covered here, but if you follow the thought process that went into these examples, you should be able to experiment your way to a solution.

This rounds out Part II, but it's by no means the last you'll see of the for command in the pages ahead. Many more applications of this command are yet to come, but in the next chapter, I'll step back and explore some important pseudo-environment variables.

PART III

ADVANCED TOPICS

Part I covered bat file essentials, and Part II explored the all-important for command. Part III will include techniques that require the use of this vital command, along with some useful and advanced topics.

In this part of the book, you'll learn about pseudo-environment variables, writing reports, recursion, text searches, automatic restarts, and bat files that build other bat files. Other topics will delve into conditional execution (again), arrays, hash tables, and testing and troubleshooting. I'll finish up with object-oriented design and an application of it in the form of data structures called stacks and queues. Many of these topics weren't envisioned by the creators of Batch. That hasn't stopped us before and won't stop us in the following chapters.

21

PSEUDO-ENVIRONMENT VARIABLES

I introduced environment variables in Chapter 2 with the set command, and they have found their way onto nearly every page since. You can define and resolve a simple variable and then maybe reset and use it again in various ways. *Pseudo-environment variables* are similar but also quite distinct. You can resolve them just like regular environment variables, but their origins or how they are set are substantially different.

We've already discussed a few pseudo-environment variables, including path, pathext, cd, and errorlevel. All pseudo-environment variables share some characteristics, but many have unique qualities. There are different means of setting many of them, and some you should never set at all. Some are active before you run a bat file, and the interpreter updates others repeatedly during an execution.

Each pseudo-environment variable has an intrinsic quality in the Batch universe that you must understand before properly using it. In this chapter, I'll explain the intricacies of some pseudo-environment variables already touched on and explore some useful ones that we'll use in future chapters. I'll also provide the long-promised explanation of the primary difference between bat and cmd files from the coder's perspective.

Date and Time

You can easily retrieve the current date and time with the aptly named date and time pseudo-environment variables, respectively:

```
> con echo Date = "%date%";  Time = "%time%"
```

This command would have produced the following output if executed shortly after the Boston Red Sox snapped their 86-year championship drought:

```
Date = "Wed 10/27/2004";  Time = "23:39:12.34"
```

The date variable contains the current date, formatted as day of week, month, day, and year. The day of the week always presents as a three-character mixed-case abbreviation, followed by a space, a two-byte month, a forward slash, a two-byte day, another slash, and a four-byte year. For instance, Sun 06/08/1986 is an example from the early Batch era.

The time variable contains the current time, formatted as hours, minutes, seconds, and hundredths of seconds. It uses military time or a 24-hour clock, so 11:39 PM translates to 23:39:00.00. If the hour is a single digit, Batch precedes it with a space instead of a leading zero; just before the stroke of 10:00 AM, time resolves to a space followed by 9:59:59.99, and midnight presents as a space followed by 0:00:00.00.

It's certainly an oddity, but keep in mind that time has a leading space in lieu of a zero, while date has a leading 0 for all the one-digit months and days of the month.

Since date and time are nicely formatted, you can easily use them to enhance reports and logfiles, and because date is consistently formatted, it's easy to substring out a datestamp, formatted as CCYYMMDD, as shown in Listing 21-1.

```
set #=%date%
set datestamp=%#:~10,4%%#:~4,2%%#:~7,2%
```

Listing 21-1: Two commands in the Datestamp.bat *bat file to build a datestamp*

(To save keystrokes I like to use the pound sign as a very short variable name, but only for a very concise and limited use. Using this variable much later in the bat file would be confusing, but using it immediately within the next line or two is a nice way to condense the code. Though I must admit that %#:~7,2% is esoteric and not to everyone's liking.)

Using a different technique, here's the code to build a timestamp formatted as HHMMSSss:

```
set timestamp=%time: =0%
set timestamp=%timestamp::=%
set timestamp=%timestamp:.=%
```

The first command replaces the leading space, if it exists, with a 0. The next two commands remove the two colons and the decimal point.

Unless coding and testing before 10 AM, it's disturbingly easy to forget about the leading space, but it's critical. If you miss it while testing in the afternoon, the variable will suddenly contain a space at the stroke of midnight, and depending on how you plan to use it, failures could ensue at a very inopportune time of day. Consider this one more batveat.

Datestamps and timestamps have many uses. You can use them in filenames to indicate their creation date and time. In an if command, you can compare them to other datestamps or timestamps to turn on logic at a specific date and time. You can even capture them before and after some process to measure elapsed time.

Prompt

The prompt pseudo-environment variable does double duty as a command. Just as path is a command to change the path variable, prompt is a command to change the prompt variable.

In Chapter 12, when discussing the interpreter-generated output (stdout), I mentioned that the interpreter prefixes the output from every command, whether it ends up on the console or redirected to a trace file, with the prompt. By default, the prompt is the current directory followed by a greater-than symbol. For instance, if the two lines of code producing a datestamp in *Datestamp.bat* from Listing 21-1 were run from the *C:\Batch* directory, it might generate the following output to a trace file:

```
C:\Batch>set #=Wed 10/27/2004
C:\Batch>set datestamp=20041027
```

But defaults are made to be changed. The prompt variable contains hardcoded text and/or special codes that define the content of the prompt seen in stdout, and the prompt command is the tool that updates the prompt variable. The command's lone argument is the new prompt variable, which'll change what we see in stdout.

To demonstrate, if I were particularly self-absorbed and wanted my signature on every line of executed code, this simple command would assuage my ego:

```
prompt Jack's$SCode$G
```

Two pieces of hardcoded text are in the argument, `Jack's` and `Code`. Additionally, two special codes insert a space (`$S`) in between the words and a greater-than sign (`$G`) at the end. Running the same two lines of code on the same date now produces this output:

```
Jack's Code>set #=Wed 10/27/2004
Jack's Code>set datestamp=20041027
```

But this command and variable were not created for vanity; they were created to populate the prompt with customized information. Consider this far more complex and esoteric example:

```
prompt %~NX0$A$N:$$$C$D$B$T$F$G
```

This `prompt` command isn't the easiest to read, but here it's broken down:

%~NX0   Bat filename and extension; perhaps resolves to `Datestamp.bat`

$A   Ampersand; resolves to &

$N   Drive letter; perhaps resolves to `C`

:   Hardcoded text; appears as :

$$ Dollar sign; resolves to $

$C   Open parenthesis; resolves to (

$D   Date; perhaps resolves to `Wed 10/27/2004`

$B   Pipe; resolves to |

$T   Time; perhaps resolves to `23:39:12.34`

$F   Close parenthesis; resolves to)

$G   Greater-than sign; resolves to >

After you assign this `prompt` variable, executing the same two lines might result in this output:

```
Datestamp.bat&C:$(Wed 10/27/2004|23:39:12.34)>set #=Wed 10/27/2004
Datestamp.bat&C:$(Wed 10/27/2004|23:39:12.35)>set datestamp=20041027
```

Of these entities in this `prompt` variable, all but a couple are special codes specific to the `prompt` command. One byte, the colon, is hardcoded, and the first item, `%~NX0`, is just a resolved variable. It happens to be the name and extension of the bat file being executed, but most any variable would work here.

The special code for time (`$T`) allows you to see exactly when each and every command executes. If a bat file seems to take longer to execute than it should, this is a simple means of pinpointing the bottleneck. In the previous example, the fact that the second command executed a hundredth of a second after the first is displayed in the prompt, while the rest of the prompt is unchanged.

Also, notice that the greater-than sign ($G) is the last character in the prompt. Without it, the prompt bleeds into the command following it, producing a rather unreadable stdout. It isn't required, but it's good form to conclude the prompt with the greater-than sign or some sort of special character.

You can even add a space or two after the greater-than sign to further distinguish the prompt from the output. Regardless of the current prompt variable, this command will add two spaces to it:

```
prompt %prompt%$S$S
```

This command clearly shows the two uses of prompt. Assuming that the default prompt was active, the prompt variable resolves to PG (current directory and greater-than sign). The command then appends this with SS and uses it as the argument to the prompt command:

```
C:\Batch>prompt $P$G$S$S
```

This command activates the new prompt with trailing spaces for the execution of any subsequent commands:

```
C:\Batch>  set #=Wed 10/27/2004
C:\Batch>  set datestamp=20041027
```

With hardcoded text and all the characters available with the special codes, you can easily customize the prompt to virtually any text imaginable to suit any need. I showed a number of the special codes earlier, but the help command provides a complete list.

Random Numbers

The random pseudo-environment variable resolves to a random number between 0 and 32,767, inclusive. You can use this to simulate a coin flip; an even number is heads, and an odd is tails. If you want to randomly launch a process on one of any number of servers, this pseudo-environment variable gives you that ability.

To demonstrate one use of random, in Chapter 15 I demonstrated interactive Batch with a bat file that offered up a joke, pun, or riddle—but just one of each. Unfortunately, it didn't take long to exhaust the material. Now imagine a library of 100 bat jokes, 100 bat puns, and 100 bat riddles. Unfortunately (or fortunately), I won't list them here. Imagine further that when the user asks for a pun, we randomly select one of the 100 puns from the library.

To make this happen, we need a couple of things. First, we need to put the 100 puns into an array so that we can select them individually. (That'll come in Chapter 29.) More important at this moment, we need a means of generating one random number out of 100 possible numbers. The following `set /A` command uses the `random` pseudo-environment variable and the modulo operator to generate a *random* number between 0 and 99 (sort of):

```
set /A punNbr = %random% %% 100
```

If the puns are labeled 0 through 99, we can simply choose the pun based on the value of `punNbr`. If the puns are labeled 1 through 100, we merely need to add 1 to the result:

```
set /A punNbr = %random% %% 100 + 1
```

There are two reasons I mentioned that this "sort of" works. First, like the vast majority of computer-generated random numbers, this is actually a pseudo-random number and not truly random. (Yes, this is the pseudo-random pseudo-environment variable.) When the bat file first starts, the interpreter seeds the random function with the current time, which it uses in the algorithm that generates all future random numbers on request. This means that two bat files starting at the very same moment will see the same set of pseudo-random numbers generated—even two bat files launched within seconds of each other will see very similar *random* numbers, at least for the first few invocations. It's important to be aware of this, although pseudo-random numbers are more than acceptable for most applications.

The second reason `punNbr` isn't truly random is that 32,768, the total number of random numbers, isn't divisible by 100. If you executed the first set command in this section 32,768 times (once for each number from 0 to 32,767), 0 would be the result 328 times. Likewise, 1 through 67 would be the result 328 times each. But you would see 68 as the result only 327 times, and the same goes for all of the numbers up to and including 99. The upshot is that some numbers will be *randomly* selected just slightly more often than other numbers.

The remainder of this section is the inevitable result of a just slightly obsessive-compulsive mathematician becoming a coder who ultimately deals with random numbers. The vast majority of the time a pseudo-random number and modulo arithmetic will more than get the job done, but if you want to find out how to get as close as possible to a truly random number, read on.

AN ARITHMETIC DIGRESSION FOR MY
FELLOW MATH GEEKS

Since 32,768 is a power of two, the modulo function weights all results equally when finding a random number out of possible values equaling a power of two, that is, 2, 4, 8, 16, and so on. If the library has 128 bat puns, `%random% %% 128` weights each pun equally. In the case of 100 puns, it selects 68 numbers

---

slightly more often than the other 32. A popular alternative method involves multiplying the pseudo-random number by the desired number of possible values and dividing by 32,768:

```
set /A punNbr = %random% * 100 / 32768
```

Although this method is widely used, it offers only a slight improvement. The same number of results still occur more often, but instead of being grouped together as the first few numbers in the set, they're now dispersed throughout the set. Out of 100 puns, 68 will still be selected more often; the fact that those 68 aren't consecutive numbers offers little solace.

The following is an example of overthinking in most instances, but these few lines of code ensure that every number from 1 through 100 is weighted equally. Each has 327 chances of being selected:

```
set nbrPossVal=100
set /A maxRandNbr = 32768 / %nbrPossVal% * %nbrPossVal% - 1
:GetAnotherRand
set randNbr=%random%
if %randNbr% gtr %maxRandNbr% goto :GetAnotherRand
set /A punNbr = %randNbr% %% %nbrPossVal% + 1
```

You can set the number of possible values, nbrPossVal, to any reasonable number, but I'm still using 100 here. When we divide 32,768 by this number, the decimal part vanishes into the ether, leaving a whole number; multiplying the result by the same number provides the greatest multiple of nbrPossVal less than or equal to 32,768; subtracting 1 provides the maximum random number that we'll accept, maxRandNbr. In this example, that's 32,699: 32,768 / 100 = 327; then 327 × 100 = 32,700; finally, 32,700 − 1 = 32,699.

With the use of a do...while command, we'll simply get another random number after throwing away the rare random number between 32,700 and 32,767, inclusive. Those are the 68 values that gave the results of 0 through 67 each one extra possibility of being chosen. With those gone, we can perform the modulo operation in the last command to get a number between 1 and 100. We haven't eliminated the issue of the variable being a pseudo-random number, but this is as random as random can get in most coding languages without a cryptographic algorithm.

The cmdcmdline Variable

Another interesting pseudo-environment variable is cmdcmdline, or *command command line*. It looks redundant, but it's the command line command that originally started the current execution. On Windows computers, the *.bat* extension is associated with the Windows *cmd.exe* program by default, and when you open a bat file, this program executes it. To demonstrate, assume that the *DateTime.bat* bat file contains this command:

```
> con echo %cmdcmdline%
```

Executing the bat file might write this to the console:

```
C:\WINDOWS\system32\cmd.exe /C ""C:\Batch\DateTime.bat" "
```

When you open or double-click a bat file, behind the scenes Windows is calling the *cmd.exe* program with the /C option and the bat file as its argument. If this bat file calls another bat file, the value of cmdcmdline won't change. It's consistently the command that started the high-level process.

You can parse this variable to get some useful information. Even from a called bat file, you can retrieve the original parameter list. If you have redirected stdout to a trace file, the path and name of the trace file are at the end of the variable's value, ready to be extracted. A bat file might be designed to run in two different modes, stand-alone or invoked by another bat file, with slightly different logic needed in each mode. To intelligently determine the mode, compare the contents of this variable to the %0 hidden parameter. If you find the name of the same bat file in both fields, it's the high-level bat file and, therefore, stand-alone. If not, it must be a called bat file.

System Variables

Another class of pseudo-environment variables informs you about the machine where a bat file executes. They are called *system variables*.

A sampling of these system variables includes USERNAME, USERPROFILE, PROCESS_ARCHITECTURE, NUMBER_OF_PROCESSORS, and others that'll be meaningful to anyone familiar with the workings of a Windows computer. The variable ProgramFiles resolves to the root directory where Microsoft has installed its 64-bit program files, and ProgramFiles(x86) does the same for its 32-bit counterpart.

After all of these verbosely named variables, it might seem odd, but OS is a severe abbreviation of *operating system*. The directory for holding *temporary* files is special enough to warrant two system variables, TEMP and TMP, while you can reference the root *Windows directory* via windir.

The USERDOMAIN variable is very handy when your bat file can run in different domains, perhaps even different physical locations. Each domain likely has differing infrastructure, such as pathing for certain resources, and this one variable is the key to making the code intelligent enough to run in those multiple locations. Another system variable that I've used often is COMPUTERNAME. If a process can be launched on any one of dozens of servers, you can use this variable to easily determine exactly where the bat file is being executed.

NOTE *Despite appearances, I'm not being arbitrary with the capitalization of the system variable names in this section. You're probably aware that all Batch variables are case-insensitive and that I typically use camel case, but I show each pseudo-environment variable as Microsoft presents them—that is, what would be displayed by running a* set *command with no arguments at the command prompt to avoid any confusion. Some are entirely uppercase, some entirely lowercase, some are camel case, some are even snake case (words separated by underscores), and a couple even have parentheses in the variable name. It's truly a nightmare for anyone yearning for consistency.*

Explore further on your own. Pull up the command prompt and enter the three-byte command, **set**, to see a list of all the variables set on your machine. All of them are available at the onset of any bat file's execution on that particular computer.

Bat Files vs. cmd Files

In Chapter 1, I introduced bat files and cmd files. At the time, I mentioned that the only significant difference from a coder's perspective concerned how and when the interpreter sets the return code. Here I'll detail those differences.

We've discussed three commands that set errorlevel to a nonzero value when the command fails to execute properly: set, path, and prompt. Actually, most commands do this, but these differ in that when the command executes successfully, they don't set errorlevel to 0. The upshot is that you can't trust the value of errorlevel after you execute one of these commands.

In a cmd file, however, executing these commands successfully always sets errorlevel to 0, and when they fail, they always set errorlevel to a nonzero value. (I said that this was *the* biggest difference. I didn't say it was a *big* difference.)

Most coders, including myself, rarely interrogate the return code for these commands. Even if you pass a nonexistent directory to the path command, it won't fail; it fails only when it can't reset the variable with a valid path for some reason, and I've never seen that happen. Likewise, the prompt command accepts pretty much anything as the prompt variable, and I've never seen it fail either. Setting a simple variable with the set command is also difficult to get wrong. The one possible exception is when using set /A to do some arithmetic. For instance, a missing operand or division by zero generates nonzero values of errorlevel.

That said, if you want to interrogate errorlevel after executing one of these commands, there are two solutions. First, when using a bat file, in some way, shape, or fashion, you need to reset errorlevel to zero before executing the set, path, or prompt command. If the command fails, the interpreter resets errorlevel to a nonzero value; if it succeeds, errorlevel will still be zero. The other option is to use a cmd file.

There's one hurdle to overcome with setting the return code to zero in a bat file. In general, the issue is how to set pseudo-environment variables.

More specifically, errorlevel should never be set to anything with a set command, but there's always a way.

Setting Pseudo-Environment Variables

You have the power to set and reset some pseudo-environment variables. You've learned that path, cd, and prompt act as both commands and variables, where the command resets the variable of the same name. They're set to defaults when a bat file starts, but you can change the values.

Other pseudo-environment variables, such as windir, are already set when a bat file starts, and it would be foolish to reset them. The interpreter sets and resets still other such variables during a bat file's execution, perhaps many times. For instance, most commands reset errorlevel; the time variable takes on a new value every 100th of a second, and if the bat file is running at midnight, date will change as well. You should never set those variables. Notice that I didn't write that you *cannot* set these variables. There's nothing to stop you from executing this command:

```
set errorlevel=0& rem Never Never Never Do This... Ever
```

There's no compiler to prevent this hubris. The interpreter doesn't abort and crash the execution. It essentially says, "So you want to set errorlevel now? This was my variable, but if you want it, fine, it's yours now. But I'll have nothing more to do with it." I probably personify the interpreter more than I should, but it can be so very passive-aggressive.

This simple yet ill-advised set command transforms the variable into a simple user variable and removes it from the domain of the pseudo-environment variables. Subsequent commands will succeed or fail, commands that would normally generate a return code, but since errorlevel is no longer a pseudo-environment variable, it'll remain as is, unchanged from its erroneously assigned value, until the run stream ends or another ill-advised set command erroneously resets it again.

Some of the pseudo-environment variables that should never be set with a set command are errorlevel, date, time, cmdcmdline, and random. When in doubt, it's best to assume that any pseudo-environment variable shouldn't be reset. It wouldn't make sense to reset most of these variables, but there's just one that you might want to reset: errorlevel. In the prior section, I detail just such a scenario.

The following command resets errorlevel to 0 without even mentioning errorlevel:

```
cmd /C exit 0
```

The cmd command opens a new command shell, and the /C option tells the interpreter to execute the command that comes after it and then terminate the new command shell when it's through. In this example, it executes a simple exit command returning 0. The result is that it sets errorlevel to 0—without a set command.

If this looks oddly familiar, that's because I mentioned the *cmd.exe* program earlier in this chapter. You can invoke the same program, which also happens to be the interpreter, with the `cmd` command to execute a bat file or another command.

Summary

Truly understanding pseudo-environment variables will give you more tools, allowing you to complete more tasks. I didn't provide an exhaustive list, but I touched on the important ones. You learned how to manipulate the prompt, how to generate random numbers, and about the dangers of erroneously setting certain pseudo-environment variables. I also discussed the `errorlevel` pseudo-environment variable in two contexts. You can reset it to any number, but not how you probably imagined, and it behaves a little differently in bat files compared to cmd files.

In the next chapter, you'll learn how to create and format reports in Batch using the `date` and `time` pseudo-environment variables.

22

WRITING REPORTS

Even if squinting hard enough to provoke an aneurysm, no one will ever mistake Batch for Power BI or other similar report writers, but when you want a simple formatted text report, Batch is one tool that's up to the challenge.

In this chapter, we'll build a report with real-world data from a pipe-delimited input file. With two pseudo-environment variables from the previous chapter, you'll learn how to build a title with the current date and time, and formatted column headers. You'll also create detail records by reading the input file with a certain command you learned about in Part II. I'll share a few techniques for right- and left-justifying strings, integers, and floating-point data into nicely aligned columns when viewed in a fixed-width or monospace font. Finally, you'll learn how to tally the data to create trailer records with total and average quantities.

And if you are looking to generate a pie graph, histogram, or scatterplot . . . there are other tools.

The Data and Report

For this exercise, we'll start with a simple pipe-delimited file containing three important health measures for a short list of selected wealthy countries from the year 2019. The first token in each record is the name of a country, followed by the percentage of the country's gross domestic product spent on healthcare. This is a great measure of how much money a country spends on healthcare out of its overall wealth. The third token is life expectancy, and the final is the number of avoidable deaths for every 100,000 residents. Avoidable deaths are defined as deaths resulting from a lack of access to effective and quality healthcare for conditions such as diabetes, hypertension, and certain cancers. These last two measures are very good indicators of the effectiveness of a healthcare system. The *HealthStats.dat* file can hold any number of records, but for brevity's sake, I'm including only seven countries and their statistics, as shown in Listing 22-1.

```
Australia|9.3|82.6|62
Canada|10.7|82|72
France|11.2|82.6|60
Germany|11.2|81.1|86
Sweden|11|82.5|65
UK|9.8|81.3|84
US|16.9|78.6|112
```

Listing 22-1: The pipe-delimited HealthStats.dat file containing health statistics

Notice that the first two numeric tokens are floating-point values, but someone (me) didn't include the .0 for a couple of entries' values. We'll have to take that into account in the code. (The data in this file is from the Commonwealth Fund, used with permission, at *https://www.commonwealthfund .org/publications/issue-briefs/2020/jan/us-health-care-global-perspective-2019.*)

It's wonderful data, but pipe-delimited files are not known for their readability. Our task is to convert the data in Listing 22-1 into the far more readable and descriptive report shown in Listing 22-2.

```
                A Comparison of National Health
                Expenditures and Outcomes, 2019
                 Date: 03/23/2020  Time: 14:30


                    % of         Life        Avoidable
    Country         GDP       Expectancy     Deaths/100K
    -------         ----      ----------     -----------
    Australia       9.3          82.6            62
    Canada         10.7          82.0            72
    France         11.2          82.6            60
    Germany        11.2          81.1            86
    Sweden         11.0          82.5            65
    UK              9.8          81.3            84
    US             16.9          78.6           112
    -------         ----      ----------     -----------
    Averages       11.4          81.5            77
```

Listing 22-2: The HealthRpt.txt bat file–generated report

At worst, you might call this report functional. It doesn't have the different font sizes, boxes, highlighting, automatic centering, or other features you might find in an HTML-created report viewed in a browser, but it's useful, informative, and well-formatted.

A report such as this has three distinct parts: introduction, body, and summary, consisting of header, detail, and trailer records, respectively. I'll share the entire bat file to build this report, but I'll break it down into those three parts. At the conclusion of this chapter, you'll be able to build your own data files and create your own reports.

Header Records

The obvious place to start is with the introduction, which consists of the title and column headers. Here's the first part of the bat file that creates the report:

```
    setlocal EnableExtensions EnableDelayedExpansion
❶  set rpt=C:\Batch\HealthRpt.txt
❷  set cnt=0
    set totPerGDP=0
    set totLifeExp=0
    set totDeaths=0

❸ >  %rpt% echo                     A Comparison of National Health
    >> %rpt% echo                     Expenditures and Outcomes, 2019
    >> %rpt% echo                      Date: %date:~4%  Time: %time:~0,5%
    >> %rpt% echo.
❹  >> %rpt% echo                     %% of           Life        Avoidable
    >> %rpt% echo Country             GDP         Expectancy     Deaths/100K
    >> %rpt% echo -------             ----        ----------     -----------
```

After the opening setlocal command, we define the rpt variable ❶ with the path and name of the report file. I'm keeping the variable name succinct because we'll be using it every time we write a record to the report, which will be often. Next, we initialize four variables ❷ to 0. The cnt variable keeps a count of the number of detail records, and the other variables are totals for each of the three quantities in the report, which we'll use in the next two sections of the bat file.

The introduction is actually composed of two parts: the title ❸ and the column headers ❹. In this particular report, they account for seven header records overall, and we'll create them with seven echo commands redirected to the report file.

We start the report by redirecting the beginning of the title to the file defined by the rpt variable ❸; a single redirection character is used for only this command, so if an existing file is present, we overwrite it. We next append the remainder of the title, followed by the date and time and a blank line with the echo. command.

We're populating the date and time in the third record from the aptly named date and time variables, respectively. These pseudo-environment variables introduced in Chapter 21 offer an easy way of documenting when the report was generated. Notice I'm extracting portions of each value to remove the day of the week from the date and the seconds from the time. Sometimes there's such a thing as too much data.

The final three echo commands are writing out the column headers ❹. Most of this data is hardcoded, but notice that I'm escaping the percent sign with another percent so the interpreter doesn't think that it's the start of a very awkward variable name (see Chapter 14).

Some of the data in the title and the column headers appear to be off-kilter, but this is just a result of variable resolution and escaping. The best way to line up everything is to type the title, headers, and a sample data line into a text file using a fixed-width font and line up everything as desired—that is, type up a sample of the report in Listing 22-2. When satisfied with the alignment, copy the resulting headings into the bat file, preceding each with the redirection and an echo command. Then add any escape characters and replace any temporary text such as the sample date and time with the variables that will take their place.

Throughout this last step, let the data shift; everything will realign in the final output. For instance, the record with the date and time ❸ appears to be shifted to the right, but that's only because the variable name with the substringing syntax and the encasing percent signs is longer than the time it will eventually display. Likewise, the extra percent sign ❹ skews the rest of the data in the first column header record. Life and Avoidable don't appear to be lined up with the next two lines, but after the interpreter consolidates the two percent signs into one, everything will again realign.

Detail Records

There's much to unpack, but the following code writes one formatted detail record for each record in the input file and keeps track of the record count and the running totals of the three fields:

```
❶ for /F "usebackq tokens=1-4 delims=|" %%a in ("C:\Batch\HealthStats.dat") do (
  ❷ set ctry=%%a                    eol
  ❸ for /F "tokens=1-2 delims=." %%m in ("%%b") do (
      set dcml=%%n0
      set perGDP=      %%m.!dcml:~0,1!
  )
  ❹ for /F "tokens=1-2 delims=." %%m in ("%%c") do (
      set dcml=%%n0
      set lifeExp=              %%m.!dcml:~0,1!
  )
  ❺ set deaths=              %%d
  ❻ >> %rpt% echo !ctry:~0,15! !perGDP:~-5! !lifeExp:~-14! !deaths:~-15!
  ❼ set /A cnt += 1
    set /A totPerGDP += !perGDP:.=!
    set /A totLifeExp += !lifeExp:.=!
    set /A totDeaths += deaths
)
```

The for /F command ❶ introduced in Chapter 19 is the obvious solution to pull out the four tokens (tokens=1-4) from each record of the pipe-delimited data file (delims=|). This logic assigns the country from the data file to the for variable %%a, which implies that the percent of GDP is %%b, the life expectancy is %%c, and the number of avoidable deaths is %%d.

Aligning Columns with Justified Data

I'm padding the ctry variable ❷, which contains string data, with a number of spaces and ultimately the text eol that doesn't appear in the report. To make the columns line up, I'll make this a left-justified field and ultimately substring out just its first 15 bytes, but for this to work, the field must be at least 15 bytes in length—hence, the space padding.

The eol tag at the end is simply there to demonstrate to the reader that the field has trailing spaces. I'll strip it off before writing the record, so any text would work, but it does stand for *end of line*. (If you are really proud of the report, you can sign your work by entering your name instead.) Without some sort of a marker, a future coder might someday remove the trailing spaces, especially if they're more familiar with languages that ignore trailing spaces, which is almost any language not named Batch.

WARNING   *In Chapter 2, I mentioned that you can place an ampersand, or the command separator, after trailing spaces, but due to a frustrating batveat, that doesn't work in a code block, or at least not the same way. The interpreter balks when you use the ampersand in a code block without an actual command after it, which means you could replace* eol *with* &rem. *In what's even more of an oddity, if escaped, the ampersand works in a code block without a second command, so you can also replace* eol *with* ^&.

Contrast the country variable with the variable corresponding to the last column detailing avoidable deaths per 100,000 people. Instead of trailing spaces, I'm adding 15 *leading* spaces to deaths ❺. This is an integer and unlike the string data items that we should line up by the first character, we should line up avoidable deaths by its final character, or the ones digit.

To right-justify a number, I do the opposite of what I did for a string. I *prepend* the value with a number of spaces so that I can later extract the desired text from the end of the field. To maintain the spaces needed for the report, I'll extract 15 total bytes from this field, so if this field isn't at least 15 bytes long, the resulting data will be askew.

Working with Floating-Point Data

Decimal or floating-point values represent the two middle columns, and since we'll be treating both the same way, I'll focus on just one. The data in the input file expresses life expectancy ❹ as a decimal with a tenths place for all values except for Canada, which happens to be an integer, but we want a decimal place for each value in the report, and we want to line up the numbers on that decimal place.

I'm resolving life expectancy from the third token, %%c, of the outer for command ❶ and using it as the input string to one of the inner for commands ❹. Delimiting on the dot breaks the value up into the whole number before the decimal and the decimal part after the decimal point. I'm assigning the latter value to the dcml or decimal variable while appending 0. Batch syntax can be so esoteric it's easy to miss, but in the four bytes %%n0, the first three are the second token of the inner for loop, and the last is a hardcoded number.

In the second and final command inside the code block of the inner for command, I'm extracting the first byte of the decimal: !dcml:~0,1!. For most countries, we append 0 to the decimal value and immediately strip it off. That seems pointless until Canada is considered. Since its life expectancy is 82 with no decimal value present, the 0 tacked onto the end becomes the sole decimal byte. Finally, I string together the whole number, %%m, a dot, and the first digit of the decimal value. Lest we forget, this must all follow a number of leading spaces for right-justification. If we had wanted to format numbers with two decimal points, such as dollar amounts, we could have appended two zeros and extracted the first two bytes.

(In this example, %%n0 represents a for variable followed by the hardcoded 0, but changing just one byte produces something quite different: %~n0. The n now turns into a modifier for the hidden parameter, %~0. Hence, %~n0 resolves to the extensionless name the bat file. Oh, the vagaries of Batch.)

The logic for the percentage of each country's GDP spent on healthcare ❸ is nearly identical to the logic for life expectancy. Because of how the columns line up, the only difference is the number of leading spaces we attach to each value.

Writing a Detail Record

These four variables culminate in the line that actually writes the formatted text string to the report file ❻. This is a redirection of an echo command similar to what we've seen earlier in this chapter, resolving the four variables and extracting portions via substringing, each separated by a space.

To left-justify the ctry variable, I use an offset of 0 and length of 15, thus extracting the first 15 bytes and dropping everything else (including the eol marker). The next three values, perGDP, lifeExp, and deaths, are to be right-justified numbers, so I substring with negative offsets to grab the last 5, 14, and 15 bytes, respectively.

The various lengths are dependent on the layout. The best way to format the detail record and determine the proper layout is to type up the same type of sample line I suggested for the header records. Figure out the lengths of each justified field, experiment, and expect the need for some tweaking. Just be careful to make sure there are at least *n* bytes in a string if you plan to extract *n* bytes from it. Put more plainly, the country is 15 bytes, so make sure you append 15 spaces to ensure perfect alignment.

Working with Counters and Totals

The last four lines of the code block ❼ all perform some arithmetic with the augmented assignment operators from Chapter 6. The first is a simple counter, cnt, keeping track of the number of entries. The last three, totPerGDP, totLifeExp, and totDeaths, are cumulative totals of the three quantities in the report. I've named these variable names with tot, for *total*, prepending a familiar variable name.

The logic is straightforwardly incrementing the variable for total deaths by the number of deaths in each record. The other two are decimals, and as you learned in Chapter 6, floating-point arithmetic requires a little ingenuity. The text replacement syntax removes the decimal point before adding each to the total—for example, !perGDP:.=!. This effectively multiples the total by 10, so we'll need to address this discrepancy when calculating the averages and writing out the trailer records.

I didn't do it in this report, but you may want to create a page break after a certain number of detail records. Typically, you might want a page number at the bottom followed by a few blank lines before reproducing the headers followed by another page of detail lines. To do this after every 25 detail lines, interrogate cnt %% 25 at the end of the loop. If equal to 0, the record count is a multiple of 25, so you can initiate a page break. You can also create another counter for the page number and write it as part of the page trailer information and move the header logic to a callable routine so that you can invoke it one to many times.

Trailer Records

The third and final section of the bat file finds and formats the averages before writing them to the report:

```
❶ set /A avePerGDP = (totPerGDP * 10 / cnt + 5) / 10
  set /A aveLifeExp = (totLifeExp * 10 / cnt + 5) / 10
  set /A avgDeaths = (totDeaths * 10 / cnt + 5) / 10
❷ set avePerGDP=      %avePerGDP%
  set aveLifeExp=            %aveLifeExp%
  set avgDeaths=            %avgDeaths%

❸ >> %rpt% echo -------        ----   ----------   -----------
  >> %rpt% echo Averages      !avePerGDP:~-5,-1!.!avePerGDP:~-1!^
   !aveLifeExp:~-13,-1!.!aveLifeExp:~-1! !avgDeaths:~-15!
  goto :eof
```

To find the averages, we could simply divide the totals by the number of detail records, but since Batch truncates the decimal part of the solution, everything is in effect rounded down. To compensate, each set /A command ❶ first multiplies the value by 10 and divides by cnt. Adding 5 to this number corrects for the rounding so that dividing by 10 produces the rounded average. For example, 77.4 deaths should round down: 77.4 + 0.5 = 77.9, which is 77 when the decimal is truncated. Then 77.6 should round up: 77.6 + 0.5 = 78.1, which becomes 78. Because we can't add the decimal 0.5, we are instead multiplying by 10, adding 5, and dividing by 10.

The next section of code ❷ appends leading spaces to each of the three averages in anticipation of the substringing for data alignment. The final section of the code ❸ writes the trailer records to the report with two echo commands. The first writes hardcoded dashes identical to a header record. The second command replaces the name of a country with the hardcoded text, Averages, and the remainder of the command displays the three averages with such dense substringing that I've had to continue the command on the next line.

I'm extracting the last 15 bytes from the avgDeaths variable, but since the other two totals are actually 10 times greater than their actual values, it follows that their corresponding averages, avePerGDP and aveLifeExp, are also increased by a factor of 10. We can't correct this by dividing these by 10, because that would lose the decimal parts. However, by inserting a decimal point into the number as it's being written, we are presenting the number as it should be, effectively dividing by 10 while also showing the decimal part, which is a win-win. Notice that !avePerGDP:~-5,-1!.!avePerGDP:~-1! resolves to the four bytes prior to the last byte, a hardcoded dot, and that last byte.

Other datasets may lend themselves to simply displaying totals instead of averages, meaning that the floating-point arithmetic will be lessened or nonexistent. Even with this example using averages, we were able to create a fairly impressive report without a great deal of code.

Summary

In this chapter, I stepped through the three sections of a typical text report formatted with Batch. If you were expecting a nifty routine to automatically line up columns with ease, I'm sure I've disappointed you, but with a little attention to the details, you can create a quality report. You learned how to build a title, headers, any number of detail records, and a trailer record with totals and averages. Along the way, I demonstrated techniques for aligning columns with justified data items and tips for handling floating-point data. This isn't a heavy-duty utility, and I'm sure that no one is making a living solely producing Batch reports, but when a simple text report is needed, a compiled program is not.

The next chapter changes gears and delves into a subject that's dear to my heart: recursion. You'll learn how to build Batch code that calls itself, along with some interesting applications.

23

RECURSION

This chapter covers one of my favorite topics: recursion, or code that calls itself. I'll start with a much more detailed definition, but the only way to truly understand this concept is through examples, so we'll step through multiple instances of Batch recursion. One will be the calculation of a factorial, a truly classic example, with another being the conversion of a decimal to a hexadecimal. The last example will be something that's quintessentially Batch: a recursive search through directories and their subdirectories. Then you'll learn an important limitation to be aware of before you write code that calls itself.

Defining Recursion

Recursion is the technique where a bit of code invokes or calls itself. You can do this in the vast majority of coding languages. In a more object-oriented language, a command inside a method calls that particular method. Even in a procedural language like COBOL, a command inside a program calls that particular program. Batch is no different. In recursive Batch, a routine typically contains a `call` command that calls that particular routine. Less frequently, a bat file contains a `call` command that calls that particular bat file.

There's a simple logical beauty to recursion that can best be summed up with one word: *elegance*. I was trained as a mathematician before becoming a coder, and in both disciplines elegance is the greatest praise, and *functional* is a back-handed compliment at best, whether it be in reference to a proof in the former discipline or a program in the latter. There are many words and phrases of compliment for a piece of code—well-constructed, slick, nifty, smart, well-thought-out—but elegant stands alone as the best adjective a coder can hear. But when someone calls your code functional, the conceit is "It'll work, but it's supremely ugly, even logically offensive, and I could've done far better." In the Venn diagram of descriptive terms for code and supermodels, the intersection set is a set of one: elegant.

If your first instinct is that recursion sounds like the makings of an endless loop, your caution is prudent. If the call is done unconditionally, yes, the result will be an endless loop (or a crash when the call stack blows up). Recursion must have some sort of conditional logic, usually an `if` command, that'll execute code for either the recursive case or the base case.

The *recursive case* performs the recursive call, and the *base case* does not. A properly designed recursive call will get you one step closer to the base case. Several executions of the recursive case usually lead to a call that executes the base case, starting the process of backing out of the recursive calls. The best way to understand this is through examples (to come), stepping through each recursive call and keeping track of the state of each variable for each call, often with pencil and paper.

Recursion is quite different from the `while` and `do...while` commands introduced in Chapter 9. The `goto` command branched backward in the code to re-execute some code that just executed, but nothing was being called; there was no intent of control being returned. Instead, the technique of recursion calls or invokes the code of which it's a part.

Recursion is the coding equivalent of the Ouroboros, the mythological serpent or dragon eating its own tail (see Figure 23-1). The beast has convergent roots dating back to ancient China, Egypt, and Greece. It often symbolizes "eternal cyclic renewal," infinity, eternity, and even alchemy. I've long viewed it as an excellent metaphor for code invoking itself, even before knowing it by name.

Figure 23-1: A representation of the Ouroboros

Salvador Dali expressed his typically atypical interpretation of the creature in his work *The Ouroboros*. It's certainly presumptuous, but when I'm done coding a bit of recursive logic, I feel a very small affinity to an artist such as Dali, imagining the pride he must've felt in sharing his works with the world. A great painter rightly wants to showcase his works for others to view as a preeminent chef surely looks forward to diners sampling her plat du jour. Instead of a gallery showing or a restaurant opening, I anticipate the date of the next code review with my peers. I'm embellishing to a degree (and not comfortable admitting to what degree), but I do take pride in a fine bit of recursion, and I hope that you do or will as well.

Factorials

The classic example of recursion in any math or programming text is the factorial, and I see no reason to counter tradition. The factorial of n, represented by $n!$, is $n \times (n-1) \times (n-2) \ldots 2 \times 1$, or more informally, the product of the successive multiplication of the integer and all the integers less than it down to 1.

NOTE   *When asking a mathematician how old he was turning, I received the reply, "my last factorial birthday." He was nearing 24 and didn't expect to make it to 120 or 5!. I was once guilty of decorating a 30th birthday cake with 6! / 4!. Factorials can be fun as well as useful, but I digress.*

The factorial of 4 is the product of 4 and the factorial of 3, which is the product of 3 and the factorial of 2, which is the product of 2 and the factorial of 1, which is simply 1. The pattern begs for recursion. A routine that accepts a number as input and returns its factorial can multiply that number by the factorial of the number one less than it. And, the best way to find that second factorial is for the routine to call itself. When finding the factorial of an integer greater than 1, we invoke the recursive case, and when finding the factorial of 1, we have satisfied the base case and elegantly return the number 1. That's recursion! Now we must turn this into code.

The :Factorial routine accepts a numerical input parameter and passes back the number's factorial as the variable name we pass in the second parameter. Before getting to the routine itself, the following call to it populates factorial with the factorial of 4:

```
call :Factorial 4 factorial
> con echo The Factorial of 4 is %factorial%.
```

You might be expecting a more complex routine, but here it is in its simplicity. Take note of the call command recursively invoking the :Factorial routine:

```
:Factorial
if %~1 equ 1 (
    set %~2=1
) else (
    set /A nbrLessOne = %~1 - 1
    call :Factorial !nbrLessOne! lessOneFact
    set /A %~2 = %~1 * !lessOneFact!
)
goto :eof
```

If the input parameter, %~1, equals 1, the if command asserts that the base case is satisfied and we set the second parameter, %~2, to 1, because the factorial of 1 is 1, and we are done.

If the integer is greater than 1, control goes to the code block under the else keyword, where the logic for the recursive case executes. We next find the number one less than our input value: nbrLessOne. To determine the factorial of nbrLessOne, we recursively call the same exact routine that we are currently in and retrieve the result as the lessOneFact variable. Finally, we multiply the routine's input value by the factorial returned from the recursive call, assign the result to the second parameter, %~2, which we return to the calling code, and we are done.

This top-down reading of the routine is helpful and a great first step, but it glosses over what happens in the successive recursive calls. To really understand what's happening, let's explore the logic again by stepping through a sample execution with the input parameter of 4.

Because 4 is greater than 1, we immediately jump down to the else code block, find the prior number of 3, and do the recursive call. Let's put a breadcrumb down and come back to it later.

The second time through the routine, the input parameter is 3, so we call recursively again to find the factorial of 2. Place a second breadcrumb at the call command.

The third time through the routine, the input is 2, so we perform yet another recursive call, this time to find the factorial of the number 1. Place a third breadcrumb.

Finally, the if command is true, the base case is satisfied, and we return the value 1 as the second parameter, %~2.

Now we can pick up the breadcrumbs in reverse order as we find our way back to the original call. At the third breadcrumb we get back the factorial of 1 in the lessOneFact variable, and we multiply it by that call's input parameter, %~1, which is 2. We assign the product of 2 to the return parameter and pass it back.

We now find ourselves back at the second breadcrumb where we multiply that call's input parameter of 3 by lessOneFact, which holds the just returned value of 2. The routine passes back the result of 6, or the factorial of 3, to the site of the first breadcrumb.

The logic multiplies the original input parameter of 4 by lessOneFact, which now holds 6. We return the result of 24 to the original call. That last point is subtle and critical: we aren't passing the result back to one of the recursive calls in the routine; we're finally passing the result back to the original call. And we are done.

The concept may be a bit confusing at first, and there is no shame in rereading the last few lines more than once. Curiously, the variables seem to have multiple states at one time. The nbrLessOne and lessOneFact variables contain three different values each, the input parameter took on four values, and we assigned the output parameter four times. Batch accomplishes this with the *call stack*. Before performing a recursive call, it stores pertinent data on the call stack, and it can do this for multiple calls.

The interpreter places all active variables on the call stack before it does the first recursive call. During that call, the variables may take on new values that it again places atop the call stack before the next recursive call. When control returns from each call, the interpreter simply restores the corresponding values from the top of the call stack and continues processing.

By the way, there are means to calculate factorials without recursion, but they are uninspired and far less enjoyable.

Decimal to Hexadecimal

Before converting a decimal number (base 10) to a hexadecimal number (base 16) with recursive Batch code, let's consider how to do it mathematically. For decimal numbers less than 256, start by dividing the number by 16, leaving a quotient and a remainder. These two numbers will be the two digits of the hexadecimal number, with one catch. Either number is in the range from 0 to 15, but we want a single character. The numbers 0 through 9 are fine, but if the value is a two-digit decimal number, we must map it to a hexadecimal digit. That is, 10 maps to A, 11 maps to B, and so on, up to 15 mapping to F.

If the decimal number is between 256 and 4,095, it maps to a three-digit hexadecimal number. This requires two rounds of division. The remainder of the first division provides the rightmost hexadecimal digit, and we divide the quotient again by 16. The remainder becomes the second rightmost hexadecimal digit, and the new quotient is the leading hexadecimal digit. As the numbers get larger, the same pattern holds; for instance, a six-digit hexadecimal number requires five divisions.

This is exactly the type of pattern that also screams out for recursion. The following Batch routine converts a decimal number into a hexadecimal number. Similar to the factorials example there are two parameters: the first is the decimal input, and the second is the variable containing the hexadecimal output. Here's the code:

```
:GetHex
 set hexChars=0123456789ABCDEF
 set /A quotient = %~1 / 16
 set /A remainder = %~1 %% 16
 if %quotient% equ 0 (
    set %~2=!hexChars:~%remainder%,1!
 ) else (
    call :GetHex %quotient% recur
    set %~2=!recur!!hexChars:~%remainder%,1!
 )
 goto :eof
```

I'm storing the 16 hexadecimal characters in hexChars for later use. The routine divides the decimal number by 16, giving us quotient, while modulo division by 16 gives us remainder. If the quotient is 0, the result is a single character. This is the base case. We substring the appropriate character out of hexChars, using remainder as the offset. Notice that 0 maps to 0, 1 maps to 1, and so on, until 9 maps to 9. Then 10 maps to A, 11 maps to B, and, ultimately, 15 maps to F. We return this single digit as the value of the second parameter to complete the base case.

The recursive case occurs when quotient is greater than 0. The quotient variable needs to be converted further, so we perform a recursive call of :GetHex and get back its hexadecimal value in the recur variable, which can be one to many characters. We assign the return parameter a concatenation of this value and the same mapping of the remainder to a hexadecimal digit that we just witnessed.

(By the way, notice the two concatenated values. We resolve the recur variable with exclamation marks because it's assigned in the code block as part of the call command. The rightmost byte is resolved from this text: !hexChars:~%remainder%,1!. This time I'm employing delayed expansion with the exclamation marks after first resolving the offset, or remainder, with percent signs.)

To really understand this logic, let's step through it to convert 700 to a hexadecimal number. First, let's do it mathematically: 700 / 16 = 43 with a remainder of 12. The 12 maps to the hexadecimal digit C, which will be the rightmost byte of the final result. Next, 43 / 16 = 2 with a remainder of 11, which maps to the next byte from the right in the final result, B. The quotient of 2 is a one-digit number, so it represents itself. The result is the hexadecimal number, 2BC.

The following call command returns the value 2BC as the hexVal variable:

```
call :GetHex 700 hexVal
```

Taking this step by step, since the input parameter is 700, the quotient variable is 43, and the remainder variable is 12. Because quotient isn't 0, the recursive case logic executes. The interpreter puts the `remainder` of 12 on the stack for now and passes 43 as the first parameter of a recursive call.

In this pass, `quotient` is 2, and `remainder` is 11. Again, the recursive case logic executes, and 11 finds its way onto the stack as we pass 2 in another recursive call.

In what'll be the final pass, `quotient` is 0, and `remainder` is 2. Since `quotient` equals 0, the base case logic finally executes. The decimal digit 2 maps to the hexadecimal digit 2, and we pass it back as the output parameter.

Now let's reverse direction and step back through the calls that we just made. The interpreter restores `remainder` to its value of 11 before the set command concatenates two values. The first is the just returned value of 2, and the second is B, which we mapped to from the 11. Hence, the routine passes back 2B as the output parameter.

Back in the initial pass, the interpreter restores the `remainder` variable of 12 from the call stack. We concatenate two values, the just returned 2B and C, which is the hexadecimal value corresponding to the 12. Finally, the routine passes back 2BC as the output parameter to the original `call` command.

With each call, the recursive logic is determining another hexadecimal digit, ultimately returning a multibyte hexadecimal value. At first glance, these few lines of code might not look like much, but under close inspection the routine turns out to be quite involved and interesting.

Recursive Directory Searches

The last two examples offer great demonstrations of recursion, allowing us to step through the recursive calls, but for my last example I want something that has Batch in its DNA, something not easily done in other languages. We'll recursively search a directory and all of its subdirectories to produce a report detailing the total number of bytes and files in each folder.

If that sounds familiar, you learned about the `for` command with the /D (directory) and /R (recursion) options in Chapter 18. This command easily created a simple list of all the subdirectories, but it handled the recursive call for you and didn't leave much room for modifications. True recursion provides much more flexibility and power over the output, and that's what we'll do here.

Before coding the recursive routine, we need a plan and some analysis. To produce the detail records, we'll use a `dir` command targeting a directory and use it as the input to a `for /F` command. The routine will write the totals for the directory to the report and recursively call itself, passing each subdirectory. Then it will process each subdirectory, making recursive calls for any subdirectories of subdirectories.

The only way to write code like that is to see the output of the embedded command, in this case a `dir` command. Depending on the contents of the directory, the `dir C:\Batch\*` command might produce the following output:

```
Volume in drive C is OS
Volume Serial Number is 2E6D-DBF0
```

```
Directory of C:\Batch

10/31/2002  10:05 AM    <DIR>          .
10/31/2002  10:05 AM    <DIR>          ..
05/01/2001  11:18 AM               197 FourBrits.txt
02/14/2001  03:37 PM               178 FourBrits.csv
02/06/2002  12:47 PM    <DIR>          OrphanedFolder
06/20/2000  05:52 PM            89,402 outFile.dat
10/27/2002  08:36 AM    <DIR>          Subfolder
07/02/2002  02:03 PM             2,828 test.bat
               4 File(s)         92,605 bytes
               5 Dir(s)  147,918,372,864 bytes free
```

We'll need to skip seven lines, the five header records plus the two entries showing directories of one or two periods. Of the remaining records, if the second token equals File(s), we've found the entry with the total number of files (token 1) and total bytes of those files (token 3). If the fourth token equals <DIR>, we've found a folder name for a subdirectory (token 5). We don't know much about the subdirectory yet, but a recursive call will bring up the same type of information about it. We can ignore the other records detailing each file and the final trailer record.

We could write the data to the console, but let's use our report writing skills from Chapter 22. The first section of code creates the header data and makes the initial call to the recursive :GetFldrSz routine that gets the folder information starting with the contents of *C:\Batch*:

```
set rpt=C:\Report\FolderSizes.txt
>  %rpt% echo  ==== In Search of Lost Disk Space ====
>> %rpt% echo        Total Bytes     Files  Folder
>> %rpt% echo        -----------     -----  ------
call :GetFldrSz C:\Batch
goto :eof

:GetFldrSz
for /F "usebackq tokens=1-4* skip=7" %%a in (`dir "%~1\*"`) do (
    if /i "%%d" equ "<DIR>" (
        call :GetFldrSz "%~1\%%e"
    ) else if /i "%%b" equ "File(s)" (
        set ttlFiles=       %%a
        set ttlBytes=                  %%c
        >> %rpt% echo !ttlBytes:~-17! !ttlFiles:~-8!  %~1
) )
goto :eof
```

Focusing on the :GetFldrSz routine, the for /F command uses a dir command as its input, and that command uses the routine's sole parameter, a directory, appended with a wildcard as its argument. The for /F command uses five tokens (tokens=1-5) and skips the unwanted header records (skip=7).

If the fourth token, %%d, equals <DIR>, we've found the recursive case; the recursive call passing as its argument the input directory appended with the name of the subfolder from the fifth token: %~1\%%e. Otherwise, the base case looks for the second token, %%b, to match the text File(s). If so, we store the total number of files and bytes in the folder in variables padded with leading spaces. Using those recently learned formatting techniques, we write a record to the report detailing the three pieces of information.

If the directory structure isn't very complex, this code might write the following recursively generated report:

```
==== In Search of Lost Disk Space ====
    Total Bytes    Files  Folder
    -----------    -----  ------
         24,533       12  C:\Batch\OrphanedFolder
      2,419,998        4  C:\Batch\Subfolder\SubSub\Child
         67,150        3  C:\Batch\Subfolder\Sub
            242        3  C:\Batch\Subfolder
         92,605        4  C:\Batch
```

The last line contains the information from the dir command we executed to get a feel for the expected output, and it also shows the root directory argument from the initial call command. The other four detail lines are products of the recursive calls.

The beauty of this design is that the code makes a call for each subfolder, regardless of how many exist, if any at all. This routine is a framework, and there are countless auxiliary processes possible with minor modifications. Perhaps only directories in excess of a certain number of files or bytes should make the report. Shifting attention to files, perhaps you want to flag recently modified files to be part of an entirely different report, or maybe archive them. Perhaps you want to delete old or excessively large files, or maybe files fitting a certain mask or having a certain attribute. The list goes on.

There are a couple of caveats, however. The previous code doesn't work on a root directory such as *C:* because we are skipping the first two detail records produced by the dir command (the <DIR> records with one or two dots for the directory). Remember from Chapter 13 that this command doesn't display those two records when the argument is just a drive letter. With some modifications, we can account for that issue, but the other caveat is more of a batveat, and it applies more generally to recursion. It's the possibility of a stack overflow.

Recursion Stack Overflow

The primary batveat concerning recursion is important, yet very avoidable. With each successive recursive call, the interpreter places data onto the call stack, allowing you to use a variable that may have scores of values, one for each invocation. But memory is finite, and the interpreter doesn't allocate much of it for the call stack. When it reaches 90 percent of its allocation, the interpreter aborts with a message such as this:

```
****** B A T C H   R E C U R S I O N exceeds STACK limits ******
Recursion Count=507, Stack Usage=90 percent
******        B A T C H   PROCESSING IS   A B O R T E D      ******
```

Setting aside all justified critiques of Batch's seemingly random use of capitalization and space-delimited lettering, this failed after 507 recursive calls, but 506 isn't the limit. I've used recursion quite a bit and have never seen it blow up with 300 or fewer recursive calls, but it varies greatly from machine to machine and from situation to situation. Every language has a limitation on recursion, but most usually allow far more levels. This is manageable, but you must take this limitation into consideration when coding a solution.

If the code is part of a larger process in an environment where an abort might result in a substantial financial loss with the possibility of you and others being woken up in the middle of the night to address the fallout, then you should limit recursive calls to situations where the call stack will max out well below the threshold of a possible overflow. But please don't let this scare you off from such a wonderful technique. Well-designed recursion will easily stay inside these guardrails.

For instance, the conversion of an integer to a hexadecimal number requires 10 or fewer recursive calls for numbers less than nine trillion. Even the recursive code traversing a directory structure isn't in danger of overflowing the call stack. Some directories might hold hundreds of subdirectories, but a close reading of the code in the previous section shows that sibling folders are never on the call stack at the same time. The interpreter continually adds and removes items from the call stack so that it's never deeper than the level of the deepest folder from the root, rarely more than a dozen. You can safely code these solutions in any language, including Batch.

Summary

I hope that you enjoyed this chapter as much as I did. You've learned how recursion works from a coder's perspective and the interpreter's perspective—that is, I demonstrated how to execute recursion and also discussed how the interpreter is using the call stack behind the scenes.

I also demonstrated the usefulness of stepping through the code, recursive call by recursive call, with detailed examples. You must be careful of overflowing the recursion stack, but recursion is a wonderfully elegant tool when used wisely. Be on the lookout for problems in need of a recursive solution. For any process that iterates through a finite number of repetitive steps, a loop is usually the first solution that comes to mind, but look for the recursive case and the base case. If you see them, you can write some recursive logic. (For more on this topic, see Chapter 23.)

Recursion is great for searching directories. In the next chapter, I'll also discuss searches, but with a far more narrowed focus. Instead of searching every directory on your computer, you'll learn how to search for a string inside a larger string, a file, or even multiple files.

24

TEXT STRING SEARCHES

In previous chapters, you've seen a number of searches, such as for files, directories, and even lost disk space. In this chapter, I'll discuss the many ways of searching for text strings and possible applications for text searches. You'll see searches for a single word, searches for one out of multiple possible words, and searches for a literal string containing multiple words. Another search flavor will look for a list of words and considers the search a success only if each and every word is found. I'll show how to perform these searches against a file, multiple files, and other strings.

For performing these searches, I'll compare and contrast two very different techniques. One is far more flexible, and the other executes much faster, so they're both extremely useful. I'll also discuss regular expressions and how you can use them to build some very impressive Batch searches.

Searching within a File

To demonstrate how to search each record in a file for a string, the first requirement is a file to search. In the real world, you might have a logfile containing tens of thousands of records with many clients interspersed; searching for a client name can extract all relevant entries for a more targeted report. Daily report files might each have totals at the end; a search on the Totals text can extract each of those trailer records from all of the report files in a certain directory. Better yet, you can search all files satisfying a file mask, maybe targeting files from the prior month or year.

For this demonstration, I'll use a much smaller (and I hope more interesting) input file, a file called *12Movies.txt* containing a not-so-random list of a dozen movies spanning three decades, organized by release date. Look closely for any commonalities with the titles. Here are its complete contents:

```
Here Come the Littles
Little Shop of Horrors
Big Trouble in Little China
Big
The Little Mermaid
The Big Lebowski
Stuart Little
Big Momma's House
My Big Fat Greek Wedding
Little Miss Sunshine
Big Hero 6
The Big Short
```

Some are great movies, some not so great, and some I've never seen, but we'll be using this file in many examples throughout this chapter.

A Simple String

The findstr command is the primary Batch tool for finding a text string inside one or more files. Despite the abbreviation, coders refer to it as the *find string* command. You'll soon see how versatile this command is, but I'll start with a simple optionless command that searches for the word Little in the input file. The first argument is the search string, and the second argument is the file to be searched:

```
findstr Little C:\Batch\12Movies.txt
```

This command writes every record from the file containing the six consecutive letters in the search string to stdout:

```
Here Come the Littles
Little Shop of Horrors
Big Trouble in Little China
The Little Mermaid
Stuart Little
Little Miss Sunshine
```

Notice that the interpreter returns the first title even though it contains the search word appended with an s; the command isn't searching for whole words. Also, this particular command sets the pseudo-environment variable errorlevel to 0, indicating that it found at least one instance of the search string. If it finds no matches, errorlevel takes on the value of 1.

Typically, coders handle the output from this command in one of three ways. If you simply want to know whether one or more records exist, you need only interrogate errorlevel and move on. In other instances, you can redirect the list of returned records written to stdout to the console or an output file for later use or viewing. The last use is to programmatically process every returned record, which you can do by using a findstr command as input to a for /F command. For most of the upcoming examples, I'll describe what's written to stdout, but understand that the output has many different uses.

Now let's make a subtle change to the prior command and make the search string entirely lowercase:

```
findstr little C:\Batch\12Movies.txt
```

This returns nothing because the findstr command performs case-sensitive searches, by default anyway, and every instance of the word in the file starts with an uppercase L. The other interesting result is that because the command returned nothing, 1 is the value of errorlevel. Often, a case-sensitive search is exactly what you want; many other times, that's exactly what you don't want.

Customizations

Fortunately, this command has a large number of options to customize each search. I'll discuss many of them in this chapter, starting with a few options that change the behavior of the findstr command in simple yet powerful ways.

Just as the /i option invokes case-insensitivity of the if command, the same option works for the findstr command. (As mentioned in Chapter 4, I use lowercase for this one option, but /I also works.) Notice the option and the odd capitalization of tHE:

```
findstr /i tHE C:\Batch\12Movies.txt
```

I'm not recommending a capitalization scheme such as this, but I do it here to unambiguously demonstrate the fact that the interpreter returns all four titles containing these three letters in this order, regardless of the case, as you can see in the output:

```
Here Come the Littles
The Little Mermaid
The Big Lebowski
The Big Short
```

Another useful option is /E. With it, the command returns only the records it finds where the search string is at the *end* of the record. Consider this command:

```
findstr /i /E little C:\Batch\12Movies.txt
```

The only title returned is *Stuart Little*. Also notice this command uses multiple options for further customization; with the /i and /E options, it performs a case-insensitive search for records ending with the search string.

Similarly, the /B option returns only the records it finds where the search string is at the *beginning* of the record. You can team up this option with /i as well as the /N option, which prepends the *line number* to the returned record, delimited by a colon:

```
findstr /i /B /N big C:\Batch\12Movies.txt
```

This findstr command returns the following four titles, all starting with big, case-insensitive, prepended with their corresponding line numbers:

```
3:Big Trouble in Little China
4:Big
8:Big Momma's House
11:Big Hero 6
```

Another useful option is /V, which negates the search logic. The following command is identical to the previous one, except it includes the /V option:

```
findstr /i /B /N /V big C:\Batch\12Movies.txt
```

The four records that were returned previously are now missing from the output, replaced with the other eight records not satisfying the search criteria. The line numbers are still at the front of each record because of the /N option, but the /V option alters the logic so that the output consists of all records *not* starting with big, case-insensitive:

```
1:Here Come the Littles
2:Little Shop of Horrors
5:The Little Mermaid
6:The Big Lebowski
7:Stuart Little
```

```
9:My Big Fat Greek Wedding
10:Little Miss Sunshine
12:The Big Short
```

Rounding out these options is /X, which finds only records that match the search string in their entirety:

```
findstr /i /X big C:\Batch\12Movies.txt
```

This command returns a single title, the Tom Hanks film *Big*.

The one-character codes in the /i, /B, /E, and /N options are representative of their function, but /V, /X, and some others aren't as obvious. Plan to make ample use of the help when working with the findstr command.

Multiple Words

There are multiple variants of a two-word search (when the search string has an embedded space). We can search for all records that have either word, both words, or a literal string of the two words separated by that space (or spaces). The findstr command handles all of them, although the variant searching for both words requires a little extra work. We can extrapolate these solutions to searches of more than two words.

Any Words in a List

Instead of a one-word search string, the following findstr command has two words encased in double quotes. If you haven't seen something like this before, you're probably expecting it to return all titles with the word the followed by the word big, but that's not the case:

```
findstr /i "the big" C:\Batch\12Movies.txt
```

In actuality, the double quotes encase the set of space-delimited search strings. The interpreter searches each record in the file for each word in the set of search strings, returning all records with at least one match. This command returns nine titles; all but three movies in the list contain either the word the or the word big, or both.

Adding three specific words to the set of search strings returns all 12 titles:

```
findstr /i "the big art hop sun" C:\Batch\12Movies.txt
```

The three additional words in the set of search strings are part of the words *Stuart*, *Shop*, and *Sunshine*, respectively, and each of those words is in one of the previously missing titles. Although, if you haven't noticed yet, the two-word set of search strings, "big little", returns every record in the file more efficiently.

A Literal String

With a simple modification, you can alter the command searching for either of two words to search for a single string: the, followed by a space and big. The /C option defines a literal search string, and you must use it when the search string includes at least one space.

You've already seen a case-insensitive search of *12Movies.txt*. In this example, I've inserted the /C: option in front of what's now a literal search string encased in double quotes:

```
findstr /i /C:"the big" C:\Batch\12Movies.txt
```

This findstr command returns just these two titles:

```
The Big Lebowski
The Big Short
```

Both of these titles happen to start with the text, but a record with this literal string later in the title would've also been part of the output.

The literal search string doesn't have to contain entire words. The following command

```
findstr /i /C:"y big fat greek wed" C:\Batch\12Movies.txt
```

returns the title *My Big Fat Greek Wedding*.

All Words in a List

There's just one movie title in the *12Movies.txt* file that contains two particular words of interest, Big and Little. Unfortunately, the findstr command cannot perform a single search to find all records containing both words, but with some ingenuity, you can meld two findstr commands together to get the job done:

```
findstr /i big C:\Batch\12Movies.txt | findstr /i little
```

This pipes the output of one findstr command—via the pipe character—to another findstr command (another application of the piping technique introduced in Chapter 12). The first findstr command performs a case-insensitive search for the word big using the *12Movies.txt* file as its input. As you have seen by now, this command by itself writes seven titles to stdout.

But this isn't a simple command. The interpreter writes the output, those seven records, to an unnamed temporary file and pipes, or feeds, it into the second findstr command, which is doing a case-insensitive search for the word little. Notice that I'm not defining an input file in the second command. It doesn't need one, because its input is the output from the first findstr command. As the following output shows, of the seven titles that contain the word big, only one also contains the word little:

```
Big Trouble in Little China
```

The upshot is a search that returns only records containing both strings.

The intermediate file is lost, but if you desire an audit trail of what transpired, you can redirect the output into a file. Then you can pipe a type command of that file into the second findstr command:

```
findstr /i big C:\Batch\12Movies.txt > C:\Batch\BigMovies.txt
type C:\Batch\BigMovies.txt | findstr /i little
```

The two commands find the same title, but now *BigMovies.txt* contains the seven records found with the first search string.

You can use this technique with any number of search strings. The following command again finds the one title, because it contains all four of the search strings, even if the third word is only a portion of a word in the title:

```
findstr /i big C:\Batch\12Movies.txt | findstr /i little ^
                                     | findstr /i chi ^
                                     | findstr /i trouble
```

The trickiest part of this technique is making it readable. In this example, I've lined up all of the search strings, other than the first, by continuing the command on multiple lines with the trailing carets.

Searching Multiple Files

Up to this point, I've performed the findstr command using a single input file, but you can search any number of files with a single invocation. The command accepts multiple files to search as additional arguments, and it also accepts file masks. The following command is looking for the miss text, regardless of the case, in the file we've been using and in any file that satisfies either of the two file masks:

```
findstr /i miss C:\Batch\12Movies.txt C:\Flicks\*Movies.txt C:\Movies\*
```

This example raises an issue of concern about the output because prior invocations have simply written each record found to stdout. That worked great when searching a single file, but when searching multiple files, this output would leave you no way of knowing the file of origin for each output record. The interpreter smartly detects the difference and outputs the path and filename with the record found:

```
C:\Batch\12Movies.txt:Little Miss Sunshine
C:\Movies\Some Other File.dat:  Will findstr miss this record?
C:\Movies\Some Other File.dat:  Sorry, that was misserable. Sorry again.
```

The command found *Little Miss Sunshine* in the *12Movies.txt* file as expected, and it also found the text in two records belonging to a file satisfying the trailing file mask, resulting in the last two lines of the output. The formatting leaves much to be desired. It's hard to see where the filename ends and the record starts despite the colon delimiter. When writing the output to the console, the /A option highlights the path and filename to a color scheme of your choosing, but that obviously does nothing when you redirect the output to a file or pipe it to another command.

The colon itself is an unfortunate choice for the delimiter because it's often part of the path after the drive letter, as it is in this instance. If you want to parse this data, you could use a findstr command as input to a for /F command and delimit the output on the colon. But given this output, the path and filename would span the first two tokens with the actual record in the third. A delimiter that can't be in a path or filename, such as a pipe, would've been a better idea, but you can still parse this with a little extra work.

The /S option expands the search to include subdirectories. I often use it with wildcards to search all files in a directory tree or all files of a certain extension in a directory tree, but in the following example, I'm using an explicit filename:

```
findstr /i /S /N miss C:\Batch\12Movies.txt
```

The interpreter searches *C:\Batch* and all of its subfolders for files named *12Movies.txt*. Then it searches each file found for records containing the search string.

Also, notice that I reintroduced the /N option mentioned previously. The output now contains the path and filename, the line number (delimited on either side with a colon), and the full record containing the search string:

```
C:\Batch\12Movies.txt:10:Little Miss Sunshine
C:\Batch\Subfolder\12Movies.txt:2:The misspelling of miserable was painful.
C:\Batch\Subfolder\12Movies.txt:3:It should be a missdemeanor.
```

Two files in two directories have the same name, but the result of this command shows that their contents are quite different.

WARNING *When the findstr command doesn't find any files that fit a file mask, it writes an error message to stderr saying it Cannot open the specific mask. If you have redirected both stdout and stderr to a trace file, the command intermingles the message with the desired output. If a mask might not be valid, suppressing stderr with the 2> nul syntax anticipates the possibility of the batveat and cleans up the output:*

```
findstr /i miss C:\Batch\12Movies.txt C:\NotADir\* 2> nul
```

The interpreter returns any records it finds in the valid file, but it sends the error message concerning the nonexistent directory to the nul file. This technique even works inside a routine or bat file with its stderr already redirected.

Auxiliary Search Files

When your searches start to get more complex, you can more easily manage them with two auxiliary files, one that contains a list of search strings and another that contains a list of files to search.

File of Search Strings

I mentioned earlier how you can search for any of the strings in a list by encasing multiple space-delimited search strings in double quotes. That works great for a handful of strings, but when the list gets long enough to make a mess of the command, you can use the findstr command with a file containing the list of search strings. You define this file by entering it after the /G option, delimited by a colon. The following example performs case-sensitive searches for Little and four of its synonyms, and you can easily add many more:

```
>  SearchStr.temp echo Little
>> SearchStr.temp echo Small
>> SearchStr.temp echo Short
>> SearchStr.temp echo Minuscule
>> SearchStr.temp echo Tiny
findstr /G:SearchStr.temp C:\Batch\12Movies.txt
del SearchStr.temp
```

I'm building the temporary file with hardcoded strings, but they could easily be variables or even come from user input, and because it's a temporary file, I'm deleting it when I'm done with it. The output consists of all records containing at least one of these five strings, which in this case includes the six titles containing Little, plus *The Big Short*, with nothing found for the other three search strings.

This technique is also helpful when the search criteria changes from execution to execution. You can generate a file dynamically in the code, or even update it manually, and you can run the same code with differing results.

File of Files to Search

Taking this a step further, I'll use the file just created containing the list of the search strings in tandem with another file containing the list of files to be searched. This *file of files (FOF)* is defined by the findstr command with the /F option. Similar to the /G option, the file comes after the option, delimited by a colon:

```
findstr /i /G:C:\Batch\SearchStrings.txt /F:C:\Batch\SearchFiles.txt
```

Oddly, you can use the /F option only when using the /G option.

If the list of files to search will be known only at the time of execution, you can build this FOF dynamically at runtime. This technique is also useful when you can't easily define a set of files with a file mask. For instance, these options are ideal if you plan to search one of multiple sets of files, perhaps production or test sets of files partially named with a datestamp. You can also create the file of search strings with data entered by the user, perhaps a list of client names. If, however, the list of files to search is more consistent, you can use a static file instead.

Searching a String

Most compiled languages include a method that returns a boolean indicating whether a string is contained in part or in whole inside another string, because the need arises often in very disparate situations. In Batch, you can search a variable holding a path for a specific node or server name, or you might examine the path variable to see whether it holds a particular directory. You can even use this technique to validate user input, verifying that the response contains at least one word on a list.

There are two very different methods of finding out if a string contains another string. The makers of Batch designed the findstr command to search files, but the first method manipulates it to search a string. The second method is based on the text replacement syntax from Chapter 5, and they each have significant advantages over the other.

The findstr Method

Finding love can be difficult, but with the findstr command, finding the love string requires only a few lines of code. For this exercise, I'll set the aString variable to one of two similar text strings giving advice to anyone planning a winter trip to one of two neighboring countries on the Adriatic Sea:

```
set aString=Bring mittens and a sweater to Croatia.
set aString=Bring gloves and a pullover to Slovenia.
```

I'll step through a couple of upcoming code listings twice, with the variable set to each of these strings to demonstrate very different behaviors.

Can you find love in either string? The findstr command can:

```
echo "%aString%" | findstr love
if %errorlevel% equ 0 (
    set bLove=true==true
) else (
    set bLove=false==x
)
```

To search aString for the love text, I employ the same piping technique used earlier, with the only difference being that instead of piping a multirecord file to the findstr command via a type command, I'm piping a variable via an echo command. In essence, I'm treating the contents of the variable as a single-record input file to the findstr command. The end result is that the command searches the string for the text.

Remember that the findstr command sets errorlevel to 0 when it finds the search string; otherwise, 1 is the value. If it's 0, the code sets the bLove boolean to true; if not, the result is false.

First envision this logic with aString set to the Croatian string. The love text isn't in the string, so the command returns 1, and we set the boolean to false. Now do the same with the string set to the Slovenian text. The love text is embedded in three different words in the short string—Bring g**love**s and a pul**love**r to S**love**nia. One or more matches sets errorlevel to 0, so we set the boolean to true.

Also notice how easily we can convert this to a case-insensitive search:

```
echo "%aString%" | findstr /i love
```

Much of the flexibility present when searching a file is still available when searching a string. The options for targeting the beginning or ending of the string, negating the logic, and others work perfectly well in this context.

The Text Replacement Method

The idea behind the text replacement method is as straightforward as its execution. The technique compares a resolved variable to itself with the search string removed. If they differ, we've found the search string; if they're equal, we haven't found the text. The following code uses this method to determine whether a string contains another string, in this case love, setting the same boolean from the prior example to true or false:

```
if "%aString%" neq "%aString:love=%" (
    set bLove=true==true
) else (
    set bLove=false==x
)
```

The left side of the inequality is pedestrian by now, a resolved variable in double quotes. The if command compares it to "%aString:love=%", the same resolved variable, but with all instances of the love text replaced with null; notice that nothing comes between the equal sign and the terminating percent sign. The upshot is that if aString contains at least one instance of the love string, these two values differ, and we set the bLove boolean to true; if the search string isn't inside the string we're searching, the two values are identical, and we set bLove to false.

Let's execute this code with both possible values of aString. Assuming that it contains the Croatian text, the two values are identical because the love string isn't to be found, and we set bLove to false. However, the text replacement syntax alters the Slovenian text by removing each of the three instances of the love string, resulting in this mess on the right side of the inequality: "Bring gs and a pulr to Snia." This clearly doesn't equal the original text, so we set bLove to the value of true.

Delayed expansion makes this technique more generic, allowing you to use variables for both the search string and the string to search:

```
if "%stringToSearch%" neq "!stringToSearch:%searchString%=!" (
    set bLove=true==true
) else (
    set bLove=false==x
)
```

Now the search string and the string to search are variables, allowing you to determine both in the Batch code prior to performing this search.

When searching a string, both methods have a definitive place in the Batch universe. The biggest advantage of the findstr method is its flexibility, primarily its ability to perform case-sensitive searches, and you can use those options discussed earlier to easily customize any search. In contrast, the text replacement method is intrinsically case-insensitive because you can't easily change the fact that the interpreter ignores the case of the text being changed.

The text replacement method has advantages of its own. First, I consider it a bit simpler to use. Neither method is complex, but an if command, even with delayed expansion, is even more straightforward than an echo piped to a findstr. But by far its primary advantage is performance.

When you call the findstr command, you're actually calling a program, *findstr.exe*, and any program invocation involves more overhead than a simple comparison of two variables. They both happen in a fraction of a second, but the text replacement method happens in a much smaller fraction. You wouldn't notice the distinction performing a handful of searches, but I tested both methods extensively and found the text replacement method to be more than 200 times faster than the findstr method. There are many variables to consider when testing performance and my testing is far from definitive, but it's safe to say that a major advantage of the text replacement method is that it's much faster.

In the final analysis, if your code is to perform a search repeatedly, say in a loop with possibly hundreds or even thousands of invocations, the replacement text method is the better choice. However, if efficiency isn't a big concern or if you need a more complex search, even just a case-sensitive search, the findstr method is the better choice.

Regular Expressions

Throughout this book I've more than hinted that Batch syntax can be esoteric and counterintuitive, even for someone who has coded in the language for many years. But somewhere out there someone of a contrarian bent is saying, "It isn't that bad" or "Who among us hasn't memorized all the options of the findstr command?" To this person I have two words: *regular expressions*, or *regex*.

Regular expressions are not unique to Batch. Many languages and editors use them as an incredibly powerful tool for searches. With regex, you can search for numeric values, non-numeric values, and very intricate patterns and ranges of characters. The /B and /E options of the findstr command allow you to search for text at the beginning or ending of a record, but regex allows you to do both in one command—that is, search for one string at the beginning and another string at the end of a record. Let's see regex in action with a couple of examples.

Searching for Any Number

The following findstr command using the regex option, denoted appropriately enough by /R, searches the *12Movies.txt* file to find all movies with at least one number in the title:

```
findstr /R "[0-9]" C:\Batch\12Movies.txt
```

The regular expression [0-9] denotes all characters from 0 to 9, inclusive. Given the input file that we've been using throughout this chapter, the command returns just one title:

```
Big Hero 6
```

If we were working with a more complete list of movies, the titles returned might include *2001: A Space Odyssey*, *12 Angry Men*, *The 12th Man*, and *Ocean's 11*, but not the remake *Ocean's Eleven*.

Regular expressions also are effective when searching a string as opposed to a file. Consider the following example that uses negated logic (/V) for a regex (/R) search:

```
:TryAgain
> con set /P reply=Enter a movie title that does NOT include a number:
echo %reply% | findstr /R /V "[0-9]"
if errorlevel 1 (
    > con echo Invalid response. Please try again.
    goto :TryAgain
)
```

The code prompts the user for a movie title without a number anywhere in the title. If they enter a typical movie sequel or a title such as

28 Days Later, this logic prompts them to enter a different title until they finally abide by the instructions.

Searching with Complex Criteria

For a search that would be far more difficult without regex, consider the following:

```
findstr /R "^The..........*Man$" C:\Batch\12Movies.txt
```

The leading caret isn't an escape character in this context, but part of a string encased in double quotes. The caret is a regex indicator noting that the text after it is anchored to the beginning of the string, and the trailing dollar sign indicates the text before it is anchored to the end of the string. The 11 dots are wildcards, and the asterisk indicates that the wildcard just before it can be of any length, zero and up.

Putting this all together in a language that a non-regex-coder can understand, the search is looking for all records that start with The and end in Man, case-sensitive, with at least 10 characters, spaces included, between them.

If you execute this command using a file containing a more complete list of movies, it might return the title *The Invisible Man* and even *The Amazing Spider-Man*. However, *The Amazing Spider-Man 2*, *The Music Man*, and the aforementioned *The 12th Man* are out of the mix. (The first has a number appended to the title, and the other two are too short.)

To perform this same search without regex, you could pipe one findstr command using the /B option into another findstr command using the /E option, but you'd still need to filter out all of the titles with fewer than 10 characters between the two words; it's possible, but oh so messy. Many other difficult to nearly impossible searches are more than possible with regular expressions.

The topic of regular expressions commands its own book. I've demonstrated a couple of examples useful in Batch, but the next time one of your searches starts to get overly complex, look up the regex syntax for your problem in a book or on the internet, and give it a try with the findstr command and the /R option. Even experienced coders sometimes shy away from regex because of the complexity, but the power illustrated in these relatively simple examples is a window into other applications.

To make things a little more intriguing, Batch supports only a subset of the common regex functionality, so some regular expressions that work elsewhere don't work in Batch. To state the obvious, rigorous testing is a must, with both positive and negative cases.

Finding the Record Count of a File

Hoarding may be a vice, but nothing ever gets truly thrown out in Batch. The copy command is useful for creating an empty file even though the xcopy and robocopy commands have long since superseded it for all copy-related functionality. Likewise, the `find` command is pretty much useless when compared to the `findstr` command, so I'll forgo the discussion of how you would use it to perform a search. It does have one useful feature, however: getting the record count of a file. Consider the following:

```
find "" /V /C C:\Batch\12Movies.txt
```

This command performs a search for the null string between the double quotes, using *12Movies.txt* as its input. The /V option negates the search logic just as it does with the `findstr` command. It returns all records not containing the null string, which in effect returns every record in the file. The /C option gives the *count* of records returned, which is the number of records in the file since every record is returned, but what it writes to stdout is a bit more verbose than what we need:

```
---------- C:\BATCH\12MOVIES.TXT: 12
```

Conveniently, and also oddly, the `find` command behaves differently when we pipe the input file into it via the type command:

```
type C:\Batch\12Movies.txt | find "" /V /C
```

This command succinctly writes the count, 12 in this instance, to stdout.

To capture that value in a variable, we can execute the two piped commands as input to a `for /F` command, but we must escape the pipe before the `find` command:

```
for /F usebackq %%c in (`type C:\Batch\12Movies.txt ^| find "" /V /C`) do (
    set recCount=%%c
)
```

(Notice the `usebackq` keyword and the back quotes encasing the input component of the `for /F` command, a combination that clearly shows command input.)

This might seem like an awfully long walk to get a record count. Yes, with the use of escaping we are piping the output of one command (`type`) into a second command (`find`) and using its output as input to a third command (`for`) that has a code block containing a fourth command (`set`) that actually sets the variable. Phew. But it works and is elegant in its own special way.

Summary

In this chapter, I discussed many facets of Batch text searches. You learned how to perform searches for many different types of strings, how to search each record of a file, and how to search for one string inside another string.

I also compared and contrasted two different techniques for performing text searches. The `findstr` method is extremely powerful and flexible, and the text replacement method is easy, efficient, and lightning fast. You now know when to use each. I introduced regular expressions and demonstrated how immensely useful they are in complex searches. You even learned how to determine how many records are in a file.

In the next chapter, I'll introduce another fascinating and useful topic—code that writes code, specifically bat files that create other bat files.

25

BAT FILES BUILDING BAT FILES

In our post-industrial age, manufacturers can build a toaster with relative ease, but no one has ever built a toaster that can build another toaster, and I'm going out on a very short limb to say no manufacturer ever will. Robots, at least in part, can build robots, but cars don't build cars, and smartphones aren't smart enough to build phones of any intellect. In the realm of software, however, code conceives code, programs propagate programs, and bats beget bats.

This chapter isn't about flying mammal procreation, but instead discusses the technique of one bat file creating another bat file. Several languages offer an automated code generator, but those typically create a template or a good starting point from which to do the interesting coding.

Here I'm referring to one bat file creating another fully functional and ready-to-execute bat file.

If this sounds like a parlor trick, it isn't. You might need information from one Batch process before you can write the code for a later process. Instead of writing the bat file for that second process, you can make the first bat file smart enough to write the second with all the needed information. This will also allow one bat file to intelligently break up large processes on the fly, dynamically creating any number of processes based on the size of the input.

I'll first jump right into a complete step-by-step example of a bat file building a bat file, from the parent bat file to the created child bat file and ultimately to the child's output. I'll also detail how to populate a dynamically created bat file with static data, resolved variables, and yet to be resolved variables. I'll put this all together with a real-world application, demonstrate multigenerational bat files, and, most important, discuss useful applications of this technique.

Dynamically Creating a Bat File

The best way to explain how a bat-file-building bat file works is through a simple yet (I hope) interesting example, so I'll start with a demonstration of *Mother.bat*. When it executes, it'll display its name to the console, which is nothing new, and then proceed to something that might have sounded like alchemy not long ago: building the aptly named *Daughter.bat*, a bat file that will write its name to the console along with the name of the bat file that gave it life when it itself executes.

Listing 25-1 isn't a code snippet; it shows the complete contents of *Mother.bat*, the parent bat file.

```
   @setlocal EnableExtensions EnableDelayedExpansion
   @echo off
❶ > con echo ***** This bat file is "%~NX0".
   > con echo.

   set batDtr=C:\Batch\Daughter.bat
❷ >  %batDtr% echo    @setlocal EnableExtensions EnableDelayedExpansion
   >> %batDtr% echo    @echo off
❸ >> %batDtr% echo    ^> con echo ***** This bat file is "%%~NX0".
❹ >> %batDtr% echo    ^> con echo ***** It was created by "%~NX0".
❺ >> %batDtr% echo    ^> con echo.
❻ >> %batDtr% echo    pause
❼ pause
```

Listing 25-1: The parent bat file, Mother.bat

The bat file starts with a `setlocal` command (as all my bat files do). It turns the echo to off, thus keeping the console display clean. The first section of code ends with two `echo` commands, writing the name of the bat file to the console followed by a blank line ❶. Since we aren't in a routine, `%~0` resolves to the hidden parameter of the path and name of the bat file being executed (Chapter 11). With the use of two modifiers, `%~NX0` extracts just the filename and extension from the hidden parameter (Chapter 17).

The final section of the bat file is where it gets interesting. Six echo commands write one line each to build the child bat file. The first echo command ❷ with a single redirection character creates the child bat file, writing the `setlocal` command to it. (I've mentioned that every bat file I write starts with this command, and that also goes for bat files I indirectly write via other bat files.)

Nothing here is executing the `setlocal` command; this code treats it as simple text as it redirects or writes it to *Daughter.bat*. Don't think of it as a `setlocal` command, but as a *proto*-`setlocal` command. Three spaces follow the name of the echo command; the first space delimits the command itself from the text it's writing, and the next two spaces are part of the text it writes to the file. Functionally, the two additional spaces aren't necessary, but for aesthetics I always indent, again even in dynamically created bat files.

Multiple commands performing redirection appear to have two echo commands each. Taking the last of these commands ❺ first, the initial echo writes a line to the child bat file, a line consisting entirely of the `> con echo.` text. The caret escape character is critical here. Without it, the interpreter would treat the greater-than sign after it like a second redirection operator, which obviously wouldn't be good. With the caret, the greater-than sign is just another character written to the child bat file.

The two prior commands look quite similar to each other. Both are writing a record to *Daughter.bat*; both records will be echo commands writing something to the console, and both are using the caret as an escape character for its redirection character. There is, however, a critical difference between them.

Each writes distinctive text after the asterisks, but that's trivial. The first command ❸ has a second percent sign in what looks to be the resolution of the filename. Don't be fooled by the subtlety; it's the crux of this entire chapter. The text in the second command ❹ does in fact resolve to the name of the parent bat file. But in the first command ❸, the first percent sign is the escape character for the second percent sign, meaning that the interpreter resolves the two characters to a single percent sign and writes it as a simple text character to the file. Thus, the tilde and other characters that come next have no special meaning to Batch in this context, so the interpreter also writes them unchanged as text to the child bat file.

Not to put too fine a point on this, but here's how the interpreter handles these similar text strings when writing the child bat file:

- The `"%%~NX0"` text ❸ becomes `"%~NX0"`.
- The `"%~NX0"` text ❹ becomes `"Mother.bat"`.

The parent bat file writes one last line, which will become a pause command ❻, to the child bat file. Finally, an actual pause command ❼ rounds out *Mother.bat*.

Now we can execute *Mother.bat*, the bat-file-building bat file shown in Listing 25-1. The "%~NX0" from the first section of its code ❶ resolves to "Mother.bat", and the following appears on the console:

```
***** This bat files is "Mother.bat".

Press any key to continue . . .
```

That pause command at the very end of *Mother.bat* holds the console open so that we can read this message.

More interesting, *Mother.bat* creates *Daughter.bat*, a fully functional bat file. This point cannot be stressed enough; the bat file shown in Listing 25-2 was *not* created directly by a human.

```
@setlocal EnableExtensions EnableDelayedExpansion
@echo off
> con echo ***** This bat file is "%~NX0".
> con echo ***** It was created by "Mother.bat".
> con echo.
pause
```

Listing 25-2: The child bat file, Daughter.bat

The child bat file has six records with the two most interesting ones in the middle. As expected, the interpreter resolved "%%~NX0" from *Mother.bat* (Listing 25-1) to "%~NX0" in the first of these echo commands in *Daughter.bat*. This will be important when *Daughter.bat* itself (herself?) executes. Likewise, the next echo command in the child bat file contains the "Mother.bat" text, which the interpreter resolved from "%~NX0" in the parent bat file.

This culminates in the execution of the child bat file, *Daughter.bat*. Run it as you would any other bat file, and it writes the following to the console:

```
***** This bat file is "Daughter.bat".
***** It was created by "Mother.bat".

Press any key to continue . . .
```

When the child bat file executes, the interpreter resolves "%~NX0" in the first redirected echo command to "Daughter.bat". The next line of output comes from the echo command containing the already resolved "Mother.bat".

As a recap, let's follow the flow from the parent to the child to the child's output. When the parent bat file executes, "%%~NX0" becomes "%~NX0" in the child bat file—again, two percent signs resolve to one due to escaping. Then when the child bat file executes, "%~NX0" resolves to "Daughter.bat" in the final output.

Contrast that with "%~NX0" in the parent bat file, which becomes "Mother .bat" in the child bat file. At that point it's hardcoded text, at least from the perspective of the child, and when the child bat file executes, it writes "Mother.bat" to the console.

This example demonstrates two important points. First, it's very possible for a bat file to create another fully functional bat file. Second, some text containing escape characters can become a *resolvable* variable in the child, not a resolved variable. Put another way, the parent can write some text to the child, and when the child executes, that text resolves a variable to its value. But this example just touches on what's possible.

No one will confuse this process with the artificial intelligence that might someday kill or enslave all of humanity, but I wouldn't call *Mother.bat* a dumb bat file.

Variable Resolution

You can now resolve the hidden parameter in either the parent or child bat file, but resolving ordinary variables in either bat file is equally if not more important.

Variables delimited by percent signs and exclamation marks behave a bit differently. To demonstrate, the following listing uses two system variables set on all Windows computers: computername is the name of the computer, and os is the machine's operating system (Chapter 21). This code creates a small bat file named *Dynamic.bat*.

```
  set batDyn=C:\Batch\Dynamic.bat
  > %batDyn% echo    @setlocal EnableExtensions EnableDelayedExpansion
  >> %batDyn% echo    @echo off
❶ >> %batDyn% echo    ^> con echo This bat was built on %computername%,
  >> %batDyn% echo    ^> con echo      using the operating system !os!.
❷ >> %batDyn% echo    ^> con echo This bat is running on %%computername%%,
  >> %batDyn% echo    ^> con echo      using the operating system ^^!os^^!.
  >> %batDyn% echo    pause
```

I've encased the first reference to computername in a single set of percent signs ❶, and in the next command, I've set the first reference to os between a single set of exclamation marks. (Either delimiter works for either variable; I'm merely comparing and contrasting the two.) Both variables resolve to their respective values when these two echo commands execute, perhaps writing the following to the dynamic bat file:

```
> con echo This bat was built on JACKLAPTOP,
> con echo      using the operating system Windows_NT.
```

However, the next two echo commands ❷ write the following two lines:

```
> con echo This bat is running on %computername%,
> con echo      using the operating system !os!.
```

When the interpreter encounters %%computername%%, it doesn't see a variable. Since the percent sign is the escape character for itself, each pair resolves to a single percent sign, and the text between them isn't a variable name; it's just along for the ride, at least for now. As detailed in Chapter 14, escaping the exclamation mark is a bit trickier, but ^^!os^^! similarly resolves to !os!.

Execute the child bat file, *Dynamic.bat*, on any computer, and the first pair of echo commands write what is now hardcoded text to the console—that is, they write the information derived from the machine where the first bat file ran. The next two echo commands, however, have two variables that resolve when *Dynamic.bat* executes, and their values reflect the computer name and operating system of the computer on which this child bat file runs.

Let's look at a real-world application to demonstrate when it makes sense to resolve variables as we write them to the child bat file and when it makes sense to resolve them as the child executes.

A Real-World Application

The prior examples show how you can resolve variables and parameters in a dynamically created bat file, but these examples are pedagogical at their core. There's no practical use for a bat file that does nothing more than announce its lineage and current status. A real-world bat-file-building bat file will do much more and be far more useful.

For instance, it will likely transmit variables from the parent to the child. As any bat file executes, it accumulates and modifies variables, but nothing automatically imbues those variables to a dynamically created bat file. A simple way of ensuring that a variable is preserved in its scion is to write a set command defining that variable to the child. When that bat file runs, the set command executes, and the variable is available for the remainder of its execution or until it's reset.

I've already demonstrated how to write a single line of code with an echo command, but you can also write the contents of an entire file into a dynamically created bat file with a type command (Chapter 12). Typically, I start a child bat file with a prologue static file and end it with an epilogue static file.

The prologue static file probably starts with a setlocal command (because most bat files should), and it likely sets some variables, but after that the contents could be anything. What's important is that this file contains the hardcoded Batch code that'll begin each bat file the process dynamically creates. Likewise, the epilogue static file contains all of the common code needed to complete all child bat files. At the very least it usually contains some callable routines and error handling.

Static bat files don't have to come at the beginning and ending of dynamically created bat files. You can insert others with multiple type commands interspersed with the echo commands. You can even store just a few lines of code in a static file to avoid the need for escaping.

The following listing contains a template for a real-world bat-building bat:

```
   set batDyn=C:\Batch\Dynamic.bat
❶ >  %batDyn% type C:\Batch\StaticPrologue.bat
❷ >> %batDyn% echo.
❸ >> %batDyn% echo    set someVar=%someVar%
   >> %batDyn% echo    set someOtherVar=%someOtherVar%
❹ >> %batDyn% echo    set parentPath=%path%
   >> %batDyn% echo.
❺ >> %batDyn% echo    %someExe%
❻ >> %batDyn% echo    if %%errorlevel%% neq 0 ^(
❼ >> %batDyn% echo       ^> con echo Some EXE FAILED
   >> %batDyn% echo       pause
   >> %batDyn% echo       goto :Abort
❽ >> %batDyn% echo    ^)
❾ >> %batDyn% type C:\Batch\StaticEpilogue.bat
```

At first glance, the redirection ❶ that begins the creation of *Dynamic
.bat* might look like the first of many echo commands, but this is the first
of two type commands in the listing. This one writes the entirety of the
StaticPrologue.bat file into the dynamically created bat file.

Two echo commands ❸ demonstrate the technique for maintaining
a parent variable in the child bat file. The argument of each burgeoning
set command has the variable name to the left of the equal sign and its
resolved value to the right. It looks redundant, but this turns into a hardcoded set command assigning a value to a variable in the child bat file.

The next echo command ❹ demonstrates a twist on this technique; the
new variable gets a new name. The child bat file might need to know the
path variable used by the parent bat file, but we don't want to impact the
child's own path variable. This command writes a set command that will
eventually assign the full contents of the parent's path variable to a variable
named parentPath when *Dynamic.bat* executes.

There are two reasons to use the technique of escaping when creating a
dynamic bat file. First, percent signs and exclamation marks used to resolve
variables need escaping—sometimes. It all depends on when we should
resolve the variable.

Dynamic.bat will invoke some executable and then check the return
code. In this example, let's assume that the executable is known when we
create the dynamic bat file. For that reason, I'm simply resolving the variable as %someExe% ❺ and writing it directly to the dynamic bat file where it
will be hardcoded text.

The return code ❻ is a very different story; clearly, we should *not*
resolve it until this command executes as the dynamic bat file runs, so I'm
using escape characters for the delimiters. The interpreter sees %%errorlevel%%
and writes %errorlevel% to the file. Without the escape characters, the variable would have simply resolved to its state at the time it was written, likely
0, resulting in a perpetually false conditional clause: if 0 neq 0. The escape
characters leave this as a variable yet to be resolved.

The second reason to use escaping in a dynamic bat file is when the
character has some other special significance in Batch. For instance, always
escape pipes and ampersands when they are to be part of the dynamic

code. In this example, we need to escape the open ❻ and close ❽ parentheses around the code block, as well as the redirection symbol or greater-than sign ❼ inside of the code block.

Assuming that someExe is set to a particular value, the interpreter might write the section of code between ❺ and ❽ to the dynamic bat file as:

```
C:\Batch\SomeExecutable.exe
if %errorlevel% neq 0 (
    > con echo Some EXE FAILED
    pause
    goto :Abort
)
```

The second type command ❾ rounds out this listing and writes the entirety of *StaticEpilogue.bat* to the dynamic file. It probably uses the three variables that the earlier code explicitly wrote to the dynamic bat file. Given the goto command inside the code block, I'm also very confident that there is an :Abort label somewhere in this file. Whatever its contents, they'll complete the dynamic bat file.

But the writing of static files to child bat files has one subtle batveat. I've passed over one very critical command in the code, so critical that I've saved it for last. Immediately after the first type command writes the static prologue data to the dynamically created bat file, a simple echo command ❷ appends a blank line to *Dynamic.bat*.

You might assume that I did this to simply separate the static code and the coming set commands in the new bat file, and that would've been a wonderful justification in its own right. After all, a blank line after the set commands ❹ also creates some whitespace solely for this purpose, but the first blank line is for much more than aesthetics.

To explain the problem that this blank line is fixing, I once shared this bat-building bat technique with a co-worker who ended the equivalent of his *StaticPrologue.bat* with the setting of a critical variable:

```
set criticalVar=criticalValue
```

This data is the very end of the file; there isn't even a trailing blank line. It will be crucial momentarily.

After the type command in his main bat file, he didn't write a blank line. Instead, he set a variable:

```
>> %batDyn% echo    set someVar=%someVar%
```

The ultimate result was this line of code in the middle of his dynamic bat file:

```
set criticalVar=criticalValue  set someVar=Whatever
```

What looks to be a second set command isn't a command at all; it's just more text, including the spaces, appended to the intended value of the *actual* set command. The result is dynamic code that doesn't set `criticalVar` to the intended value and doesn't set `someVar` at all. It's pretty obvious that the result is garbage, but what caused this?

When the interpreter performs an `echo` command redirected to a file, it appends the text to the very end of the target file. Then the interpreter immediately appends the two characters for a carriage return line feed, or more informally, it adds a CRLF. (I detailed the CRLF in Chapter 14.) The end result is that when you view it in an editor, there's an empty line at the bottom of the file. When you redirect multiple `echo` commands one after another, each command appends a line of text and a CRLF so that the next command appends its text as a new record.

That works great when you create the file exclusively with dynamically generated code via `echo` commands, but the `type` command writes an entire file just as it is into the target without adding a CRLF. That causes a potential problem if the creator of the static bat file didn't append a CRLF onto the final record of the file. (That is, they didn't position the cursor at the end of the last record, hit ENTER, and save the file.) When the interpreter writes the static file missing that CRLF to the dynamic bat file and then tries to append a record via an `echo` command, it actually appends that record to the final record of the copied static data instead, resulting in the dog's breakfast we see here. (It also results in a frustrated co-worker trying to figure out why a couple variables aren't resolved as expected.)

The `echo.` command ❷ writes a null or blank record (not even any spaces) and, more important, a CRLF. Its inclusion here ensures that if the CRLF is missing from the last record of the static file, the code will insert another CRLF in the dynamically created bat file, and if it isn't missing, it writes a null record, which nicely separates the sections of code. If you're really counting on that whitespace, write two blank lines.

It seems like a never-ending battle to make code bullet-proof and to anticipate every possible condition that can break it, but there are two primary means of avoiding this issue: ensure that every static file you use ends with a CRLF, or write the blank line after every `type` command that doesn't complete the child bat file. I find it far easier to control this in the code with the latter option, but it's not a bad idea to always do both.

Multigenerational Bat Files

The quote "Give me a lever long enough and a fulcrum on which to place it, and I shall move the world" is attributed to Archimedes. I'd like to think that if the ancient Greeks had Batch, the great thinker would've said, "Give me enough escape characters and disk space, and I shall create an infinite bat-file-creating bat file." Undoubtedly, this quote pales in comparison to the original, but escape characters can be escaped, and bat files aren't limited to a single generation of offspring.

Stripped of everything superfluous, this bare-bones version of *Mother.bat* will create a child bat file that'll create a progeny of its own:

```
set batDtr=C:\Batch\Daughter.bat
>  %batDtr% echo    set batGDtr=C:\Batch\GrandDaughter.bat
>> %batDtr% echo    ^> %%batGDtr%% echo   @echo off
>> %batDtr% echo    ^>^> %%batGDtr%% echo   ^^^> con echo I am "%%%%~NX0"
>> %batDtr% echo    ^>^> %%batGDtr%% echo   ^^^> con echo Begat by "%%~NX0"
>> %batDtr% echo    ^>^> %%batGDtr%% echo   ^^^> con echo Begat by "%~NX0"
>> %batDtr% echo    ^>^> %%batGDtr%% echo   pause
```

Executing *Mother.bat* produces *Daughter.bat*:

```
set batGDtr=C:\Batch\GrandDaughter.bat
>  %batGDtr% echo    @echo off
>> %batGDtr% echo    ^> con echo I am "%%~NX0"
>> %batGDtr% echo    ^> con echo Begat by "%~NX0"
>> %batGDtr% echo    ^> con echo Begat by "Mother.bat"
>> %batGDtr% echo    pause
```

Notice that ^> escapes to > and %% escapes to %, but by escaping the escape character, ^^^> becomes ^> and %%%% becomes %%.

Executing *Daughter.bat* produces *GrandDaughter.bat*:

```
@echo off
> con echo I am "%~NX0"
> con echo Begat by "Daughter.bat"
> con echo Begat by "Mother.bat"
pause
```

Running *GrandDaughter.bat* produces the following output to the console where %~NX0 resolves one last time, this time to "GrandDaughter.bat":

```
I am "GrandDaughter.bat"
Begat by "Daughter.bat"
Begat by "Mother.bat"
Press any key to continue . . .
```

I have an admission to make. This last example is nothing more than an egregious instance of the author shamelessly showing off—the coder's equivalent of an endzone dance or a geek version of trash talk after a dunk. I've been coding in Batch for many years, and this is the first time I've ever even thought to code a bat that builds a bat that builds a bat. I've done it here only to show what's possible and am hard-pressed to come up with a real-world application for it, but there are many uses for a bat file that creates a second bat file.

Recommendations

You can use the real-world application discussed earlier as a template for more complex dynamic bat files. It has all the pieces you'll need: it assigns variables, using existing and new names; it uses escaping to allow variables to be resolved later; it escapes other special characters to be used in the child bat file; and it uses partial static bat files in tandem with the dynamically generated code.

This technique is great when a process grows to the point where you need to break it down into smaller chunks and execute them independently. Perhaps you'll base the breakdown on the size of the input so you can write a bat file to build one to many dynamically created bat files after inspecting that input. Put another way, you can dynamically create a dynamic number of subprocesses.

The different subprocesses might even end up running on different servers to balance the load. You might be able to use static bat files for those subprocesses, but when you dynamically generate the other bat files, you can imbue them with information gathered during the execution of the original bat file.

Some might protest that you can pass the dynamic information as arguments to the second bat file, but that works only if the first bat actually calls the second. Some completely different process might execute your dynamically created bat file. That process doesn't have to pass any arguments or even understand the contents of the bat file or its function. You can even create a bat file, hold it, and execute it at a later time.

Summary

In this chapter, I showed how a bat file can build another bat file. After a detailed demonstration, I discussed how to write resolved variables and resolvable variables to a dynamic bat file. I also shared some techniques that I use for creating variables in a dynamic bat file and building these bat files with both dynamic and static code. You learned situations in which dynamically created bat files are most useful and applicable.

In the next chapter, I'll demonstrate an intriguing application of a bat-building bat. After discussing a very useful technique of automatically restarting an intermittent failure, I'll apply lessons from this chapter to perform an even more difficult task, killing and restarting a hung execution. We'll dynamically create a second bat file to call the process susceptible to hanging and monitor it from the first bat file. It's amazing how problems start to find solutions in tools from an expanding toolkit.

26

AUTOMATIC RESTARTS AND MULTITHREADING

In this chapter, I'll explore solutions to a couple of vexing issues for any coder: intermittent failures and hangs, specifically the type that usually execute successfully if restarted. I'll detail how to automatically restart an intermittent failure of any process in a bat file. Hangs are a little trickier, but I'll introduce a technique for terminating or killing the hung process before restarting it. For both types of issues, I'll step through how to create a solution, including design considerations, specifications, coding, and even testing.

Along the way, I'll introduce some interesting commands that have applications beyond automatic restarts. One puts a bat file to sleep for a defined period of time. Another one monitors all of the processes running on a computer (think of it as Task Manager inside a bat file). Yet another command terminates any specific process or multiple processes on a computer. Ultimately, this discussion will lead to the seemingly unrelated technique of multithreading or concurrency.

Five Stages of Intermittent Failures

The bane of a coder's existence is the intermittent failure. It might be a simple xcopy command that fails because of a temporary network or server communication issue. You might have to call a program written by someone else that sometimes fails to connect to a web service or simply fails for no apparent reason from time to time. Simply rerunning the process "fixes" the issue, but doing so wastes resources and causes delays. I've been involved in a number of these episodes, and every last one has followed these "Five Stages of Intermittent Failures" (loosely based on the "Five Stages of Grief"):

Stage 1: Denial   "This looks like a fluke. I can't find anything wrong. Just rerun it."

Stage 2: Anger   The operator who's tasked with tracking down and restarting the failures is peeved; the Batch coder who has no control over the network or the executable they're invoking is cross; the mid-level manager with even less control is vexed. Each failure makes the situation worse until everybody is just plain angry.

Stage 3: Finger Pointing   "It's the fault of networking. Our servers are held together with duct tape and chicken wire." "No, the vendor product is malfunctioning." "No, your environment can't support our product." "It's a problem with our internet provider." "That guy who retired a couple of months ago left us with junk."

Stage 4: Exploration   A manager harrumphs, "I don't want a Band-Aid. We need to find the root cause." This is something everyone can agree on, because no one wants to be the lone member of the Band-Aid caucus—at least initially. Extra logging is put in place and diagnostic tools are installed on any piece of hardware that might be remotely involved in the issue. Different groups dive into their codebase and develop theories. Sometimes the root cause is found, sparing everyone the last stage, but more often than not the ghost in the machine remains an enigma.

Stage 5: Acceptance   Finally heeding Voltaire's proverb, "The best is the enemy of the good," the Batch coder fixes the issue with an automatic restart of the suspect process.

As long as one person holds onto the hope of finding the root cause, it's difficult to move on to the final stage of acceptance. It might take days, weeks, or months, but when it becomes obvious that a root cause won't be forthcoming or would be exceedingly expensive or difficult to fix, the only option is to attack the problem at its manifestation. Notice that in the fifth stage I didn't put the word *fixes* in quotes. Some holdouts will still call it a

Band-Aid or a work-around, but a well-designed automatic restart process will correct the problem so that no one will be bothered by it again. I call that a *fix*.

The timeout Command

Before building an automatic restart, I'll introduce a new command that'll be very helpful in its design. Prior to initiating an automatic restart, I'll want to put the bat file to sleep for a short period of time to allow any momentary server or connectivity issues to clear. Doing nothing is easy for humans; for some it's our default state, but a computer program is designed to execute as fast as possible. Fortunately, Batch has given us the `timeout` command, possibly modeled after the timeout taken in sports or enforced upon a misbehaving youth.

It's a simple command that accepts a single argument: the length of the timeout in seconds. This command will sleep for one minute:

```
timeout 60
```

Batch allows for a maximum timeout of 99,999 seconds, which translates to more than 27 hours. When this command is used interactively, the user sees a countdown on the console until processing resumes and has the option of pressing any key to end the timeout early and continue.

There are a couple of mild oddities with the `timeout` command. First, it accepts an argument of 0. This would make no sense as a hardcoded value, but consider this command:

```
timeout %sleepSeconds%
```

If you are determining the sleep time in the code, it offers an easy way of essentially turning off the command without wrapping it up in an `if` command. Set `sleepSeconds` to 300 for a five-minute break or to 0 if you want to skip the command. An argument of -1 results in an indefinite wait time until any key is pressed, which is really just a glorified `pause` command.

The Automatic Restart

Let's step through the process of building an automatic restart of some process that fails intermittently. Design considerations will inform the specifications that'll lead to writing and testing the code.

The Design Considerations

The basic concept of an auto-restart is straightforward. When any process generates a bad return code, the main logic normally aborts the execution in an orderly fashion. An auto-restart instead circles back and reruns the offending process. In Batch, that might sound like nothing more than an if command and a goto command, but the details quickly become involved and in need of a well-thought-out design.

Ideally the restart works, and the process continues to completion, but sometimes the auto-restart also fails, and if it continues to fail, the prospect of an endless loop mounts. Someone has to make a decision concerning the number of times to restart the process before conceding defeat and initiating an abort.

If a process fails without explanation one time in 100, the restarted process will likely fail one time in 100 as well. Basic probability theory dictates that if an event occurs once in 100 attempts, the odds are 1/100. To find the odds of this randomly occurring twice in succession, the ratio is squared, giving us 1/10,000. Cubing the original odds gives us one chance in a million of the event occurring in three consecutive attempts. An exponent of five tells us that just one in 10 billion events should see this fail five straight times.

This means that five or six attempts should get us to a point where the failures will realistically no longer happen if—and this is an enormous if—the one failure in 100 attempts is truly random.

Oftentimes failures are not random, and that also factors into the design considerations. Failures might happen when a server or a database is busy during peak processing times. Occasionally, for no apparent reason two servers will lose connectivity for a split second or a couple of seconds or several minutes. If a copy from one of these boxes to another one fails, the next 10 auto-restarts might happen in less time than it takes you to read this sentence, meaning that all 10 happen during the window of lost connectivity. This isn't random.

For that type of failure, you'll need more analysis. How long does it take for the issue to typically clear itself? In most situations, it's best to go to sleep for a few seconds before the first auto-restart, as mentioned previously. After subsequent failures, we can initiate longer and longer wait times. If the issue typically clears in a minute, the total restart attempts should finish up in about three or four minutes, with the time frame adjusted from there.

If this seems overwhelming, does it make sense to just go with hundreds of auto-restart attempts over the course of several hours? No, it doesn't. If the auto-restart process makes an excessive number of attempts or if the sleep time between attempts is too great, the solution can become self-defeating. If a server loses connectivity at noon on a Friday, excessively generous auto-restarts might mask the problem until the evening. Processes might be hours behind schedule before anyone is even aware of the problem. A compromise is needed.

Another consideration is the nature of the failure. You should make every effort to differentiate between legitimate failures and restartable failures. If a program aborts because of a data condition that won't differ on a restart, an auto-restart will simply be a waste of time and CPU cycles. Sometimes you can divine the nature of the error from the return code. If so, you can use it to determine the next course of action. If not, that also factors into the calculus; maybe you should attempt fewer restarts.

The Specifications

For this exercise, I'll invent a scenario requiring an auto-restart and write some specifications with all of the just-considered design considerations in mind.

A compiled executable communicating with a database on a remote server works great most of the time. It runs more than 30 times daily, but every three days or so it fails, returning an errorlevel of 7. The first few times it happened, someone restarted it, but a couple failures a week became a nuisance. Then a Sunday morning failure that went unnoticed until later in the week became a huge embarrassment for everyone involved. Something had to be done.

The fictitious failure happens about once in every 100 attempts, which is fortuitous because I just did some math assuming that exact frequency. After we have gathered all of the statistics, some failures appear to be truly random, but the unexplained connectivity with the database seems to clear up in less than five seconds, so we won't need long sleep times.

Fortunately, whoever wrote the executable did a good job with the return code. Other failures, such as the inability to find certain entries in the database, generate return codes other than 7, and a successful invocation always returns 0.

We now have what we need to write the specifications. The first one is obvious, but the other two require a little finesse, as you might come up with slightly different numbers:

1. Initiate an auto-restart if errorlevel is 7. Continue if 0, and abort for all other returned values.

2. Attempt up to four auto-restarts for a total of five executions of the program, aborting after the fifth.

3. Pause for 2 seconds after the first attempt and double it for each subsequent attempt, meaning that the wait times will be 2, 4, 8, and 16 seconds.

After little more than 30 seconds (plus however long the executable runs), the fifth failure will initiate an abort. In an endeavor that is as much computer art as computer science, this should be a good compromise. Now, we're ready to code.

The Auto-Restart Code

Listing 26-1 meets the defined specifications. The only prerequisite to this code executing is that we must set the flakyExe variable to the program or process experiencing the intermittent failure.

```
❶ prompt $T$G
  if not defined sleepIncrmt  set sleepIncrmt=2
  if not defined maxAttempts  set maxAttempts=5
  set attempt=0

❷ :Restart
  set /A attempt += 1

  %flakyExe%

❸ if %errorlevel% equ 7 (
  ❹ if %attempt% lss %maxAttempts% (
    ❺ timeout %sleepIncrmt%
      set /A sleepIncrmt *= 2
      goto :Restart
    ) else (
    ❻ goto :Abort
    )
  ) else if %errorlevel% neq 0 (
  ❼ goto :Abort
  ) else (
  ❽ > con echo Successful Call of the Flaky Executable
  )
```

Listing 26-1: Code that initiates up to four auto-restarts of a flaky executable

In the first section of the code, the prompt command ❶ (introduced in Chapter 21) embeds the time into the prompt string that's prepended to each executed line in stdout, making it easier to verify that the process is pausing for the requisite amount of time. I define the variable for the sleep increment as 2 seconds and the variable for the maximum attempts as 5 attempts. I also initialize the attempt variable, which tracks the attempt being executed, to 0.

To add flexibility to the code, I use the technique of setting sleepIncrmt and maxAttempts only if they aren't already defined. Much effort has been put into the specifications, but if the compromise between averting an abort and minimizing the time it takes to perform the auto-restarts isn't quite right, a user can set these variables prior to calling this logic or set them globally on the computer. If one abort is still occurring each month, anyone can increase the sleep increment or the maximum attempts without changing this code, but I'll assume the defaults for this exercise.

The logic proceeds past the :Restart label ❷ and increments the attempt variable to 1, before resolving flakyExe and thus executing the program. (In this exercise, the variable contains the flaky executable that's failing, but this invocation could instead be an xcopy command to or from a remote server; it could be a call to a flaky bat file or whatever process might fail and need restarting.)

I next evaluate the errorlevel the executable returned. If the code encounters the bad return code of 7 ❸, I look to see whether I've made the requisite 5 attempts ❹. Since this is the first attempt, the execution enters the code block ❺ and executes the timeout command to sleep for 2 seconds.

Then I double the increment, `sleepIncrmt`, so that the process will sleep for 4 seconds if invoked again. Next, I break out of this logic, backward, via the `goto` command.

This brings us back to the `:Restart` label ❷ that the execution processed past just a moment ago. Here's a great application of the `do...while` command from Chapter 9. Notice the strategic placement of the label. I increment the total number of attempts to 2 after invoking the first restart and then execute the flaky process again.

If 7 is again the return code ❸, the same process executes another restart, this time upping `attempt` to 3, which is still less than 5 ❹. Back in the code block ❺ and after taking the four-second timeout, I double the sleep increment to 8 and return again to the `:Restart` label ❷.

If this fails four times, I'll sleep for 16 seconds ❺ and make one last attempt. If this also fails, `attempt` resolves to 5 and is no longer less than the target value in `maxAttempts` ❹, so the code will abort via the `:Abort` routine ❻ that isn't shown.

We need to think like the interpreter for two more scenarios. You already know what happens when `errorlevel` is 7. Now imagine that the flaky process returns anything but 0 or 7. The `else if` clause, `%errorlevel% neq 0`, is true, and the code invokes the `:Abort` routine ❼.

As the final scenario, imagine that 0 is the return code. This is the only possible way to get to the code block ❽ after the default `else` clause that verifies that the execution was successful.

The abort routine should distinguish between the two types of aborts. One failed after multiple auto-restarts ❻, and the other failed due to something unrelated to the restarts ❼ after just a single failure.

The Testing

This is clearly some advanced Batch coding, but after you've grasped the concept and coded up something such as what's in Listing 26-1, what might seem like an even more difficult task awaits: testing. If you run this code 100 times, you're likely to see at least one failure, but there's still a better than one chance in three of seeing no failures at all. Billions of executions wouldn't even guarantee seeing five failures. (Look up the Poisson distribution if you're curious about the math.)

We need a means of simulating the failure, and entering this command prior to Listing 26-1 will do exactly that:

```
set flakyExe=cmd /C exit 7
```

When the interpreter resolves `flakyExe` in the code, the `cmd` command (introduced in Chapter 21) executes, running the `exit` command that sets `errorlevel` to 7. If the main logic was coded correctly, this'll trigger an auto-restart, and then it'll repeat the same process a total of five times before aborting.

After you are satisfied with that testing, change `exit 7` to `exit 4` and run it again; expect to see a different abort, one that doesn't invoke a restart.

Change it again to exit 0, and you should see a successful run (or at least a simulated successful run).

An ideal test might invoke two auto-restarts after two failures return 7 and then succeed with a return code of 0 on the third call. You could replace the cmd command in this setting with a call command of a simple bat file containing some conditional logic to set the return code based on the attempt being executed. Better yet, just use this setting:

```
set flakyExe=if ^^!attempt^^! lss 3 (cmd /C exit 7) else (cmd /C exit 0)
```

As you learned in Chapter 14, I escape the exclamation marks so they'll be stored in the variable. Then when the code resolves flakyExe, the value contained in the attempt variable will be part of the conditional clause. It'll be true the first two times it executes, resulting in a return code of 7; then on the third execution, the conditional clause will be false. Hence, the return code will be 0. I recommended against messy if commands like this in Chapter 4, but it's perfect for this type of testing.

The Central Log

The previous example is stripped down and perfectly functional, but when actually implemented, another key feature is a central log of each auto-restart. When this process completes, we can interrogate attempt; anything greater than 1 means that the code executed at least one auto-restart. With this information we can write a timestamped entry to a logfile with details about the auto-restart, especially the number of attempts.

You might become a victim of your own success if the auto-restart completely masks the failures. There's still an underlying and unresolved issue, so it's important to keep a record of the aborts avoided. After a month, you can use the log to definitively state that some number of processes would have aborted without the auto-restart. It might be just two or three or a dozen or maybe hundreds.

Whatever the number, you can use this log as a testament to the successful implementation of the auto-restart process. It'll also monitor the underlying root problem. The frequency of the issue might decrease or vanish after the installation of new hardware, or it might happen more as existing hardware ages. This information can help determine the urgency of a solution targeting the root cause. (It may also be hard numbers for your annual review.)

Hangs

I've discussed automatically restarting a failed process that returns a certain value or set of values for errorlevel. An even bigger challenger is a hang; a *hang* occurs when a called process fails to terminate and never returns a value for errorlevel—even worse, hangs never return control to the Batch code.

A hang can be the result of an endless loop that would happen again on a restart, but sometimes a faulty process will hang when a connection drops or it can't find a resource. In short, if you can go into Task Manager, kill the hung process, restart it, and have it process successfully with no other intervention, then the process is a great candidate for an automatic kill and restart.

But any auto-kill-and-restart process has one major obstacle. An auto-restart is fairly straightforward in concept. When you get back certain bad return codes, you simply invoke the restart logic. But with a hang, the Batch code is, well, hanging. The process has taken its ball home and promised never to share it again. By definition, a hang will not return control to the Batch code, so the bat file that called it can't do anything, much less kill and restart the process. But there's always a way: something or someone must kill the hung process. Hence, the coder must anticipate and code for the possibility of a hang.

To accomplish this, we'll need some important commands that aren't in an everyday bat file. The start command (detailed in Chapter 10) will spawn a second command window that'll actually run the process that might hang. The tasklist command will monitor the spawned bat file that may possibly hang, and the taskkill command will . . . I think this one is self-explanatory.

Just listing these commands sketches out the broad underpinnings of the plan, but before getting into details, I must properly introduce these two new commands.

Retrieving a List of Processes

The tasklist command provides much of the information that you can find on a Windows machine "manually" with Task Manager. It retrieves a list of all or some of the current processes running on a machine. We'll be using it in a bat file, but first bring up a command prompt and type **tasklist** and you'll get a list of everything running on the machine, including the memory usage, session information, and process indicator (PID). Scores of processes will be running at any given time, but here's an example of just a few rows:

Image Name	PID	Session Name	Session#	Mem Usage
System Idle Process	0	Services	0	8 K
System	4	Services	0	3,168 K
Registry	120	Services	0	51,168 K
cmd.exe	8692	Services	0	432 K

The PID is a number that the operating system assigns to a process when its execution starts. The System Idle Process is always running, and its PID is always 0; System usually runs with a PID of 4 or 8, depending on the operating system, and all other processes are assigned a unique number divisible by 4. At some point PIDs are reused, but not until thousands of different processes have run on the machine. The tasklist command displays each executing bat file with an image name of *cmd.exe* as seen in the fourth and final entry.

The command has some very useful parameters. When parsing through the output of the command (which we'll be doing shortly), we'll want to avoid the first two header lines of the output. The /NH option (for *no headers*) removes the first line of header information as well as the cosmetic second line of equal signs.

The /FO option (for *format*) alters the presentation of the data. The available formats are comma-delimited (/FO:CSV), list (/FO:LIST), and table (/FO:TABLE), which is also the default shown in the sample output.

The /FI option will *filter* out unwanted entries or include only wanted entries. You can include or exclude certain window titles or build filters involving the CPU time, PID, image name, and more. For example, the following command brings up all instances of Notepad++ running on a machine:

```
tasklist /FI:"ImageName eq notepad++.exe"
```

(Please don't ask why this option uses the equality operator eq instead of equ, but it does.)

Using the wildcard (*) brings up all instances of Notepad, Notepad++, and anything else that might start with those seven letters:

```
tasklist /FI:"ImageName eq notepad*"
```

The following command uses the greater-than operator to display all processes currently being memory hogs:

```
tasklist /FI:"MemUsage gt 250000"
```

Use the help for more details on the /FI option; what I've shown here is just a sampling of the operands and operators.

Killing Processes

The taskkill command can terminate a specific process or several at one time. Some of its parameters are shared with the tasklist command, most important, the /FI option. The following command attempts to kill all instances of Notepad running on a machine:

```
taskkill /FI:"imagename eq notepad.exe"
```

This command tries to close all opened Notepad files, immediately doing so for all that are saved. Notepad generates a pop-up window for all unsaved work, kindly asking the user to save the file, but the /F option *forcefully* kills the processes. Using the option will unapologetically terminate the processes unsaved. The /T option kills not only a process but also any processes that it may have started. Before long, we'll kill the spawned bat file with both of these options to ensure that it, and everything associated with it, is truly terminated.

Used with the /PID option, the taskkill command terminates one or more specific processes based on the process indicator. For instance, this'll terminate two processes:

```
taskkill /PID 12348 /PID 6784
```

You can also forcefully kill processes with very specific window titles. (Foreshadowing isn't just for fiction.)

The Automatic Kill and Restart

Just as we did with the automatic restart, let's step through the building of an automatic kill and restart of a process prone to occasional hangs, including design, specifications, coding, and testing.

In this fictitious scenario, the flaky executable will continue to work perfectly well 99.9 percent of the time, but one time in 1,000 it hangs. We know that the root cause isn't a simple endless loop, because we can manually kill and restart it and see it run successfully. The team theorizes about how interacting with the database could cause the problem, or maybe it has nothing to do with the database. It happens so infrequently, it's nearly impossible to troubleshoot, but it happens frequently enough to be a problem, and no one can find the root cause.

After cycling through the five stages, we've decided to fix the issue with an auto-kill-and-restart. We'll put the call to the offending process into a dynamically created bat file and spawn it in lieu of calling the process directly. The spawned process will execute completely independently of the main bat file, which will then monitor the spawned bat file, killing and restarting it if we determine that it's hung.

The Design Considerations

By far the trickiest part of the design is determining exactly how long to wait for the executable to finish up before assuming a hang. How long does it typically take? What's the maximum time that it can take when there isn't a hang? Is the execution time consistent, or does it fluctuate? If it fluctuates, can we predict it by the size of an input file, or is it more random? If a process typically takes 3 or 4 minutes to execute, it's reasonable to set the maximum execution time to 10 minutes. But this will kill and restart a particularly slow-running execution that needs 10 minutes and a second to complete just as it's about to finish up.

We must complete a great deal of analysis before settling on a length of time. I usually set this to be three times the length of time of a typical run if the execution times are fairly consistent. If the execution time is dictated by an input file size, you can wait longer for larger files. If the execution times seem to be random, add even more time, but don't make the maximum time so long that it's self-defeating.

The number of attempted restarts before aborting is another factor you must determine. The same considerations that applied with the auto-restart process also apply here. In short, how frequent and random are the hangs?

An additional design consideration of a proposed auto-kill-and-restart is how often to check the status of the spawned bat file. If a process usually takes 3 or 4 minutes and the maximum execution time is set at 10 minutes, it doesn't make sense to wait the full 10 minutes before checking on it. We can check on it every 15 seconds; if it's done, we can move on without waiting any longer; if it isn't done, we can wait another 15 seconds for up to a total of 10 minutes. It's important to note that the interval selected is the maximum amount of time that we might add to any one execution.

The Specifications

Continuing with this imagined scenario, the executable typically runs in 10 or 20 seconds. After much testing, even concurrent testing, 35 seconds is the maximum runtime we've observed. A reasonable maximum wait time seems to be 60 seconds; it's three times longer than a typical long execution and comfortably exceeds the longest observed execution time.

Checking the spawned bat file every 10 seconds seems to make sense. A quick run will finish up just before the first check, most others will be done by the second check, and all but a few will be completed by the third, which will add no more than 10 seconds to any execution compared to a direct call of the flaky executable.

A total of four attempts before aborting should also work. Since it fails once in 1,000 attempts, four completely random failures would happen once in a trillion attempts. This might sound like overkill, but we've observed multiple hangs at roughly the same time, meaning that these failures aren't truly random. They might be happening during a period of lost connectivity.

At worst, four failed attempts will take a little over four minutes before we initiate an abort. This process aims to mitigate the threat of a hang in as short of a timeframe as possible. As with the auto-restart, there is an art to these specifications. Reasonable co-workers might want longer or shorter wait times, or more or fewer restarts.

The Core Auto-Kill-and-Restart Logic

Before sharing the code, I'll discuss the process that's at the heart of this entire enterprise—the spawning, tracking, and possible killing of a second bat file.

At a very high level, I'll launch the spawned bat file via the start command, not the call command, so that the two bat files will execute independently. The spawned bat file will change its title to some unique text also known to the main process. This'll allow the main process to track or monitor the spawned bat file with the tasklist command, and if it's taking an excessive amount of time to finish up, we'll kill it with the taskkill command. Then we'll spawn the dynamically created bat file again, monitor it again . . . and possibly kill it again.

In Chapter 15, I introduced the `title` command to change the title displayed in the top-left corner of the command window when we ran an interactive bat file. It never hurts to title the command window so that we humans can differentiate one window from another, but the uses of the `title` command go beyond cosmetic. I'll use it here to attach a tracking device.

Just as marine biologists might attach an electronic tracking device to the shell of a sea turtle, we'll attach a tracking device to the spawned bat file. The biologist uses satellite telemetry to track the sea turtle's movements for many years throughout the world's oceans and beaches, following them as they mate, forage, and lay eggs. Our goal is less ambitious; we're simply tracking the life of an executing bat file on one machine.

If the `title` command attaches the tracking device, then the `tasklist` command is analogous to the satellite tracking the sea turtle. In the main bat file, the `tasklist` command will use the same unique title used by the `title` command in the spawned bat file. The following command will track the spawned bat file with the unique title contained in the `uniqTitle` variable:

```
tasklist /FI:"WindowTitle eq %uniqTitle%" /NH
```

The `/FI` option allows us to filter on many different characteristics of the various processes running on a machine. For example, the `ImageName` of the spawned bat file will be *cmd.exe*, but this is true of all bat files, including the main bat file doing the tracking, so that's of no use here. But filtering on the `WindowTitle` will return the one and only process with that title. (For this reason, it's critical that the unique title truly be unique in this design.)

The `/NH` option gets rid of those pesky headers, so if the spawned bat file is running when the previous command executes, it will return something such as this to stdout:

```
cmd.exe                      9736 Console                1      4,996 K
```

This shows the image name, PID, session name, session number, and memory usage. We aren't interested in most of this information, but we do care about how this entry contrasts to what this command returns if the process isn't running:

```
INFO: No tasks are running which match the specified criteria.
```

The obvious differences will tell us whether the spawned bat file is still running. A `for /F` command can pull out the first token for interrogation; if it's *cmd.exe*, the bat file with the unique title is running, and if it's `INFO:`, nothing with the title is running.

After taking great care to positively identify the hung process, the following `taskkill` command will kill or terminate it with surgical precision.

Using the same /FI option looking for the same WindowTitle from the tasklist command ensures that we don't overreach and kill anything else:

```
taskkill /F /T /FI:"WindowTitle eq %uniqTitle%"
```

The /F and /T options will forcefully kill the spawned bat file and any child processes that it might have initiated.

By the way, this is where I end my sea turtle analogy. We don't want to harm sea turtles in any way. They're some of the most beautiful and fascinating animals in existence, other than bats, of course.

Now let's put this all together.

The Auto-Kill-and-Restart Code

Listing 26-2 is clearly one of the most complex in the book, but even so I've stripped it down of most error handling and used hardcoded values that really should be parameterized. I'll address these concerns a bit later, but Listing 26-2 meets all of the specifications assuming that flakyExe is assigned the executable that occasionally hangs.

```
   set spawnedBat=C:\Batch\Spawned.bat
   set uniqTitle=Spawned Bat - %date% %time%
❶> %spawnedBat% echo    setlocal EnableExtensions EnableDelayedExpansion
 >> %spawnedBat% echo    title %uniqTitle%
 >> %spawnedBat% echo    %flakyExe%
 >> %spawnedBat% echo    goto :eof

   set totHangs=0
❷ :Restart
   set totSleep=0
❸ start /MIN %spawnedBat%
   timeout 1
❹ for /F usebackq %%i in (`tasklist /FI:"WindowTitle eq %uniqTitle%" /NH`) do (
       if /i "%%i" equ "INFO:" (
           call :Abort "%uniqTitle% Not Spawned"
   ) )

❺ :WaitMore
   timeout 10
   set /A totSleep += 10
❻ for /F usebackq %%i in (`tasklist /FI:"WindowTitle eq %uniqTitle%" /NH`) do (
       if /i "%%i" equ "cmd.exe" (
     ❼ if %totSleep% lss 60 (
             goto :WaitMore
         ) else (
           ❽ taskkill /F /T /FI:"WindowTitle eq %uniqTitle%"
             set /A totHangs += 1
           ❾ if !totHangs! lss 4 (
                 goto :Restart
             ) else (
                 call :Abort "%uniqTitle% - 4 Hangs"
   ) ) ) )
```

```
❿ > con echo The Spawned Bat Has Completed.
  pause
  goto :eof

:Abort
  > con echo Aborting: %~1
  > con pause
  exit
```

Listing 26-2: Code that initiates up to three auto-kill-and-restarts of a flaky executable

There are three main sections to this code centered around the spawned bat file: creating it, starting or executing it, and monitoring it. I'll take a closer look at each section.

1. Create *Spawned.bat*: Using the bat-building-bat technique from Chapter 25, I'm creating *Spawned.bat* with four echo commands ❶. It's a simple bat file that does little more than define a unique title, uniqTitle, and invoke the flaky executable. There isn't even any error handling.

   The complete contents of *Spawned.bat* might look like the following, depending on the contents of date, time, and flakyExe:

```
setlocal EnableExtensions EnableDelayedExpansion
title Spawned Bat - Mon 11/01/2004 10:30:59.33
C:\Batch\Flaky.exe
goto :eof
```

   We assign the unique title its value before creating the spawned bat file so that both bat files know what it is. By using the date and time in the uniqTitle variable, I'm assuming that two processes won't be invoked within one hundredth of a second, but ideally, there should be some unique variable in each execution of the bat file that you can add to the title. (For the purposes of this example, I'm assuming that this title is truly unique.)

2. Start *Spawned.bat*: The :Restart label ❷ has no impact on the code as of now, but we'll eventually use it to restart the process after terminating the hang. I initialize the total number of hangs, totHangs, to 0 prior to the label, ensuring that a restart won't reset it. I'm also setting the total sleep time measured in seconds, totSleep, to 0, but after the label. If and when this builds up to 60 seconds of wait time, I'll initiate a restart and re-execute this command, thus reinitializing totSleep to 0.

   The start command ❸ starts, spawns, or launches the dynamically created bat file independently of the main process. So as not to inundate the desktop with extra windows, the /MIN option immediately minimizes the spawned window.

To verify that the spawned bat file is off and running, I'll pause for just a second to give it time to execute its title command, allowing this code to find it. This assumes that the spawned process will run for at least a second. (If there's even the remotest possibility that this isn't true, I can always add the timeout 1 command to the end of spawned bat file, ensuring that it runs for at least a second.)

The input to the for command ❹ is the same tasklist command detailed earlier, by default passing just the first token into the code block. If that token is equal to INFO:, something is wrong—the spawned bat file hasn't started, and it's far too soon for it to be done—and we go to the abort routine passing it an appropriate error message; otherwise, we continue.

3. Monitor *Spawned.bat*: Finally, we get to the core logic. Another timeout command ❺ sleeps for 10 seconds as defined in our specifications, and we add those 10 seconds to totSleep, which represents the total time spent waiting for the spawned bat file to finish. Next, another for command ❻ similar to the prior one executes, but the code block is now looking for the first token to be equal to *cmd.exe*, an indication that the process is still running. If so and if evaluating the next if command ❼ shows that we haven't slept for 60 seconds, the goto command circles back to the :WaitMore label ❺.

After the total wait time has reached or exceeded 60 seconds ❼, the taskkill command ❽ terminates the spawned bat file. We increment and interrogate the total number of hangs, totHangs. After four attempts ❾, there must be a larger issue at play, so we initiate an abort. But otherwise, we go back to the :Restart label ❷ and restart the entire process again.

Notice that the code contains two overlapping do...while commands, a twist on the technique introduced in Chapter 9. The more modest one goes back to wait another 10 seconds until a minute has passed (:WaitMore ❺ ❼). The other restarts the entire process after it encounters a hang (:Restart ❷ ❾).

If all goes well, the tasklist command embedded in the for command ❻ eventually won't find the instance of *cmd.exe* running with the specific title. This indicates that the spawned bat file has finished up, and we fall through to the echo command noting its completion ❿.

The Testing

If testing an intermittent failure that occurs 1 percent of the time is difficult, then testing an intermittent hang that occurs 0.1 percent of the time is nearly impossible without some intervention. To fix a hang, we first need to create a hang for testing. You could write a program that occasionally executes an endless loop (at one time or another every coder has done this without even trying). But since this is a book about Batch, let's write a bat file that'll go into an endless loop about 20 percent of the time. *OccasionalHang.bat* will do just this; here are its complete contents:

```
 timeout 15
 set /A rand = %random% %% 5
:EndlessLoop
 if %rand% equ 0  goto :EndlessLoop
 exit
```

The timeout command simulates a program that runs for 15 seconds. Without this, the bat file would usually complete in a small fraction of a second. The set /A command captures a pseudo-random number between 0 and 4 in the rand variable by modulo dividing the random pseudo-environment variable (Chapter 21) by 5. If rand is greater than 0, we exit the bat file successfully, but roughly one time in five the value will be 0, and we'll fall into an endless loop. If rand equals 0, the goto command repeatedly loops back to the :EndlessLoop label on the prior line with no hope of liberation. To make this bat file hang more often, you can tweak the modulo division; for instance, %% 2 will hang about half of the time.

To call this bat file instead of the flaky executable, simply enter the following command into the main bat file prior to the code in Listing 26-2:

```
set flakyExe=call C:\Batch\OccasionalHang.bat
```

The call command is part of the variable's value, so when flakyExe resolves, the interpreter calls *OccasionalHang.bat*.

Real-World Tweaks

Even though Listing 26-2 is extremely involved, I've left out some error handling and used hardcoded values where I normally wouldn't, all to keep the focus on the auto-kill-and-restart logic, but I have a number of suggested tweaks or enhancements for a real-world application.

Three hardcoded values in the code should have been variables. I hardcoded them purely for the sake of readability, but I should have set up the sleep interval, maximum number of hangs, and maximum sleep time with overridable defaults like this:

```
if not defined sleepIntrvl  set sleepIntrvl=10
if not defined maxHangs     set maxHangs=4
if not defined maxSleep     set maxSleep=60
```

Just as with the auto-restart, these variables should replace the hardcoded numbers in the code. If a user wants to change any of these values, they can do so with a set command prior to executing this logic.

I mentioned earlier that you might be able to predict the expected execution time of the process based on the size of an input file. The following code will set the maximum sleep time to a baseline of 30 seconds, adding

1 second for every 1,000 bytes of data in the input file, but only if someone hasn't defined it already:

```
if not defined maxSleep (
    for %%s in (C:\Batch\InputFile.txt) do (
      set /A maxSleep = 30 + %%~Zs / 1000
) )
```

You can fine-tune this algorithm with a little analysis comparing file sizes and typical runtimes.

Sometimes you can identify a hang by looking at the expected output file. If it doesn't appear after so many seconds, you may already know the process is hung. You can capture the size of the file periodically, and if it doesn't get any larger during some interval, that might also be an indication of a hang. A little analysis will greatly enhance the process, finding the balance between not killing a good yet long-running execution versus pausing the execution for as little time as is necessary.

Another possible tweak is to increase the maximum sleep time before the last attempt. Even after all the analysis done in the scenario we've tackled here, one execution might legitimately require more than a minute to execute. If you've killed the process three times after 60 seconds each, it might not be a bad idea to allow 2 minutes for the final attempt. Just multiply maxSleep by 2 if the values of attempt and maxHangs are equal. If future logging shows that a number of failures are succeeding on the final attempt, you can reevaluate the maximum sleep time.

If the hangs seem to happen when two runs kick off simultaneously, there's a good chance of a contention issue, and if we kill and restart the two runs on the same schedule, it might just happen again because they'll still be synced up. A way around that situation is to put in a wait of a few seconds just after the kill. Staggering the sleep times can be tricky because the random pseudo-environment variables will also be in sync in the two bat files if they were started at the same instant, but with a little effort, you can ideally find a unique number in each of these executions.

A glaring omission in Listing 26-2 is the error handling inside the spawned bat file. The code in the main bat file can tell us when the spawned bat file has finished, but it has zero visibility into whether it executed successfully. It's tantamount to running a program and not checking the return code. One solution is for the spawned bat file to write errorlevel and maybe even a status message to a small file. The main logic can then read the file and proceed based on its contents.

A good solid design will make the end product much more usable and stable. This is the type of process that really needs to be thought out in great detail with all the possibilities of what can happen in both threads as they run simultaneously. Speaking of threads . . .

Multithreading

Before moving on to the next chapter, let's take the components we've used to build the automatic kill and restart process and reimagine them as pieces for something completely different: *multithreading* or *concurrency*.

This is another feature of Batch not envisioned by its creators but realized by later coders. To fully implement the multithreading found in other languages, we'll need to perform three tasks. First, we'll need to spawn two or more processes called *threads*. Second, we'll need to monitor those processes to determine when each completes. Third, we'll need to allow those spawned processes to communicate with each other and the main process, even sharing data.

You can perform the first two tasks with what you've learned in this chapter. The start command will start or spawn any number of other bat files, which I'll now refer to as threads. You can use the title and tasklist commands to track the uniquely named threads in the same way you tracked a spawned process prone to hanging. The only difference is that you'll now spawn and monitor multiple processes instead of just one. If the number of processes might vary, you can keep track of them in an array. (I'll get to arrays in Chapter 29.) Languages with built-in multithreading tools often have a means of killing all threads if they're still running after a certain amount of time, and you can do the same in Batch with the timeout the taskkill commands.

Admittedly, the one piece that is difficult to fully implement is the ability for the main process and the threads to talk to each other. It should come as no surprise that there is no such thing as a block of asynchronous Batch code accessible from multiple threads, but some communication is possible. Each thread can record its status and high-level information such as the number of records processed in a simple text file named after its title. Since the main process also knows the title for each thread, that main process can find and process this information as each thread completes or even as each thread executes.

Multithreading is a wonderful technique for breaking down time-consuming processes into more manageable chunks, and with a little work, you can make it happen in Batch.

Summary

Coders can rate all intermittent failures and hangs on a scale of irritant to catastrophe. In this chapter, you've learned some advanced Batch coding techniques to mitigate these issues. I've detailed the auto-restart and the auto-kill-and-restart processes to deal with them. For both, I walked through design considerations, specifications, the coding, and even the testing. You also learned about some new and useful commands and new applications for others already discussed, and I even introduced multithreading.

Above all else, I hope you have gained an appreciation for the nuance required to build these solutions. Even before getting into the many details of a particular solution, we had to perform much analysis just to determine if an automatic restart is appropriate. And remember, it's a real fix, not a "fix."

In the next chapter, I'll delve into a topic that sounds like something that should have been a very short section in Chapter 4, namely, using the and and or operators in the conditional clause of an if command. I won't spoil here why this is Part III material.

27

AND/OR OPERATORS

In this chapter, I'll discuss what may be the most glaring shortfall in all of Batch. It doesn't support an and operator, nor is there an or operator. After a brief problem statement, I'll detail a few techniques to simulate or mimic these two operators, handling both the true and false cases. The and is fairly straightforward, but the or requires more ingenuity.

As is often the case with Batch, you can look at a deficiency with frustration or as an inspiration for creativity. These techniques are a must for any Batch coder because without them, you can't write even moderately interesting if commands.

The Problem Statement

A certain conversation is a rite of passage for anyone learning Batch:

> *Bobby*: I have a syntax issue. I'm trying to code an if command with an and operator—you know, do something if `variable1` equals A and `variable2` equals B—nothing complex. I'd hoped that the syntax was simply the word *and*. That didn't work, so I tried an ampersand and then two ampersands. I know that Batch can be unintuitive, so there must be some sort of funky syntax for the and operator, maybe an at sign with a tilde or some nonsense like that. So how do I code this?
>
> *Jack*: Sorry, Batch doesn't have an and operator.
>
> *Bobby*: Seriously? That makes no sense.
>
> *Jack*: Seriously, there is none.
>
> *Bobby*: You're messing with me, aren't you? Every programming language with an if command has an and operator. I think there's a law.
>
> *Jack*: No, not every language. I can't name another offhand, but Batch isn't following the crowd on this one.
>
> *Bobby*: That's like selling a car that doesn't turn left. What are you supposed to do?
>
> *Jack*: Take three rights. Oh . . . and by the way, the or operator . . . also not a thing.
>
> *Bobby*: I'm still not sure if you're yanking my chain. It's nowhere near April Fool's Day, and I really need to get this thing working. Any suggestions?
>
> *Jack*: I agree, Batch should have these operators, but this is where some creativity comes in handy. Anyone can code an and in Java or Perl, but doing it in Batch will fill you with a great sense of pride and accomplishment. The or operator is even more fun— or problematic, depending on your perspective.

I still remember playing the part of the novice in this conversation, and I've since experienced déjà vu countless times in the opposite role. I fear that some will think that I'm overstating the issue, but it has perplexed many. This and operator irredeemably does *not* return true if both comparisons are true:

```
if "%var1%" equ "A" and "%var2%" equ "B" (
    > con echo This is junk code.
)
```

That's not to say that the command inside the code block never executes; in fact, the interpreter typically performs it after discarding the invalid if command. To further complicate matters, the invalid command might generate an error message to stderr, or not, and errorlevel might end up as a nonzero value, or not.

The same is true for this *invalid* or operator:

```
if "%var1%" equ "A" or "%var2%" equ "B" (
    > con echo This is more junk code.
)
```

It doesn't return true if either or both of the comparisons are true.

But enough of what won't work. There are solutions, some elegant and some functional, for building these operators.

Replicating the and Operator

The first and most obvious technique to code around the lack of an and operator is the nested if command:

```
if "%var1%" equ "A" (
    if "%var2%" equ "B" (
        > con echo Nesting works but is oh so uninspired.
) )
```

This is the only possible solution if either conditional clause uses the exist keyword to determine whether a resource exists or the defined keyword to see whether a variable is defined. But if you are examining multiple variables for equality to constants or other variables, I'll share a far more elegant solution. The following if command, with two resolved variables on one side of the equ operator and two values on the other, is functionally equivalent to the nested commands in the previous example:

```
if "%var1%-%var2%" equ "A-B" (
    > con echo This if command has an AND operator even if the AND is implied.
)
```

The lefthand side of the equality, %var1%-%var2%, has three parts inside the double quotes: the resolution of the first variable, a dash, and the resolution of the second variable. If the two variables are set to A and B, respectively, then "%var1%-%var2%" resolves to "A-B", and equality is found. If either variable (or both) is set to anything else the conditional clause is false.

The dash delimiter serves two important purposes. Without the delimiter, we will erroneously find equality if one of the two variables resolves to AB and the other resolves to null. Also, it's just far easier and more pleasant to read, especially when the comparisons become more complex. For example, the following two if commands—each containing a trio of compares—are very similar, but which one would you rather read?

```
if /i "%writer%%coworker%%admin%" equ "jackbobbysteve" (
    > con echo These variables and values are smushed together.
)

if /i "%writer%-%coworker%-%admin%" equ "jack-bobby-steve" (
    > con echo We can all agree this is far more readable.
)
```

I'm using a dash as the delimiter, but most any understated character also works. Dots are another good option, but above all else, the delimiter that you choose should be a character that you don't expect to be part of the data. (I'm hesitant to open this can of worms, but the conditional clause, "%A%-%B%" equ "%X%-%Y%", will incorrectly register as true if A and Y are set to a dash and B and X are null. While this theoretically is an issue, if you know your data and choose your delimiter wisely, it won't be an issue in practice.)

Notice also that the two comparisons in the previous listing are case-insensitive. You can do the same for any multiple comparison with the addition of the /i option, but it applies universally—that is, to all three comparisons in this example. If you want to do a mix of case-sensitive and case-insensitive compares, nesting is your best option.

The prior logic would have required two and operators in most other languages. In Batch, you could have done it with three nested if commands, but the technique connecting operands with a dash is more succinct and readable than it would have been even with a true and operator.

Replicating the or Operator

The or operator is as complex and varied as the and operator is straightforward and uniform. I'll demonstrate the techniques best suited for different situations.

Comparing One Variable to Multiple Values

A common application of the or operator is to determine whether the contents of a variable is equal to one out of two or more values. For instance, you can glean quite a bit from a state postal code. If it's equal to WA, OR, or CA, the state is on the Pacific coast of the contiguous United States, and any one of a list of 10 values indicates that the state is on the Mississippi River.

To build an or operator looking for one of multiple values being assigned to a single variable, I'll once again turn to the eminently useful for command:

```
for %%p in (ND SD) do (
    if "%postalCode%" equ "%%p" (
        > con echo This is an OR operator of a variable and multiple values.
)   )
```

The echo command executes if and only if the variable represents the postal code for one of the Dakota states.

The for command executes its code block twice, passing ND and then SD as the %%p variable. The code block contains just an if command comparing the contents of postalCode to what's passed in as the for variable. Thus, the first execution of the if command looks to see if the variable resolves to ND, and the second execution compares the value of postalCode to SD. If the variable equals either ND or SD, the if command evaluates to true, triggering the execution of its block of code. This in essence is a Batch or operator.

The previous example was for two possible values, but since the for command takes in a space-delimited list, you can pass any reasonable number of values. Here's an example of a Batch or operator matching a variable on any one of six names:

```
for %%p in (Cleese Gilliam Jones Chapman Idle Palin) do (
   if /i "%name%" equ "%%p" (
       > con echo %name% is a Python
) )
```

A single variable, such as postalCode or name, can't take on two current values at once, meaning that with this technique, the conditional clause in the if command can evaluate to true at most once. This isn't true of other variants of the or operator, meaning that other considerations and modifications come into play.

Comparing Multiple Variables to One Value

Let's flip the last example so that we compare multiple variables to a single hardcoded value. Perhaps a particular program has two functions, and we want to execute it if either of two variables is set to some common value.

In this example, the for command is using the resolved values of the two variables as its input, and it's passing each to the if command and comparing them to A:

```
 for %%i in (%var1% %var2%) do (
    if "A" equ "%%i" (
        > con echo This OR operator compares a value to multiple variables.
        goto :OrDone
) )
:OrDone
```

In this scenario, there's the possibility for both variables to be equal to A. A true or proper or operator won't execute the code inside the code block of the if command twice if both are true. To mimic this behavior, we must break out of the logic after the first true condition is satisfied and the code block is executed, and this is accomplished by the goto command branching control to the label just after the for loop.

Many times, it's perfectly acceptable to execute the code block multiple times. For instance, if you're setting some variable or variables when the condition is true, it won't hurt to simply reset them to the same values, and in those situations, you can simplify the code by removing the goto and the label. Even so, this code isn't bulletproof in all situations.

The technique in the previous example assumes that the variables don't contain any embedded spaces. Since the for command accepts a space-delimited list, the interpreter treats a single value with an embedded space as two distinct values. The following listing accounts for the limitation:

```
for %%i in ("%var1%" "%var2%") do (
    if "A" equ "%%~i" (
        > con echo This OR operator compares a value to multiple variables.
        goto :OrDone
) )
:OrDone
```

I've encased each resolved input variable in double quotes, ensuring that we pass each one in its entirety into the code block. To account for what I've just added, I've also included a tilde to the resolution of the for variable to remove these double quotes while doing the comparison: %%~i.

Only a double quote in the contents of one of these variables could break this code. Know your data.

Comparing Multiple Variables and Values

The prior examples demonstrate common yet fairly narrow cases. They won't work for more complicated conditional clauses containing an or operator comparing multiple variables to various hardcoded values or comparing different variables to each other.

As a specific example, a desired conditional clause might evaluate to true if one variable equals a particular value or if a second variable equals a third variable. That is, we might try to execute something like the following, but again this does *not* work in Batch:

```
if "%var1%" equ "A" or "%var2%" equ "%var3%" (
    > con echo This is one last example of junk code.
)
```

There are two ways to mimic this variant of the or operator:

The else if Solution

With some brute force you can evaluate the first condition and use the else if construct from Chapter 4 to evaluate subsequent conditions:

```
if "%var1%" equ "A" (
    > con echo This executes for only one of multiple conditions.
) else if "%var2%" equ "%var3%" (
    > con echo This really needs to be the same code as what's above.
)
```

This works but has a major drawback that I more than hinted at in the code itself. You must repeat the code block to be executed if the conditional clause in the if command is true. If this code consists of a single statement, that may be more than acceptable, but if the logic is more complex, even two or three lines of code, the code will quickly get messy. In such cases, it's best to put that code block into a labeled method and call it from multiple locations:

```
if "%var1%" equ "A" (
    call :CommonLogic
) else if "%var2%" equ "%var3%" (
    call :CommonLogic
)
```

The :CommonLogic routine may contain some involved logic and live elsewhere in the bat file, but if it's only a handful of commands, I suggest placing it immediately after the else if construct inside a perpetually false if command. (See Chapter 20 for more on this technique. Hint: if 0 equ 1.) However, if the code block really doesn't justify its own method (or even if it does), there's another technique worth exploring.

The Nested for Command Solution

This last technique for implementing an or operator isn't a simple one, but it's elegant, and I've employed it often. It mimics multiple compares of two items where just one match satisfies the condition, but where the two items can be any combination of resolved variables and hardcoded values. It even handles embedded spaces in any of the values.

In this solution, I've wrapped the if command inside two nested for commands:

```
for %%i in ("%var1%:A" "%var2%:%var3%") do (
    for /F "tokens=1-2 delims=:" %%j in ("%%~i") do (
        if "%%j" equ "%%k" (
            > con echo A complex OR conditional clause has evaluated to true^^!
            goto :IfOrDone
) ) )
:IfOrDone
```

The input of the outer for command is a space-delimited set of colon-delimited pairs of values, where each pair is encased in double quotes. This means that each execution of the outer code block resolves a pair of values delimited by a colon as %%~i. The pair of values can be a combination of a resolved variable and a hardcoded value such as in the first pair: %var1%:A. In contrast, the second pair demonstrates a different possibility, that of two resolved variables: %var2%:%var3%.

The inner for /F command successively accepts each pair resolved by %%~i and treats it as string input because of the encasing double quotes. (Notice that "%%~i" strips off and then adds back a set of double quotes. I could have used %%i, but the explicit double quotes make it clear that the input to the for /F command is a string.)

The tokens and delims clauses separate the pair by the colon delimiter into the %%j and %%k tokens (Chapter 19). Finally, the if command compares them for equality and executes the code block if true.

I'm using the same technique I employed earlier to break out of the logic so that it doesn't execute multiple times. Once again, you can drop the goto command and the label if there's no harm executing the code block more than once. If a colon might be in one of the values being compared, you can choose a different delimiter. Likewise, if a double quote might be in one of the values, you can drop the double quotes around each pair in the input list, but this will expose spaces and special characters in the data.

After you get a grasp on how it works, take another look with fresh eyes and ask yourself whether this looks like an if command with an or operator. Some may call it cryptic, and to be clear, an explanatory remark is definitely in order, but what I've presented here represents the most comprehensive complex Batch or operator you're likely to encounter.

The else Keyword

There's one last pertinent topic related to any if command that we must not forget: the else keyword. I've discussed executing one code block if multiple conditions are all true or if at least one of them is true, but often you'll want to execute another code block if the ultimate result of the and or or conditional clause is false. Traditionally, this is the code block coming after the else keyword.

The simulated and operator with multiple resolved variables and hardcoded values strung together lends itself to the use of an else code block:

```
if "%var1%-%var2%" equ "A-B" (
    > con echo Both are true.
) else (
    > con echo One of these variables doesn't match the value, or both don't.
)
```

This also works with the else if construct that can mimic the or operator. But you can only mimic the else keyword in the other situations, and I'll share two very useful methods here:

The Preemptive Action Method

The easiest way to execute the else logic is to do it preemptively:

```
set result=NoMatchFound
for %%p in (ND SD) do (
   if "%postalCode%" equ "%%p" (
      set result=Match
)  )
```

Clearly, this works only if upon finding a match, you can easily undo the preemptive logic. If the else logic is copying or deleting a file, this technique is of no value, but if the logic is simply setting a variable to one of two values, you can do the else logic first and undo it if the if command evaluates to true. In essence, this is an if...else construct.

The Branch Over Method

Another method is to use that bit of space before the label used to break out of the code block on the first match:

```
for %%p in (ND SD) do (
   if "%postalCode%" equ "%%p" (
      set result=Match
      goto :OrDone
)  )
set result=NoMatchFound
:OrDone
```

The goto command already ensures that the logic just above it executes no more than once, but now it also branches over the logic just after the completion of the for command. If this logic finds one match, it sets the variable to Match, but if the if command doesn't find a match after exhausting the list in the input, only then does control fall to the set command setting the variable to NoMatchFound.

This method offers far greater flexibility. Instead of setting a variable, you can call a program if one match is found, and if not, delete a directory. The code isn't doing anything preemptively, so it doesn't have to undo anything. For this reason, the branch over method is a truer form of the if...else construct. The fact that the else logic comes last makes it look even more like the traditional construct. After seeing enough of these, you'll start to interpret those two close parentheses as a kind of else keyword.

Summary

In this chapter, I've detailed a couple of methods to mimic the and operator of a conditional clause, and you've learned multiple techniques for simulating the or operator that satisfy many differing situations. I also demonstrated ways to mimic the else keyword, so as to execute logic that traditionally executes when a conditional clause is false.

It's certainly true that the techniques discussed in this chapter are completely unnecessary in most languages, but they are a necessity for any Batch coder wanting to code more than rudimentary logic. They also fill the most prominent lacuna in the Batch universe as elegantly as possible.

Bobby shouldn't be faulted for trying to use && as an and operator; nor should he be faulted if he tried using || as an or operator. Both are commonly used for these purposes in other languages. I haven't mentioned it yet, but the && and || operators do have a place in Batch, but in relation to a completely different topic, conditional execution. In Chapter 4, I detailed the most commonly used technique of conditional execution (the if command), but in the next chapter, I'll return to this topic to share some lesser-known alternative techniques.

28

COMPACT CONDITIONAL EXECUTION

In this chapter, I'll discuss conditional execution . . . and no, this isn't a chapter about the if command. It's true that the if command is the quintessential example of executing code conditionally, and this chapter will revisit that discussion from Chapter 4, but with a very different take. Batch has a funky construct simply called *conditional execution* that executes one or more commands based on the success or failure of a prior command. It's a compact and streamlined alternative to the if...else construct, but there are striking differences, and it's crucial that you understand them before using it.

I'll introduce the two operators used in the conditional execution syntax, and you'll see something that's very similar to, but not identical to, an if...else construct. I'll demonstrate how to successively execute several commands where if any one command fails, the rest won't execute. Flipping the script, I'll then show how to successively execute several commands where if any one command *succeeds*, the rest won't execute.

Conditional Execution Operators

In many languages, the double ampersand (&&) is the and operator and the double pipe (||) is the or operator, and in Chapter 27, I detailed how Batch doesn't support this functionality. Instead, the conditional execution syntax employs the double ampersand and the double pipe as operators, which produces a level of cognitive dissonance for coders versed in other languages, but these operators offer a unique and very succinct alternative to the if command:

The && Operator

In the following general syntax, command1 always executes, and command2 executes only if the value of errorlevel is 0 after the completion of command1:

```
command1 && command2
```

A single ampersand separates two commands that execute unconditionally, but the extra ampersand invokes the conditional logic. For lack of a better term, this is the positive conditional execution operator.

The || Operator

Replacing the ampersands with pipes negates the logic. In the following example, command2 executes only if the value of errorlevel is *not* 0 after the completion of the first command:

```
command1 || command2
```

A single pipe (appropriately enough) pipes the output of one command to another, but here nothing is being piped to the second command, which might not even execute at all because of the negative conditional operator.

DEFINING SUCCESS AND FAILURE

Before getting into some examples and usages, I must share a major batveat. Much of the documentation on this subject simply states that if two commands are separated by double ampersands, the second command executes only if the first is successful. Likewise, the second of two commands separated by

---

double pipes executes only if the first fails. That's a simplified version of the truth; success and failure are based on the state of errorlevel.

This might sound like splitting hairs, but some commands don't conform to the general programming standard of returning zero on a successful invocation and a nonzero value on a failure. The robocopy command is a great example. The interpreter assigns errorlevel the value of 0 when no errors occurred, but only when nothing is copied. A successful copy of one or more files returns a value of 1 (or greater). Additionally, the set, path, and prompt commands don't reset errorlevel to 0 after executing successfully in a bat file.

Using a Single Operator

As an alternative to an if command, you can often use a single conditional execution operator to streamline your code, but first you need to compare and contrast the two methods.

Positive Conditional Execution

To demonstrate, Listing 28-1 offers this straightforward and easy-to-read example that creates an empty file and checks the return code.

```
copy nul C:\Batch\Empty.dat
if %errorlevel% equ 0 (
    > con echo Empty.dat Created Successfully
)
```

Listing 28-1: Empty file creation with error handling

Using conditional execution, this one line of code is functionally equivalent:

```
copy nul C:\Batch\Empty.dat && > con echo Empty.dat Created Successfully
```

If the copy command creates the empty file and returns 0, the echo command writes the message to the console. In essence, the && is synonymous with if %errorlevel% equ 0. If the copy command fails to create the empty file, it returns a value other than 0 as the return code, and the echo command doesn't execute.

Because errorlevel is only implied in the conditional execution syntax, its value doesn't find its way into stdout, sometimes obscuring whether certain code ever executed. If it's important that you can find the value of the return code in the trace file, the more verbose option is the wise choice.

The conditional execution syntax can be a very succinct (some may say cryptic) alternative to an if command, but when you rewrite it to span multiple lines, it's more readable and more closely resembles an if command.

You can initiate a code block by placing an open parenthesis after the && operator. Then you can make your code block out of one or more commands before terminating it with a trailing close parenthesis. The following is functionally equivalent to both of the prior listings:

```
copy nul C:\Batch\Empty.dat && (
   > con echo Empty.dat Created Successfully
)
```

Comparing this to Listing 28-1, I've reduced the code by one line and replaced the if command along with its conditional clause with the && operator. The code is clearly condensed, but whether it's simplified depends on the reader's knowledge of conditional execution.

Negative Conditional Execution

Now, let's make some modifications to this logic to experiment with the negative conditional execution operator. First, let's use a folder that doesn't exist. (Spoiler alert: the copy command fails to create an empty file.) Second, let's change && to the || operator and make the message reflect a failure:

```
copy nul C:\NonExistentFolder\Empty.dat || (
   > con echo Empty.dat NOT Created
)
```

Now the echo command executes only when the copy command fails, because when it fails, it also sets errorlevel to 1. If the command creates the file successfully, it sets the return code to 0, and the interpreter writes nothing to the console.

Real-World Applications

There's no shortage of applications; I'll detail a couple here that use a single conditional execution operator.

Text Searches

One scenario starts with a variable holding a program name. If you can find a particular server name in its path, you might want to call a certain process contained in an internal routine.

The following code searches the contents of progName for the value of svrName, calling a routine if it finds the server:

```
echo "%progName%" | findstr %svrName% && call :ServerFound
```

The echo command pipes the program name into the findstr command, which sets errorlevel to 0 if it finds the server name in the input text. Don't be fooled by the single pipe; that's not conditional execution, but the double ampersands do represent this technique.

Similarly, using the || operator instead results in the following code calling a different routine, but only when it doesn't find the text:

```
echo "%progName%" | findstr %svrName% || call :ServerNotFound
```

This example also starkly illustrates the difference between a pipe and double pipes.

Calling Another Bat File

One popular usage of conditional execution is the validation of a call command when the argument is a variable containing the name of a bat file to invoke, but there are some common pitfalls to avoid.

For this demonstration, the calledBat variable might contain the path and name of a valid bat file, but it might also contain junk resulting in a failed call command. A failure triggers the interpreter to set errorlevel to a value of 1, so it's quite understandable if you were to use the || operator with the following error handling:

```
call %calledBat% || (
    > con echo Called Bat File Invalid: %calledBat%
)
```

However, if the call command successfully calls the bat file, the interpreter doesn't set errorlevel to 0—in fact, it doesn't change the return code at all. It's probably a bug, but that doesn't change the coder's plight. If the call command is successful, the return code holds the value returned by the last command to update it.

I'm making note of this because it's very easily overlooked. You can test this code with a bad bat file, and it'll work—that is, it'll write out the error message. Then you can test it again with a good bat file, and it'll probably appear to work—that is, it won't write the message—but it *worked* only because errorlevel just happened to be set to 0 before the call command executed, which is something you might not always be able to count on. Earlier, I had suggested against using conditional execution with the robocopy command because of its unconventional return code. I'm not suggesting the same when using commands that don't universally reset the return code, such as the call command, but I do recommend a certain level of diligence. There's a potential, yet very correctable, problem lurking with this type of command and conditional execution.

The return code issue should in no way preclude your use of this technique. In fact, the same issue exists if you were to evaluate the return code in a traditional if command after the execution of the call command. Remember that this technique is a glorified way of comparing the contents of errorlevel to a specific value, namely, 0. To make this work, you need the value of the return code to be 0 before the call command executes. The following `cmd` command ensures that you reset the return code just before the `call` command:

```
cmd /C exit 0
call %calledBat% || (
    > con echo Called Bat File Invalid: %calledBat%
)
```

The final concern here is that some command in the called bat file might set `errorlevel` to a nonzero value upon its completion. Unfortunately, this error handling treats the bad return code no differently than a failed `call` of the bat file. In this context, both present simply as a nonzero `errorlevel` after the `call` command, resulting in the possibility of an unrelated failure in the called bat file incorrectly triggering the `echo` command stating that the bat file is invalid.

The best solution is an agreement between the two bat files. The called bat file can use an `exit /B 0` command to ensure that it always returns `0` at the end of a successful invocation. Error handling between the two bat files might take on another form, perhaps a parameter containing a descriptive error message, where the called bat file sets it to null as an indication of a successful execution.

It's a very useful tool, but you must consider all possible values of `errorlevel` at different stages of the process flow. This advice is even more critical when multiple conditional execution operators are used in tandem.

Using Multiple Operators

Alone, these operators are fairly straightforward, but it gets interesting and useful when you use them together.

A Pseudo if...else Construct

You've learned that a pseudo-random number isn't random, but it's close; likewise, a pseudo `if...else` construct isn't really an `if...else` construct, but it's close. The following code looks remarkably similar to just such a construct, and it acts quite a bit like one as well:

```
copy nul C:\Batch\Empty.dat && (
    > con echo Empty.dat Created Successfully
) || (
    > con echo Failure to Create Empty.dat
)
```

I'm using the `&&` operator in place of the `if` command and its conditional clause; even more oddly, the `||` operator is taking the place of the `else` keyword (and looking a little like a failed attempt at an emoji nestled in between the close and open parentheses). In practice, this usually behaves like an `if...else` construct. The copy command tries to create an empty file; if successful, the first `echo` command executes, and if not, the second `echo` writes a different message. That's exactly what an if...else construct would do, but this technique has a major batveat.

If something inside the first code block sets errorlevel to a nonzero value upon its completion, this construct also triggers the second code block. In this example, each code block consists of a single echo command, but it isn't hard to imagine more complex logic between the parentheses.

This is incredibly counterintuitive; if this code successfully creates *Empty.dat*, the first echo command executes, but if that command fails, the echo command from what might be thought of as the else code block also executes. An if...else construct that can execute both code blocks isn't a true if...else construct.

In this particular instance, this behavior might be perfectly acceptable because it's unlikely if not impossible for a simple echo command to the console to produce a failure, but anything complex enough to reset errorlevel in the first code block is ill-advised. Because of this batveat, I don't use this particular technique often, but the next couple of examples demonstrate its true usefulness.

Multiple && Operators

Conditional execution is most powerful and useful when you execute multiple similar commands consecutively and want to address the error handling en masse. For instance, you can copy four distinct files to a target path with four distinct xcopy commands. The goal might be to abort the execution if any one of the four copies fails, but it doesn't matter which one fails. At the same time, I don't want to redundantly interrogate the return code four different times. You can accomplish that with two different methods, one with and one without conditional execution.

In lieu of conditional execution, this method concatenates the value of the errorlevel variable from each copy attempt. For this demonstration, I'll just write an error message to the console instead of aborting. Assuming that the four source files and the target path are defined earlier in the code, this listing performs the task:

```
xcopy %sorc1% %targ%\ /Y /F
set cmlRC=%errorlevel%
xcopy %sorc2% %targ%\ /Y /F
set cmlRC=%cmlRC%%errorlevel%
xcopy %sorc3% %targ%\ /Y /F
set cmlRC=%cmlRC%%errorlevel%
xcopy %sorc4% %targ%\ /Y /F
if %cmlRC%%errorlevel% neq 0 (
    > con echo One or more of the four copies FAILED
)
```

After the first xcopy command, I set cmlRC (cumulative return code) to the value of errorlevel. Then I concatenate the errorlevel returned from the next two commands onto the end of cmlRC. Finally, I concatenate the three return codes of cmlRC with the errorlevel from the last xcopy command and compare it to 0 in the conditional clause of the `if` command. The interpreter is smart enough to perform a numeric compare—four zeros are considered to be equal to one zero. (If each side of the conditional clause had been encased in double quotes, Batch would've treated them like strings, unequal strings to be precise—that is, 0000 equals 0, but "0000" doesn't equal "0".)

If only the second xcopy fails, the left side of the conditional clause might resolve to 0400. Since that isn't equal to 0, the error handling logic initiates. This works, it's readable, and it has its place in the Batch canon, but now let's compare it to a solution using conditional execution.

The syntax has a couple variants. The first requires all of the commands to be on one line, which we can make more readable with carets acting as continuation characters, as shown in Listing 28-2.

```
xcopy %sorc1% %targ%\ /Y /F ^
  && xcopy %sorc2% %targ%\ /Y /F ^
  && xcopy %sorc3% %targ%\ /Y /F ^
  && xcopy %sorc4% %targ%\ /Y /F ^
  || > con echo Exactly one of four possible copies FAILED
```

Listing 28-2: Multiple && operators followed by a || operator

Conditional execution allows us to streamline this logic quite a bit compared to the prior method, but it isn't nearly as intuitive.

Each && operator separates a pair of xcopy commands, meaning that if the first command succeeds, the next one executes, and if it succeeds, the third executes, and if all of these did not fail, the final xcopy command also executes. The || operator at the front of the last line of code indicates that the echo command executes only if—and immediately after—any one of the xcopy commands fails. This is a subtle and important point resulting in these two methods *not* being functionally equivalent.

In the concatenation method, all four xcopy commands execute before we examine the complete set of return codes, regardless of any earlier failures. In the conditional execution method, if one command fails, execution skips immediately to the error handling after the two pipes. But how exactly does it work?

Assume for a moment that the first xcopy works. Seeing the && operator before the next xcopy command, the interpreter checks the return code. It's 0, so that second command also executes, but assume that it fails because of a lack of disk space. The && operator in front of the third command again tells the interpreter to check the return code. This time it isn't 0; the interpreter skips over the third command to find the third and last && operator. Since errorlevel is still nonzero, the fourth command doesn't execute. Next, the interpreter finds the || operator and executes the echo command precisely because errorlevel isn't equal to 0. Only if all four xcopy commands execute successfully (that is, each returns 0) will the echo command not execute.

So, if there's any value in executing all of the commands even if one fails, the return code concatenation method is preferred. But typically, if one failed copy means that you will abort the execution, it's pointless to even attempt the other copies. In this instance, it's more efficient to not bother with the other attempts; hence, the conditional execution method is optimal. Choose the one that works best for your situation.

I hinted earlier about an alternate syntax for this application of conditional execution. For those who appreciate the aesthetics of parentheses over carets, the following version of the code is functionally equivalent to the prior listing:

```
xcopy %sorc1% %targ%\ /Y /F && (
  xcopy %sorc2% %targ%\ /Y /F) && (
  xcopy %sorc3% %targ%\ /Y /F) && (
  xcopy %sorc4% %targ%\ /Y /F) || (
    > con echo Exactly one of four possible copies FAILED
  )
```

Which one is easier to read is subject to debate. I like both and don't have a strong opinion on the matter (which in itself may be as odd as either syntax).

NOTE   *When using conditional execution with multiple operators, I usually indent the continued line just two spaces to differentiate it from a code block, which I usually indent three spaces. Sometimes I'll indent a continued line more than three spaces, but I never indent it exactly three.*

Multiple || Operators

Let's turn the last scenario on its head. We'll have the same xcopy commands, and we don't necessarily want all of them to execute. The difference is that we need just one of the copies to work. Perhaps a resource file has multiple possible locations, with a hierarchy dictating the order of selection. If we successfully copy one file, we'll want to skip over the later copy attempts and call some process that uses the file, but to keep this as simple as possible an echo command will simply declare the success instead.

Once again, assuming that the source files and the target path are defined earlier in the code, the code in Listing 28-3 copies at most one file.

```
(
  xcopy %sorc1% %targ%\ /Y /F ^
    || xcopy %sorc2% %targ%\ /Y /F ^
    || xcopy %sorc3% %targ%\ /Y /F ^
    || xcopy %sorc4% %targ%\ /Y /F
) && (
  > con echo Exactly one of four possible copies SUCCEEDED
)
```

Listing 28-3: Multiple || operators followed by a && operator

Compared to Listing 28-2, the most striking difference here is that multiple || operators separate the xcopy commands and a && operator comes before the trailing command. A more subtle difference is that the xcopy commands make up the entirety of a code block.

Let's step through the logic assuming that none of the source files exists. The first xcopy command executes unconditionally, and it fails, setting errorlevel to 4; the nonzero return code and the first || operator trigger the second xcopy command, which also fails; two more || operators and two more failures result in the final two xcopy commands executing and failing. The last failure sets errorlevel to 4 as control exits the first code block. The interpreter immediately finds the && operator, quickly checks errorlevel, sees that it isn't 0, and does *not* execute the echo command.

It gets even more interesting when one of the copies works. Imagine that the first xcopy command successfully copies the file denoted by sorc1 to the target path. Because of the good return code and the first || operator, the interpreter doesn't execute the next xcopy command. Furthermore, it doesn't even recognize the third and fourth commands. This is easier to visualize when you consider that the four xcopy commands are really all part of the same line of continued code. Once the interpreter determines that the command after a || operator won't execute, nothing that comes after it will execute.

More interesting yet, control now exits the first code block after the one successful copy where the interpreter finds the && operator. Since errorlevel equals 0 from the first xcopy command, which was successful, the code block with the echo command executes.

If the first xcopy command fails and the second is successful, the third and fourth don't execute because of the second || operator, but the echo command executes because of the && operator trailing the first code block. Likewise, if the third or fourth xcopy commands are the first to copy a file successfully, the echo command also executes.

The parentheses are crucial in this example. In the prior section, four commands were separated by && operators, with the last command coming after the || operator. In this example, the operators are reversed, demonstrating a significant difference between them. I'll address why the parentheses are in place momentarily, but first, since one of the primary reasons to use this conditional execution syntax is to condense the code, notice the following five lines of code are functionally equivalent to the prior listing:

```
(xcopy %sorc1% %targ%\ /Y /F ^
  || xcopy %sorc2% %targ%\ /Y /F ^
  || xcopy %sorc3% %targ%\ /Y /F ^
  || xcopy %sorc4% %targ%\ /Y /F
) && > con echo Exactly one of four possible copies SUCCEEDED
```

I'm not fond of this syntax, because it does violate my convention concerning the alignment of the open and close parentheses of a naked code block (Chapter 16). However, it's nothing if not concise, but I find the version with more whitespace more readable.

Here's the same basic logic with a pseudo if...else construct to write a message indicating either the success or failure to copy one file:

```
(
   xcopy %sorc1% %targ%\ /Y /F ^
      || xcopy %sorc2% %targ%\ /Y /F ^
      || xcopy %sorc3% %targ%\ /Y /F ^
      || xcopy %sorc4% %targ%\ /Y /F
) && (
   > con echo Exactly one of four possible copies SUCCEEDED
) || (
   > con echo One or more of four copies FAILED
)
```

This does come with the obligatory batveat that if the first echo command somehow manages to reset errorlevel to a nonzero value, the second echo command will also execute.

Multiple && vs. Multiple || Operators

I promised more details on why the parentheses are in place when using multiple || operators in Listing 28-3 but not with the multiple && operators in Listing 28-2.

To understand, first take this generic syntax of multiple commands separated by && operators with a trailing || operator:

```
command1 && command2 && command3 && command4 && command5 || command6
```

Assume that command1 returns 0. If so, command2 executes; assume it fails to return 0. Because of the && operator prior to command3, the interpreter doesn't execute the command, skipping over it instead to find another && operator; errorlevel is still nonzero, so it also skips command4. It finds yet another && operator, so command5 doesn't execute. But then the interpreter finds the || operator, and the nonzero errorlevel from the second command triggers the execution of command6.

Now let's flip each of the conditional execution operators. This is more like the scenario where we wanted a single command to execute successfully, but no more than one:

```
command1 || command2 || command3 || command4 || command5 && command6
```

This time let's assume that command1 returns something other than 0. Because of the || operator before command2, the second command also executes; now assume it executes successfully and returns 0. Because of the || operator after it, the logical flow skips command3. This is where it gets interesting.

The interpreter does *not* continue to look for another operator. The line is abandoned right there, regardless of the subsequent commands and operators.

That's significant and the reason why I included the parentheses in Listing 28-3 along with the multiple || operators. Consider this apparently minor tweak to the prior syntax:

```
(command1 || command2 || command3 || command4 || command5) && command6
```

With a set of parentheses surrounding the commands separated by || operators, the first command again executes unconditionally. The other commands in the parentheses execute only if the one prior to it fails. It doesn't matter how many execute; after any one of these commands succeeds or after they all fail, control exits the logic inside the parentheses. The interpreter immediately encounters the && operator, where command6 executes only if one command (the last command to execute) returned 0.

Don't assume anything when using multiple conditional execution operators; always test.

Summary

If nothing else is to be taken away from this chapter, && isn't an and operator and || isn't an or operator. They are the conditional execution operators that evaluate errorlevel being equal to 0 or not equal to 0, respectively. I've detailed in depth how each works alone, together, and in series.

Conditional execution is similar to the if command, but you've learned the important differences that you must know before you can use this technique successfully. Although it isn't ideal in all situations, it does offer a very concise alternative syntax. I also explained an important difference between how the interpreter handles both operators and demonstrated some real-world applications.

In the next chapter, I'll return to the concept of building tools in Batch that were not imagined at its onset, namely, arrays and hash tables.

29

ARRAYS AND HASH TABLES

"Arrays? Batch doesn't have arrays!" After daring to mention the use of this data structure in Batch code, I've received an array of incredulous responses. Technically, these skeptics have a point. Arrays are not intrinsic to the language, and the creators of Batch never anticipated their use.

However, over the years, some innovative coders have found ways to build something that looks like an array, walks like an array, and even quacks like an array (if arrays could quack . . . and walk). In this chapter, I'll explore multiple ways of building fixed- and variable-length arrays in Batch. You'll learn how to iterate through an array and access any given element in it, as well as how to initialize an array. I'll also discuss hash tables, detailing their similarities and differences with arrays, and then show how to populate them with data and retrieve that data. Most important, you'll learn applications for both of these tools that you can use to better organize and house small and large sets of similar data during a bat file's execution.

Arrays

Regardless of the coding language, an *array* is a data structure that holds multiple like variables of the same name, differentiated by an index. You can think of *like variables* as items or elements in a list; some commonality must tie them together. One array might hold the names of your co-workers. Countries of the world might be in another, and a third array might contain members of a basketball team. These are all examples of arrays of string variables, but an array can contain other data types. Three more arrays might represent statistics in each game of the season for that basketball team: points scored (whole numbers), point differential (integers), or offensive efficiency (floating-point numbers).

An array has a unique name, and each element in the array is denoted by a combination of the array name and a number or *index*. In most modern languages, the index counts up from 0, which is a *zero-offset array*. In contrast, arrays that count up from 1 are *one-offset arrays*. I'll be working solely with the more common zero-offset arrays. (If you're a dyed-in-the-wool COBOL coder, you can build one-offset arrays just as easily in Batch, but at the risk of being labeled a dinosaur by your younger co-workers.)

One of the arrays just mentioned might be named `coworker` and another `points`. The value of `points[0]` would be the number of points scored in the first game of the season, `points[1]` would correspond to the second game, and so on. Your co-workers won't be as ordered, but `coworker[0]` would be one person and `coworker[1]` would be another. If you work with 100 people, `coworker[99]` will be the final element of the 100-element array.

In many languages, you can define arrays in memory, assigning all of the elements of the array to a certain data type. As detailed often since Chapter 5, Batch simply doesn't allow you to define variables as certain data types, and that doesn't change with arrays, but you can set the following variables:

```
set celtics[0]=Bird
set celtics[1]=McHale
set celtics[2]=Parish
```

Any coder would tell you that this certainly looks like the first three elements of an array named `celtics`, and that's exactly how it behaves. It's important to note that there's no unifying data structure in memory containing the three elements. Instead, the interpreter considers these to be just three different and ordinary variables whose names all just happen to start with the text `celtics[`, followed by a number and a trailing `]`.

Because Batch is so accommodating when it comes to which characters are permissible in variable names, you can easily embed most characters on the keyboard into the variable name itself. Other coders have different conventions on how to name arrays, but I use the square brackets, also called hard brackets, around the index. And behold, an array is born.

Creating Arrays

You can create arrays in many different ways. In the previous section, I created the celtics array with three elements. That code snippet defined three elements of the array by assigning three hardcoded values to three hardcoded variables. But you can build arrays of fixed or variable sizes from multiple different sources.

Fixed-Size Array from User Input

Sticking with the basketball theme, it doesn't take much code to build an array of exactly five elements, the starting five players, with data a user enters from the console. A fixed-size array requires a specific number of assignments, which begs for an iterative loop made possible with a for /L command (Chapter 18). Likewise, user input begs for the set /P command (Chapter 15). Here's the code:

```
> con echo Please Enter the Starting Five:
for /L %%i in (0,1,4) do (
   > con set /P myTeam[%%i]=Enter Array Value %%i = &rem
)
```

The trailing &rem is just there to spotlight the space before it.

This loop executes the command requesting user input five times, iterating the index, %%i, from 0 to 4. One of the advantages of Batch coding is that variable names can contain other variables, something you can't easily do in many other languages. Notice that the variable myTeam[%%i] has three components:

- The text string ending in the open square bracket: myTeam[
- The number resolved from %%i: 0 through 4
- The single character of text for the close square bracket:]

The first time through the loop, the variable name resolves to myTeam[0] as the code assigns it the first value retrieved from the console. Then myTeam[1] accepts the second value entered, and so on until myTeam[4] takes on the value of the fifth and final entry. I'll be using the same basic technique in the upcoming examples of element assignment.

Variable-Size Array from a Parameter List

I defined the previous array to be a set size, but you often don't know the ultimate size of an array. The following routine uses an optionless for command (Chapter 17) to process all the parameters passed to it, %*, adding each one to the parmArr (parameter array).

```
:BuildParmArray
 set parmArrSize=0
 for %%i in (%*) do (
    set parmArr[!parmArrSize!]=%%~i
    set /A parmArrSize += 1
 )
 set parmArr
 goto :eof
```

Instead of an iterative loop with a built-in index, this code is executing the code block of the for command once for each parameter. As a result, I first define or initialize the index, defined as parmArrSize, and then increment it with each enumeration of the loop. Since I set it to 0 initially, the first pass of the loop assigns the first parameter to parmArr[0]. If there are 20 parameters, the for loop assigns 20 elements, up through parmArr[19].

This is a subtle point, but notice that I'm incrementing parmArrSize at the end of the loop to the index value of the next parameter, whether or not another one exists. The upshot is that if this code assigns elements 0 through 19, the ultimate value of parmArrSize is 20, which is the actual size of the array. Many languages have a method that returns the size of an array; in Batch the next best thing is a variable with that data item.

This code builds a zero-offset array, but you can build a one-offset array with one minor tweak. Swap the two set commands in the code block to assign parmArr[1] as the first element, and parmArrSize will still contain the correct array size.

If the call to this routine passes no parameters, parmArrSize remains as 0, and this logic adds nothing to the array because the code block of the for command doesn't execute at all. Thus, this code successfully creates an empty array.

Also, I don't want to give short shrift to the set command after the code block. Immediately after building or populating an array, I usually like to document its current contents. This command writes all the variables starting with the parmArr text and their values to stdout or the trace file. Since all of the elements of the array start with this text, they'll all be displayed.

I highly recommend doing this for all arrays that aren't too large. You'll usually ignore this data, but when a need to troubleshoot arises, it'll make the task far more pleasant. For diagnostic purposes, it provides a great audit trail of how this code loaded the array, and you can easily repeat it elsewhere in the code after later manipulating the array in any way.

As a final note on this listing, you may take issue with the variable name I'm using for the index. It's usually best to define indices succinctly, but parmArrSize is an awfully verbose, even clunky, name for a reason. Since this variable name is the concatenation of the name of the array and the Size text, the set parmArr command displays it and its value along with the array contents. If the array has even a fairly unique name, it's unlikely that anything else will meet the criterion, resulting in this command cleanly displaying everything you want to know about the current state of this array: its elements and its size.

Symbiotic Arrays from a File

I'll demonstrate a couple intriguing concepts in this next example that you can use together or on their own. One is loading an array from a data file, and the other is building symbiotic arrays. Two arrays are *symbiotic* when they are the same size and synced up by their indices. For example, two arrays, one of co-workers and one of phone numbers, might each contain 10 entries. That doesn't make them symbiotic, but if the phone number at index 0 belongs to the co-worker at index 0 of the other array and if the same is true of all 10 sets of elements, the arrays are symbiotic.

In Chapter 15, I presented an interactive bat file that told a joke, a pun, or a riddle. In Chapter 21, when discussing the random pseudo-environment variable, I expanded on this by imagining dozens of jokes, puns, and riddles, all in memory and randomly accessible—ostensibly giving the users hours of entertainment. The last piece to this puzzle is reading a library (also known as a file) containing dozens of jokes and loading them into memory to be accessed randomly. That sounds like an array . . . or maybe two arrays.

Let's focus solely on the jokes for now and put the puns and riddles aside, knowing that we can do something similar for them later. Mercifully, I'll include only the first three lines of the *BatJokes.txt* file (not to be confused with the *BadJokes.txt* file), but just imagine hundreds of lines of material. Each record contains a joke followed by its answer, delimited by a pipe:

```
Why are bats so active at night?|They charge their bat-teries by day.
How do bats flirt?|They bat their eyes.
What's a good pick-up line for a bat?|Let's hang.
```

The code in Listing 29-1 loads this comedic gold into two arrays, the jokes into the joke array and the answers into the answer array.

```
set jokes=0
for /F "tokens=1-2 delims=|" %%b in (C:\Batch\BatJokes.txt) do (
    set joke[!jokes!]=%%~b
    set answer[!jokes!]=%%~c
    set /A jokes += 1
)
set joke
set answer
```

Listing 29-1: Symbiotic arrays built from a data file

These are symbiotic arrays in that the joke located at a specific index corresponds to the answer of the same index. As the for /F command reads each record, it delimits on the pipe to tokenize the text for the joke and its answer. The first two set commands assign each string to an element of the appropriate array using the pluralized jokes index. I'm using this index for both arrays because they're symbiotic arrays, while incrementing it at the end of the code block.

The set commands outside of the loop write the following to the console verifying that both arrays were loaded successfully:

```
C:\Batch>set joke
jokes=3
joke[0]=Why are bats so active at night?
joke[1]=How do bats flirt?
joke[2]=What's a good pick-up line for a bat?

C:\Batch>set answer
answer[0]=They charge their bat-teries by day.
answer[1]=They bat their eyes.
answer[2]=Let's hang.
```

This also verifies that 3 is the total number of jokes.

I've built both arrays from a single file, and the contents of answer[1] is the punchline for the contents of joke[1]. If the file had a thousand entries, both symbiotic arrays would have had a thousand elements, and all of their elements would have been synced up. I can set up two more arrays for the riddles, although I must use something other than answer for the name of the riddle punchline array. Puns don't have punchlines, so I can load each entire record into a pun array.

We now have almost everything needed to build a truly usable user interface of bat jokes, puns, and riddles. We can build libraries of humor, and we can load those libraries into memory as arrays. We can get a request from the user for a type of humor, and we can randomly determine which of the many jokes, puns, or riddles to select. The last piece is the ability to access the arrays—that is, to extract a joke and its answer to be displayed.

Accessing Array Elements

In order for this to be a *real* array, we must be able to iterate through it, reassign elements, assign elements to other variables, resolve elements, and more. To demonstrate how to access array elements, I'll first assign 14 elements of the myChar array:

```
set myChar[0]=B
set myChar[1]=a
set myChar[2]=t
set myChar[3]=c
set myChar[4]=h
set myChar[5]= &
set myChar[6]=i
set myChar[7]=s
set myChar[8]=%myChar[5]%
set myChar[9]=C
set myChar[10]=o
set myChar[11]=!myChar[10]!
set myChar[12]=l
set myChar[13]=.
```

I'm assigning each element a single character. Most are straightforward, but a few are a bit more interesting. The sixth set command assigns element

5 to a single space terminated by a command separator, making it obvious that it isn't being set to null or multiple spaces. Elements 8 and 11 are taking on the value of elements defined earlier, so element 8 is a space, and elements 10 and 11 are both the letter o.

The two resolutions of elements with a hardcoded index illustrate that both delimiters work equally as well. Using percent signs, %myChar[5]% resolves to the 6th element, and with exclamation marks, !myChar[10]! resolves to the 11th element. The syntax is more limited when the index is a variable, as you'll soon witness.

Now we can write a for /L command that will iterate through this array, concatenating all the values together into a sentence:

```
set mySentence=&
for /L %%i in (0,1,13) do (
    set mySentence=!mySentence!!myChar[%%i]!
)
> con echo %mySentence%
```

After building the string, the last command writes Batch is Cool. to the console.

Backing up, the for command iterates %%i from 0 to 13, where !myChar[%%i]! successively resolves to each of the 14 elements. The interpreter first resolves the %%i index and then the array element. For instance, the first time through the loop, the intermediate result is myChar[0]. Since that's surrounded by exclamation marks, the interpreter resolves it to B and assigns it to mySentence. The second time through the loop, myChar[1] resolves to a, which the interpreter concatenates to the prior result giving us Ba. This repeats another dozen times until we've constructed the entire sentence.

This is yet another example of the power of delayed expansion, and with delayed expansion, you must use exclamation marks as the outside delimiters; percent signs simply won't work. It's quite tempting to try %myChar[%%i]%, but if you think as the interpreter does, you won't see an array. You'll see two discrete variables to resolve: myChar[and i]. In this example, a for variable is the index, but delayed expansion works the same with a common variable as the index. Consider the following where percent signs encase the idx index and exclamation marks encase the outer array element for the second level of delayed expansion:

```
set idx=9
> con echo The Tenth Element is: !myChar[%idx%]!
```

This writes the capital C to the console.

Similarly, to extract a joke and its answer from the symbiotic arrays built in Listing 29-1, you can enter a random non-negative number less than the number of jokes into an index variable such as jokeIdx. Then you can resolve the joke with !joke[%jokeIdx%]!. Because these are symbiotic arrays, you can retrieve its answer with the same index: !answer[%jokeIdx%]!. You now have all of the tools necessary to update the bat file in Chapter 15 to randomly display one of any number of jokes, puns, and riddles.

Initializing an Array

Languages with proper arrays usually offer a simple one-line command for creating an array or even re-initializing all of the elements of an existing array. There's no instantiation of variables, much less of arrays, in Batch, so once again ingenuity is a must.

Before building the joke array, it makes sense to initialize it just as I have often initialized a variable to 0 before entering a loop. It's true that it's highly unlikely that any active variables start with the joke[text, but there are definitely instances when you'll want to re-initialize and rebuild an array already in use. The following wipes out all elements of the joke array:

```
for /F "usebackq delims==" %%j in (`set joke[`)  do (set %%j=)
```

The for /F command accepts as input the set command listing every existing element of the array and its value. By delimiting on the equal sign and passing only the first token—that is, the variable or element name but not its value—we're setting each element to null in the code block. If there aren't any variables to reset, the second set command never executes, and the end result is the same.

In prior examples, I've simply assumed that no elements already existed when building arrays. To be certain, it's best to execute a command such as this to initialize the array before building and using it.

INDEX OUT OF BOUNDS

The best thing about Batch arrays is that they'll never throw the dreaded *index out of bounds* abort that's ubiquitous in other languages. And the worst thing about Batch arrays is that they'll never throw the dreaded *index out of bounds* abort.

For better or worse, the interpreter sees elements as simple variables, thus resolving any unset elements to null, allowing the process to continue unabated. If the joke array mentioned earlier contains 100 elements, indexed by 0 to 99, resolving the value of joke[100] won't result in an abort; it'll simply resolve to nothing.

This can be an asset. You can enumerate through an array until a null alerts you to the end of the array. In other instances, you might not care to differentiate between an empty element and an undefined element. But the lack of an abort can also cause problems. If you're expecting an element to contain a valid value but it doesn't, an abort in some other language will set you on the path of fixing the error. In this instance, the lack of distinction between a purposely set null element and an unset element does matter.

In the final analysis, use this behavior to your advantage when appropriate, but take care to set and resolve any and all intended elements correctly.

Implementing Multidimensional Arrays

This technique even extends to building and accessing multidimensional arrays. Single-dimensional arrays are largely possible in Batch because you can embed square brackets into a variable name. For multiple dimensions, we just need one more character: the comma. The following command sets row 1 and column 2 of the my2dArray array to a hardcoded value in what unmistakably resembles an element assignment of a two-dimensional array regardless of the language:

```
set my2dArray[1,2]=Row1Col2Data
```

As a demonstration, I'll briefly re-imagine two prior examples as two-dimensional arrays:

User Input

Returning to the array built with user input, the following nested for /L commands build a two-dimensional array of three rows and four columns:

```
> con echo Please Enter 2-Dimensional Array Data for 3 rows and 4 columns:
for /l %%r in (0,1,2) do (
    for /L %%c in (0,1,3) do (
        > con set /P my2dArray[%%r,%%c]=Enter Row %%r, Column %%c = &rem
) )
```

The outer for variable, %%r, loops through the three rows, while %%c loops through the four columns for each row. This code accepts exactly 12 values before continuing.

If rowIdx is set to 2 and colIdx is set to 3, the following resolves to the last data element entered by the user:

```
!my2dArray[%rowIdx%,%colIdx%]!
```

The two indices resolve first with the percent signs, resulting in !my2d Array[2,3]!. Then the exclamation marks and delayed expansion finish the job.

File Input

Earlier, we built the two symbiotic arrays, for the joke and answer, from each record of an input file. Instead, we can load the data into a single two-dimensional array where the second-level index of 0 is the joke and 1 is the answer:

```
set jokes=0
for /F "tokens=1-2 delims=|" %%b in (C:\Batch\BatJokes.txt) do (
    set joke[!jokes!,0]=%%~b
    set joke[!jokes!,1]=%%~c
    set /A jokes += 1
)
set joke
```

You can think of this array as having exactly two columns; notice the hardcoded index for the second dimension in both assignments: 0 and 1. The set /A command increments the jokes index. The number of rows is dictated by the number of records in the input file. Finally, the single set command at the end of the listing produces the following audit trail given the same three-record input file used earlier:

```
jokes=3
joke[0,0]=Why are bats so active at night?
joke[0,1]=They charge their bat-teries by day.
joke[1,0]=How do bats flirt?
joke[1,1]=They bat their eyes.
joke[2,0]=What's a good pick-up line for a bat?
joke[2,1]=Let's hang.
```

Arrays of even greater dimensions are only a comma or two away: my4dArray[1,2,3,4]. I don't remember ever coding anything quite like this, but single-dimensional arrays and even two-dimensional arrays have many applications in Batch.

Regardless of the dimension, if you need an extremely large array or if you plan on accessing it many thousands of times, compiled code is a far more efficient solution. But when used wisely, Batch arrays are quite helpful and surprisingly easy to manage.

Hash Tables

It turns out that Batch does support arrays, or at least we can fashion an array out of the rudimentary tools at our disposal. But surely a hash table isn't possible? You've probably intuited the answer to this question given the title of the chapter and the section that you're now reading, but before building a hash table, let's define what it is.

A *hash table* (sometimes called a *hash map*) is a data structure that stores data in pairs: a key and a value. The *value* can be of any data type, even other data structures. The *key* is similar to the index of an array, but it doesn't have to be an integer. In fact, in the Batch universe, arrays and hash tables behave very much alike; in fact, the best way to compare and contrast them is to transform an array into a hash table.

Arrays vs. Hash Tables

Imagine an array where the index is the date formatted as CCYYMMDD and the data is the number of steps a person might take in a day. If this otherwise active individual was sedentary on the first pandemic Christmas doing little more than opening presents and drinking eggnog in solitude, the steps array might contain these three entries:

```
set steps[20201224]=15842
set steps[20201225]=987
set steps[20201226]=13009
```

These indices are quite large, even though we're using only a small number of elements. It's a good thing that we didn't define this array in memory like we would have in many other languages, because its size would have been upward of 20 million elements. One advantage of a Batch array is that it uses memory only for the elements that are defined. Memory has gotten mighty cheap, but there's still no reason to be profligate.

The minimal usage of memory is a direct result of the array element (for example, steps[20201225]) being a simple variable with a name consisting of some text, a number, and a couple square brackets. Another advantage of the underlying nature of Batch elements is that the index doesn't have to be a number at all; in fact, it needn't even be a true index. To demonstrate, let's format the date as MM/DD/CCYY for readability:

```
set steps[12/24/2020]=15842
set steps[12/25/2020]=987
set steps[12/26/2020]=13009
```

Because the index is not an integer, this is no longer an array; we've transformed it into a hash table. Period, just like that. We can't iterate through it like we could an array, but we can look up the number of steps given a formatted date. We can no longer retrieve an element for a given index; instead, the lookup involves a key between those brackets.

Taking this a step further, let's add text for the day of the week and even an embedded space to the key:

```
set steps[Thu 12/24/2020]=15842
set steps[Fri 12/25/2020]=987
set steps[Sat 12/26/2020]=13009
```

Not incidentally, that key is starting to look a lot like what we can resolve from the date pseudo-environment variable.

One small problem with this syntax is that it falsely looks like an array. The non-numeric key, in lieu of an index, might make it clear that it isn't an array, but the key will more than likely be a variable, thus obscuring its data type. For this reason, a different convention is ideal. Personally, I've settled on using curly brackets, also called braces:

```
set steps{Thu 12/24/2020}=15842
set steps{Fri 12/25/2020}=987
set steps{Sat 12/26/2020}=13009
```

This is just one convention, and there are others that work just as well. For instance, you can prepend hash table variables with ht. What's important is that you make the data structure look like something unique and something other than an array. Anyone who reads the code, even quickly, should notice the difference. Even if the reader doesn't know the convention, the uniqueness of the syntax will raise curiosity, which in turn cracks open the door to understanding.

Consider this simple, and at the same time not so simple, set command:

```
set steps{%date%}=987
```

This command is setting one element of the steps hash table, and the key is the formatted date of whenever the command executes.

If you choose to use my convention, I'll summarize it as array[index] and hashTable{key}, but as always, use the convention that makes sense to you and stick with it.

Basic Hash Table Functionality

Another example of a basic hash table contains multiple pairs of a person and their occupation, where the person's name is the key, and their job is the value. For instance, the Darwin key retrieves the Naturalist value. Lincoln, Poe, and Braille are the respective keys for the President, Poet, and Inventor values. Here's the hash table in tabular form:

Key	Value
Lincoln	President
Darwin	Naturalist
Poe	Poet
Braille	Inventor

Notice the lack of an index and any semblance of order to the elements.

Every key must be a unique value. If there are two people in this hash table named Darwin, we'll need to distinguish them in some way, perhaps by adding first and middle names. However, multiple people can hold the job of Poet; that is, the value doesn't have to be unique.

The syntax for building and accessing elements of a hash table in Batch is very different from that of many other languages, where after declaring the jobs hash table, you can define a single key-value pair via some variant of the *put* method. For instance, this is how to do it in Java:

```
jobs.put("Lincoln", "President");
```

There's no dot notation or built-in methods in Batch, but the following set command assigns the same hardcoded pair to the hash table:

```
set jobs{Lincoln}=President
```

More typically, the key and value are both variables. The following code creates the same entry:

```
set person=Lincoln
set aJob=President
set jobs{%person%}=%aJob%
```

Extracting the value in many languages requires some variant of the *get* method. Again, this is from Java:

```
String job = jobs.get("Lincoln");
```

The corresponding Batch code retrieves an element much like we did from a Batch array, only with curly brackets and a key instead of square brackets and an index. Both of these commands work equally as well:

```
> con echo The Job is: !jobs{Lincoln}!
> con echo The Job is: %jobs{Lincoln}%
```

But the key is more often a variable, which requires the now familiar delayed expansion:

```
> con echo The Job is: !jobs{%person%}!
```

If person is set to Braille, the output is The Job is: Inventor.

We now have a simple hash table to which we can add more keys (people) and values (occupations) as pairs. We can remove one specific entry if someone is laid off and reconsiders their occupation:

```
set jobs{Jack}=&
```

The following assigns a value to a key only if it doesn't yet exist in the hash table:

```
if not defined jobs{Kai}  set jobs{Kai}=Chef
```

This for /F command mimics three different methods available in many other languages that get the size of a hash table and extract lists of keys and values:

```
set hashSize=0
set listKeys=&
set listValues=&
for /F "usebackq tokens=2-3 delims={}=" %%x in (`set jobs{`) do (
    set /A hashSize += 1
    set listKeys=!listKeys! "%%x"
    set listValues=!listValues! "%%y"
)
```

Both lists are space-delimited with each element in double quotes. With a little more work, we can use these results to determine whether the hash table is empty:

```
if not defined listKeys  > con echo The jobs hash table is EMPTY.
```

The following code tells us whether a particular key exists in the hash table:

```
echo %listKeys% | findstr "Poe" && > con echo Quoth the Raven, "Nevermore."
```

The echo command writes the famous refrain to the console if "Poe" is contained in listKeys. Poe is encased in double quotes because that's how we added each key to the hash table, and we can similarly search listValues for a specific value.

Complex Hash Tables

A more complex hash table might also be keyed by a person's name, but instead of a simple string as the value, it might have something more resembling an object from a more modern language. For example, it might contain a more complete set of information on that person such as occupation, state, hobbies, and more. (I'll have much more to say on the topic of objects in Chapter 32.)

Once you understand that hash tables and arrays in Batch are built by simply stringing together text, partial variable names, resolved variables, indices, and brackets, it's not a huge leap to create a people hash table keyed by a person's name attached to signifiers for job and state, and even an array of hobbies:

```
set people{Lincoln.job}=President
set people{Lincoln.state}=Illinois
set people{Lincoln.hobbies[0]}=Wrestling
set people{Lincoln.hobbies[1]}=Cats
set people{Lincoln.hobbies[2]}=Storytelling
```

Don't confuse this with dot notation; people{Lincoln.hobbies[1]} is just a variable name, either a messy one or an elegant one, depending on your perspective.

After the prior commands execute, the following code extracts the second hobby from the array inside the hash table:

```
set info=hobbies[1]
set person=Lincoln
set hobby=!people{%person%.%info%}!
```

Delayed expansion resolves the two variables encased in percent signs first. Then the exclamation marks resolve the intermediate result to Cats. (The 16th US president shared the White House with Tabby and Dixie.)

The same considerations that I mentioned earlier for arrays apply to hash tables. This technique isn't meant for heavy duty processing, but in many instances, a quick and relatively simple solution in the form of a hash table might be hiding in plain sight.

In Chapter 3, I introduced the idea of using delayed expansion to store and retrieve transmission paths in variables containing city abbreviations, such as pathNYC, pathNash, and pathSTL. This is really a thinly disguised hash table; consider these three elements: path{NYC}, path{Nash}, and path{STL}. Treat the city as a variable and use it to extract the corresponding transmission path with !path{%city%}!.

Summary

With a little ingenuity, we can make Batch do many things for which it wasn't first designed, like repurposing an old tire and some rope as a swing. In this chapter, I illustrated how to load arrays from hardcoded data, user data, parameters, and data from a file. You learned the importance of delayed expansion in accessing elements of an array and the possibilities opened with multidimensional arrays. I then extended this technique to build and access hash tables, explaining the similarities and differences between them and arrays, with applications of both.

I hope these examples have demonstrated the flexibility that's possible in Batch. In the next chapter, I'll switch gears and cover a few disparate yet useful topics that are intrinsic to the language.

30

ODDS AND ENDS

Throughout this book, I've endeavored to write short, concise chapters about pointed topics, while introducing a few related commands along the way. In this chapter, I'll discuss a few interesting topics that couldn't find a home in any of the other chapters and were too short to constitute chapters of their own, but these topics are no less important or helpful than the others.

With these odds and ends, you'll learn how to sort files and interrogate the registry for useful information. You'll also learn how to retrieve and set the attributes of files and directories, and I'll discuss bit manipulation to round out the book's coverage of Batch arithmetic.

Sorting Files

The sort command does exactly what you would likely expect it to do; it sorts input files into output files. To demonstrate, consider a small file containing the names of the first eight future captains of the starship *Enterprise*, listed in the order in which they'll serve in the post. The first 15 bytes contain a first name, followed by one byte for a middle initial (if they use a middle initial, and only one does). The last name starts in byte 17 and may or may not be followed by a few trailing spaces:

Jonathan	Archer
Robert	April
Christopher	Pike
James	TKirk
Willard	Decker
John	Harriman
Rachel	Garrett
Jean-Luc	Picard

(*Star Trek* is famous for its alternate universes and timelines, but this is the list for *our* universe with one significant omission. Spock, or Mr. Spock, was left off the list for two reasons. First and foremost, he has only one name, which is neither a first nor a last name, but sometimes treated as either, hopelessly complicating the format of the data file. Second, he was captain for only about three minutes of screen time at the beginning of *Star Trek II: The Wrath of Khan*. As seriously as I take getting every fact about Batch as accurate as possible, I also strive to stay true to the *Star Trek* canon.)

The following command accepts the file as its first argument, and the /O option precedes and defines the *output* file that follows it:

```
sort C:\Batch\Captains.txt /O C:\Batch\SortedByName.txt
```

The command very easily sorts the small input file into an output file of the same size. Here's the complete contents of the *SortedByName.txt* file following the execution of the prior command:

Christopher	Pike
James	TKirk
Jean-Luc	Picard
John	Harriman
Jonathan	Archer
Rachel	Garrett
Robert	April
Willard	Decker

The captains are sorted by their first names, because the sort command starts sorting at the first byte of the record by default. If two captains had shared the same first name, they would have been sorted on middle initials and finally on last names, but we can alter the initial character of the sort easily with the /+ option. The following command starts sorting in byte 17 where the last name starts:

```
sort C:\Batch\Captains.txt /O C:\Batch\SortedByLastName.txt /+17
```

The *SortedByLastName.txt* file is sorted by last name, as its name more than suggests:

```
Robert       April
Jonathan     Archer
Willard      Decker
Rachel       Garrett
John         Harriman
James        TKirk
Jean-Luc     Picard
Christopher  Pike
```

The command has a few other useful options for customizing sorts. The /R option *reverses* the order of the sort, so Pike would have come first and April last if you had added /R to the last command. The /UNIQ option writes out only *unique* lines, which is another way of saying that it drops duplicate records. If some records in the input file might exceed the default maximum length of 4,096 bytes, use /REC to define a different maximum *record* length up to 65,535 bytes.

NOTE *I must state my displeasure with any option, parameter, or setting denoted by a single letter O; users will invariably enter a zero by mistake. After a blunder in my coding youth, I stay away from this and other ambiguous characters (I and 1), but unfortunately, this is what we have with the* sort *command.*

The performance of the sort command is far from great on large files, and you can't define multiple sort fields, but the command offers an easy way to perform simple sorts on small-to-medium-sized files.

Commercially available sort utilities are much faster and offer far more functionality than the sort command. With a little effort, you can set up a bat file to execute one or the other depending on whether a utility is registered on a machine. For instance, the bat file can execute a commercial sort utility, such as Syncsort, if it exists; if not, it will execute the slower but still functional sort command. In this way, you'll reap the benefits of the faster sort utility on the machines where it's registered, but the primary challenge in this plan is determining whether the utility is installed and registered on a particular machine. Conveniently, this leads directly to our next topic.

The Windows Registry

The Windows Registry is a hierarchical database storing configuration settings and options for the operating system and all installed applications. It's structured similarly to Windows itself with what looks like a folder structure, but each apparent folder is really a registry key one or more levels beneath a root key or hive.

If an application is installed on a particular computer, you can find information about that application in the registry. The existence or lack of that information on other machines indicates whether the application is installed on that particular computer, and we can determine this with a few lines of Batch code.

For instance, if Syncsort is installed on a Windows computer, it has a registry key in the registry, and eventually we'll interrogate the registry for that key associated with the application with some Batch code. If we find it, Syncsort is installed; if we don't find it, it isn't installed. But before we can use that logic, we need to know the registry key associated with the application. The best way to find the key is to look for it in the registry of a computer where you know the software (in this example, Syncsort) is installed.

Exploring the Registry

The regedit command, which stands for *Registry Editor*, offers a portal into the registry that looks a bit like Windows Explorer. At the command prompt, enter the following and press ENTER:

```
regedit
```

The Registry Editor should open.

WARNING *On second thought, hold off a minute. When first using this editor, I felt as though I had stumbled into a secret room behind a trapdoor in an old mansion, but the potential to do some damage exists. There's no need to be paralyzed with fear, but unless you have a deep understanding of the registry, don't delete or modify anything from inside the Registry Editor. Caution is a must, but investigating the registry can be illuminating even if much of the data is cryptic.*

All of the software loaded onto a computer is in the registry under *HKEY_LOCAL_MACHINE\SOFTWARE*, so this is the first place to look for an application. If one of the many keys under the *SOFTWARE* key isn't obviously for the product in question, you can also right-click the *HKEY _LOCAL_MACHINE* root key or hive, select **FIND**, enter the application name or any other search string, and press ENTER. The first key to match the string appears, and pressing F3 takes you to the next matching key.

For the sake of this demonstration, assume that we find the following registry key for the application in question:

```
HKEY_LOCAL_MACHINE\SOFTWARE\Syncsort
```

The regedit command is one of the few commands you'll find in this book that's used almost exclusively at the command prompt and is of little use inside a bat file. If you were to use it in a bat file, it would simply open the Registry Editor and pause the execution of the bat file until a human closes the Editor. But with this command and a little work, we now have the registry key. What we need next is some Batch code that can determine whether this key exists in the registry of other computers.

Querying the Registry

The solution to this challenge is the reg command, which simply stands for *registry*. From a bat file, the reg command can do quite a bit of damage in the registry in its own right. If you go to the help for this command, you'll see that it sports several operations that can manipulate the registry, including add, delete, copy, and import, that someone with ill intent could easily exploit to build a bat virus. It's important to know that these commands exist but use them only if you truly and fully understand the registry and any possible impacts of your actions. I'll be strictly focusing on reading from or querying the registry—that is, performing the query operation of the reg command.

The most basic reg query command accepts a possible registry key as an argument. Conveniently, Batch allows us to abbreviate the HKEY_LOCAL_MACHINE root key as HKLM. This command is looking for Syncsort in the registry:

```
reg query "HKLM\SOFTWARE\Syncsort"
```

This command returns a list of the argument's registry key values and other registry keys immediately subordinate to it. More important for our purposes, if this command finds the argument key in the registry, it sets errorlevel to 0; if it doesn't find it, the value returned is 1. With this in mind, consider this code using the same command with conditional execution to set a boolean:

```
reg query "HKLM\SOFTWARE\Syncsort" && (
   set bSyncsort=true==true
) || (
   set bSyncsort=false==x
)
```

After this executes, you can reference the boolean elsewhere in the process flow to determine whether the particular application is installed and available.

We can also interrogate the registry for other types of information. For instance, the following command uses the /V option to look for one specific registry key *value*, ProductName, of the current version of Windows:

```
reg query "HKLM\SOFTWARE\Microsoft\Windows NT\CurrentVersion" /V ProductName
```

Without the /V option, the command will likely write many key values and subordinate keys to stdout, but with this option in place, it writes precisely two lines of output if it finds the key value. One example might be:

```
HKEY_LOCAL_MACHINE\SOFTWARE\Microsoft\Windows NT\CurrentVersion
    ProductName    REG_SZ    Windows 10 Home
```

The registry key in the argument is the first line of output, and the desired information about the ProductName is contained in the second.

The following for /F command nicely parses out the Windows version and assigns it to a variable:

```
set key=HKLM\SOFTWARE\Microsoft\Windows NT\CurrentVersion
for /F "usebackq tokens=1,2*" %%i in (`reg query "%key%" /V ProductName`) do (
   if /i "%%i" equ "ProductName" (
      set winVersion=%%k
) )
```

Since the for /F command processes two lines of text and we care only about the second, the if command isolates just the line containing ProductName as the first token. (We also could have ignored the first line with the skip=1 clause from Chapter 19.)

Because of the asterisk in the tokens clause, the third token, %%k, contains everything, including embedded spaces, after the unused and discarded second token. Thus, the value of winVersion becomes Windows 10 Home. If you were to run this on a different machine, this code might assign Windows 7 Enterprise to the variable.

Much more can and has been written about the registry. I've just touched on it here from the perspective of Batch to show how you can safely interrogate it for some very useful information. The help for the reg command provides far more information for the curious.

File Attributes

Just as you can use the reg command for evil as well as good, you can do the same with another interesting command, the attrib command. Its name is short for *attribute*, and it both retrieves and assigns file and directory attributes. Ne'er-do-wells can use this command to create and hide malignant files on a computer for any number of nefarious purposes, although such actions do violate the Batch coders' oath to use their powers only for good.

Retrieving Attributes

If the command's only argument is a file, it returns the file's attributes. Consider this:

```
attrib C:\Batch\SomeFile.txt
```

This command writes the following result to stdout if the file is, from left to right, ready to archive (A, byte 1), a system file (S, byte 4), hidden (H, byte 5), and read-only (R, byte 6):

```
A    SHR              C:\Batch\SomeFile.txt
```

The second and third bytes are always blank.

Each position in the string represents a predefined attribute. For instance, the value of H in the fifth byte means that the file is hidden or that you can't see it in Windows Explorer, at least by default. In contrast, a space in that position means that the file isn't hidden.

To determine whether a particular file is read-only, the following for /F command uses the attrib command as its input:

```
for /F "usebackq tokens=*" %%a in (`attrib C:\Batch\SomeFile.txt`) do (
    set attrs=%%a
    if "!attrs:~5,1!" equ "R" (
        set bReadOnly=true==true
    ) else (
        set bReadOnly=false==x
    ) )
```

The logic in the code block sets the bReadOnly boolean to true or false based on the existence or nonexistence of the file attribute associated with the sixth byte.

A file mask with wildcards can return results for multiple files. The /S option matches the filename or mask on all files in the directory and all of its subdirectories, giving the results for each. Also, the /D option handles directory attributes in lieu of the attributes of a file.

Setting Attributes

The command's real power comes in its ability to reset attributes. A negative sign in front of the attribute character turns the attribute off, and a plus sign turns it on. For instance, the following command ensures that the file isn't a system file (-S) and not a hidden file (-H), while also being read-only (+R):

```
attrib -S -H +R C:\Batch\SomeFile.txt
```

This can be very useful. If you create a Batch process that creates or modifies a file where users might have access to it and if those users are not to be trusted with the file, you can protect and hide it when not in use with the attrib command. To make the file accessible, run the command with the -H -R argument string just before updating the file, followed by another command with the +H +R argument string after the update, thus leaving the file hidden and read-only until the code needs it again. It's the digital equivalent of unlocking the shed, getting and using the mower, putting it away, and relocking the shed until the lawn grows long again.

Interestingly, the `attrib` command fails to set attributes when a file is a system file or a hidden file—except for the actual system and hidden file attributes themselves. Thus, if a file is hidden and you use +R alone in the argument string, the `attrib` command fails to set the file to read-only. However, the previous command with the -S -H +R argument string ensures that these two file attributes are not set, thus enabling the use of the last attribute. If need be, you can execute a second `attrib` command to reset the system and/or hidden attributes: +S +H. You'll find the full set of attributes that you can set and unset with the `help` command.

To demonstrate a final use, the `del` command (Chapter 7) does a great job of deleting a particular file, but not of deleting everything *but* a particular file. Assuming that your work directory doesn't have any hidden files, these three lines of code delete everything except the lone file:

```
attrib +H C:\Work\Noah.txt
del C:\Work\* /Q /A-H
attrib -H C:\Work\Noah.txt
```

The first `attrib` command flips the *Noah.txt* file to hidden; then the `del` command deletes everything in the directory that isn't hidden thanks to the /A-H option. Finally, the second `attrib` command restores the file to its prior state without a scratch on it and without any other files in the directory.

Once you've mastered the art of manipulating the attributes of a file, you can move on to the manipulation of bits.

Bit Manipulation

In Chapter 6, I promised to return to the last remaining arithmetic operators supported in Batch: three bitwise operators and two logical shift operators. These operators work on the bit level, so you need to make a cognitive shift to the binary world to understand their behavior. A *nibble*, or half of a byte, is comprised of four bits, each representing a decreasing power of two. Setting a bit's value to 1 turns it on, and setting its value to 0 turns it off.

When you turn on the first or leftmost of the four bits, it represents the decimal 8—the second bit is 4, the third bit is 2, and the final bit is 1. Therefore, the binary number 0001 equals the decimal number of 1, and binary 1000 is equivalent to decimal 8.

You can derive other numbers by turning on a combination of bits. Binary 1111 is equivalent to decimal 15—that is, $8 + 4 + 2 + 1$. The complete byte consisting of two nibbles has 256 unique values, but for this discussion, I'll stay with the much more manageable nibble and its 16 unique values for most of the upcoming examples.

Bitwise Operations

The *bitwise and* operation accepts two operands and returns a 1 in each bit position for which the corresponding bits of both operands are set to 1. For this example, consider the decimal numbers 3 and 6. The decimal number

3 equals binary 0011, having the bits for 2 and 1 turned on, and the decimal 6 equals the binary 0110, having the bits for 4 and 2 turned on. The only common bit set to 1 is the third bit, which has a value of 2, so the result of a bitwise and of 3 and 6 is binary 0010 or decimal 2.

The *bitwise or* operator looks for bits being set to 1 in *either* operand. There are three such bits between 3 and 6, resulting in binary 0111 or decimal 7. The *bitwise exclusive or* turns on the bits that *differ* in the two operands. Using the same numbers, only the second and fourth bits differ, so the result is binary 0101 or decimal 5 (that is, $4 + 1$).

This is much easier to visualize in tabular form. Table 30-1 also introduces the Batch operator for each bitwise arithmetic operation.

Table 30-1: Bitwise Arithmetic and Operators

	Operator	Example
Bitwise and	&	3 & 6 = 0011 & 0110 = 0010 = 2
Bitwise or	|	3 | 6 = 0011 | 0110 = 0111 = 7
Bitwise exclusive or	^	3 ^ 6 = 0011 ^ 0110 = 0101 = 5

After grasping the machinations of bitwise logic, you might balk at the choice of operators. One ampersand usually terminates a command, the caret is an escape character, and the character used for the bitwise or is most often used to pipe data from one command to another (and I haven't even mentioned conditional execution). Surely, you can't use these characters in arithmetic calculations?

You can, but you need to take some action to ensure that these characters don't trigger their other uses. There are actually three different methods, all of which I show in these three functionally equivalent examples of bitwise and arithmetic:

```
set /A bitAnd = "3 & 6"
set /A "bitAnd = 3 & 6"
set /A bitAnd = 3 ^& 6
```

My preference is to encase just the arithmetic in double quotes as demonstrated in the first example. You can also use double quotes to surround the variable name, the equality operator, and the arithmetic, as shown in the second example. Finally, you can escape the operator with a caret.

The following demonstrates all three bitwise arithmetic operations using my preferred method:

```
set /A bitAnd = "3 & 6"
set /A bitOr = "3 | 6"
set /A bitXOr = "3 ^ 6"
```

After these commands execute, bitAnd, bitOr, and bitXOr contain the values 2, 7, and 5, respectively, the same results calculated earlier.

This is where I usually detail the many uses for what I've just discussed, but I can't say that I manipulate bits on a daily basis. Actually, I've never used any of the bitwise operators in Batch. In the early days of computing, coders would often concatenate a set of flags at the bit level to create just one condensed field. They could then set and retrieve the individual bits representing individual flags with bit manipulation.

Cheap and plentiful memory has made this technique a distant memory, but I can still share one use. The following code determines whether a particular number is a power of two:

```
set /A bitAnd = "nbr & (nbr - 1)"
if %bitAnd% equ 0  > con echo %nbr% is a power of 2.
```

Only if nbr equals 0, 1, 2, 4, 8, 16, and so on, does the echo command write its message.

Any number that's a power of 2 has exactly one bit turned on, and the number one less than it has that bit turned off with all the bits to its right turned on. For instance, decimal 8 = binary 1000, and 7 = 0111. The result of a bitwise and operation on these two operands is 0, because there are no common bits turned on or set to 1. But if a number isn't a power of 2, at least one corresponding bit is turned on in both it and the number one less than it. For instance, 6 = 0110, and 5 = 0101; the second bit is turned on in both numbers, so the result of the bitwise and operation is nonzero: 4 = 0100.

Logical Shift Operations

Batch has two more tools for manipulating bits. The *logical left shift* operator shifts all of the bits in the first operand to the left by an amount dictated by the right operand, replacing the bits on the right with zeros. The *logical right shift* operator behaves similarly except that it shifts to the right and replaces the vacated bits on the left with zeros while discarding the same number of bits on the right.

Here are the logical shift operators, both with an example:

	Operator	Example
Logical left shift	<<	3 << 2 = 0011 → 1100 = 12
Logical right shift	>>	9 >> 1 = 1001 → 0100 = 4

The bits that the logical shift inserted into the result are shown in bold. The first command appends two zeros after shifting the bits two places to the left. The second command prepends one zero after shifting the bits one place to the right, while also dropping the rightmost 1 in the process.

The following two commands implement both of these examples in Batch:

```
set /A logicLeftShift = "3 << 2"
set /A logicRightShift = "9 >> 1"
```

(To handle the less-than and greater-than signs, we either need escape characters or one of the two double-quote techniques mentioned in reference to the bitwise operators.)

I'm equally nonplussed attempting to find logical shift applications because I've never used these operators in the real world. However, since Batch doesn't support exponentials, we can use the logical left shift to raise a number to a power . . . if that base is two. Think of it as a very narrowly defined power function. Consider these examples that compute 2^3 and 2^9:

```
set /A TwoCubed = "1 << 3"
set /A TwoToTheNinth = "1 << 9"
> con set Two
```

Every bit in a nibble (and a byte) represents a power of 2, so the first command shifts 0001 to the left 3 bits, resulting in 1000 or the decimal number 8, which is two cubed. The trailing set command writes the following to the console:

```
TwoCubed=8
TwoToTheNinth=512
```

The second command uses more than one nibble in its calculation. Notice that a binary 1 followed by 9 zeros equals 512 or two to the ninth power.

If you have used these operators in the wild, drop me a line and I'll see about adding your application to the next edition of this book.

Summary

In this chapter, I discussed a set of topics that I simply had to share even though they're too short for chapters of their own. You learned how to sort small-to-medium-sized data files and how to customize that sort. I gave a brief overview of the Windows Registry and demonstrated how to interrogate it with a couple interesting commands. You also learned how to set and retrieve file attributes and how to manipulate bits with the bitwise and logical shift operators.

The next chapter might be the most important and, eventually, the most referenced in this book. Troubleshooting tips and testing techniques are important in any language, but especially in a scripting language without a compiler—and without an animator or debugger.

31

TROUBLESHOOTING TIPS AND TESTING TECHNIQUES

When I first started to share with a small number of friends and colleagues the fact that I was writing the book that you are now holding, what they wanted to see in it more than anything was a chapter on testing and troubleshooting because of the unique development challenges posed by Batch.

I've mentioned often that there's no Batch compiler, and maybe this goes without saying, but there's no animator or debugger either. Stepping through some Batch commands, stepping over others, setting breakpoints, and inspecting or modifying variables are pure fantasy, or a very bad novel in the making (or maybe my next project). There are two steps in the life-cycle of Batch code: it's written, and it's executed. That's the list; there's no compilation and no animation. But this doesn't mean you can't test bat files. In fact, it makes testing all the more crucial.

In this chapter, I'll step through a number of tips, discussing the various techniques I've learned and developed over my years of coding Batch applications, small and large.

(If the alliterative title doesn't sit well with you, be thankful that I pared it down from "Tantalizingly Tidy Troubleshooting Tips and Timeless Testing Techniques"—a veritable tsunami of Ts.)

Capture stdout and stderr

Without a doubt, the first step in testing and troubleshooting any bat file is capturing stdout and stderr to a trace file. While other languages offer an animator, Batch offers the next best thing—a detailed accounting of the results of most every command as each one executes. In some limited ways the trace might even be better than animation. It's true that you can't step through the code and manipulate variables as the bat file executes, but you can see the value of variables throughout the run and easily go in the reverse direction by simply scrolling up.

However, the trace can be daunting. If a loop executes 1,000 times, all 1,000 executions are in the trace file, possibly spanning tens of thousands of lines. For this reason, most tips in this chapter will revolve around how to interpret the trace. The information in it is so invaluable, if you don't remember how to capture stdout and stderr, return to Chapter 12 and reacquaint yourself with the process before reading on.

Now that you can capture the trace, being able to read it is paramount.

How to Navigate the Trace

Always navigate the trace while referencing the bat file or files that generated it. It's exceedingly easy to get lost in the trees of the trace file, and the original Batch code contains the map of the forest. This tip might seem obvious, but at times the trace may bear little resemblance to the bat code. For instance, in the trace you might see myVar being set like so:

```
C:\Batch>set myVar=finalValue
```

But that doesn't tell you whether finalValue was hardcoded or set by other means, such as resolved from an intermediate variable. The original bat file will, however:

```
set myVar=%intermediate%
```

Also, traces can become so long and dense that performing a search is the only reasonable means of finding the desired section of output, but doing so can be trickier than you might imagine. Consider this code:

```
rem Execute the Database Purge Program
 %_pgmPurgeDB%
 if %errorlevel% neq 0 (
    set errorMsg=The Database Purge Program Failed
    goto :Abort
 )
```

The resulting trace might appear like so:

```
C:\Batch>rem Execute the Database Purge Program

C:\Batch>DatabasePurge.exe

C:\Batch>if 0 NEQ 0 (
set errorMsg=The Database Purge Program Failed
 goto :Abort
)
```

The interpreter shows the variables as resolved, so you can't find this section of the trace by searching for the _pgmPurgeDB variable name from the bat file. Several sections of the code often look similar. For instance, multiple programs might execute, trailed by similar error handling.

The two most readily identifiable portions of this Batch code are the remark and error message. Let's take advantage of these bits of hardcoded text. To manage this issue, make sure that each program has a unique remark before it and/or a unique error message in the error handling code block after it. Now to find this section of the code in the trace, just copy the remark or error message from the bat file and search for it in the trace. And you'll be documenting your code to boot—a true win-win scenario.

Successful executions are similar and boring, but failures are often unique and interesting. Let's execute the same code again, but this time imagine a user has asked us to investigate why the database wasn't purged despite the apparent success of the bat file's execution. The clues are in the trace:

```
C:\Batch>rem Execute the Database Purge Program

C:\Batch>if 0 NEQ 0 (
set errorMsg=The Database Purge Program Failed
 goto :Abort
)
```

First comes the comment. Then the errorlevel variable resolves to 0 in the conditional clause of the if command, so the program must've executed successfully, right? No, this only means that the last process to set the variable set it to 0. Was that last process the executable? Hold on . . . where's the executable? It isn't showing up in the trace after the remark. That's a clue.

This demonstrates why it's so important to reference the original Batch code when reading the trace and doing so line by line by line. Doing that clearly exposes the missing content, which in this case is a program invocation. Without the original bat file, it would've been very difficult to see that something was missing.

Getting back to our specific issue, its proximate cause is probably the variable for the program resolving to null or to one or more spaces, but what's the root cause? Maybe the variable was misspelled in this code; maybe someone misspelled it earlier when defining it; maybe it was never defined at all; maybe some other process wiped it out. (But maybe someone prefixed the contents of _pgmPurgeDB with @, thus suppressing the executable name from the trace even though it did execute, or maybe I'm overthinking this.) What you can be assured of is that the execution of the program isn't showing up in the trace, and that with a little more digging you'll find the actual root cause.

Remember, this is uncompiled code; using an undefined variable is the type of issue a compiler would catch, but Batch coders don't have that luxury.

Don't Be Fooled by the Ghost Trace

I've witnessed more than one novice Batch coder fixating on a portion of the trace similar to the following example, convinced that the program failed:

```
C:\Batch>if 0 NEQ 0 (
set errorMsg=The Database Purge Program Failed
 goto :Abort
)
```

After all, the trace clearly shows a line with the errorMsg variable being set to a string definitively stating that the program failed, but this is part of the "ghost trace." The line above the message contains the if command and the conditional clause that triggers the logic: if 0 NEQ 0. This is false; hence, the code block didn't execute, and any apparent execution is an apparition. If an else keyword and code block had been present, the code in that code block would have executed, but in this instance, after the interpreter evaluated the if command, control skipped to whatever came after the code block.

For better or worse, the interpreter doesn't suppress such unexecuted code blocks. Not everything in the trace actually executed. If a command in the code block generates output to stdout, the existence or nonexistence of that output in the trace verifies whether it executed. Many times, however, nothing in the code block generates output, so you must behave like the interpreter and attempt to evaluate the conditional clause.

Frustratingly, even this has limitations. You can't always evaluate the results of some conditional clauses from the trace. For example, an if exist command determining the presence of a file is impossible to evaluate from just the conditional clause in the trace. You have little means of knowing whether the file existed when the code executed or whether connectivity to the file was momentarily lost.

If the code branches significantly, you can infer the result of the `if` command from what happens next in the trace. For instance, if that error message had been set, control would have immediately jumped to the `:Abort` label due to the goto command. Ask yourself if the next few lines in the trace look like the code under this label or the code after the code block. (This is another reason for one of those descriptive remarks I mentioned earlier.) However, if the code in the code block does nothing more than set a variable or two, you'll be hard-pressed to determine whether it actually executed given the trace (although the next tip might help).

If nothing else, you can begin the code block that executes when the conditional clause is true with an `echo true` command. I hesitate to suggest this inelegant cluttering of the code, but this writes the true text, or whatever text you desire, to the trace immediately after the execution of the `if` command, but only if the code block executes, definitively showing the result of the `if` command. For instance:

```
C:\Batch>if exist C:\Batch\MysteryFile.txt (
echo true
 set errorMsg=The Database Purge Program Failed
 goto :Abort
)
true
```

The `echo true` command in the code block always finds its way into the trace. After all, the point of this tip is that the ghost trace contains unexecuted commands. But the true text coming immediately after the close parenthesis shows that the code block executed and that the mystery file definitely existed at the time the `if` command looked for it.

Create an Audit Trail of Variables

An audit trail of all the variables set, reset, or unset during the execution of a bat file can greatly aid your troubleshooting. As mentioned in the prior tip, this might be the only way to know whether a code block executed. To this end, near the beginning of a long-running bat file, I usually add the following two lines:

```
rem \- All Variables in Effect Before Execution:
   set
```

This one simple command, the set command with no arguments, writes all existing variables to the captured trace. At the end of the same process, you can execute the same command but with a refence to `After Execution` in the remark.

The remarks make both lists of all populated variables easy to find. The initial command details all variables set on the machine as the execution begins, and the latter shows what changed during the execution. You can do this only when debugging or as an audit trail for every execution.

I more than hinted at this technique in Chapter 29 in relation to arrays and hash tables. You might populate these data structures by various means, and it doesn't take many entries for the building of these data structures to make a mess of the trace. In that chapter, I recommended dumping the contents of an array or hash table to the trace with a more targeted set command. For instance, we built a hash table by the name of people. Since every entry in the data structure starts with people{, the following command displayed the entire contents of the hash table after the load or at any other point in the process flow:

```
rem - The Contents of people{key}:
  set people{
```

Similarly, if your convention is to prepend all variables containing an executable program with the _prog text, the following displays the complete list of all such variables:

```
rem - All Program Variables:
  set _prog
```

The command without an argument works best at the start and end of a long process because it provides you with the global set of variables, and the targeted command works great for a shorter list of variables at strategic locations in a bat file, perhaps just after some tricky code.

Understand the stdout of the for Command

The complexity of the trace generated by a for command grows in relation to the complexity of the for command itself, but even a simple example demonstrates what can be a common misconception. The following code is from Chapter 18, but instead of summing the integers from 1 to 100, it sums the integers from 1 to the number defined by the count variable:

```
for /L %%i in (1,1,%count%) do (
    set /A sum += %%i
)
```

To cut down on the length of the trace, assume that count is set to 3, meaning that it executes three times even though the following trace shows four set commands:

```
C:\Batch>for /L %i in (1 1 3) do (set /A sum += %i )

C:\Batch>(set /A sum += 1 )

C:\Batch>(set /A sum += 2 )

C:\Batch>(set /A sum += 3 )
```

The first line is the entire for /L command—but *not* its execution. Notice that count along with the encasing percent signs resolves to 3 in the input and that both references to %%i have changed to %i. This is actually how you would enter the variable in a for command at the command prompt, and for whatever reason this is how it appears in stdout. The next three lines show the three actual executions of the code block with the for variable resolved to 1, 2, and 3, respectively.

Because variables such as count are resolved in the first line, it can appear to be an actual execution. This is especially true with more involved examples using complex code blocks or many more executions of the loop. But understand that it's just an informational setup for the executions yet to come. Think of it as an inarticulate introduction to a book, with chapters to follow, one for each execution of the loop.

The next tip demonstrates another source of confusion concerning the trace of the for command.

How to Interpret Unresolved Variables

This is very frustrating, but the interpreter resolves some variables in the trace, but not others. In the last tip I teased that the trace of the for command can get quite complex, and it doesn't take much. To demonstrate, here's a different take on a file that I used frequently when discussing the for /F command in Chapter 19. I'm doing nothing more than putting the entire record of a file into a variable and writing that record to both stdout and the console:

```
for /F "tokens=*" %%r in (C:\Batch\FourBrits.txt) do (
    set inRec=%%r
    echo Writing to Stdout: !inRec!
    > con echo Writing to the Console: !inRec!
)
```

(If you're asking why I didn't simply directly write the %%r token instead of incorporating the superfluous inRec variable, I'm demonstrating the resulting trace of a variable set and used inside a for command's code block with as little else going on as possible. This condition occurs naturally and often with even moderately complex logic.)

As in the last tip, the trace first shows the for command largely, but not entirely, unchanged compared to the actual code. But in contrast, the interpreter displays this more complex command and its associated code block on multiple lines, making it easier to read:

```
C:\Batch>for /F "tokens=*" %r in (C:\Batch\FourBrits.txt) do (
set inRec=%r
 echo Writing to Stdout: !inRec!
 echo Writing to the Console: !inRec! 1>con
)
```

Next, the first record in the files generates the following in the trace. Everything inside the parentheses is the code being executed, while the last line is the result of the first echo command:

```
C:\Batch>(
set inRec=English    John      Paul      George    Richard
 echo Writing to Stdout: !inRec!
 echo Writing to the Console: !inRec! 1>con
)
Writing to Stdout: English    John      Paul      George    Richard
```

By the way, each record in the file generates something very similar to this, so you can see how the trace can get very big very quickly; 100 records would have generated 600 lines of text.

The previous trace clearly shows the input record resolved from %%r and its assignment to the inRec variable, but—and this is important—the next two lines of the trace don't show the resolution of !inRec! at all. Was it set and resolved correctly? In this instance, I use it in the first echo command to clearly show the contents of the variable in the trailing line of output, but you can't see many other usages of the variable in the trace. For example, the second echo command is writing the same text to the console, but it doesn't appear in the trace. (Think of this as the opposite of the ghost trace.)

Simply put, any variable assigned inside a code block and resolved with exclamation marks, also inside the code block, presents as the variable name surrounded by exclamation marks, that is, unresolved. When executed, it resolves as expected, but the trace gives you no indication of this fact.

This is an immensely unnerving batveat. There are nearly countless reasons to set and use a variable inside of the code block of a for command—and this is usually where the most interesting code resides—but what's happening is lost into the ether. Delayed expansion, executed inside and outside of code blocks, is another victim of this issue.

There are a few ways to handle this. The first is do nothing at all; once this behavior is understood, a good coder can navigate these idiosyncrasies with the knowledge that they need to perform a certain amount of extrapolation to read the trace.

Second, strategically placed echo commands can show the results of a few lines of logic. You can write the text to the console for troubleshooting (more on this to come) or simply to the trace file. That's in effect what I did in the prior listing with the first echo command.

Third, if the line-by-line results of each command are required, you can move the interesting code block to a called routine and invoke it with a call command, passing the needed tokens as arguments. The routine can then treat the tokens like parameters with the upshot being functionally equivalent code that's now fully resolved in the trace.

I have some professional history with this issue. After implementing a very involved nested for structure culminating in the rename of a file, some continually raised questions as to whether the rename actually occurred. To ultimately settle the debate, I rewrote the code using a called routine. Unfortunately, we all must compromise elegance for functionality at times.

As a side note, this trace contains some oddities. The first line inside the code block has no indenting, and the others are indented one space, regardless of the indentation in the bat file. The redirection syntax, `> con`, precedes the echo command in the bat file, but in the trace, it's moved to the end. I can't explain these discrepancies, but I know they exist, and we must come to accept that what's in the trace is a tortured rendering of the actual code.

Recognize Inconsistent Command Outputs

Due to the vagaries of Batch, the messages produced from command to command varies, thus compounding the already nasty batveat from the prior tip. For example, if an xcopy command executes inside of a code block using variables set and resolved in the code block, the trace won't show the resolved filename or names in the xcopy command. But if you use the /F option, the command writes a clear message to the trace detailing the result of the command, listing the file or files copied.

In contrast, a similar ren command produces no message from a successful rename, meaning that you can rename a file with no mention of it in the trace other than a ren command with unresolved filenames. A failed ren command writes a generic error message to stderr, but unlike the xcopy command, it doesn't contain the filename. The end result is that if a failed ren command uses exclamation marks inside a for loop or it uses delayed expansion, an error message states that the rename failed without noting the file or giving any other information.

With experience you'll learn what output to expect and when to expect it from commands that you commonly use. For other commands, expect the unexpected.

Write Variables to the Console

Unless you've skipped directly to this chapter and to this tip, you're more than familiar with an echo command redirecting its output to the console via the > con syntax. I've used the technique many times to show the results of code listings, and it's very handy when troubleshooting, especially for complex for loops.

The trace can be both cryptic and large, which isn't a good combination for readability. To tease out just the important data, I often place a temporary redirected echo command inside a loop to see the state of one or more variables during each pass.

For instance, the logic to add up a series of integers in "Understand the stdout of the for Command" on page 380 is difficult to test, because while we see the sum variable being set, we never see it resolved in any of the iterations of the loop in the trace. You won't see the value of sum until you use it somewhere in the code after the loop, but if you aren't getting the expected result, you'll likely want to see those lost intermediate values. You can add a single line to the summation code so as to get a summation of events. See if you can spot it:

```
for /L %%i in (1,1,%count%) do (
    set /A sum += %%i
> con echo ---- index = %%i ---- sum = !sum! -----
)
```

Assume that count is set to 4 before this executes; the final sum should be 10, but we're getting 35.

The trace still hasn't gone anywhere if you need more detail, but the additional command writes the following plain and comprehensive text to the console. The variables are labeled clearly, and the dashes just make them stand out and look nice:

```
---- index = 1 ---- sum = 26 -----
---- index = 2 ---- sum = 28 -----
---- index = 3 ---- sum = 31 -----
---- index = 4 ---- sum = 35 -----
```

The index variable should increment (no surprise there), but a close inspection of the sum variable for each entry reveals the issue. The code never initialized sum, and it can be 26 in the first line only if it were 25 coming into the loop. An earlier process must be using the same generically named variable. After adding a quick set command initializing the variable to 0, the code displays the following:

```
---- index = 1 ---- sum = 1 -----
---- index = 2 ---- sum = 3 -----
---- index = 3 ---- sum = 6 -----
---- index = 4 ---- sum = 10 -----
```

Another close inspection of the sum variable now reveals that all is working as intended; that is, the prior sum plus the current index does in fact equal the current sum in every entry after the first, where it's just 1. Once the testing and troubleshooting is complete, you can and should delete the echo command before moving on.

I've demonstrated this technique on one of the simplest for commands possible, but for commands can quickly become opaque. A simple redirected echo command or two can quickly and easily generate a synopsis of some tricky and repetitive logic to greatly aid your troubleshooting.

In Chapter 9, I expressed some very definitive views on indenting that I appear to have flouted with this echo command. As a quick recap, remarks have no indent, labels are indented one byte, and everything else is indented two bytes or more. In my opinion this is a must for the finished product, but this particular echo command is temporary, and it's best to make that obvious. Otherwise, there's a good chance that you unnecessarily and accidentally leave it in the code. This gaudy unindented command is all but begging to be deleted.

Decipher Different Types of Syntax Errors

The interpreter writes two general types of error messages to stderr: errors generated by a command and syntax errors. Failed xcopy or del commands display the command itself in the trace followed by a clear error message stating why it couldn't copy or delete a file.

Unfortunately, syntax errors don't present consistently. One example of a syntax error is the use of the nonexistent and operator in a conditional clause. As mentioned in Chapter 27, the interpreter might just ignore it and go on to execute whatever's in the code block without even writing a message to stderr. A slightly different conditional clause with the same bad operator might write the if command to the trace followed by an error message:

```
C:\Batch>if "" NEQ "A" and "" equ "B" (
'and' is not recognized as an internal or external command,
operable program or batch file.
```

But this still plows ahead executing the code block and beyond. By the way, the text of this error message means that the interpreter is mistakenly trying to execute something in the command as if it were a program, but it's often a syntax error instead.

There's at least one more way that syntax errors can manifest themselves. To demonstrate, let's consider this slightly modified version of the code discussed earlier in this chapter that does little more than execute a program and check the return code:

```
%_pgmPurgeDB%
if %errorlevel% neq 0
    set errorMsg=The Database Purge Program Failed
    goto :Abort
)
```

As simple as this code appears to be, the execution crashes, and the command window closes, leaving the following text at the bottom of the trace:

```
C:\Batch>DatabasePurge.exe
The syntax of the command is incorrect.

C:\Batch>  if 0 neq 0
```

A pessimist might point out that the generic error message is completely devoid of details. An optimist might point out that the interpreter definitively informs you of a syntax error, but when you begin to analyze the message, you realize that its digital author is unintentionally sinister.

The error message stating that the syntax is incorrect immediately follows the execution of the program; there isn't even a blank line between them. It certainly suggests that the preceding line has the bad syntax. But no, the interpreter is something of a fortune teller. It's stating that the following line—the one separated by a blank line—is the source of the gaffe, even though it looks like an uncontroversial if command.

To recap, syntax errors sometimes write an error message to the trace, and sometimes they don't. Sometimes the interpreter blows past syntax errors, executing the commands coming next, and sometimes it doesn't. Error messages sometimes come after the offending command, and sometimes they come before. My best advice is to find the general vicinity of the error. Look at the code before and after the message and avoid tunnel vision.

Before moving on, what's wrong with the syntax in that if command anyway? This is where a compiler giving a succinct and pointed error message would be manna from heaven, but we're armed with little more than our wits and an interpreter that has shrugged its binary shoulders and said, "Something's wrong. Figure it out." A heads-down interrogation of the line of code following it reveals a command name nearly impossible to misspell, if; a valid operator, neq; and two numbers to compare. D'oh! The open parenthesis is missing.

Modularize Wherever Possible

The act of creating small bat files that perform definitive tasks has many benefits, not least among them is testing. You can easily set up another bat file to call the new bat file many times with various input parameters, each time verifying any and all outputs, which can take the form of returned parameters, data written to the console, or some action, such as a copied file.

To see an example of this simply flip back to Chapter 11. After building the *MadLib.bat* file, I called it several times with many different input parameters. Turning to Chapter 29, if you're creating an array or hash table in a section of code in an already large process, one option is to code it in the existing bat file. But most of the time, a far better option is to create a new called bat file with all of the interesting logic. Then you can test the new bat file quickly and repeatedly with call commands from another bat file to work out any bugs. Finally, you'll need to do little more than add a call command or two to the existing bat file containing the larger process.

You'll soon see more examples of this. In Chapter 32, after creating an object-oriented bat file, I'll invoke it with multiple call commands from another bat file. Then in Chapter 33, I'll create a single bat file to handle stacks. Subsequent calls to it will then push items onto the stack and pull items off the stack. Modularize whenever possible.

Test Snippets in a Test Bat File

Unfortunately, sometimes modularization isn't possible. A large application might need a tweak to an existing for command. If it's in a large bat file that's part of an even larger process, it's probably impractical to incorporate the change into a new module. To complicate matters, the lack of a compiler greatly increases the chances of you introducing errors when making even the most trivial of changes. If this is a long-running process, it might take an hour or longer just to learn that you omitted a parenthesis, and more complex changes often require multiple rounds of the coding-testing-tweaking triumvirate. It would be far better to test just the code in question, being able to run it repeatedly and quickly.

What we need is a way to mimic the actual environment of the new or updated logic in a simple and controlled setting. As a means to this end, every computer I work on has a *C:\Batch* folder containing a bat file named *Test.bat* with these complete contents, at least to start:

```
@setlocal EnableExtensions EnableDelayedExpansion
@call :GetTrace > C:\Batch\Trace.txt 2>&1
@pause
goto :eof

:GetTrace
rem --- Variables Set Prior to Code Snippet
rem --- Code Snippet Goes Here
rem --- Variables Set After to Code Snippet
  goto :eof
```

As it stands, this bat file will execute a very boring routine of three rem commands, capture stdout and stderr in a trace file, and hold the console open with the pause command. But this bat file is merely a shell. To test a code snippet from a larger bat file, paste it after the second rem command. Examples might include a complex for command or even a much longer snippet that builds and uses arrays while also reading from and writing to multiple files.

If the code expects certain variables to be set before the snippet executes, you can enter them as hardcoded values after the first rem command. If a file is to be read, mock one up and add its file connector in this section.

Similarly, if the process being tested is to set certain variables in the environment for later use, you can interrogate them with echo commands redirected to the console after the third rem command. Not only will you see these resolved variables on the console, but they'll also be in the detailed trace (unless the issue of unresolved variables rears its head).

To demonstrate, if you were to use this technique to test the summation logic detailed earlier in this chapter, you might update the internal routine in the shell bat file like so:

```
:GetTrace
rem --- Variables Set Prior to Code Snippet
  set count=100

rem --- Code Snippet Goes Here
  for /L %%i in (1,1,%count%) do (
    set /A sum += %%i
  )

rem --- Variables Set After to Code Snippet
  > con echo sum = %sum%
  goto :eof
```

The code to be tested goes in the middle section, but this is just the starting point. You'll need to define the count variable before the core logic executes, and since the ultimate result of this code is the value of one variable, you'll want to resolve and display sum to the console in the third section of the routine.

You can now test, tweak, retest, and tweak again quickly, efficiently, and often. This isn't a final test, but once this testing is satisfactory, you can copy and paste the listing into the main process. Now you can perform a full end-to-end test with a high level of confidence.

I also use this very same bat file for testing the modularized code that I introduced in the prior tip. You can easily add one or more call commands of other bat files to the middle section, while still using the first section for setup and the third for validation. Cutting and pasting is never elegant, but without a doubt, testing snippets in a test bat file is supremely effective.

Summary

I cannot overstate the importance of mastering techniques for testing and troubleshooting Batch code. In this chapter, I plugged in the amplifier from *This Is Spinal Tap* and turned it up to 11. With these 11 tips, I demonstrated how I develop and maintain bat files. In one sentence: capture and be able to read the trace, write output to the console, modularize when possible, and use *Test.bat* whenever appropriate.

I'm sure that others have useful additions to this list, and I encourage you to seek them out. The only alternative to solid Batch testing is eventually giving up and writing some compiled code to perform a task that could've been done, and should've been done, with just a few lines of Batch.

The next chapter tackles an exciting and interesting coding methodology: object-oriented design, a topic that you may not currently associate with Batch, but soon will.

32

OBJECT-ORIENTED DESIGN

In preceding chapters, I've explored many topics that aren't typically associated with Batch from booleans to hash tables, with many others in between. In this chapter, I'll tackle the holy grail of Batch user-built tools: object-oriented design.

After explaining the difference between procedural and object-oriented coding, I'll lay out the four pillars of object-oriented programming. Then I'll present a fully functional model of Batch object-oriented design, complete with bat files representing parent, intermediate, and child objects. After you've learned how to invoke the object-oriented code, I'll share many recommendations and analyze how well this model satisfies the basic tenets of object-oriented design.

Procedural vs. Object-Oriented Coding

In the very early days of computers, all coding was *procedural*—that is, all programs consisted of a series of computational steps. The methodology is still very much in existence with possibly more than a trillion lines of such code still in use and many more written every day. By default, variables are accessed globally in procedural code. Sometimes many hundreds of variables are defined in a section near the beginning of a program, and at other times, such as in Batch, they come into being when first referenced. Even when an internal routine or procedure is invoked, the set of active and available variables doesn't change. Certain measures can often be invoked to limit scope, such as the setlocal discussed in Chapter 3, but in procedural coding, a variable typically can be set or reset anywhere in what is often a very large program file.

Before long, some smart people came up with the concept of *object-oriented programming (OOP)*, where the code is broken into small, easy-to-manage *objects*, each containing data in the form of variables and executable code in the form of methods. A *method* is similar to an internal routine in Batch; it can be invoked, and when it completes its execution, control is returned to the point of the call, but a method can also be called externally; that is, code inside another program file can call the method directly. Regardless of the source of the call, the method accepts well-defined inputs and returns equally well-defined outputs. However, most of the data inside a method is typically inaccessible from elsewhere in the program file and especially from other program files.

The compartmentalization of the code into individual objects streamlines the logic and guards against the unintended consequence of some portion of the code adversely affecting another portion. Additionally, if one of these objects is of use in a different context, it can easily be used by both processes without modification or duplication. An equivalently useful portion of a procedural program might end up being copied and pasted into another program.

If I were to construct a list of great personal irritants—and for the sake of brevity, I'll limit this to work/coding-related peeves—atop my jeremiad is procedural code disguised as object-oriented code. Certain languages and frameworks are designed to support each coding paradigm. Java and C# are object-oriented languages; COBOL and Batch are procedural languages. But contrary to what many believe, it isn't that simple; procedural code can easily be written in Java, and with some work, object-oriented principles can be implemented in Batch.

PROCEDURAL VS. OBJECT-ORIENTED MINDSETS

For much of my coding career, I've split my time between COBOL, Java, .NET, and of course, Batch. Many years ago, a .NET coder, who knew me only as

---

a COBOL coder, pedantically went on at length about the virtues of object-oriented coding with the utmost condescension. When I had the displeasure of opening an example of his work, I found a single program file (or class) running into the thousands of lines predominated by global variables and many gratuitous examples of cut-and-paste code snippets with minor tweaks. He clearly fancied himself an object-oriented coder simply because he managed the modicum of knowledge necessary to achieve a clean compile in a language considered to be object-oriented.

Shortly thereafter I abruptly interrupted his next harangue, "You're no object-oriented programmer. You are the worst type of coder; you're a procedural coder masquerading as an object-oriented coder, and you don't even know the difference. If by analogy we were woodworkers, you've been provided with only the most modern cutting-edge tools—industrial caliber lathes and miter saws—and yet you produce a rickety chair that would earn a pity D– from a disappointed middle-school shop teacher, while I've built a finely crafted mahogany chair with dovetailed joints using nothing more than stone knives and bearskins."

To be completely honest, that isn't exactly how it happened . . . or really at all how it happened. I did have to work with this individual, so during a code review I provided some mild constructive criticism while laboring to find more positive comments about his atrocious code than negative remarks so as to soften the blow.

The Four Pillars

Any coding language that purports to be object-oriented must fully support the four pillars of object-oriented programming. Languages considered to be object-oriented implement these in different ways, but they all have built-in mechanisms to guide the coder into writing code with these four characteristics.

The first pillar is *abstraction*, which simplifies the code's interface with the outside world. It shows only the necessary or relevant features to the user, while shielding the implementation details and any information irrelevant to the functionality's use.

This segues into the second pillar, *encapsulation*, which restricts access to certain methods and variables in an object, wrapping up data and code into multiple small units. Data hiding, or treating some variables and methods as private, is a significant part of this pillar. Another significant part is simply the act of creating compact, readable, and reusable modules.

Inheritance, the third pillar, allows for the creation of a base or parent object. Then derived objects can use the parent object while extending it to fit the more specific needs of the child. The classic example is a base or parent object of an Animal, defining all that is common throughout the animal kingdom. Then intermediate objects defined as Reptile and Mammal can inherit data and routines from the Animal object and add to it information about their respective zoological classes. Then objects of Cat, Rat, and even Bat can inherit from the Mammal object, which is already inheriting from the Animal object. More than 1,000 child objects, one for each bat species on the planet, can then inherit from the Bat object. Finally, each of the inheriting objects can use the data and code in its parent objects for its own use.

The fourth pillar, *polymorphism*, which means the condition of occurring in several different forms, derives literally from the Greek words meaning *many forms*. This allows a call to a routine to behave differently in different situations. Reusable code is always awesome, but this pillar takes the concept of reuse to its zenith. A method in the parent object might be invoked by multiple child objects, where each invocation is unique to the child.

In the pages ahead, I'll attempt to mimic these four pillars of abstraction, encapsulation, inheritance, and polymorphism.

Batch Object-Oriented Design

This chapter is about Batch object-oriented design and not Batch object-oriented programming for two reasons. First, and more trivially, BOOP is a horrible acronym, reminiscent of the noise one might make when affectionately poking a baby's nose. BOOD isn't much better, but I do have a Brilliant Acronym Team (or BAT) diligently working on something batter . . . sorry, something better.

Far more important, Batch has none of the built-in features that are intrinsic to more modern languages that implement object-oriented programming. I'll demonstrate how to mimic each of its four pillars, and the level of success in creating object-oriented bat files may very well surprise many, but I'll craft some of its functionality more completely than other functionality. True object-oriented programming won't be possible in Batch, but I encourage you to incorporate these design elements, in whole or in part, in the design of your Batch code.

In Batch, a variable cannot be defined as public or private; in fact, variables can't be defined at all. There is no keyword to invoke inheritance found in other languages, such as "extends" or "implements." In OOP, a child object can override methods in the parent object; you'll soon see how to perform many of these tasks in Batch, but they won't be done automatically. Remember that this is a language without booleans, floats, the while and do...while commands, the and and or operators, arrays, and hash tables. I've demonstrated how to build all of those things with the tools at hand (and I'll do the same with stacks and queues in Chapter 33), so it should be of little surprise that Batch has nothing off the shelf for anything like object-oriented programming.

However, object-oriented principles can be used, and should be used, regardless of the provided toolkit. Someone coding in an "object-oriented language" can easily define excessive class-level variables, make all data items public, and put the lion's share of the code into a "god object" (a single object that does too much and is too big to be managed efficiently). But regardless of the coding language, this design with large modules and excessive global variables is essentially procedural coding. More modern languages have object-oriented guardrails, but guardrails can be breached.

Conversely, there's an expectation among many that Batch coders should create only large uninteresting modules. But while Batch procedural code is the standard, there's no Batch police requiring it. When object-oriented programming or design is thought of as a technique and not as a characteristic associated with only some languages, scales will fall from your eyes as if on the road to Damascus. Batch doesn't possess the sturdy guardrails offered elsewhere, but you can craft object-oriented techniques using any coding language, just as it's more than possible to reach the summit driving up a mountain road with shear drops. The infrastructure or plumbing might not exist in Batch and not everything will be possible, but the elegance of object-oriented design in Batch offers the same benefits realized in other languages.

Classes and Objects

One of the differences between OOP and Batch object-oriented design is that traditionally each module or file is defined as a *class*, and an *object* is an instantiation of that class. Instantiating an object is much like defining a variable. Just as a variable can be defined as a string or as an integer in many languages, an object is instantiated to be one specific instance of a class.

To demonstrate, imagine again a class defined as *Bat*, representing all flying nocturnal mammals, where each species of bat would have its own class inheriting from *Bat*. One such species is the Madagascan fruit bat, and its class might be defined as a *MadFruitBat*. This class represents all bats of this one species, and it can be instantiated many times, each time representing one specific creature. A cave containing 500 Madagascan fruit bats could be populated with 500 objects, each one an instantiation of the *MadFruitBat* class individually named for a particular bat.

This is where Batch has its first object-oriented limitation. Remember that this is a language without the ability to define variables as strings and integers. Obviously then, a variable can't be defined or instantiated as a data type corresponding to a class module. In Batch, the distinction between classes and objects doesn't exist. A module or bat file is itself an object. It doesn't have to be instantiated, nor can it be instantiated.

For this reason, the word *class* isn't part of the Batch object-oriented design vernacular. I'll soon share bat files that are fully constituted objects, each one ready to be invoked, and I'll be referring to them as *objects*. The Madagascan fruit bat defined as the *MadFruitBat* class in OOP would be the *MadFruitBat.bat* object bat file in Batch. To implement the 500 individual Madagascan fruit bats, you would need to create a small bat file for each, and each would inherit from *MadFruitBat.bat*.

Actually, *oMadFruitBat.bat* is a better name for the object bat file. To distinguish an object bat file from its more pedestrian brethren, I always prepend its name with a lowercase *o* as a visual cue. The *obj* text also works.

Batch Object-Oriented Design Model

The best way of describing object-oriented design is with an example or model. I'll lay out here the broad strokes of the example of Batch object-oriented design that I present in this chapter. Then I'll show the parent object with examples of intermediate and child objects, all the while explaining the object-oriented concepts implemented in each module. In the next section, "Executing Object-Oriented Batch," I'll discuss exactly how to invoke this model, and in a later section, "The Four Pillars in Batch," I'll explore how closely this model mimics each of the central concepts of object-oriented principles.

At the top of the pyramid is the base or parent object. Other objects inherit from it, but it's the one object in this model that doesn't inherit from another object. Beneath the parent are the intermediate objects that inherit directly from the parent object. Other intermediate objects can inherit from the first level of intermediate objects, culminating in child objects at the bottom of the pyramid. Intermediate and child objects are both called *derived objects* because they inherit or are derived from another object. (Technically, an intermediate object is also a child object because it is a child of another object, but I use the term *child* for what might more accurately be called a "childless child object.")

In this chapter's Batch object-oriented design model, Movie is the parent object to dozens of different film genre objects, such as SciFi, RomCom, and Action, although only two are shown: Comedy and Drama. Individual movies are their own specific object, each one inheriting from a particular genre object. More than two million movies have been released, but I'm showing only three here, two of which are the greatest movies ever released, and *The Godfather* is a great film as well. The objects that I'll present in this chapter, I've marked with an asterisk in Figure 32-1.

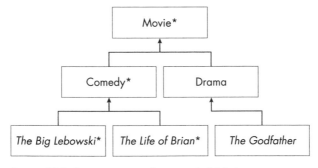

Figure 32-1: Parent, intermediate, and child objects

The Movie object contains data and methods that are common to all movies, or are at least the defaults for all movies. (Echoing the parlance of OOP, I'll use the term *method* in place of *routine* from this point forward.) The Comedy and Drama objects each inherit from the Movie object and extend it, defining data and methods particular to each genre. The individual movie objects inherit from the genre objects, and thus indirectly from the Movie object, and contain detailed data about their specific flick. (Each arrow extends from the derived object to its parent object.)

But this isn't a rigid hierarchy. A movie franchise object such as StarTrek could inherit from the SciFi genre object (neither is shown), and the individual *Star Trek* movies could be child objects of the movie franchise object.

More important, all objects are bat files. The Movie object in its most concrete form is the *oMovie.bat* bat file, and the Comedy object is the *oComedy .bat* bat file. Likewise, one of the child objects will be *oBigLebowski.bat*.

Some object-oriented languages offer multiple inheritance; that is, a derived object can inherit from two or more different objects. For instance, the Dramedy object might inherit from both the Comedy and Drama objects. While that is theoretically possible even in Batch, I'm restricting this model to single inheritance, so the Dramedy object is just another genre object inheriting from the Movie object, and individual dramedies will then inherit from the Dramedy object.

The Parent Object

Once all of this makes sense conceptually, you'll want to see everything in action. Starting with the base or parent object, Listing 32-1 shows the contents of *oMovie.bat*. Note that this and the other object bat file don't start with a setlocal command because they'll always be called from other bat files that contain the command.

```
  set meth=%~1
❶ for %%m in (Constructor DispInfo Set Get) do (
      if "%%m" equ "%meth%" (
      ❷ call :%meth% "%~2" "%~3" "%~4"
      ❸ goto :eof
  ) )
❹ > con echo ABORT - Invalid Method Invoked: %meth%
  pause & exit

❺ :Constructor
  set gauge{%~1}=35mm
  set clrOrBW{%~1}=color
  goto :eof

❻ :Set
  set %~1{%~3}=%~2
  goto :eof

❼ :Get
  set %~2=!%~1{%~3}!
  goto :eof
```

:DispInfo

```
> con echo "%~1" is a !year{%~1}! !clrOrBW{%~1}! !gauge{%~1}! film.
> con echo       Genre: !genre{%~1}!
> con echo        Plot: !plot{%~1}!
> con echo    Starring: !star{%~1}!
> con echo        Cast: !cast{%~1}!
> con echo     Country: !cntry{%~1}!
> con echo    Language: !lang{%~1}!
> con echo.
goto :eof
```

❾ :PrivateMeth

```
rem - some private method code goes here
goto :eof
```

Listing 32-1: The base or parent object, oMovie.bat

There are many interesting pieces of this object.

Hiding Methods

Encapsulation, one of OOP's pillars, includes the hiding of methods. By default, all methods of a bat file are hidden because there's no built-in means of creating multiple entry points into a bat file; when a bat file executes, it starts at the top every time. Hence, the task here isn't to hide certain methods but to make certain methods publicly accessible, while leaving the others hidden.

The for command ❶ acts as a "traffic cop"; it contains a list of the bat file's public methods as its input: Constructor, DispInfo, Set, and Get. The if command inside its code block compares the first parameter received, meth, to this list. If it matches one of the methods listed, the parameter, prepended with a colon, becomes the argument of the call command ❷, and we pass the remaining parameters as additional arguments.

Upon its completion of the called method, control immediately returns to the calling bat file via the goto :eof command ❸ at the end of the for loop. Notice that the last method ❾ isn't on the list. As its name suggests, it's a private method, callable exclusively from methods inside the object. If a calling bat file tries to invoke any other method not on the list or some text that isn't even a method, the code writes out an abort message ❹ and exits the entire process after a pause. (More robust error handling would be preferable, but this works as a demonstration.)

Constructor

When coding in a language with object-oriented guardrails, the act of instantiating an object automatically calls the constructor method belonging to the class. In fact, it isn't even possible to call the other public methods until you've invoked the constructor. The constructor might set some variables or open a file or two, but its general purpose is to set up the object so you can use it going forward. This model mimics this behavior with the :Constructor method ❺ near the top of every Batch object.

This constructor method of the parent object simply sets two variables to defaults so that the majority of the individual movie objects won't have to set them. The vast majority of movies released in the past several decades were shot in color and on 35-millimeter gauge film. This particular constructor accepts only one parameter, the movie title, so for one film in particular, the two set commands assign the values of 35mm and color to the variables defined as gauge{The Big Lebowski} and clrOrBW{The Big Lebowski}, respectively. The variable names have spaces, and if that's a problem for any reason, you can remove them with the replacement syntax, as long as you do so consistently.

We'll also want variables for the plot, year of release, and other characteristics, but these clearly don't have defaults, so we'll set them elsewhere. However, you'll soon see how the object for a 70-millimeter black-and-white film will be able to override these default values set in the parent object constructor.

Setters and Getters

In strict object-oriented coding, classes typically have many setter and getter methods; that is, for each defined data item one method sets and another method gets its value. For instance, there might be a pair of methods to get and set the gauge and another pair for the plot, and so on. But due to delayed expansion and Batch's lack of defined data types, we can consolidate all of the setter methods into a single :Set method ❻, and we can handle all of the getter methods with a solitary :Get method ❼.

The :Set method has a single line of interesting code that a calling bat file can use to set any variable for the object. It's a set command using three parameters: the characteristic being set is %~1, the value being assigned is %~2, and the movie title is %~3. The variable name being set is a combination of the first and last parameters: %~1{%~3}.

To demonstrate how this works, you can invoke the :Set method with the following call command:

```
call :Set plot "A day repeats ad infinitum" "Groundhog Day"
```

The result of this call sets the value of the plot in the second argument to the plot{Groundhog Day} variable, but notice that there's no explicit call to the :Set method to be found in this bat file. I'll eventually show how to make this call from outside of this parent bat file.

The :Get method flips the assignment around, returning the value in lieu of assigning it. The parameters for the setter and getter methods are the same with the notable exception that the second one for the getter is the name of the variable to which we assign the plot, instead of the plot itself. Conveniently, resolving the other two parameters inside of exclamation marks extracts the value of the plot as part of the assignment: !%~1{%~3}!.

Here's one possible invocation of the method:

```
call :Get plot plotVar "Groundhog Day"
```

This returns the plotVar variable set to the value A day repeats ad infinitum or the same string we passed to the :Set method earlier.

It's easy to miss how sublime this really is. Yet again, delayed expansion offers us a useful and elegant solution not available in most languages. Astonishingly, an object with dozens of variables needs only one setter and one getter method. In at least one small facet, Batch offers a better solution than traditional object-oriented languages.

App-Specific Public Methods

In traditional OOP, constructors are a must, and setters and getters are ubiquitous, but there are usually other public methods specific to an application, and I've included one example of just such a method in the *oMovie* *.bat* object. The :DispInfo method ❽ displays detailed information about a film to the console. A series of echo commands in the method write the movie title and several other pieces of data to the console. For instance, its first line mentions the movie itself and details the year of release, whether it's color or black and white, and the gauge.

These last two variables are set in the constructor, but the variable for the year and others aren't. In fact, their only mention in the parent bat file is here. (I'll share their origins before long, but it has something to do with inheritance.) Regardless of where this data comes from, this one method displays information for any movie object that is derived directly or indirectly from this object. That's polymorphism.

> **NOTE** *If variables such as plot{Groundhog Day} remind you of hash table elements, that's because they are in fact elements of hash tables (Chapter 29). You don't need to understand the data structure to understand this model, but after executing the logic to build 17 plots for 17 different movies, the plot hash table contains 17 elements.*

The Intermediate Object

In this model, the genre objects are all intermediate objects, with the *oComedy.bat* object being one example. It's a child of *oMovie.bat*, but it also has children of its own, two of which are shown in Figure 32-1.

Listing 32-2 shows the complete bat file object for *oComedy.bat*.

```
❶ set extends=C:\Batch\oMovie.bat
  set meth=%~1
❷ for %%m in (Constructor PublicMeth) do (
      if "%%m" equ "%meth%" (
❸     call :%meth% "%~2" "%~3"
          goto :eof
  ) )
❹ call %extends% %*
  goto :eof

❺ :Constructor
  call %extends% %meth% %*
❻ set genre{%~1}=Comedy
  goto :eof
```

```
❼ :PublicMeth
   :: some public method code
❽ call :PrivateMeth
   goto :eof

❾ :PrivateMeth
   :: some private method code
   goto :eof
```

Listing 32-2: The intermediate object, oComedy.bat

At a glance, this looks to be structured much like the parent object, but there are differences. The very first line defines another bat file, and immediately after the traffic cop is a `call` command instead of an abort. The constructor also calls another bat file, and the setter and getter methods are missing along with the method to display information about a movie.

Strict object-oriented languages have reserved words and syntax allowing one object to seamlessly inherit from another. Not to be confused with Batch, this is how a child class would use the extends keyword to inherit from a parent in Java:

```
public class oComedy extends oMovie {}
```

In Batch, without similar built-in syntax, we do it quite differently. The first statement in the *oComedy.bat* object defines the parent object bat file from which it inherits, namely, *oMovie.bat* ❶, which is also the object it extends. Then the traffic cop, looking much like the one in the parent object, has its own list of public methods maintained in the `for` command ❷. If the first parameter matches either of the two public methods in the list, the `call` command invokes it ❸. But where the parent class aborts when the method to be invoked isn't public, the child object instead calls the parent class defined by extends, passing the same arguments along ❹. That's inheritance.

An intermediate (and child) object can define its own methods not already in the parent object. It can also inherit the methods from the parent object by doing nothing more than what I've already shown. If the first parameter isn't in the list of public methods, this bat file becomes a simple pass-through as it makes the identical call to the parent object ❹. The %* syntax ensures that the same parameter list received by this bat is the argument list passed to the parent.

We'll soon be able to call the important methods in the parent object (:DispInfo, :Set, and :Get) with the Batch inheritance just described. Elegantly, all of the genre objects and their children can easily use these methods. Not only does the intermediate object not have to reproduce them, but it doesn't even need to mention them. And what happens when someone errantly passes this object a method not made public here or by its parent? The intermediate object passes it along, and the parent performs the error handling for all its children in one place.

This object does more than inherit methods from the parent. The constructor offers an example of *extending* a method already defined in the parent object. There is a :Constructor method in the parent, but the inheritance set up with the traffic cop doesn't call it. Instead, the intermediate object's :Constructor method ❺ supersedes it, but this doesn't mean that we never invoke the parent constructor logic.

The very first line of the :Constructor method calls the parent object to invoke its method of the same name, that is, its constructor. This is another built-in feature of traditional object-oriented languages that we must mimic. After calling the parent's constructor, the derived object's constructor puts its own spin on the data. Remember that the *oMovie.bat* object defined the movie as color and 35mm in its constructor. Here the *oComedy.bat* object accepts those two values and also defines the genre as Comedy ❻. As we'll soon see, its child objects will extend this even further.

Finally, notice two aptly named methods, one public ❼ and one private ❾. The private method isn't listed in the traffic cop, so we can invoke it explicitly only from somewhere inside this bat file, such as from inside the public method ❽.

The Child Objects

Finally, we come to the objects for the individual movies. Listing 32-3 is the entire bat file for one movie object, *oBigLebowski.bat*.

```
❶ set extends=C:\Batch\oComedy.bat
  set meth=%~1
❷ set title=The Big Lebowski

❸ for %%m in (Constructor) do (
      if "%%m" equ "%meth%" (
          call :%meth% "%~2" "%~3"
          goto :eof
  ) )
❹ call %extends% %* "%title%"
  goto :eof

❺ :Constructor
❻ call %extends% %meth% "%title%"
❼ set plot{%title%}=The Dude seeks recompense for a valued rug micturated upon.
  set star{%title%}=Jeff Bridges
  set cast{%title%}=John Goodman, Julianne Moore, Steve Buscemi
  set lang{%title%}=English
  set year{%title%}=1998
  set cntry{%title%}=United States
  goto :eof
```

Listing 32-3: The child object, oBigLebowski.bat

The traffic cop ❸ at the top of this child object looks much like the one from the intermediate object, but it now extends the *oComedy.bat* object ❶, and the new title variable ❷ defines the movie. We're passing the title to its parent object as the final argument ❹, where it's used to set variables such as gauge{The Big Lebowski} in *oMovie.bat* and genre{The Big Lebowski} in *oComedy.bat*.

This child object has only one public method and no private methods, but it could easily have multiples of either type. (Since there's only one entry in the list of public methods, we could remove the for command and leave just an if command.)

The :Constructor method ❺ is even more interesting than the constructor in the intermediate object. It first calls the constructor of its parent, *oComedy.bat* ❻, and we've already seen that the constructor in the intermediate object will in turn call the constructor of its parent, *oMovie.bat*. Both parents set a variable or two before returning control to the constructor of the individual movie object where it sets everything that's particular to its actual movie, such as the plot, star, and cast ❼.

We can now set up similar object bat files for other movies. Notice the differences and similarities between the previous object and the following object, *oLifeOfBrian.bat*, which contains data and a constructor method for another great film in Listing 32-4.

```
set extends=C:\Batch\oComedy.bat
set meth=%~1
set title=The Life of Brian

for %%m in (Constructor) do (
    if "%%m" equ "%meth%" (
        call :%meth% "%~2" "%~3"
        goto :eof
) )
call %extends% %* "%title%"
goto :eof

:Constructor
call %extends% %meth% "%title%"
set plot{%title%}=A very naughty boy is taken for the Messiah in old Judea.
set star{%title%}=Graham Chapman
set cast{%title%}=John Cleese, Eric Idle, Michael Palin
set lang{%title%}=English
set year{%title%}=1979
set cntry{%title%}=United Kingdom
❶ set troupe{%title%}=Monty Python
goto :eof
```

Listing 32-4: The child object, oLifeOfBrian.bat

Both constructors are setting the plot, star, members of the cast, language, year of release, and country, but this one is also setting troupe{%title%} ❶. *The Life of Brian* was created by a comedy troupe, but this variable doesn't apply to most other comedies. Each constructor is unique to a particular move and bat file; while it should define a certain set of variables in this model, it can contain additional logic pertinent to its movie, as the object demonstrates.

I more than hinted earlier that you can override variables defined in the parent's constructor in the child, and the child's constructor is where that happens. For instance, the constructor in *oRagingBull.bat* would reset the `clrOrBW{Raging Bull}` variable to `Black` and `White`. Likewise, for a movie shot in something other than `35mm`, such as `digital`, we can reset the gauge in the child's constructor.

Another feature of object-oriented design is the ability of a child object to override methods defined in a parent class. You've seen methods inherited and extended. The constructor just discussed is a great example of extending a method. Now imagine that method without the call to its like-named method in its parent. That's a *method override*. The child object will never call the public method in its parent object because the child has overridden it with a method of its own.

To demonstrate, let's consider one last child object with this as the title variable:

```
set title=Star Wars: Episode I - The Phantom Menace
```

If `DispInfo` is in the list of public methods defined for this particular child object, the coder of this object could add the following method to the bat file:

```
rem - Override Method
 :DispInfo
 > con echo "%title%" is the worst movie ever released. Members of an
 > con echo accomplished cast are reduced to one-dimensional characters
 > con echo upstaged by the uniquely annoying Jar Jar Binks in a plot so
 > con echo tortured it evokes war crimes. It's little more than a big budget
 > con echo excuse to unveil the technology to meld animated characters into
 > con echo live action. Only the most ardent Star Wars apologists and young
 > con echo children found it enjoyable, but the racist tropes made it
 > con echo unsuitable for viewing by anyone of any age.
 > con echo.
 goto :eof
```

A comment stating that this method is an override isn't required, but it's good form.

Notice that this method doesn't invoke a corresponding method in its parent class. It simply writes a few lines of commentary, followed by a blank line, and does nothing more. It has completely superseded or overridden the like-named method in the parent class. Unlike other movies, this title won't see the plot, cast, and other information written to the console as we've seen for other movies using the `:DispInfo` method in *oMovie.bat*. The author of this bat file obviously felt that something special was needed for the informational display for such a singular film. (Please, no hate mail; the original trilogy was fine, even better than fine.)

Executing Object-Oriented Batch

We've created the *oMovie.bat* parent object and the *oComedy.bat* intermediate object that extends or inherits from the parent. In theory, we could create more intermediate (or genre) objects and more than two million child objects for individual movies, but before us we have two child object bat files representing two comedies, each extending the *oComedy.bat* object. Finally, we can execute this object-oriented code. If nothing else, you can use the *Test.bat* file mentioned in Chapter 31, but you need to place all calls to this code into a bat file not already in the model.

The implementing code calls only the child objects; the parent and intermediate objects are called only from their children. Let's start with these four commands:

```
call C:\Batch\oBigLebowski.bat Constructor
call C:\Batch\oLifeOfBrian.bat Constructor
call C:\Batch\oBigLebowski.bat DispInfo
call C:\Batch\oLifeOfBrian.bat DispInfo
```

Remember that you must call the constructor before you can call any other method in an object. These first two commands are the Batch equivalent of instantiating objects.

We first call *oBigLebowski.bat*, and its traffic cop invokes its :Constructor method; as we've already seen, that constructor invokes the constructor method in its parent object, *oComedy.bat*, which invokes the corresponding method in its parent, *oMovie.bat*. Each of the three bat files contributes to the creation of the nine variables that describe this movie. Immediately after that, we do the same with *oLifeOfBrian.bat* to create a second set of movie variables.

The constructors don't generate any output, but the last two call commands display the information shown in Listing 32-5 to the console.

```
"The Big Lebowski" is a 1998 color 35mm film.
    Genre: Comedy
     Plot: The Dude seeks recompense for a valued rug micturated upon.
 Starring: Jeff Bridges
     Cast: John Goodman, Julianne Moore, Steve Buscemi
  Country: United States
 Language: English

"The Life of Brian" is a 1979 color 35mm film.
    Genre: Comedy
     Plot: A very naughty boy is taken for the Messiah in old Judea.
 Starring: Graham Chapman
     Cast: John Cleese, Eric Idle, Michael Palin
  Country: United Kingdom
 Language: English
```

Listing 32-5: Output from two DispInfo calls using two different child objects

The third command calls *oBigLebowski.bat*, passing `DispInfo` as its only argument. This child object doesn't find a public method named `:DispInfo`, so the inheritance kicks in with a call to its parent, *oComedy.bat*, where the method also doesn't exist. Once again because of inheritance, we call the base object, *oMovie.bat*, where we finally find and execute the public method. It displays a concise summary of information about *The Big Lebowski* to the console in seven lines of text.

The final command also shares a wealth of information, but about a different movie, because it calls the *oLifeOfBrian.bat* object. We are ultimately invoking the exact same method, `:DispInfo`, in the exact same object, *oMovie .bat*, but notice the stark differences in the output. The output describes two entirely different movies. That's polymorphism.

Batch has one critical and fairly unique characteristic that lends itself to the implementation of polymorphism: delayed expansion. Resolving variables is straightforward in most coding languages, but Batch allows you to resolve one or more variables to create a variable name that can then itself be resolved.

Both sets of output come from the `:DispInfo` method in the parent object *oMovie.bat* (Listing 32-1). Taking just one variable as an example, delayed expansion first resolves the parameter embedded in `!plot{%~1}!` to be the movie title. In our first call, this results in `!plot{The Big Lebowski}!`, which then resolves to the plot of that movie. The second time through, this exact same code results in `!plot{The Life of Brian}!`, which resolves to a very different plot. This is Batch polymorphism at its finest.

Whoever wrote the *oBigLebowski.bat* object left an Academy Award–winning actor off the cast list. The late Philip Seymour Hoffman had a relatively small role as the title character's smug toady of a personal assistant, Brandt, but he played it with a brilliance and nuance that foretold greater roles. The following two commands add him to the current cast:

```
call C:\Batch\oBigLebowski.bat Get cast lebowCast
call C:\Batch\oBigLebowski.bat Set cast "%lebowCast%, Philip Seymour Hoffman"
```

The first argument of both `call` commands is the name of the method to be invoked, and the second argument is the type of variable pertinent to the call, which is cast in both instances. The first command will `Get` the current cast members, returning the value as the contents of the `lebowCast` variable. The second command will `Set` (or reset) the list of current cast members to the just-returned value concatenated with Mr. Hoffman's full name. If you were to invoke the *oBigLebowski.bat* object again with the `DispInfo` argument, you'd see all four actors included in the cast as opposed to the three in Listing 32-5.

Recommendations

To keep this complex example as comprehendible as possible, I've resisted the mention of some possible tweaks, up until now.

I shared that strict OOP dictates that you must invoke the constructor before you can use an object. This model leaves that restriction to the honor system, but you can remedy the issue with an "instantiated" switch. First, the child constructor would set the switch when it executes. Then you could interrogate that switch before any attempt to invoke a public method, throwing an abort if it hasn't yet been set. This is almost certainly overkill, but it wouldn't be difficult (or elegant). I prefer the honor system here.

I never used the comedy troupe variable set for the Monty Python film, but you can define a :DispInfo method in the *oLifeOfBrian.bat* object to extend the like-name method from *oMovie.bat*. After the child calls to inherit the display performed by its parent (or parent's parent), it can append a similar line for the troupe. Even better yet, since a troupe applies only to some comedies, the new method could go into the *oComedy.bat* object, where you'd display the troupe only if it exists.

The most significant element of OOP that we haven't successfully duplicated in Batch is data hiding. When a variable is set, it's available in the environment until it's reassigned or the process ceases, and there's no realistic means of preventing its reassignment by some other code. We can use the setlocal and endlocal commands to hide variables, but after the execution of the endlocal command, the variables will be lost into the ether. As I mentioned in Chapter 16, variables can survive an endlocal command, but doing so would make them available globally, and that doesn't lend itself to "data hiding." We could hide the variables in a temporary file and restore them the next time through the code, but this most definitely is overkill.

Not being able to declare private variables is a limitation that precludes the ability to make a Batch object available to a great number of users, as is the case with other languages. But let's take a step back to gain some perspective. Making an object generally available for the masses is not part of the design I'm positing; this is Batch, and there's no realistic infrastructure for something on that type of scale anyway.

I'm suggesting the building of objects for use by oneself and maybe a small group of friends or co-workers working on the same network. This isn't something you'd want to make callable from a web service. Thus, the only real ramification of not being able to hide data is that a small cohort of coders must be aware that they shouldn't step on the variables used in certain objects.

Batch object-oriented design is a methodology that I highly recommend. You might not implement it as extensively as in the model that I've presented here, nor should you. (More on this in the next and final chapter.) Even just portions of this methodology may very well be useful to you. Even without the use of inheritance, you can write a module with polymorphic code that behaves differently based on the caller. A simplified version of inheritance might rely on one central bat file for a few important tasks. Just writing small and reusable modules is redolent of object-oriented design and is an enormous step forward.

The Four Pillars in Batch

You've already seen that in this Batch model we've been able to simulate many of the characteristics of OOP surprisingly well. Let's step through each of the four pillars one more time, detailing how close we've actually come to our goal.

Abstraction, the first pillar, simplifies the code's interface, shows only the necessary or relevant features, and shields implementation details. Take another look at the two complete child objects in Listings 32-3 and 32-4. The methods to get and set variables, along with the method to display movie information, have all been abstracted away. Other than the logic at the top of each object listing public methods and handling the inheritance, there's really just a single method, the constructor, and everything in it is pertinent to the object. Abstraction in Batch object-oriented design gets high marks.

Smaller, more plentiful modules present a superior design regardless of the language or coding methodology. Each file has a distinct purpose, and the code is more maintainable and extensible. The model I've shown in this chapter lends itself to writing short, compact, and reusable code modules, and this is one of three components that define the second pillar, encapsulation, along with data and method hiding. Method hiding is trivial in Batch; in fact, we had to do some work to expose public methods. Data hiding, however, isn't supported at all in this model. All of the variables set for all of the different movies float around the environment for anyone to modify at any time. Two out of three is a passing grade.

Examples of inheritance, the third pillar, are strewn throughout the previous pages. Child objects are inheriting constructors from intermediate objects, which in turn inherit the same from parent objects. The method for displaying information to the console and the setter and getter methods are all quality examples of inheritance. We coded them once in the parent object for use by up to two million child objects. I've even demonstrated how to override a method in a child object. We need a bit of redundant code at the top of each bat file to make this work, but this model clearly scores near the top of its class when it comes to inheritance.

The fourth pillar, polymorphism, allows code to behave differently in different situations, with the method displaying movie information being a prime example of this functionality. We use a single method in a single bat file to write the unique information for a couple million movies—and two of those variables displayed were originally set in the parent object's polymorphic constructor. The setter and getter method take this a step further. Traditional OOP requires a pair of these methods for each and every defined variable. In this model, a single setter and a single getter handle all variables for each and every individual movie object. Batch polymorphism is what many students call a *curve buster*.

I'll leave it to you, the reader, to give this model a final grade. I'll concede that due to the lack of data hiding, the mark of an A is out of reach, but I hope not too far out of reach.

Summary

Was Batch designed as an object-oriented language? Not a chance. Is it possible to build much of object-oriented design—that is, abstraction, encapsulation, inheritance, and polymorphism—in bat files? Absolutely. Can Batch object-oriented design achieve the efficiency and scale of other languages? No. After reading this chapter, how many Batch coders will propose an enterprise-wide object-oriented project to their employer? Not many. If that number is greater than zero, how many will still be employed in three months? Most assuredly none. How many coders will try to incorporate elements of Batch object-oriented design into their code? Hard to say, but I'm hoping for quite a few.

Object-oriented design is this book's dénouement, so why is this merely the penultimate chapter of the book? In the next and final chapter, I'll introduce two data structures: stacks and queues. But I'll also use these data structures as an opportunity to further demonstrate object-oriented design, because this discussion is far from complete. The model I've detailed in this chapter implements every possible object-oriented design principle, but it isn't how I usually code Batch objects. It's better to use only what's needed and not what isn't. When building stacks and queues in the next chapter, you'll see real-world objects for each, and I'll also share some final thoughts about Batch object-oriented design.

33

STACKS, QUEUES, AND REAL-WORLD OBJECTS

In this chapter, I'll build two more Batch data structures from scratch: stacks and queues. Both hold a finite set of ordered values, with the only difference being that stacks fit the last-in-first-out paradigm, while queues are first-in-first-out. I'll detail both data structures in general and demonstrate how to build their unique functionalities. And of course, you'll learn applications of these new tools, even a Batch pseudo-compiler of other bat files.

However, this chapter is as much about real-world Batch objects as it's about stacks and queues. I'll also use what you learned in the previous chapter to construct object bat files for each data structure. The objects will allow you to maintain multiple stacks or queues simultaneously, and they'll ideally inspire future real-world Batch objects of your own. I'll even finish up with final thoughts on Batch object-oriented design.

Stacks

A *stack* is a data structure containing an ordered list of data items, organized as *last-in-first-out (LIFO)*. Undoubtedly, the best metaphor for a stack is a spring-loaded cafeteria plate dispenser. The weight of each plate pushes down a spring at the base of the dispenser so that only the top plate in the stack is available. Add more plates and the stack drops down so that only what's now the top plate is poking up. The first plate added is at the bottom of the stack, and the first one retrieved is the last one added to the top of the stack. You can't access a plate lower on the stack without first removing the plates above it, one by one. Take that top plate and the stack rises the height of a single plate, exposing the one that was just underneath it, while protecting the rest from the clumsy and possibly unhygienic hoi polloi.

Similarly, you can add or *push* a data item onto a stack, followed by more data items. At any point, you can retrieve or *pop* the data item at the top of the stack—that is, get the item added most recently. Most object-oriented languages come with a built-in stack data structure with methods for pushing an item onto the stack, popping the last item, and peeking at the last added item without actually removing it. There should also be methods to clear the stack and to determine whether the stack is empty.

Batch has no such built-in data structure, but if you're still with me in this final chapter, I'll assume that you also enjoy the challenge of creating atypical Batch functionality. The underlying structure of the stack in Batch is merely a single variable. To push the first value onto a stack, we'll simply assign it to the stack variable. Then we'll push subsequent items onto the stack by prepending to that variable, pushing the existing items down the stack.

To execute a pop request, we'll extract the leading item in the variable from the contents of the variable, leaving the rest. A peek request will be similar, except we'll leave the stack undisturbed. To make this work, we'll need a delimiter between each item guaranteed not to be in the data. Spaces, pipes, and commas are good options, depending on the expected data, but my preference is the tab character. If it's possible that your data might have tabs, you should choose something else as the delimiter; it can even be a variable itself set by the user.

To demonstrate the different pieces of functionality needed to implement a stack, I'll construct and use a stack of friends. The first task is to come up with a variable name; any will do, but I'll use the stkFriends variable. My convention is to prepend the name of the stack with stk, making it clear to anyone that stumbles across it (who also happens to know this convention) that the variable is the manifestation of a stack. In short order, I'll bring all of this functionality into an object, but first I'll step through the methodology for the push, pop, and peek functions.

Push

The logical place to start is with the *push*, and this solitary set command is all you need to push Walter onto the stack:

```
set stkFriends=Walter▶%stkFriends%
```

Here, as well as in future listings, I'm using a solid arrow to represent the tab character. By default, it is indistinguishable from one or more spaces in most editors, but if using Notepad++, you can show tab characters as arrows by selecting **View ▸ Show Symbol ▸ Show Space and Tab**. (Other editors have a similar feature, and if you've gotten this far into the book using Notepad, you are clearly a glutton for punishment.)

I'm using the stkFriends variable twice in the command, assigning it to itself, resolved with percent signs and prepended with the item I'm adding, Walter, and the delimiter, a tab character. This has, in effect, added the value to the top of the stack. Instead of the hardcoded data item, you can easily use a resolved variable in its place for the friend being added.

If the stack is already empty, this command populates it with its first value, followed by a tab and nothing else.

Peek

The *peek* function finds the item on the top of the stack without altering the stack. It just takes a peek, without popping. We don't know how many values are on the stack, if any at all, but we do know that if stkFriends is populated, its first tab-delimited value is at the top of the stack.

The following code populates aFriend with whatever's on top of the stack:

```
set aFriend=&
for /F "delims=▶" %%s in ("%stkFriends%") do (
    set aFriend=%%s
)
```

The parsing of delimited data is clearly a job for the for /F command. I'm using the stack variable as text input, and since we've delimited the variable by tabs, I'm setting the delims keyword to a tab. The tokens=1 clause is implied, meaning that the for variable defined as %%s resolves to the first token in the string, and since that first token is the last item placed onto the stack, we'll simply capture it as aFriend.

Also notice that I'm wiping out the aFriend variable prior to the for command. If the stack is empty, the for /F command doesn't execute, so initializing the variable ensures that an empty stack returns a null value.

Pop

The *pop* function is remarkably similar to the peek function with one significant difference; it also removes the returned data item from the top of the stack. Notice that the logic for this task mimics the previous listing with two additions: the tokens clause and the final set command:

```
set aFriend=&
for /F "tokens=1* delims=▶" %%s in ("%stkFriends%") do (
    set aFriend=%%s
    set stkFriends=%%t
)
```

Instead of using the implied tokens clause, I'm setting the keyword to 1*. This has no impact on the for variable, %%s, itself. It still resolves to the top item on the stack, but now the interpreter assigns the remainder of the text field to the second token, %%t. Since the rest of the text field is the entire stack minus the first item, I'm simply reassigning the abbreviated stack to the stack variable with the last set command. The entire process is analogous to breaking one square off the end of a chocolate bar and pushing the rest of the bar back into the wrapper.

Queues

Stacks and queues go together like chocolate and peanut butter. At its core, a *queue* is the *first-in-first-out (FIFO)* version of a stack. (This is the same as last-in-last-out, but LILO has never caught on.) The metaphor for a stack took us to a cafeteria, but the metaphor for a queue takes us to a restaurant. If you're the first to show up without a reservation at a busy time, the host staff will likely put your name at the top of a list. They'll add others to the list, and when a table frees up, you'll be sat first from the list. Each of the others on this list will move up and continue to wait their turn in order.

Here's a truly horrible business idea. I'll open a pancake restaurant, call it Stacks, and use a stack for those waiting for a table. The group that arrives just as we get busy is first onto the stack, where they'll wait, perhaps patiently, as others are added to and removed from the stack (that is, sat). Even if there are 20 groups on the stack, the people who just showed up get the next table. Obviously, this is a far better application for a queue.

Implementing a queue in Batch is almost identical to implementing a stack. The one significant difference is that when adding a data item to the queue, you'll want to append it to the end of the variable instead of prepending it:

```
set queFriends=%queFriends%▶Walter
```

There are also a couple of differences in nomenclature. First, because the variable represents a queue, I've changed its leading text from stk to que, but again, this is just one convention. Second, the terms *push* and *pop* make sense only when thinking about a stack, such as a plate dispenser. When adding and removing values from a queue, I'll instead use the pedestrian yet accurate terms *add* and *remove*, respectively.

Everything else is the same between the two data structures. Notice that the previous set command also uses the tab delimiter. The add and remove functions are respectively identical to the push and pop functions, other than the variable name, since both target the first delimited data item in the variable. In fact, they are so similar I'll hold off showing you these functions until I build the queue object.

WARNING *We live in a finite world, and just as the cafeteria plate dispenser can accept only so many plates, Batch has a limitation pertinent to stacks and queues. A single variable can't exceed 32,767 bytes, and since this design of stacks and queues relies on a single variable holding the entire data structure, the cumulative size of all data items and delimiters in a stack or queue can't cross this threshold. For instance, you can store 16,383 one-byte values or 1,927 sixteen-byte values. For most applications, this is sufficient, but if it isn't, you can instead build these data structures with an array and a pointer to keep track of the pertinent index.*

Real-World Batch Objects

In Chapter 32, I explored Batch object-oriented design. I detailed a model that implemented every possible piece of functionality involving the four pillars of OOP, but in truth, that model isn't representative of typical object bat files. Fortunately, the stack and queue offer instructive real-world examples of Batch objects.

The Stack Object

I'll show the stack object bat file, *oStack.bat*, in two parts, starting with the comments and mainline logic:

```
rem ****** Stack Object ******
rem parm 1 - Name of Stack
rem parm 2 - Method: Push, Pop, Peek, Clear, or IsEmpty
rem parm 3 - Input/Output Variable:
rem            Value Pushed, Variable Popped, or Variable Peeked
rem            Boolean for isEmpty

  cmd /C exit 0
  call :%~2 "%~1" "%~3" || (
    > C:\Batch\Log.txt echo ** ERROR - Invalid Method Name "%~2"
    exit
  )
  goto :eof
```

The most striking difference between this code and the objects from the prior chapter is that I've replaced the "traffic cop" hiding private methods with a `call` command exposing all the methods as public.

In Chapter 32, all object bat files had a `for` command containing the list of public methods, but the *oStack.bat* object bat file has only public methods. As a result, instead of maintaining a list, the `call` command directs the execution to the appropriate method, thus making all of the methods public. Since the second parameter is the name of the method to be called, I'm stripping it of possible double quotes and prepending it with a colon to create the name of the called label: `:%~2`.

The name of the stack is the first parameter coming into the bat file and also the first argument I pass to each of the methods. The second argument passed to each method is the third input parameter, and it has different uses dependent on the method. But instead of discussing this here, maybe I should instead just point you to the comments at the top of the bat file clearly delineating the parameters accepted by the object and its public methods.

The two pipes and the code block following the `call` command is a real-world application of conditional execution. (In Chapter 28, I provided a detailed example of this technique, including why the `cmd` command at the top of the bat file is resetting the return code to 0.) The upshot is that if the object receives a valid method, it invokes that method successfully, and if the parameter is an invalid method name, this logic writes the error message to *Log.txt* and ends the execution. Thus, all methods are public.

What happens if we don't have this conditional execution and error handling? It works perfectly fine if every call to the bat file passes a valid method name. However, if for the first argument someone errantly passes the homophone for `Peek` referring to a mountaintop, the interpreter writes the following to stderr, and the execution continues unabated:

```
The system cannot find the batch label specified - Peak
```

The interpreter neither finds nor calls the method, nor does it set the return variable, if applicable, resulting in unpredictable downstream results. Something like this deserves a hard abort to pique our attention, and that's exactly what the conditional execution and rudimentary error handling is accomplishing.

Here's the remainder of *oStack.bat* and its public methods mentioned in the prior comments:

```
:Push
 set stk%~1=%~2▶!stk%~1!
 goto :eof& rem End :Push
```

```
:Pop
 set %~2=&
 for /F "tokens=1* delims=►" %%s in ("!stk%~1!") do (
    set %~2=%%s
    set stk%~1=%%t
 )
 goto :eof& rem End :Pop

:Peek
 set %~2=&
 for /F "delims=►" %%s in ("!stk%~1!") do (
    set %~2=%%s
 )
 goto :eof& rem End :Peek

:Clear
 set stk%~1=&
 goto :eof& rem End :Clear

:IsEmpty
 if defined stk%~1 (
    set %~2=false==x
 ) else (
    set %~2=true==true
 )
 goto :eof& rem End: IsEmpty
```

I've already discussed the mechanism for the push, pop, and peek functionality in the "Stacks" section, and in this object, you'll find the polymorphic version for each under the appropriately named label. For instance, the :Push method sets the stk%~1 variable in lieu of stkFriends. For this object to work with multiple stacks, it can't explicitly reference a particular stack variable. Instead, it builds the name of the stack by resolving the first parameter and prepending it with the stk text before setting it to the concatenation of %~2, a tab character, and !stk%~1!. The second parameter is the value being pushed onto the stack, and the tab character is the delimiter. This command uses the stk%~1 variable a second time to retrieve the existing values on the stack, resolving the variable with exclamation marks and delayed expansion. Ultimately, this pushes the second parameter onto the stack.

The :Pop and :Peek methods also make use of stk%~1 for setting and/or resolving the stack. The only other new feature in these methods is that I'm setting %~2 to the return value because the second parameter for both methods is the name of the variable being returned.

For this to be a proper stack object, it must provide two more methods typical of this data structure in other languages. The first accepts the name of the stack as its only parameter and clears all data items from it. To complete the task, the :Clear method simply sets stk%~1 to nothing.

The other method returns a boolean that evaluates to true if the stack is empty or to false if anything is on the stack. The :IsEmpty method determines if stk%~1 is defined. Depending on the result, it sets the second parameter to either true or false.

Now we're ready to use the stack object. These four calls add three friends to a new stack, with Marty being the last in:

```
set stack=C:\Batch\oStack.bat
call %stack% Friends clear
call %stack% Friends push Walter
call %stack% Friends push Donny
call %stack% Friends push Marty
```

The first call is probably unnecessary, but in the off chance that the stkFriends variable is defined, this initializes it. You can think of it as a constructor even though this design doesn't have one.

Execute this multiple times, and the aFriend variable will come back as Marty every time because it peeks only at the data item:

```
call %stack% Friends peek aFriend
```

This also returns Marty when called, but only once:

```
call %stack% Friends pop aFriend
```

The next pop invocation returns Donny, the value placed on the stack just before Marty.

Now only Walter remains on the stack. You can add two more friends, but Walter remains in the bottom position:

```
call %stack% Friends push "The Stranger"
call %stack% Friends push Maude
```

Remember that arguments with embedded spaces need to be encased in double quotes and that *oStack.bat* handles them deftly with the use of tildes.

The isEmpty call returns a boolean variable:

```
call %stack% Friends isEmpty bool
if %bool% (> con echo Empty) else (> con echo NOT Empty)
```

The bool variable resolves as false since there are three items on the stack, and this logic writes NOT Empty to the console.

Lastly, to start from scratch, we can empty the stack of all its data items:

```
call %stack% Friends clear
```

Call the object again to invoke the isEmpty method, and it returns the boolean set to true.

The Queue Object

Since stacks and queues are so similar, I'm modeling the queue object on the stack object. But still, notice the many subtle differences and just one significant difference as you examine the complete contents of the stack object bat file, *oQueue.bat*:

```
rem ****** Queue Object ******
rem parm 1 - Name of Queue
rem parm 2 - Method: Add, Remove, Peek, Clear, or IsEmpty
rem parm 3 - Input/Output Variable:
rem             Value Added, Variable Removed, or Variable Peeked
rem             Boolean for isEmpty

  cmd /C exit 0
  call :%~2 "%~1" "%~3" || (
     >> C:\Batch\Log.txt echo ** ERROR - Invalid Method Name "%~2"
     exit
  )
  goto :eof

 :Add
❶ set que%~1=!que%~1!▶%~2
  goto :eof& rem End :Add

 :Remove
  set %~2=&
  for /F "tokens=1* delims=▶" %%q in ("!que%~1!") do (
     set %~2=%%q
     set que%~1=%%r
  )
  goto :eof& rem End :Remove

 :Peek
  set %~2=&
  for /F "delims=▶" %%q in ("!que%~1!") do (
     set %~2=%%q
  )
  goto :eof& rem End :Peek

 :Clear
  set que%~1=&
  goto :eof& rem End :Clear

 :IsEmpty
  if defined que%~1 (
     set %~2=false==x
  ) else (
     set %~2=true==true
  )
  goto :eof& rem End: IsEmpty
```

I've changed the stk text leading the variable name to que for obvious reasons. The :Push and :Pop methods have given way to the :Add and :Remove methods, respectively, and the comments at the top of the object clearly reflect these changes. The significant alteration is in the set command ❶ that adds a data item to the queue in the :Add method. It now adds the value to the end of the line instead of the beginning, meaning that the first item in is the first item out.

A couple of the method names are different, but the execution of this object should look familiar. Here's an example of five calls:

```
set queue=C:\Batch\oQueue.bat
call %queue% Friends clear
call %queue% Friends add Walter
call %queue% Friends add Donny
call %queue% Friends add Marty
call %queue% Friends peek aFriend
```

The last call returns aFriend populated with the value of Walter, the first data item added to the queue. Compare this to the stack object that returned Marty for a very similar call.

Stack and Queue Applications

You can find applications for the queue object wherever there's a need to process data in order. You might create a queue to hold a list of server names retrieved from a source, perhaps one or more files. Then as you remove each server from the queue, you can perform a particular task on that server. The task might be as simple as verifying that it's up and running, or it might involve the creation of directories or complex file movements. What's important is that the queue allows you to take each server in order.

With interactive Batch, you might ask the user for a list of multiple inputs. Instead of retrieving one piece of data, processing it, and then asking for another, you can ask for all of the data up front as you add all of it to a queue. Then the bat file can process each data item in order without another question.

Stack applications aren't always as obvious, but when you need one, it's usually the only adequate tool for the job. You can use a stack to reverse the order of letters or words looking for palindromes. Recursion is another application of a stack. With each recursive call, the interpreter pushes the current state of all variables onto a stack. You don't have direct access to this stack, but after making too many recursive calls, the interpreter reports that the recursion has exceeded "STACK limits" (Chapter 23). That's not a coincidence.

Using a stack, you can even create a pseudo-compiler for bat files or other uncompiled source code. I don't want to oversell this; proper compilers perform a number of tasks, and while we can go a long way toward performing just one of those tasks (the balancing of brackets), it won't be bullet-proof. The concept behind this pseudo-compiler is that an open parenthesis needs a matching close parenthesis, just as curly and square brackets must come in pairs. They can be deeply nested, but a square bracket can't close a curly bracket.

Here are the complete contents of *PseudoCompiler.bat*, a bat file that attempts to balance all sets of brackets in a bat file:

```
@setlocal EnableExtensions EnableDelayedExpansion
@echo off
set stack=C:\Batch\oStack.bat
call %stack% Compiler clear

❶ for /F "usebackq tokens=*" %%r in ("%~1") do (
     set rec=%%r
  ❷ for /L %%i in (0,1,100) do (
       set byte=!rec:~%%i,1!
     ❸ if .^!byte! neq .^" (
        ❹ for %%c in ({ [ ^() do (
            if "!byte!" equ "%%c" (
             ❺ call %stack% Compiler push !byte!
          ) )
         ❻ for %%p in ("[:]" "{:}" "(:)") do (
            ❼ for /F "tokens=1,2 delims=:" %%x in (%%p) do (
                if "!byte!" equ "%%y" (
                 ❽ call %stack% Compiler pop popped
                   if "!popped!" equ "" (
                     > con echo ABORT Unmatched Close Bracket
                     pause & exit
                   )
                   if "!popped!" neq "%%x" (
                     > con echo ABORT Bracket Mismatch
                     pause & exit
) ) ) ) ) ) )

❾ call %stack% Compiler isEmpty bool
   if not %bool% (
      > con echo ABORT Unmatched Open Bracket
      pause & exit
   )
❿ > con echo Successful Pseudo-Compile
   pause
```

At a high level, this bat file accepts one file to be pseudo-compiled as its sole parameter ❶. When this code encounters any type of open bracket (including parentheses), it pushes the character onto a stack ❺. Then whenever it sees a close bracket of any type, it pops the last open bracket off the stack ❽ and looks to see if they are a matching pair. If not, it aborts. When it's done reading the bat file, it needs to verify that the stack is empty ❾, because if it isn't, we must also abort because the input has at least one unclosed bracket.

A deeper dive demonstrates many techniques introduced throughout this book, and it's always fun to deconstruct a four-level deep nested for command. After clearing the Compiler stack, the outer for /F command ❶ accepts the lone parameter, %~1, as its input and reads each record sequentially. You can pseudo-compile any bat file by dragging and dropping it onto *PseudoCompiler.bat*.

The for /L command ❷ iterates through each of the first 100 bytes of the input record. Double quotes cause issues when resolved in later if commands, so the first if command ❸ adeptly filters out the offending character. I'm using two escape characters for the comparison, and another one in the next line, where I execute an optionless for command ❹ that passes each of the three possible open brackets into its code block. It treats the curly and square brackets as text, but I must escape the open parenthesis. If I find one of the three characters, I push the open bracket onto the stack ❺.

Another for command ❻ is the driver for finding and handling instances of close brackets. It passes all three pairs of open and close brackets, delimited by a colon, into its code block, where the final /F command ❼ breaks each pair into two tokens. If the byte from the file I'm examining matches the second token, I've found a close brackets, so I pop the last added item off the stack ❽. If that byte is a null, the close bracket is an orphan, so the code aborts and writes a rudimentary message to the console. If instead the popped byte doesn't match the corresponding start bracket, the abort message notes the mismatched brackets.

If we make it through the entire file without finding a mismatch, the trailing logic checks that the stack is empty of all brackets ❾ with the use of a boolean. If an orphan remains, the code aborts because there's at least one unmatched open bracket. After clearing this last if command, the brackets have all balanced, and the code triumphantly reports the success ❿.

This code demonstrates a great use for a stack, but it has limitations and, as mentioned, is far from bullet-proof. First and foremost, it assumes that each record is 100 bytes or less. The error handling in general also leaves much to be desired. At the very least, it should track the line of the infraction.

As the interpreter processes each record, it resolves variables delimited by exclamation marks, so this routine doesn't validate any variable names containing brackets (think arrays and hash tables). Such variables will likely resolve to nothing, but if the two bat files share any variables, that can also cause problems. For instance, when I attempted to recursively pseudo-compile *PseudoCompiler.bat* (by copying and pasting it onto itself), popped resolved to an open parenthesis, resulting in it incorrectly reporting a mismatch. This self-pseudo-compile also failed on the unpaired open brackets ❹ being treated as text data.

Even with these limitations that accentuate the *pseudo* in pseudo-compiler, this is still a solid means of tracking down most missed parentheses and brackets in a typical bat file—and a great application of a stack. Notice that this bat file calls the stack object we built earlier for four distinct tasks: clearing the stack, pushing, popping, and determining if the stack is empty.

NOTE   *As a final note on the nested* for *commands, notice that I've chosen descriptive* for *variables that don't conflict with each other. I capture the entire record (%%r) and* *iterate through it with an index (%%i), grabbing individual bytes (%%b). Then I pass a pair (%%p) of brackets into a loop, breaking them up into the open bracket (%%x) and the implied close bracket (%%y). The last two might not be descriptive, but I'm limited because they must be consecutive alphabetical characters.*

Final Thoughts on Batch Object-Oriented Design

I could have discussed the stack and queue data structures without presenting them as objects. The methods in this chapter would have been routines inside of an ordinary bat file with hardcoded names for the data structures, but as important as stacks and queues are, this chapter is also about real-world object-oriented design.

The object-oriented example in the prior chapter (Chapter 32) was pedagogical at its core. It showed as many aspects of Batch object-oriented design as possible, but the two objects in this chapter are examples of real-world Batch objects. When I code objects, they're far more likely to resemble *oStack.bat* than *oMovie.bat* or *oComedy.bat*.

I hope you can see the advantages of putting all of the stack-specific code into a single reusable and concise bat file—that is, an object. This allows you to code hundreds of future stacks with this one object without ever having to consider the details of how the stack itself is implemented. With this in mind, you can reconsider arrays and hash tables (Chapter 29), imagining an object for each with methods for adding elements, retrieving elements, and clearing all elements. Further imagine other methods for displaying the contents of the array or hash table, writing all elements to a file, or even sorting the elements of the array. If you're feeling bold, you could even use the stack object in the array object to reverse the order of the array elements.

Real-world Batch objects implement only the functionality of OOP that's needed to get a job done. In a strict object-oriented language, you can't use an object until you invoke the constructor, but in Batch, for better or worse, you have more flexibility. The objects in this chapter don't even have constructors. Since Batch is not a true object-oriented language, you're free to use only the pieces of the OOP paradigm that you choose, and there's no compiler to say otherwise. I could have created a constructor (it would've looked a lot like the :Clear method), but I left it out for no other reason than that I didn't feel it was needed.

There's also no inheritance in this chapter. You can easily use *oStack.bat* and *oQueue.bat* without it, and that's exactly how I typically implement Batch object-oriented design, but you can always extend any object. Some future coder, maybe even you, might later build a child object inheriting from one of these objects.

For instance, if you're using the queue object to maintain a list of servers to be processed in some way, you might also need to look up an IP address for each or just verify that it's on the network. You can encapsulate this new logic in an object that also inherits the data and methods from what would then become the *parent* queue object, while a procedural coder would resort to artlessly cloning the queue logic. (I hope that you can sense the great distain with which I typed that last clause.)

I've also shown that you can maintain a list of public methods or simply expose all methods in an object as public. All of this shows the flexibility of Batch object-oriented design. You can use only the design elements that you want or need and not what you don't want or need. If it makes sense to have a constructor, create one; otherwise, don't. If nothing else, small bat files with narrowly focused tasks are ideal. I encourage you to use some or all of the Batch object-oriented design paradigm that I've shown in these last two chapters in your bat files.

Summary

In this final chapter, I detailed two new data structures, namely, stacks and queues, showing you how to push and pop (or add and remove) data items. You also learned how to peek at the next value, clear all values, and determine whether the data structure is empty. I shared a few ideas about stack and queue applications, even creating a pseudo-compiler. It isn't perfect, but it's very useful and nicely demonstrated how to use a stack.

I also took all that you learned about stacks and queues and wrapped it up into two real-world Batch objects. You learned how to construct similar objects, using only the components of object-oriented design that make sense to you, and how to invoke those objects. I hope you'll make use of the stack and queue objects and look for future problems in need of an object-oriented solution.

AFTERWORD

I hope that you've enjoyed reading this book half as much as I've enjoyed writing it. For me, this project was a new, exciting, and illuminating endeavor. It's my first, and quite possibly only, book. If you had told me upon high school graduation that I'd someday be an author, I never would've believed you.

I was a math kid, and I also excelled at a BASIC coding course that was offered my senior year. I did well enough in English, but I then considered writing to be a chore. In college, I enjoyed two technical writing courses as part of my major, but the idea of a book still would've seemed absurd. After many years of reading different types of books and articles, I slowly began to appreciate the creative outlet that is writing. I dabbled here and there but never published anything, not even a blog. Sometime around my 50th birthday and after years of coding bat files, the hint of an inkling of an idea for writing this book took shallow root, but I wasn't yet ready to act upon this most bizarre midlife crisis, if that's what it was.

More than two years later, in May 2020, two events collided that left me with some spare time allowing me to put fingertips to keyboard. (By this point in the computer age, we should have a better digital euphemism for "put pen to paper.") First, the realization that the coronavirus pandemic would last more than a couple of months became glaringly obvious. I had plenty of vacation time and no travel plans. Second, after a decade and a half of intense parenting, including the coaching of several youth sports teams, my son reached an age where instead of demanding my time, he demanded the exact opposite (like most teenagers).

My wife and I (while sometimes dragging our son along) did a fair amount of hiking that summer. I also did a lot of running, but I returned to the idea of this book, especially with the knowledge that normality wouldn't be returning before temperatures dropped in the Northeast. Sporadically and in no particular order, I wrote a chapter here and there, not knowing if I'd post them on a blog or find some other medium, but before long I knew that I wanted to write a book, an actual physical book. As the mercury dropped, I wrote every weekend, and this continued through to the spring and summer . . . and the next fall, and beyond. (I code fast but write slow.) My wife to me in early June 2021: "So what do you want for Father's Day, other than to be left alone so that you can write?"

After a couple of years, I presented what I thought was a finished product to No Starch Press. To my amazement, my publisher of first choice signed me up. Being a novice, my manuscript was raw, and they had some great ideas about how I could organize and improve what I had without losing my voice. (As for my voice, I write first for myself and then consider possible critiques. Who would write "the hint of an inkling of an idea?" Is it pretentious or just inane? I don't know, but I like it and can only hope you do too.)

More than 90 percent of what's in this book represents the type of coding and techniques that I've used often personally and professionally. As for the small amount of material that I had to research, I hope that I've blended it seamlessly (and indistinguishably) with what's in my wheelhouse.

For most coding languages, the idea of a single book covering the majority of the language's functionality would be ludicrous. For instance, there are introductory Python books, others for Python and web development, and yet others for Python and databases, just to name a few. But Batch scripting is a more manageable subject. I hope that I've included most of the important features about the language for beginners and experts alike, but no book can be truly comprehensive.

Many commands haven't made it into these pages. For instance, the curl command transfers data from and to a server, cipher encrypts and decrypts files, and runas runs a bat file under a different user profile. There are other commands specific to system administration that I haven't covered, and I've left others out because I simply don't find them useful. I haven't mentioned the replace command (until now) because Batch has much better tools available for replacing one file with another.

For those remaining pieces of Batch that I haven't covered, I hope you now have the tools to perform your own research. More than once, I've mentioned that you can find a full list of commands including a description, syntax, options, and examples at *https://ss64.com/nt/*. You can scroll through the list of commands looking for something that might be useful for a particular problem or if you've heard of a certain command for configuring internet protocols and want to learn more, just click on **ipconfig** and explore. No book is going to have everything, but I hope that you've found this one to contain the essentials, and much more.

For the coders finishing this book, the next time you're working on a simple bat file that needs something a little out of the ordinary—arrays, booleans, floating-point arithmetic, stacks, maybe even an object—I hope that you don't immediately fall back on writing some compiled code. Depending on the situation, a few lines of Batch might be the most efficient solution.

For the noncoders, if you made it all the way through Part III, consider yourself an honorary coder. But more to the point, the next time you have a redundant task that must be done at certain intervals, perhaps daily, consider Batch. Run a simple bat file at the end of the day to copy your day's work to a backup server or a shared directory. If a few reports need to be merged into a single file, don't cut and paste. Impress your boss and coworkers, and maybe even yourself.

Along these lines, I have one last bat file to share. As I was writing this book, I obviously backed up to the cloud, but I also wanted a date-stamped folder of the current state of all Word documents, bat files, and anything else associated with this book, and I wanted to make this backup at the end of each day of writing. Just before logging off, I would plug a thumb drive into my laptop and run a bat file containing just this code from my desktop:

```
set @=%date%
xcopy C:\Batch\*.* D:\Batch\%@:~10,4%%@:~4,2%%@:~7,2%\ /F /S /Y
pause
```

This quick and dirty bat file builds a datestamp for the target folder name under *D:\Batch*. The xcopy command creates my backup from *C:\Batch*, and the pause command holds the window open so that I'll know if I've run out of disk space. This was an incredibly simple solution that fit my needs, but you can expand on this to build a more robust bat file.

I consider myself a scripting evangelist, in general, and a Batch evangelist, in particular. Coders too often fall back on compiled code for tasks more easily and efficiently performed with a script. In Chapter 1, I defined the word *batphile* as a "lover of nocturnal flying mammals." I'd now like to assign to it a secondary definition, "lover of bat files." (Batfilephile is painfully clunky.) I hope that if you weren't already, you're now a proud batphile—in at least one sense of the word. Some fear the flying mammals, but they're fascinating animals and rather adorable.

A

FULLY FUNCTIONAL
BATCH IMPROV

 In Chapter 15, I built a rudimentary version of *BatchImprov.bat* that shared a single joke, riddle, or pun. In later chapters, you learned several tools to enhance this process, such as reading files, loading arrays, and using a random number to select an arbitrary element from an array.

Now let's put it all together into an enhanced bat file that first reads library files containing any number of jokes, riddles, and puns, and loads them into arrays. Then the BUI will randomly retrieve and share one example of the user's requested humor before asking if they want another offering.

Starting with the data, here are the full contents of *BatJokes.txt*:

```
Why are bats so active at night?|They charge their bat-teries by day.
How do bats flirt?|They bat their eyes.
What's a good pick-up line for a bat?|Let's hang.
Why did the bat cross the road?|To prove he wasn't chicken.
```

BatRiddles.txt similarly contains the riddles:

```
This type of bat is silly.|A Dingbat.
This circus performer can see in the dark.|An Acro-bat.
This is the strongest and meanest bat in the cave.|The Alpha-bat.
This sport uses bats and is also food for bats.|Cricket.
```

The puns are formatted differently, so each record of *BatPuns.txt* doesn't contain an answer delimited by a pipe:

```
Crossing a vampire bat with a computer means love at first byte.
The first thing bat pups learn at school is the alpha-bat.
Bat pups are trained to go potty in the bat-room.
```

Finally, place these three library files in the same directory as this version of *BatchImprov.bat*:

```
@setlocal EnableExtensions EnableDelayedExpansion
@echo off
color 1F
title Batch Improv Theater

call :LoadArray joke
call :LoadArray riddle
call :LoadArray pun
pause

:Again
cls
> con echo.
> con choice /C:JPR /M:"Do you want a Joke, Pun, or Riddle"
> con echo.
if %errorlevel% equ 1 (
    call :Joke
) else if %errorlevel% equ 2 (
    call :Pun
) else if %errorlevel% equ 3 (
    call :Riddle
)
> con echo.
> con choice /M:"Do you want to try again"
if %errorlevel% equ 1  goto :Again
goto :eof

:Joke
call :GetRandNbr joke
> con echo Please give an answer to the joke:
> con set /P yourAns=!joke[%randNbr%]!  &
> con echo ** !jokeAns[%randNbr%]!
> con echo ** You said: "%yourAns%"
goto :eof
```

```
:Pun
 call :GetRandNbr pun
> con echo We hope you find this punny:
> con echo !pun[%randNbr%]!
 goto :eof

:Riddle
 call :GetRandNbr riddle
> con echo Please give an answer to the riddle:
> con set /P yourAns=!riddle[%randNbr%]!  &
> con echo ** !riddleAns[%randNbr%]!
> con echo ** You said: "%yourAns%"
 goto :eof

:LoadArray
 set %1sTot=0
 for /F "tokens=1-2 delims=|" %%b in (Bat%1s.txt) do (
    set %1[!%1sTot!]=%%~b
    set %1Ans[!%1sTot!]=%%~c
    set /A %1sTot += 1
 )
> con echo.
> con echo Results of array load of %1s:
> con set %1
 goto :eof

:GetRandNbr
 set nbrPossVal=!%1sTot!
 set /A maxRandNbr = 32768 / %nbrPossVal% * %nbrPossVal% - 1
:GetAnotherRand
 set randNbr=%random%
 if %randNbr% gtr %maxRandNbr%  goto :GetAnotherRand
 set /A randNbr = %randNbr% %% %nbrPossVal%
 goto :eof
```

Much of this bat file should look familiar, but plenty is new. I perform multiple calls to :LoadArray passing either joke, riddle, or pun as the argument. The routine, which is similar to some code in Chapter 29, uses this text to find and read a specific file in the current directory and build appropriately named arrays.

An unartful coder might get this to work for the jokes before cloning it for the riddles and puns. Instead, I use common code where the first call populates the joke and jokeAns arrays and sets jokesTot to the total number of jokes loaded into the arrays, even though the actual variable name never appears in the bat file. I create the variable by resolving the parameter as part of %1sTot.

The second call similarly populates the riddle and riddleAns arrays, along with the riddlesTot variable. But the puns are formatted differently. Since there's no pipe and no answer, there's no second parameter and the code doesn't populate the answer array. Instead, the same logic builds the pun array and sets punsTot to the number of puns in the array.

You can remove this later, but for testing purposes, I display the results of each load to the console:

```
Results of array load of jokes:
jokeAns[0]=They charge their bat-teries by day.
jokeAns[1]=They bat their eyes.
jokeAns[2]=Let's hang.
jokeAns[3]=To prove he wasn't chicken.
jokesTot=4
joke[0]=Why are bats so active at night?
joke[1]=How do bats flirt?
joke[2]=What's a good pick-up line for a bat?
joke[3]=Why did the bat cross the road?

Results of array load of riddles:
riddleAns[0]=A Dingbat.
riddleAns[1]=An Acro-bat.
riddleAns[2]=The Alpha-bat.
riddleAns[3]=Cricket.
riddlesTot=4
riddle[0]=This type of bat is silly.
riddle[1]=This circus performer can see in the dark.
riddle[2]=This is the strongest and meanest bat in the cave.
riddle[3]=This sport uses bats and is also food for bats.

Results of array load of puns:
punsTot=3
pun[0]=Crossing a vampire bat with a computer means love at first byte.
pun[1]=The first thing bat pups learn at school is the alpha-bat.
pun[2]=Bat pups are trained to go potty in the bat-room.
Press any key to continue . . .
```

The cls command clears the screen before starting the user interface portion of the bat file.

The main logic under the :Again label is unchanged from the prior version of the bat file. The :Joke, :Riddle, and :Pun routines all retrieve a random number by calling :GetRandNbr. To get the total number of elements in the appropriate array, the routine resolves its parameter as part of !%1sTot!. The rest of the logic is similar to what you saw in Chapter 21.

After getting a pointer for their array (or arrays), these routines look similar to their earlier counterparts except that these get their content from arrays. For example, !joke[%randNbr%]! resolves to a joke, and !jokeAns[%randNbr%]! resolves to its answer. (Delayed expansion is awesome.)

Now you can run *BatchImprov.bat* to retrieve multiple jokes, riddles, and puns. You can even add more content to the library files without changing the code. Better yet, use this as a template for your applications that use a BUI, arrays, delimited data files, and random numbers. Enjoy.

B

ARRAY AND HASH TABLE OBJECTS

In Chapter 29, I demonstrated how to build, access, and update arrays and hash tables. These data structures, not often associated with bat files, are great applications of the equally atypical real-world Batch objects discussed in Chapter 33.

In this appendix, I'll bring these concepts together by presenting a well-commented object bat file for each data structure.

The Array Object

Here are the full contents of the array object, *oArray.bat*:

```
:: ****** Array Object ******
:: Parm 1 - Name of Array
:: Parm 2 - Name of Method:
::       AddElemAt - Insert One Element at an Index
```

```
::               Parm 3 - Index of Element being Added
::               Parm 4 - Value of Element being Added
::       AddElem - Add One Element to the Array
::               Parm 3 - Element being Added
::       GetElem - Get the Element at an Index
::               Parm 3 - Index of Element
::               Parm 4 - Returned Variable Name
::       GetFirst - Get the First Element in the Array
::               Parm 3 - Returned Variable Name
::       GetNext - Get the Next Element in the Array; call after
::                    :GetElem or :GetFirst or gets first element
::               Parm 3 - Returned Variable Name
::       GetSize - Get the Number of Elements in the Array
::               Parm 3 - Returned Variable Name
::       RemoveElemAt - Remove One Element from the Array
::               Parm 3 - Index of Element being Removed
::       Clear - Empty the Array of all its Elements
::       IndexOf - Get the Index of a Specific Value
::                    or return -1 if Not Found
::               Parm 3 - Value of Search Element
::               Parm 4 - Returned Variable Name
::       Contains - Get a Boolean Indicating if a Value is
::                    Anywhere in the Array
::               Parm 3 - Value of Search Element
::               Parm 4 - Returned Boolean Name
::       Clone - Create a Copy of the Array
::               Parm 3 - Name of New Array
:: Global Variables:
::    <arrayName>Size = Size or Length of the Array
::    <arrayName>Index = Index or Pointer to the Next Element
::    <arrayName>[n] = Nth Element of the Array

cmd /C exit 0
call :%~2 "%~1" "%~3" "%~4" || (
   > C:\Batch\Log.txt echo ** ERROR - Invalid Method Name "%~2"
   exit
)
goto :eof


:AddElemAt
call :GetSize %~1 size
if %~2 gtr %size% (
   echo ** Invalid Index "%~2" greater than Array Size "%size%"
   goto :eof
)
set /A startIndex = !%size! - 1
for /L %%i in (%startIndex%, -1, %~2) do (
   set /A nextIndex = %%i + 1
   for /F %%n in ("!nextIndex!") do (
      set %~1[%%n]=!%~1[%%i]!
) )
set %~1[%~2]=%~3
set /A %~1Size += 1
goto :eof
```

```
:AddElem
 call :GetSize "%~1" size
 set %~1[!size!]=%~2
 set /A %~1Size += 1
 goto :eof

:GetElem
 set %~3=!%~1[%~2]!
 set /A %~1Index = %~2 + 1
 goto :eof

:GetFirst
 set %~2=!%~1[0]!
 set %~1Index=1
 goto :eof

:GetNext
 if not defined %~1Index  set %~1Index=0
 call :GetSize "%~1" size
 set targIndex=!%~1Index!
 if %targIndex% geq %size% (
    set %~2=No More Elements
 ) else (
    set %~2=!%~1[%targIndex%]!
    set /A %~1Index += 1
 )
 goto :eof

:GetSize
 if not defined %~1Size  set %~1Size=0
 set %~2=!%~1Size!
 goto :eof

:RemoveElemAt
 call :GetSize "%~1" size
 if %~2 geq %size% (
    echo ** Nothing to do, Index "%~2" greater than Array Size "%size%"
    goto :eof
 )
 set /A %~1Size -= 1
 for /L %%i in (%~2, 1, !%~1Size!) do (
    set /A nextIndex = %%i + 1
    for /F %%n in ("!nextIndex!") do (
       set %~1[%%i]=!%~1[%%n]!
 ) )
 set %~1[!nextIndex!]=&
 goto :eof

:Clear
 for /F "usebackq delims==" %%a in (`set %~1`) do (
    set %%a=&rem
 )
 set %~1Size=0
 goto :eof
```

```
:IndexOf
  set %~3=-1
  set /A sizeLess1 = %~1Size - 1
  for /L %%i in (0, 1, %sizeLess1%) do (
      if "%~2" equ "!%~1[%%i]!" (
          set %~3=%%i
  ) )
  goto :eof

:Contains
  call :IndexOf "%~1" "%~2" indexOf
  if %indexOf% equ -1 (
      set %~3=false==x
  ) else (
      set %~3=true==true
  )
  goto :eof

:Clone
  call :Clear "%~2"
  for /F "usebackq tokens=1,2 delims==" %%p in (`set %~1`) do (
      set oldArrayItem=%%p
      set !oldArrayItem:%~1=%~2!=%%q
  )
  goto :eof
```

This bat file should be called often, so I'm using :: (two colons) for the remarks instead of the rem command just to cut down on what the interpreter writes to stdout.

Every call to this object passes at least two arguments: the name of an array and the method or action being invoked; depending on the method, another argument or two might be required. You can add elements to the end of an array or at a specific index; you can retrieve the first element, the next element, or an element at a particular index. The object has methods for removing an element at a certain index, getting the size of the array, and clearing or emptying the array. You can get the index of the first instance of a specific value or retrieve a boolean telling you whether that value exists anywhere in the array. You can even clone or copy the array.

Instead of stepping through each method, I'll let the comments do the talking. Notice that I've included a brief description of each method along with their required arguments.

There are, however, a few interesting bits of code worthy of mention. You'll find plenty of examples of delayed expansion in this listing. In fact, a couple methods use nested for commands solely because of delayed expansion; each for command transforms a variable assigned in the outer for command into a variable resolvable with percent signs (Chapter 20). Also, the :IndexOf and :Contains methods perform similar functions. Instead of duplicating work, the latter calls the former, converting the result into a boolean. Likewise, multiple methods retrieve the array size by calling :GetSize. The :Clone method assigns all variables associated with one array to another, taking advantage of text replacement and the fact that array elements are thinly disguised ordinary variables.

You can call the object from another bat file to perform all of these functions. Here's a small sampling:

```
call C:\Batch\oArray.bat friends AddElem Walter
call C:\Batch\oArray.bat friends AddElem Donny
call C:\Batch\oArray.bat friends AddElemAt 1 Maude
call C:\Batch\oArray.bat friends RemoveElemAt 0
call C:\Batch\oArray.bat friends GetFirst oneFriend
call C:\Batch\oArray.bat friends GetNext anotherFriend
```

This code populates oneFriend and anotherFriend with Maude and Donny, respectively.

For the sake of readability, this object has minimal error handling and validation of the incoming parameters, but these relatively few lines of code stand ready to create, modify, and access any number of arrays.

The Hash Table Object

Here are the full contents of the hash table object, *oHashTable.bat*:

```
:: ****** Hash Table Object ******
:: Parm 1 - Name of Hash Table
:: Parm 2 - Name of Method:
::        Clear - Empty the Hash Table of all its Keys and Values
::        Put - Put One Key-Value Pair into the Hash Table
::                Parm 3 - Key being Added
::                Parm 4 - Value being Added
::        Get - Get a Value Given a Key
::                Parm 3 - Search Key
::                Parm 4 - Returned Variable Name
::        GetSize - Get the Number of Key-Value Pairs in the Hash Table
::                Parm 3 - Returned Variable Name
::        Remove - Remove One Key and its Value from the Hash Table
::                Parm 3 - Key being Removed
::        ContainsKey - Get a Boolean Indicating if a Key is
::                      Anywhere in the Hash Table
::                Parm 3 - Search Key
::                Parm 4 - Returned Boolean Name
::        ContainsValue - Get a Boolean Indicating if a Value is
::                      Anywhere in the Hash Table
::                Parm 3 - Search Key
::                Parm 4 - Returned Boolean Name
::        Clone - Create a Copy of the Hash Table
::                Parm 3 - Name of New Hash Table
:: Global Variable:
::    <hashTable>Size = Size or Length of the Hash Table
```

```
cmd /C exit 0
call :%~2 "%~1" "%~3" "%~4" || (
    > C:\Batch\Log.txt echo ** ERROR - Invalid Method Name "%~2"
    exit
)
goto :eof

:Clear
for /F "usebackq delims==" %%a in (`set %~1`) do (
    set %%a=&rem
)
set %~1Size=0
goto :eof

:Put
call :ContainsKey "%~1" "%~2" bool
set %~1{%~2}=%~3
if not %bool% (
    set /A %~1Size += 1
)
goto :eof

:Get
call :ContainsKey "%~1" "%~2" bool
if %bool% (
    set %~3=!%~1{%~2}!
) else (
    set %~3=Key Does Not Exist
)
goto :eof

:GetSize
if not defined %~1Size   set %~1Size=0
set %~2=!%~1Size!
goto :eof

:Remove
call :ContainsKey "%~1" "%~2" bool
if %bool% (
    set /A %~1Size -= 1
)
set %~1{%~2}=&
goto :eof

:ContainsKey
if defined %~1{%~2} (
    set %~3=true==true
) else (
    set %~3=false==x
)
goto :eof
```

```
:ContainsValue
 set %~3=false==x
 for /F "usebackq tokens=2 delims==" %%v in (`set %~1{`) do (
    if "%%v" equ "%~2" (
        set %~3=true==true
 ) )
 goto :eof

:Clone
 call :Clear "%~2"
 for /F "usebackq tokens=1,2 delims==" %%p in (`set %~1`) do (
    set oldHashTblItem=%%p
    set !oldHashTblItem:%~1=%~2!=%%q
 )
 goto :eof
```

This object also accepts at least two parameters: the name of a hash table and the method or action being invoked. You can add a key-value pair to the data structure by invoking the :Put method and retrieve a value given a key via the :Get method. Other methods clear the entire hash table or remove just one pair. You can get the number of pairs and retrieve a boolean showing whether a key or value is present, and as in the array object, there is a clone method.

Each method and its corresponding parameters are described in the comments at the beginning of the bat file. The most interesting method is :ContainsValue, which preemptively sets the boolean to false before performing a search for the value by looking at every pair. However, determining whether a key exists in the hash table requires little more than an if defined.

Here are a few lines of code demonstrating a simple test of the object's features:

```
call C:\Batch\oHashTable.bat jobs Put Lincoln President
call C:\Batch\oHashTable.bat jobs Put Poe Poet
call C:\Batch\oHashTable.bat jobs Put Darwin Naturalist
call C:\Batch\oHashTable.bat jobs Get Poe aJob
```

The aJob variable contains the value Poet after the completion of these commands.

You can call this object from multiple bat files and even build multiple hash tables from a single process. Now look for other instances where you can keep your main code simple by placing the interesting logic in a reusable object bat file.

INDEX

The Book of Batch Scripting is set in New Baskerville, Futura, Dogma, and TheSansMono Condensed.

RESOURCES

Visit *https://nostarch.com/batch-scripting* for errata and more information.

More no-nonsense books from **NO STARCH PRESS**

**DATA STRUCTURES
THE FUN WAY**

**An Amusing Adventure with
Coffee-Filled Examples**

BY JEREMY KUBICA
304 PP., $39.99
ISBN 978-1-7185-0260-4

**THE RECURSIVE BOOK
OF RECURSION**

**Ace the Coding Interview with
Python and JavaScript**

BY AL SWEIGART
328 PP., $39.99
ISBN 978-1-7185-0202-4

**LEARN TO CODE
BY SOLVING PROBLEMS**

A Python Programming Primer

BY DANIEL ZINGARO
336 PP., $34.99
ISBN 978-1-7185-0132-4

**AUTOMATE THE BORING STUFF
WITH PYTHON, 2ND EDITION**

**Practical Programming for
Total Beginners**

BY AL SWEIGART
592 PP., $39.99
ISBN 978-1-59327-992-9

POWERSHELL® FOR SYSADMINS

Workflow Automation Made Easy

BY ADAM BERTRAM
320 PP., $29.95
ISBN 978-1-59327-918-9

THINK LIKE A PROGRAMMER

**An Introduction to Creative
Problem Solving**

BY V. ANTON SPRAUL
256 PP., $34.99
ISBN 978-1-59327-424-5

PHONE:
800.420.7240 OR
415.863.9900

EMAIL:
SALES@NOSTARCH.COM

WEB:
WWW.NOSTARCH.COM